Bodies of Modernism

Corporealities: Discourses of Disability

Series editors: David T. Mitchell and Sharon L. Snyder

Recent Titles

Bodies of Modernism: Physical Disability in Transatlantic Modernist Literature
by Maren Tova Linett

War on Autism: On the Cultural Logic of Normative Violence
by Anne McGuire

The Biopolitics of Disability: Neoliberalism, Ablenationalism, and Peripheral Embodiment
by David T. Mitchell with Sharon L. Snyder

Foucault and the Government of Disability, Enlarged and Revised Edition
by Shelley Tremain, editor

The Measure of Manliness: Disability and Masculinity in the Mid-Victorian Novel
by Karen Bourrier

American Lobotomy: A Rhetorical History
by Jenell Johnson

Shakin' All Over: Popular Music and Disability
by George McKay

The Metanarrative of Blindness: A Re-reading of Twentieth-Century Anglophone Writing
by David Bolt

Disabled Veterans in History
by David A. Gerber, editor

Mad at School: Rhetorics of Mental Disability and Academic Life
by Margaret Price

Disability Aesthetics
by Tobin Siebers

Stumbling Blocks Before the Blind: Medieval Constructions of a Disability
by Edward Wheatley

Signifying Bodies: Disability in Contemporary Life Writing
by G. Thomas Couser

Concerto for the Left Hand: Disability and the Defamiliar Body
by Michael Davidson

The Songs of Blind Folk: African American Musicians and the Cultures of Blindness
by Terry Rowden

Disability Theory
by Tobin Siebers

Fictions of Affliction: Physical Disability in Victorian Culture
by Martha Stoddard Holmes

Disability in Twentieth-Century German Culture
by Carol Poore

Moving Beyond Prozac, DSM, *and the New Psychiatry: The Birth of Postpsychiatry*
by Bradley Lewis

A complete list of titles in the series can be found at www.press.umich.edu

Bodies of Modernism

Physical Disability in Transatlantic Modernist Literature

Maren Tova Linett

University of Michigan Press
Ann Arbor

Published in the United States of America by the
University of Michigan Press
Manufactured in the United States of America
♾ Printed on acid-free paper

2020 2019 2018 2017 4 3 2 1

A CIP catalog record for this book is available from the British Library.

Library of Congress Cataloging-in-Publication data has been applied for.

ISBN 978-0-472-07331-3 (hardcover : alk. paper)
ISBN 978-0-472-05331-5 (paper : alk. paper)
ISBN 978-0-472-12248-6 (e-book)

For Ruth and Lev

Acknowledgments

I first became aware of the field of disability studies in my penultimate year of graduate school when the *Michigan Quarterly Review* published a double special issue on the topic. The issues included an array of pieces—by scholars and artists such as Tobin Siebers, Rosemarie Garland-Thomson, Joseph Grigley, Jim Ferris, Georgina Kleege, David Mitchell and Sharon Snyder, and others—that helped launch disability studies in the humanities. Although it was more than ten years before I turned to disability studies professionally, those special issues lingered in my mind and make me all the more honored now to have my book published in the Corporealities series with the University of Michigan Press.

For his unstinting mentoring ever since my time at Michigan, I am grateful to John Whittier-Ferguson, who also read sections of the manuscript and gave wise and encouraging advice. I am grateful to the following people for reading parts of the book and providing excellent feedback: Madelyn Detloff, Stephanie Kerschbaum, Rebecah Pulsifer, Aparajita Sagar, Rebecca Sanchez, and Jennifer William. For other forms of mentoring and/or consultation, I am grateful to Douglas Baynton, Michael Davidson, Lennard Davis, Rosemarie Garland-Thomson, John Gordon, Michael Groden, Janet Lyon, Suzanne Raitt, John-Paul Riquelme, Anna Snaith, and Joseph Valente.

Thanks to my Deaf academics group for weekly support and accountability: Teresa Blankmeyer Burke, Mel Chua, Stephanie Kerschbaum, and Rebecca Sanchez. And thanks to my Purdue accountability group for helping to keep me plugging along: Elena Coda, Elaine Francis, and Jennifer William. I am also grateful for the support of two lunch groups: my comrades in lunch—Elena Benedicto, Geraldine Friedman, Deena Linett, Margaret Rowe, and Aparajita Sagar—and my "reading group" (which hasn't actually discussed books in years)—Elaine Francis, Tara Johnson, Ann Kirchmaier,

Melanie Shoffner, and Jennifer William. I would like in addition to thank my Purdue colleagues Emily Allen, T. J. Boisseau, Marlo David, John Duvall, Dino Felluga, Sandor Goodhart, Daniel Morris, Nancy Peterson, Manushag Powell, and Irwin Weiser for academic advice and friendly support.

For emotional sustenance as I carry on with parenting and professing, I am grateful to my friends Fraeda Friedman, Debra Gold, Elizabeth Kiss, Nancy Kusumoto, Jennifer William, Colin William, and Elizabeth Yellen. And I cherish the memory of Rachel Levin Troxell, who died in 2008 and who, had she lived, would have continued to be a mainstay in my life.

I am fortunate to have had wonderful students in disability studies and literature classes whose ideas have influenced mine. I would like to acknowledge in particular the work of current and former students Stephanie Larson, Jessica Mehr, Rebecah Pulsifer, and Stephanie Schatz.

Sincere thanks go to LeAnn Fields, Christopher Dreyer, and Mary Hashman at the University of Michigan Press, to the series editors, David Mitchell and Sharon Snyder, and to the anonymous readers for my manuscript, whose constructive suggestions helped improve the book. LeAnn supported this project from the beginning and offered sage advice along the way.

My family has been wonderfully encouraging of my academic work. I am grateful to my brother, Peter Linett, and his spouse, Cheryl Slover-Linett, their daughters, Amelia and Sophie Linett, my father, David Linett, and his spouse, Penny Linett, my mother, Deena Linett, and my parents-in-law, Mary Naughton and Seamus Naughton, for their interest in and enthusiasm for my scholarly projects. My mother especially has given feedback on my writing and warmly celebrated my successes. My spouse, Dominic Naughton, generously prioritizes my work, offers practical and realistic feedback, and lovingly sees me through the ups and downs of academic labor. I dedicate this book to our children, Ruth and Lev, who give beautiful shape to our days and our lives.

Contents

Introduction

Disability studies explores the embeddedness of bodies within cultures. Revising the medicalized and individualized understanding of disability—an understanding that places it outside of culture and discourse—disability studies locates disability in social and political relations among bodies and minds understood as impaired, bodies and minds granted the cultural capital of normalcy, and the built and social environment. In fact, disability studies scholars point out that not only the social category of disability but also the seemingly medical category of impairment are socially constructed, in that cultures define levels of functioning that count as ablebodied and levels that do not.[1] Disability studies asks that we consider disability—along with race, class, gender, nationality, and sexuality—as a component of identity. It is therefore closely related to gender studies, contributing to, and indeed transforming, the ongoing inquiry within the humanities into the category of "the body."[2]

Bodies of Modernism engages particularly with *literary* disability studies, which examines cultural constructions and metaphoric uses of disability within artistic representations. Rosemarie Garland-Thomson puts it succinctly when she says that her book *Extraordinary Bodies* explores "how representation attaches meanings to bodies" (5). Literary disability studies considers questions that have long been ignored: What metaphoric meanings accrue to disabled characters in fiction? How does the presence of disability shape the trajectory of the narrative in which it appears? How do texts enlist disability to grapple with broader themes such as subjectivity, sexuality, and knowledge? How does disability affect the formal properties of texts? Literary criticism not informed by disability studies has treated and still treats disabled characters as *simply* flawed, *naturally* objects of pity or scorn, and thereby replicates rather than illuminates the roles disability plays in literary narrative. This project joins a body of work by scholars such as Michael Davidson, Lennard Davis, Rosemarie Garland-Thomson, Martha Stoddard Holmes, Alison Kafer, Janet Lyon, Ato Quayson, Ellen Samuels, Rebecca Sanchez, Joseph Valente, and others that explores the formal and thematic work disability performs for literary texts.

Modernist studies is now, a bit belatedly, embracing disability studies as a mode of exploring modernist texts.[3] Modernism, indeed, offers rich soil for disability analysis because of its capacious reach, its intense reflection on the relation between the mind and the body and on ways of knowing the world, and its experimentation with literary form. Because modernist authors believed fiction should be expansive, even in some cases encyclopedic, they included myriad human types in their fictional worlds (as Bernard boasts in Woolf's *The Waves*, his book will "run to many volumes embracing every known variety of man and woman" [67–68]). Because many modernist authors were focused on representing the impressions that "fall upon the mind," as Woolf puts it, they thought carefully about sensory perception. Because they wanted to break with the form of the traditional novel, they connected their attempts to reshape narrative to deformity. They therefore inquired into the metaphoric meanings disabilities had come to bear, often challenging normative understandings of embodiment.

One purpose for which modernist fiction uses disabled characters is to distinguish itself from its predecessor, Victorian realism, where disability was often saturated with pity and pathos. In Dickens's *A Christmas Carol* (1843), to take the clearest example, the disabled character Tiny Tim says "God bless us, every one!" and the narrator repeats the line triumphantly at the end of the novella. This blessing is alluded to and inverted in Joyce's *Ulysses*, where the "blind stripling" curses a man whose coat brushes his cane: "God's curse on you, he said sourly, whoever you are! You're blinder nor I am, you bitch's bastard!" (10.1119–20). The curse and the Dublin dialect signal a self-conscious revision of the roles disability might play in literary texts. Although Joyce's protagonist Leopold Bloom does think, "Poor young fellow" about the blind man, Joyce has him reconsider his own response: "Look at all the things they can learn to do. Read with their fingers. Tune pianos. Or are we surprised they have any brains. Why we think a deformed person or a hunchback clever if he says something we might say" (8.1116–17). This refusal of pathos, this effort to analyze individual and cultural responses to disabled characters, characterizes modernism's understanding of disability not as a given, but as a question.

While modernism frequently questions the ideology of normalcy, it also at times presents itself as creating new, more able, more fit forms for the modern world. In this mode it entwines itself with the eugenic thinking dominant during the period. Russian Futurist Vladimir Mayakovsky's call to "Destroy the old language, powerless to keep up with life's leaps and bounds" (qtd. in Armstrong, *Modernism: A Cultural History* 5) is representative of this metaphorically eugenic attitude. Henry James similarly links the wrong kind of writing to disability when he remarks that World War I caused "a loss of expression through increase of limpness" (qtd. in Armstrong, *Modernism: A Cultural History* 17). Woolf applies eugenic rhetoric to writing in a 1920 essay, "Men and Women," where she writes that "to try the accepted forms, to discard the unfit, to create others which are more fitting, is a task that must be accomplished before there is freedom or achievement" (*Essays* 3:195). Conversely, Michael Levenson quotes Wyndham Lewis's claim that the conflict of radical art with tradition "renders the artists and other people who create new things more agile and energetic than they otherwise would be" (139). Lewis here links the newness of art with physical ability.[4] As I demonstrate in chapter 3, modernist authors represent deafness as an antithesis to modernism's desire to forge new forms of connection and expression. And as chapter 5 makes clear, Woolf and Olive Moore use deformity to indicate types of writing they want to supersede, while aligning forms of modernism of which they approve with having, in Woolf's terms, "free use of [one's] limbs" (*Room* 76).[5] Alongside its questioning of normalcy, then, modernism does use disability to represent states of being it seeks to surpass, and in both of these modes—the antinormative and the eugenic—it casts itself as distinctively modern.[6]

Bodies of Modernism explores the ways canonical and noncanonical writers from both sides of the Atlantic used physical disabilities as means to question ideas about sexuality, intimacy, communication, knowledge, and subjectivity more broadly, and to reflect on the formal experimentation crucial to modernist praxis. In so doing, it demonstrates modernism's multifaceted dependence—for its dramatic power as well as for its self-presentation as a break from past forms—on metaphoric uses of disabled bodies. And it adds depth and shading to the picture being drawn by disability studies scholars of how different features or functions of bodies accrue meaning within literary representation. It thereby explores how literary depictions of disabled characters help shape cultural ideas (however inaccurate) about how impairments influence subjectivities.[7]

Disabled Characters

Although this study considers disabled characters, it does so in order to open up larger issues about cultural interpretations of the body. In *Enforcing Normalcy*, Lennard Davis writes that when he told people he was working on that book, they mistakenly assumed he was writing about deaf characters. He writes, "The phase of raising awareness about the treatment of disabled characters in literature has been ably carried through and continues to be studied, but finally there is a limit to what can be said—that disabled characters are usually villains or outcasts, but that when they are not they are glorified as testaments to the human spirit" (124). Certainly disability studies can profitably discuss texts without disabled characters, as demonstrated in Sanchez's recent *Deafening Modernism* and as discussed by Michael Bérubé in *The Secret Life of Stories*. Bérubé acknowledges that disabled characters are key to exploring disability: "What else would we be talking about but bodies and minds, if the subject is disability?" But as he notes, disability scholars must remain aware that "disability is also, always already, a social relation, involving beliefs and social practices that structure the apprehension of disability—and of putative human 'norms'" (25).

While keeping in mind that these social relations inform texts with and without disabled characters, I nevertheless find that Davis's dismissal takes a narrow view of what it can mean to explore disabled characters. Asserting that a character is an outcast or outsider ought to serve only as the beginning of an inquiry. Consider, for example, Douglas Baynton's explanation of the two main modes of understanding the "tragedy" of deafness in the first and second halves of the nineteenth century. In both contexts, deaf people were considered outsiders, but early to mid-nineteenth-century Christian reformers understood this status differently from late nineteenth-century nationalists because, as Baynton explains, they were thinking of quite different "insides" and "outsides." Christian reformers viewed deafness as a tragedy because it ousted deaf people from the Christian community, and sign language solved this problem by providing an avenue through which to convey the Gospel. Later assimilationists viewed deafness as a tragedy because it ousted deaf people from the *national* community, and so for them sign language exacerbated the problem and only lipreading and speaking English could begin to solve it (*Forbidden Signs* 16ff).

If Baynton had stopped after asserting that deaf people were outsiders throughout the nineteenth century, he would have missed the chance to explain not only cultural attitudes toward deafness but also how the shift from favoring sign language to campaigning against it related to broader trends in American history. In the case of literary studies, we can use our analyses of how characters are depicted as launching pads to understand both the intricacies of textual dynamics and the cultural meanings of various disabilities and aspects of bodiliness and personhood. The goal, that is, is not just to discover how a character is depicted by its author, but also how that depiction affects the overall workings of the text and what it tells us about how embodiment was understood in particular times and places.

In my chapter on deafness here, I do examine the isolation of deaf characters, but with an eye toward understanding how such isolation is artificially constructed by the texts and what functions it serves for them; moreover, I explore connections between oralism and a sense, pervading the fictions, that visuality is an inadequate mode for thinking and knowing. The notion that visual thinking is utterly alien, in turn, leads to portrayals of deaf characters' minds as inaccessible to their narrators. And the deaf characters' epistemological failure demonstrates a surprisingly strong connection in the early twentieth century between knowing and hearing, a connection usually overshadowed by the more obvious and long-standing one between knowing and seeing. So, by starting with depictions of deaf characters, we gain insight into the narrative conceits of the fictions and their broader concerns, as well as into complex and sometimes hidden cultural assumptions about relations among deaf bodies, communication, and knowledge.

In their influential 2000 book *Narrative Prosthesis*, David Mitchell and Sharon Snyder open up analysis of the ways disabled characters are represented metaphorically as well as how their presence affects textual dynamics. As they point out, "The issue of representation and what it produces in readers proves exceedingly complex" (41). While they read the disabled tin soldier in "The Steadfast Tin Soldier" as representing "social and individual collapse" (48), they also note that literary narratives use disability as a crutch to strengthen their "representational power, disruptive potentiality, and analytical insight" (49)—that is, disabled bodies can be productive for literary narrative.[8] Building on this insight, *Bodies of Modernism* demonstrates some of the ways physical disability is productive for modernism. In chapter 4 in particular I engage with "narrative prosthesis" by discussing what it can mean to turn disabled characters into metaphors.

Modernist Bodyminds

In their writings about disability, modernist authors implicitly acknowledge the constant interplay between the body and the mind, the existence of what Margaret Price suggests (following trauma studies) that we call the bodymind (269). Beginning with the body, modernist representations of physical disability end up reflecting on the whole human being. Their depictions demonstrate the remarkable degree to which bodies, including their impairments, are embedded in culture. As Elizabeth Grosz writes in *Volatile Bodies*, the body has long "remained mired in presumptions regarding its naturalness, its fundamentally biological and precultural status . . . its brute status as given, unchangeable, inert" (x). But by their nature, Grosz argues, animate bodies have an "organic or ontological 'incompleteness' or lack of finality, an amenability to social completion, social ordering and organization" (xi). Literary representations of impaired bodies form part of that process of completing the body, that "social ordering and organization." This is why, as Michael Davidson suggests, literary art "defamiliarizes not only language but the body normalized within language" (*Concerto* 118).

In the twenty-first century, especially in the wake of Foucault's discussions of biopower and docile bodies and Judith Butler's claims about the performativity of identity, it has become familiar to think of the body as encultured.[9] But even in an era when the sexed and/or raced body is understood (at least by scholars in the humanities and social sciences) to be culturally constructed, many people still take disabilities as biological givens. The attitude lingers: "either you can walk or hear or see, or you cannot. These are biological facts. What is there to discuss?"[10] This may be part of an enduring tension within social constructionism, as outlined by Chris Shilling: "While constructionism tells us much about the social forces constructing something called the 'body' . . . there is a tendency . . . to remain mute about what the body is, why it can assume such importance in society, and whether different dimensions of embodiment are open to different degrees of construction by society" (76). Indeed, Tobin Siebers argues that underneath even Foucault's constructionism lies an idealized conception of a natural, able body that has been constrained and remade by modern history. The "purer and fitter" body has been replaced by the docile body, but "if the docile body is disabled . . . it means that recent body theory has reproduced the most abhorrent prejudices of ableist society" (*Disability Theory* 58). In addition to revealing such fantasies of a natural, fit body, disability studies can also help explain how different dimensions of bodies are encultured in particular times, spaces, and bodies of literature.

Modernism's animating interest in our status as (in Aristotle's famous phrase) the "thinking animal" gives particular resonance to its examination of the interrelations between mind and body. It is important for scholars to consider the role of mental disabilities—neurological, intellectual, and psychological—in literary texts, especially those modernist texts that aim to explore the condition of living as a thinking body. Given the strong links between modernism and psychology and the history of readings of literary madness that either accept the medical model or dematerialize madness so that it stands for feminist resistance, disability studies approaches to madness in modernism will be particularly valuable.[11] And indeed there is exciting work being done about various kinds of mental disability in modernist texts.[12] In this study, however, I restrict my inquiry to the ways physical disabilities and embodiment generally are imagined to affect and even suffuse the whole person.

Modernism's representations of the relations between bodily aspects and subjectivity do not generally succeed in showing how a mobility impairment, deafness, blindness, or deformity might actually affect human subjectivity. A mixture of factors such as writers' training in compulsory ablebodiedness (McRuer 2), their ignorance—inadvertent or willful—about particular disabilities, and contemporaneous or long-standing cultural associations of particular abilities with particular aspects of subjectivity (for example, seeing with knowing) led writers to craft their representations such that they reveal far more about cultural readings of the body and disability than about disability itself. This book, then, is not about disability as anyone actually experiences it but about modernist *imaginings* of disability's effects on the bodymind.

The sociologist Zygmunt Bauman, drawing on work by Artur Sandauer, has labeled the othering of Jews, whether framed positively or negatively, as *allosemitism*. "'Allosemitism' refers to the practice of setting the Jews apart as people radically different from all the others, needing separate concepts to describe and comprehend them and special treatment in all or most social intercourse" (Bauman 143). This notion applies as well to disabled people, and in accordance with it I view ableism not exclusively as the disparagement or dehumanization of disabled people, but also as the conviction that disabled people are radically other, that their disabilities, whether congenital or acquired, change them in ways that create a gulf between "them" and ablebodied "us." David Mitchell and Sharon Snyder describe such a gulf when they write that "literary narratives . . . pos[e] disability as an 'alien' terrain that promises the revelation of a previously uncomprehended experience" (*Narrative Prosthesis* 55). We see this othering in the popular belief in disabled people's "inspiring" bravery: insisting on disabled people's bravery suggests that they need a special kind of strength to live their lives, a strength different from what ablebodied people need to live theirs, however many difficulties and losses they may face.[13]

The othering of physically disabled characters shapes modernism because of modernism's strong interest in the bodymind, in the ways our bodies shape our psychic experiences and vice versa. While any characterization of a literary movement or period must be partial and provisional, admitting exceptions, we can assert of modernism generally that it moves the focus of fiction inward, toward the human psyche, self, or soul, to explore human consciousness.[14] David Lodge has described modernist fiction as "concerned with consciousness, and also with the subconscious and unconscious workings of the human mind." Instead of chronological narration, he writes, we find "introspection, analysis, reflection, and reverie" (*Modes of Modern Writing* 45). Hugh Witemeyer lists "a fascination with the unconscious and irrational activities of the human psyche" as one of four qualities demarcating modernist literature (1). D. H. Lawrence claimed that "the real activity of life is . . . *developing consciousness*" (*Selected Letters* 428). And Woolf makes it clear in many essays that her aim was to represent the mind's experiences of life rather than the external features of that life. For example, in her review of Dorothy Richardson's *Revolving Lights* she writes, "We want to be rid of realism, to penetrate without its help into the regions beneath it" (*Women and Writing* 191).

Woolf's most famous characterization of the task of the novelist, in "Modern Fiction," further clarifies her view:

> The mind receives a myriad impressions—trivial, fantastic, evanescent, or engraved with the sharpness of steel. From all sides they come, an incessant shower of innumerable atoms. . . . Life is not a series of gig lamps symmetrically arranged; life is a luminous halo, a semi-transparent envelope surrounding us from the beginning of consciousness to the end. Is it not the task of the novelist to convey this varying, this unknown and uncircumscribed spirit, whatever aberration or complexity it may display, with as little mixture of the alien and external as possible? (189)

Here Woolf sets out the task of the novelist as recording impressions that fall upon the mind of her character noting slightly later that "for the moderns . . . the point of interest, lies very likely in the dark places of psychology" (192).

In shifting the "stuff of fiction" inward, modernists participated in developments such as the new physics—as can be seen in Woolf's use of atom imagery—and the new sciences of sexology and psychology. In these fields, surface realities had been swept aside to reveal deeper truths underneath.[15] As Mark Micale argues in the introduction to *The Mind of Modernism*, "both psychiatric medicine and the creative arts during the late nineteenth and early twentieth centuries were marked by a massive 'turn inward'. . . . [They] centered, but then destabilized, the self, and both fields were responsive to the subjectivity of individual consciousness and its relation to the external world" (2). During World War I, as doctors came to realize that shell shock did not necessarily stem from actual shell explosions, the mind similarly gained ground as a mysterious actor (Armstrong, *Modernism: A Cultural History* 20). The relationships between psychology and literature were complex and dynamic. It was not just a matter of psychology influencing literature but of cross-influences as well as misappropriations, distortions, and sometimes rejections (Micale 16).

This inward focus raised many questions for modernist authors, such as how consciousness, the interior self, relates to the body. Did modernist emphasis on the mind mean writers should ignore the body as so much materialist dross? Or did it mean they could or should redefine the body and its role in our human identity? Maurice Merleau-Ponty later rejected the first option, arguing that "one does not account for the facts by superimposing a pure, contemplative consciousness on a thinglike body" (4). Joyce similarly told Frank Budgen, "If [characters] had no body they would have no mind. It's all one" (Budgen 21). And Woolf comes to the same conclusion in her essay "On Being Ill" (1930), where she asserts that "literature does its best to maintain that its concern is with the mind; that the body is a sheet of plain glass through which the soul looks straight and clear. . . . On the contrary, the very opposite is true. All day, all night the body intervenes" (4). The possibility of ignoring the body is, she implies, an illusion fostered by physical wellness or ablebodiedness. The "creature within" must engage the world through the body: "it cannot separate off from the body like the sheath of a knife or the pod of a pea for a single instant; it must go through the whole unending procession of changes, heat and cold, comfort and discomfort, hunger and satisfaction, health and illness, until there comes the inevitable catastrophe" (4–5). Throughout the essay Woolf discusses the relation of the body to the mind, to literature, and to language.

The question of whether one can express in language what the body feels runs through much of Woolf's work. For example, in "Professions for Women" she describes a "girl sitting with a pen in her hand." The young writer's imagination "sweep[s] unchecked round every rock and cranny of the world that lies submerged in the depths of our unconscious being" until she thinks of something that brings her roaming imagination to a smashing halt. "To speak without figure she had thought of something, something about the body, about the passions which it was unfitting for her as a woman to say" (240). Gendered norms of propriety are just one factor that prevents writers from being able to speak the truth about the body. In "On Being Ill" the reasons are cast in more general terms: that we cannot communicate across bodies. "There is a virgin forest in each; a snowfield where even the print of birds' feet is unknown. Here we go alone, and like it better so. . . . In health the genial pretense must be kept up. . . . In illness this make-believe ceases" (12). When the body interposes itself through illness, Woolf claims, the truth of our aloneness is laid bare. The body, then, is a key aspect of Woolf's work, both affecting her process ("the body intervenes") and serving as a subject she seeks new methods to express.

Joyce's primary way of exploring the body's relation to the inner self is, to Woolf's famous disgust, to describe in detail aspects of bodiliness that writers had usually eschewed: to represent his characters eating, defecating, copulating, masturbating, and menstruating. He famously claimed that *Ulysses* is an "epic of the human body," with bodily rhythms determining not only the characters' trajectories but the rhythms of the episodes (Budgen 21). In her book about Picasso, Stein joins in celebrating the body as the thing itself: "for [Picasso] the reality of life is in the head, the face and the body and this is for him so important, so persistent, so complete that it is not at all necessary to think of any other thing and the soul is another thing. . . . The soul of people does not interest him, why interest one's self in the souls of people when the face, the head, the body can tell everything" (13, 47).

Lawrence considers the relation between the mind and the body by focusing, in much of his work, on the potential rejuvenation of the soul made available through heterosexual and homosocial contact. In his chapter of *Fantasia of the Unconscious* called "The Five Senses," he complains that the "orthodox view" is that the soul, if it exists at all, "sits somewhat vaguely within the machine" of the body. "If anything goes wrong with the machine, why, the soul is forgotten instantly" (64). Lawrence argues that any body must be driven, as is a bicycle by a rider, by a "central god," the soul. But his fiction everywhere suggests a more complex relation between body and soul than this metaphor of the bicycle implies. After all, a bicycle cannot experience the world or other human beings and thereby transform its rider. As Siebers points out, it's "easier to imagine the body as a garment, vehicle, or burden than as a complex system that defines our humanity, any knowledge we might possess, and our individual and collective futures" (*Disability Theory* 26).

Modernist interest in the relation of the mind to the body and its world bears out David Herman's contention that the "inward turn" is really more of a "foregrounding of the inextricable connection between 'inner' and 'outer' domains—with the scare quotes indicating the extent to which the narratives in question undermine the classical, Cartesian dichotomy between mind and body, the mental and material" (253). The mind, Herman suggests, "emerges through humans' dynamic interdependencies with the social and material environments they seek to navigate" (254). Such dynamic interdependencies also occur in and through the bodies navigating those environments. As Merleau-Ponty argues, we mustn't forget "the insertion of the mind in corporeality, the ambiguous relation which we entertain with our body" (4). Modernist writers' engagement with this ambiguous relation is played out in their representations of bodies in various impaired states, disabled bodies.

It is tempting, as Siebers acknowledges, to "view disability and pain as more real than their opposites" (*Disability Theory* 67). As John Whittier-Ferguson notes in his discussion of this idea in Siebers's work, disability "focuses attention on the fact of corporeality" (*Mortality* 183). This happens because compulsory ablebodiedness allows the nondisabled body to appropriate the neutral condition of invisibility, as do whiteness, maleness, and heterosexuality.[16] But as Siebers asserts, "the disabled body is no more real than the able body—and no less real" (*Disability Theory* 67). We are equally embodied, whether we are disabled or not; but in our ableist cultures, embodiment *seems* unequally distributed. Attitudes toward signed languages are a good example: they have consistently been seen as more embodied than spoken languages, though spoken languages, as Jennifer Esmail reminds her readers, require "the vocal organs, tongue, and lips" because "speech is as embodied as sign" (992–93).

For Wyndham Lewis, whom Whittier-Ferguson discusses, "disabled bodies signify the very fact and conditions of human embodiment" (*Mortality* 183). Without endorsing their association of the disabled body with embodiment (which implies a dissociation of the nondisabled body from embodiment), I submit that this is true also of the writers discussed here. But as becomes clear in the chapters that follow, their explorations of embodiment always circle back to become explorations of qualities that include but surpass bodiliness. The modernist body is never, as Wallace Stevens wrote of the ocean, "wholly body, fluttering its empty sleeves" (*Collected* 128). Instead, modernist bodies give rise to broad speculations about sexuality, intimacy, subjectivity, communication, knowledge, and artistic production.

Modern Bodies

In the late nineteenth and early twentieth centuries, ideas about the body and about disability changed significantly. In *Modernism, Technology, and the*

Body, Tim Armstrong traces "a revolution in perceptions of the body" over the course of the nineteenth century (2). By the early twentieth century, the body was no longer a "boundary"; instead, it "could be penetrated by a barrage of devices," from stethoscopes and speculums to x-rays (2). One change particularly relevant to modernist representations of bodiliness emerged from the fact that "Darwinian science suggested a substrata of primitive material within the body and brain, and aroused widespread fears of regression, destabilizing relations between self and world" (3). As I discuss further in chapter 2, modernism's inward turn is related to this question of how the self or psyche relates to its surroundings. While Armstrong is discussing the ways technology was enlisted to compensate for perceived lacks in human embodiment, his assertion that "modernist texts have a peculiar fascination with the limits of the body" (4) resonates for modernist representations of disability. Armstrong persuasively claims that "modernists with quite different attitudes to social and technological modernity saw the body as the locus of anxiety, even crisis" (4), and he traces the ways technology soothed this anxiety. In this study I consider another effect of anxiety about the body's role: inquiries into physical disabilities that explore and purport to explain the relations of particular functions (e.g., walking, hearing, seeing) to aspects of subjectivity.

Modernists considered disability also in part because the meanings of disabilities were quite different in the early twentieth century than they had been, say, in the mid-nineteenth. Eugenics was at its peak in the years between the two world wars, and far from being a fringe movement, it was mainstream science.[17] Now that human populations had become objects of scientific study, "defects" in individuals became "defects" in the body politic. As Siebers puts it, "eugenics weds medical science to a disgust with mental and physical variation" (*Disability Aesthetics* 27). It seemed to many that the Great War had killed off or disabled the majority of "fit" young men. Richard Overy notes that "in a foreword to Marie Stopes's *Contraception*, published in 1928, Sir James Barr, onetime president of the British Medical Association, testily observed that 'while the virility of the nation was carrying on the war the derelicts were carrying on the race'" (98). Eugenics formed a strong component of the birth control movement, as Margaret Sanger in the United States and Marie Stopes in Britain sought to popularize birth control among "undesirable" populations.[18]

In an article entitled "These Pushful Days," Douglas Baynton sets out to explain the "dramatically more negative" social attitudes toward disabled people in this period. I quote Baynton at length to give a sense of the variety of means by which discrimination against disabled people was codified:

> In the United States, as in many other industrialised countries, tens of thousands of people with psychiatric or intellectual disabilities were segregated into institutions, involuntarily sterilised, or prohibited from marrying under state eugenics laws. Popular books, articles, and silent films advocated, and some physicians practised, the euthanasia of disabled infants. A campaign to end the use of sign language among deaf people led to its prohibition in most classrooms in schools for the deaf. At the same time that widespread discrimination prevented many disabled people from earning a wage, many cities enacted "unsightly beggar" ordinances that prohibited the "diseased, maimed, mutilated, or in any way deformed" from begging. The United States, like other immigrant nations, passed a series of restrictive laws to prevent the entry of "undesirable defectives" into the country. (43)

Baynton explains this shift with an astute analysis of conceptions of time, which were themselves changing markedly because of developments in physics, geology, biology, and technology. He shows that disabilities went from being seen as static and outside of time (atemporal "afflictions") to being seen as impairments in and of time: bodies that were handicapped in the race of life or retarded in their development or moving backward along a degenerate course ("Pushful" 47–48).

Eugenics is in many ways itself about time; Jessica Mehr argues that "eugenics is about slower bodies who cannot keep pace with accelerated labor and homogenous public time; it is about seizing control of humanity's evolutionary timeline, shaping the future instead of waiting for it to unfold" (4). Eugenics aimed to speed up evolution by removing retarding forces (such as "the feebleminded") and encouraging forces thought to contribute to forward progress.[19] And as Lennard Davis demonstrates, eugenics was a manifestation of a process of normalization that began in the mid-nineteenth century with the rise of industry, statistics, and social applications of Darwin's theories (*Enforcing Normalcy* 23–39).

This atmosphere of enforced normalization or intense compulsory able-bodiedness was emblematized in immigration officials scrutinizing immigrants for any sign of physical, mental, or even "moral" anomalies. As Baynton remarks elsewhere, "the exclusion of disabled people was central to the laws and the work of the immigration service. As the Commissioner General of Immigration reported in 1907, 'The exclusion from this country of the morally, mentally, and physically deficient is the principal object to be accomplished by the immigration laws'" ("Disability" 27). In a rhetorical analysis of the process of scrutinizing prospective immigrants at Ellis Island, Jay Dolmage traces the spatial politics of visual examinations by officials placed at several angles to the approaching immigrants. He describes the inspection process as "the choreographic and architectural brainchild of Jeremy Bentham and Henry Ford—a panopticon and an assembly line" ("Disabled upon Arrival" 31–32). Although the inspection process at Ellis Island created the most direct scrutiny, an atmosphere of inspection that took in race and ethnicity, class, gender, and disability pervaded early twentieth-century cities in both the United States and Britain.

In addition to the United States working assiduously to keep out disabled immigrants, the local ordinances Baynton mentions, the "ugly laws," worked to keep "unsightly" people out of view.[20] In *The Ugly Laws*, Susan Schweik details these laws and examines their relationship to American history and attitudes toward disability. Chicago's law reads, in part, "Any person who is diseased, maimed, mutilated, or in any way deformed, so as to be an unsightly or disgusting object, or an improper person to be allowed in or on the streets, highways, thoroughfares, or public places in this city, shall not therein or thereon expose himself to public view, under penalty of a fine of $1 [about $20 today] for each offense" (Schweik 1–2). Schweik explains that the laws, passed by the majority of major American cities from the period after the Civil War through the early twentieth century, represent "a strong and unified project . . . involving both a judgment about bodily aesthetics and the use of law to repress the visibility of human diversity in social contexts associated with disability and poverty" (3).

Modernist Disabilities

In an era that valued certain kinds of bodily conformity so highly, it is no surprise that modernist writers—who often positioned themselves as rejecting conformity in favor of imaginative integrity—would reconsider disability as one angle from which to approach the role of the body within literature that revolved around consciousness. Literary treatments of disability cross lines of genre, nation, and market; this study therefore treats a range of transatlantic texts, from short stories by Flannery O'Connor, Eudora Welty, H. G. Wells, and D. H. Lawrence, to novels by less canonical modernists such as Elizabeth Bowen, Henry Green, Olive Moore, and Carson McCullers, to plays by Tennessee Williams and J. M. Synge, to Florence Barclay's popular romance *The Rosary*, to Woolf's late-modernist novel *The Years*, and to the "high modernist" classic *Ulysses* and sections of *Finnegans Wake*. Because of

Joyce's influence on other writers, his persistent attention to the multiplicity of human beings, and his patent curiosity about the role of the human body, his work serves as a sort of spine (to use a bodily metaphor) of the study, discussed in three of the chapters. But as this array of texts makes clear, overall I am relying on a capacious definition of modernism as containing "a number of divergent tendencies" (Miller 22) in accordance with what Douglas Mao and Rebecca Walkowitz have called the "new modernist studies."

Mao and Walkowitz assert that in "seeking a single word to sum up transformations in modernist literary scholarship over the past decade or two, one could do worse than light on *expansion*. In its expansive tendency, the field is hardly unique: all period-centered areas of literary scholarship have broadened in scope, and this in what we might think of as temporal, spatial, and vertical directions" ("New Modernist Studies" 737). Most of the works I consider in *Bodies of Modernism* are located temporally within what Mao and Walkowitz call the "core period of about 1890–1945" (738). This makes it possible to consider their conceptions of disability in light of contemporaneous understandings of bodies such as those outlined above.

While several of the texts included here are noncanonical or have been considered middlebrow, Mao and Walkowitz's discussion of the expansion along a "vertical axis"—"in which once quite sharp boundaries between high art and popular forms of culture have been reconsidered"—applies most to my inclusion of Barclay's *The Rosary*, a best-selling popular romance from 1909. As will become clear in chapter 2, this novel seeks to insert itself into canonical representations of blindness by building an intertextual relationship with *Jane Eyre*; and it shares with the other texts considered there an interest in blindness as part of a fully lived life that is conducive to, rather than destructive of, romantic intimacy. Treating modernism as a diverse set of responses to and reflections of modern life and modern bodies, *Bodies of Modernism* demonstrates the extent to which modernist writers relied on disability to think through the relation of the newly foregrounded mind to the inescapable body.

Moving from mobility impairments to sensory impairments to deformity, the chapters that follow explore connections in modernist texts between physical disabilities and aspects of subjectivity the authors represent as related to those disabilities. In chapter 1, "Mobility and Sexuality," I consider depictions of women with mobility impairments in the context of discourses saturated with eugenics and with the idea that walking upright—as evidenced by media coverage of archaeological finds in the early twentieth century—was a crucial indicator of humanity. Discussing Tennessee Williams's *The Glass*

Menagerie (1944), Flannery O'Connor's "Good Country People" (1955), and James Joyce's "Nausicaa" episode of *Ulysses* (1922), this chapter charts a wave-like textual dynamic in which disability recedes to make way for sexuality but then returns with force. This initial chapter demonstrates both the inverse cultural relation between disability and sexuality (the more disability, the less sexuality, especially for women, whose status as sexual commodities meant more pressure not to appear as "damaged goods") and the ways that this inverse relationship collapses, revealing a more complex relation between disability and sexuality within the fictionalized worlds and relationships.

The next three chapters focus on sensory disabilities. As Armstrong points out, "a heightened sensitivity to sensation is central to modern experience," especially as "the senses themselves are reconceived" (*Modernism: A Cultural History* 90).[21] Modernist writers' representations of sensory disability demonstrate their mixed responses to the inward turn of their literary and cultural era. On the one hand, focusing attention largely on consciousness and inner life provides an opportunity for communion with the self or soul and with individual human beings. Several modernist authors associate this set of opportunities with blindness, which to them provides a way to shut out superficial visual reality and focus on more meaningful concerns, such as romantic love. Chapter 2, "Blindness and Intimacy," traces the relationship between blindness and intimacy in five early twentieth-century texts: H. G. Wells's "The Country of the Blind" (1904), J. M. Synge's *The Well of the Saints* (1905), Florence Barclay's *The Rosary* (1909), D. H. Lawrence's "The Blind Man" (1920), and Henry Green's *Blindness* (1926). It argues that Wells and Green connect blindness to intimacy but then reject the pairing in favor of particular conceptions of individual freedom; and that Synge, Barclay, and Lawrence associate blindness both with romantic love and with some of the most valuable opportunities attendant on the inward turn: opportunities to access "life or spirit, truth or reality, this, the essential thing" (Woolf, "Modern Fiction" 188).

The inwardness of modernism, however, was also in some ways a response to and reflection of the alienation associated with increased industrialization. While turning inward could make possible deeper communion with a single other, it could on the other hand break down community and lead to isolation, with each singular person failing to "connect" or communicate with others.[22] Several modernist authors associate this set of dangers with deafness, which they saw as the condition of separateness. Chapter 3, "Deafness, Communication, and Knowledge," builds on the history of oralist attitudes around the turn of the twentieth century to explore the central role of spoken language in understandings of humanness. The chapter considers the imagined relation between deafness, communication, and access to knowledge in Eudora Welty's "The Key" (1941), Carson McCullers's *The Heart Is a Lonely Hunter* (1940), and Elizabeth Bowen's *Eva Trout* (1968). In these texts, oralism's construction of speech and hearing as absolutely necessary makes itself felt in a rejection of signed languages and, more broadly, of visuality.

Chapter 4, "Knowledge Redux: Sensory Disability in *Ulysses*," extends the book's inquiry into sensory disability by pausing to consider representations of the "blind stripling" and the deaf waiter "bald Pat" in Joyce's *Ulysses* (1922). I treat Joyce's blind and deaf characters together first because Joyce's representations of deafness and blindness differ in some key ways from those of his contemporaries, and second because Joyce connects his deaf and blind characters by casting sensory impairments as metaphors for a sort of willful suspension of knowledge. *Ulysses* deconstructs the association of sensory disabilities with not-knowing while at the same time playfully relying on it to help convey the poignancy of Bloom's predicament as he tries not to think about his wife's scheduled rendezvous with her lover, Blazes Boylan.

Not only did modernism's inwardness become linked in these complex ways to sensory disability, but its emphasis on stylistic experimentation also gave rise to disability associations. In considering how to re-form or deform the literary text, modernist authors considered the deformed body. The book therefore builds to a more sustained consideration of the relationship between modernism and disability in chapter 5. While all the chapters consider the relation of disability to modernist projects, "Deformity and Modernist Form" turns more explicitly to the metadiscursive question of how thinking about disability helped to shape modernism. While modernists were being linked to degeneracy and deformity by Nazi art historians and eugenic discourses more generally, they were also engaged in a process of de-forming the novel. As they reflected on modernist experimentation from the vantage of the 1930s, Moore, Woolf, and Joyce self-consciously linked imaginative writing to bodily deformity. As Siebers points out about visual art, there is a sense in which modernism "embrace[s] disability as a distinct version of the beautiful" (*Disability Aesthetics* 9). In *Spleen* (1930), Moore associates the deformed body with women's modernism, which she disparages, while nevertheless relying on deformity in her attempt to supersede the work of other women modernists. In *The Years* (1937), Woolf tentatively turns her back on her earlier experimental techniques, considering—in more complex ways than she had in *A Room of One's Own*—the relation between the deformed body and the modernist imagination. And in the "Shem the Penman" chapter of *Finnegans*

Wake (1939), Joyce takes his literary experimentation to a new extreme, simultaneously revaluing the deformed body as the body of the modernist text. While only Joyce went so far as to celebrate deformity as modernist textuality, all of these texts connect literary form with bodily deformity.

Ideas about bodies play key roles in social hierarchies. Garland-Thomson points out that "the gender, race, ethnicity, sexuality, class and ability systems exert tremendous social pressures to shape, regulate, and normalize subjugated bodies" ("Integrating" 339). Critiques of such systems and of the work they perform in literary texts that do not take disability into account risk reifying assumptions of wholeness and naturalness that they set out to undermine. A poignant example can be found in lesbian novelist and activist Jeanette Winterson's response to a Deaf lesbian couple who used a Deaf sperm donor in a successful effort to bear deaf children. Winterson writes, "We can make our world as friendly as possible for people with different physical capacities, but we cannot change the simple fact that it is better to have five senses than four" (np). In her expression of the ideology of normalcy, Winterson mistakes a heavily culturally constructed set of assumptions—even the notion that we have five senses is a cultural invention, with other cultures and contemporary scientists identifying more than five[23]—for "simple fact." Winterson is relying on norms she would in other contexts surely resist: norms of naturalness that act to press the variety of human beings into a single mold. As Garland-Thomson argues, "to embrace the supposedly flawed body of disability is to critique the normalizing, phallic fantasies of wholeness, unity, coherence, and completeness" ("Integrating" 351). And this in turn suggests that if we are still relying on norms of wholeness and completeness about bodies, our inclusive ideologies (such as our work against sexism, homophobia, racism, and fascism) and even our status as postmodern subjects who distrust universalizing narratives are all to some degree suspect. An analysis of disability, that is, is a necessary component of progressive scholarship. In what follows I hope to contribute to readings of modernist literature that reveal both its skepticism about and its dependence on fantasies of whole, "normal" bodies.

One

Mobility and Sexuality

In Virginia Woolf's 1927 essay "Street Haunting," the narrator, playing the flâneuse with the excuse that she wants to buy a pencil, becomes satiated with the "beauty pure and uncomposed" of the London streets and decides to enter "some duskier chamber of being where we may ask . . . 'What, then, is it like to be a dwarf?'" Since the narrator only then tells us that a dwarf is entering the boot shop, it is as if she has conjured her from her own desire for something other than beauty. From the start of the vignette, that is, disability is contrasted with beauty; the "dusky chamber" where the narrator encounters physical difference is opposed to the beauty of the "colour" and "warmth" of the city streets.

The dwarf is "escorted by two women who, being of normal size, looked like benevolent giants beside her." She wears the "peevish yet apologetic expression usual on the faces of the deformed. She needed their kindness, yet she resented it" (24). It is not clear why a woman of small stature should need to be accompanied to buy shoes; Woolf seems to have been taken in by the cultural association of physical difference with dependence.[1] Moreover, she is setting up, as Rachel Bowlby points out, two parallel trios: here a dwarf flanked by two average-sized women and, once the narrator leaves the boot shop, two blind men "supporting themselves by resting a hand on the head of a small boy between them" (25; Bowlby 216). In each trio the smaller person is in the center. But disability moves, in the second trio, from the center person to those flanking him. These artificial visual arrangements stress the role of looking, on which the narrator muses throughout the essay. They also inadvertently highlight the relationship between disability and the eye of the normate: disability emerges through the narrator's appraising eyes.[2]

Indeed, looking plays a crucial part in the vignette about the dwarf. When the shop girl brings shoes,

> the dwarf stuck her foot out with an impetuosity which seemed to claim all our attention. Look at that! Look at that! she seemed to demand of us all, as she thrust her foot out, for behold it was the shapely, perfectly proportioned foot of a well-grown woman. It was arched; it was aristocratic. Her whole manner changed as she looked at it resting on the stand. She looked soothed and satisfied. . . . She was thinking that, after all, feet are the most important part of the whole person; women, she said to herself, have been loved for their feet alone. Seeing nothing but her feet, she imagined perhaps that the rest of her body was of a piece with those beautiful feet. . . . Look at my feet, she seemed to be saying, as she took a step this way and then a step that way. (24–25)

In this passage Woolf's narrator claims to be imagining the dwarf's subjectivity, but all she imagines the woman feeling is a desire to be seen, and to be seen as normal.[3] Not only does she conclude that the woman is demanding to be looked at, but appearances matter in multilayered ways: the woman "sees nothing but her feet"; her visible manner changes as she looks at her feet; the narrator's understanding of the woman changes as *she* looks at her feet; the woman *looks* "soothed and satisfied"; and the narrator asks readers to imaginatively "behold" the woman's foot.

Amid all this visuality, however, the dwarf does not look back at the flâneuse. Although the narrator describes the woman's expression, her "peevishness" and "apology" are directed at her two companions or at the "shop girl," not at the narrator. By omitting any mention of the woman returning the narrator's gaze, Woolf cuts off the potential for the kind of encounter described by Garland-Thomson: "An encounter between a starer and a staree sets in motion an interpersonal relationship, however momentary, that has consequences. . . . A staring encounter is a dynamic struggle" (*Staring* 3). This omission forms part of the essay's, and not just the narrator's, dehumanization of its disabled characters, none of whom returns the narrator's gaze.

The narrator flaunts her condescension toward the dwarf by putting quotes around the phrase "this lady" when the "giantesses" ask for shoes to be brought, as if that label may apply only to women of a certain height or shape. But the essay does show insight into the visual dynamics of disability, the way it can be brought to the fore in some situations and moments and be allowed to fade into the background in others. As Garland-Thomson argues elsewhere, "The discrepancy between body and world, between that which is expected and that which is, produces fits and misfits. . . . A fit occurs when a harmonious, proper interaction occurs between a particularly shaped and functioning body and an environment that sustains that body. A misfit occurs when the environment does not sustain the shape and function of the body that enters it" ("Misfits" 593–94). The woman experiences a fit in the shoe store (in more than one sense) but a misfit out on the streets. Her physical difference is more visible when she walks between her taller companions, whereas when all eyes are on her feet in the shoe store, it fades into the background.

But the narrator goes further than demonstrating this dynamic quality of disability when she describes the woman leaving the shop: "the ecstasy faded, knowledge returned, the old peevishness, the old apology came back, and by the time she had reached the street again she had become a dwarf only" (25). In this passage the narrator casts the suspension of disability in the shop not as a result of differing situations or contexts, but as a result of sheer fantasy. The dwarf, she assumes, temporarily imagined that "her body was of a piece with those beautiful feet." Pointing out the fantastical nature of this transformation, Maud Ellmann describes her as "a modern-day Cinderella" ("More Kicks" 268). But now "knowledge return[s]." Disability is incompatible with being a "lady" or even a woman with beautiful feet. The woman is now a "dwarf only." This phrase crystalizes two important assumptions: that disability is the only significant thing about a person, making up the entirety of her identity and determining her psychology, and that sexuality and disability cannot coexist.[4] The woman can be momentarily a sexual being, with her arched, aristocratic feet, *or* she can, more often, be a dwarf; but she cannot be both at the same time.

This wave-like dynamic, wherein disability recedes to make way for sexuality but then returns with force, could be said to describe the narrative arc of three other modernist accounts of disabled women: Laura Wingfield in Tennessee Williams's *The Glass Menagerie* (1944), Hulga Hopewell in Flannery O'Connor's "Good Country People" (1955), and Gerty MacDowell in James Joyce's "Nausicaa" episode of *Ulysses* (1922).[5] Each text offers its own version of this dynamic, establishing but also complicating and to different degrees *collapsing* the inverse relationship between sexuality and disability for women with mobility impairments.

In his portrayal of Laura Wingfield, I argue, Williams links disability with illicit sexuality, using Laura's disability as a screen for a sexuality that is expunged from Laura's character between earlier versions of the story and the finished play. In so doing he sets up the inverse relationship between sexuality and disability evidenced in "Street Haunting": the more disability, the less sexuality. But at the same time this process of substitution establishes a relationship of identity, where disability means, or stands in for, sexuality.

In O'Connor's representation of Hulga Hopewell, disability replaces sexuality in a different way: Manley Pointer wants not Hulga's body, but her wooden leg. The story aligns Hulga's cerebral sexuality with her wooden leg and her nihilism. Pointer's symbolic rape—he steals her wooden leg—shows her, as O'Connor wrote in a letter, that "she aint so smart" (*Habit* 170) because she has embraced nihilism instead of faith. Now she has the opportunity to face her spiritual lack. But a corollary to this conclusion is that she is most complete in her physical incompleteness, without the prosthesis in which she had misguidedly invested her capacity for reverence. While O'Connor is clearly using the wooden leg as a measure of Hulga's flawed self-reliance, a disability studies reading reveals, too, a deep acceptance of disability as one facet of human limitation.

In the "Nausicaa" episode of *Ulysses*, disability replaces sexuality in that the first half of the chapter, whose style Joyce designated as "tumescence," treats Gerty as a sexual object, with disability largely absent; and the second half of the chapter, designated as "detumescence," focuses on her disability, with sex largely absent. The revelation of disability comes at the point of transition between tumescence and detumescence, fostering the text's deflation. But this dynamic of opposition is complicated by the question of who is narrating Gerty's half of the chapter. Below I consider the possibility that Bloom, seeing Gerty on the beach, uses her as a protagonist in his own narrative, "revealing" her thoughts through a derivative romance-novel discourse. If this is the case, then the revelation of her disability is Bloom's idea of narrative drama—he knew all along that Gerty limped—and disability is present throughout the sexualized section.

"The Desexualization"

Before turning to these fictions, I'd like to elaborate on the reasons disability and sexuality inform each other so strongly when it comes to representations of women with mobility impairments. The most obvious and most important reason is the general sexualization of women: since women in male-dominated cultures tend to be understood in sexual terms, sexuality is at issue with most woman characters. With regard to disabled women characters, the question of sexuality must, then, arise but is usually answered in the negative, as narrators and other characters conclude that the disabled woman is, for example, "a dwarf only" or merely "a cripple." Harlan Hahn describes this denial of sexuality to disabled women, noting that "while women have frequently been treated as sex objects, people with disabilities often have been treated as asexual objects. We become mere things" (n. pag.). In Anne Finger's story "Helen and Frida," the narrator mocks this attitude when she writes of Frida Kahlo, "But she can't be Disabled, she's Sexual," before describing the sexual passion that arises between Kahlo and Helen Keller (5). In another story, Finger considers the benefits of desexualization for disabled women in an era when sexuality was seen as incompatible with power: she has Rosa Luxemburg remark, "'I often wonder if I would have got as far in the party as I have if it weren't for—' 'The desexualization'" (67).

This desexualization is made explicit in each of the texts considered here. In *The Glass Menagerie*, Laura's mother, Amanda, has signed Laura up for business college, and only when that fails does she decide that Laura must marry. This trajectory reverses the usual one for young American women in the 1940s, who would typically attempt a career only if marriage were not in the cards. The play therefore makes it clear that Amanda believes Laura is ineligible for courtship, but when her career prospects fall apart, Amanda revisits the possibility. When she tells Laura she needs to find a husband, Laura replies, "But Mother— . . . (in a tone of frightened apology): I'm crippled!" (17). Insisting that Laura *can* marry, her mother vehemently rejects the word *cripple*; she thus assents to the presumed asexuality of "cripples" while trying, for the moment, to remove Laura from that category.[6]

In "Good Country People," Hulga's mother links Hulga's status as an amputee to her lack of romantic experience: "Mrs. Hopewell excused this attitude because of the leg (which had been shot off in a hunting accident when Joy was ten). . . . She thought of her still as a child because it tore her heart to think instead of the poor stout girl in her thirties who had never danced a step or had any *normal* good times" (274, original italics). Mrs. Hopewell's inability to think of her daughter as a grown woman demonstrates "the staggering resistance that confronts people with disabilities simply to be regarded as adults" (Kulick and Rydström 5). Her emphasis on dancing evidences the close association between mobility and sexuality, also stressed in the italicized word *normal*. And in "Nausicaa," when Bloom realizes (or reveals) that Gerty is "lame," he thinks, "Poor girl! That's why she's left on the shelf and the others did a sprint. . . . Jilted beauty" (13.772–74). Chalking Gerty up to damaged goods "left on the shelf," Bloom assumes she has been "jilted," as though romantic rejection inevitably accompanies a limp. Such dismissals of disabled women's sexuality form part of what Siebers describes as "one of the chief stereotypes oppressing disabled people," the "myth that they do not experience sexual feelings . . . that they do not have a sexual culture" (*Disability Theory* 138).[7]

A second reason sexuality is at particular issue in the case of women with mobility impairments is that archeological finds from the first half of the twentieth century led to wide circulation of the tenet that walking upright is a crucial indicator of humanity.[8] Media coverage of these discoveries contributed to popular thinking in Britain and America about where the boundaries between humans and apes might lie and about what it means to be human.[9] In 1891 debates over a set of fossils referred to as "Java Man" centered around the question of whether the fossils—a thighbone, skullcap, and tooth—belonged to a chimpanzee or an early form of human being. One key point in the debates was that the thighbone indicated "an habitual upright stance," which ruled out a chimpanzee and led to scientists positing a creature midway between humans and apes (Reader 131). In 1912 fossils were discovered in Piltdown, Sussex, that were even more prominently featured in the press, especially in Britain.[10] These fossils turned out to be a hoax (revealed in 1953), but at the time, they were considered major evidence in the debates over whether bipedalism or large brain capacity came first and which was most central to the development of human beings (Relethford 238).

Then, in 1924, Raymond Dart, an Australian anatomy professor working in South Africa, was given boxes of fossils that led him to believe that walking upright had been the first step in the evolution of hominids from an ape-like ancestor (Brain n. pag.). Dart called this creature *Australopithecus africanus* and hailed it as the intermediate species between apes and hominids. The popular press exploded with the news that the Missing Link had been found (Reader 194). Dart found himself a celebrity but also "had to endure the wrath of those who believed evolution offended religious belief. His discovery contributed to the anti-evolutionist sentiment that culminated in America with the Scopes trial, following which the State of Tennessee banned the teaching of evolution in schools" (Reader 196). Amid all this attention to scientific debate about the origins of human beings and the role of bipedalism, difficulty with walking, understood as our defining human ability, was charged with additional meaning.

These two factors—the linkage between women and sexuality and the linkage between walking upright and humanness—meant that mobility impairments had particular power in thinking about defect and procreation. The third factor built upon this conjunction: eugenics, the dominant mode of understanding human populations during this period, stressed women's role in maintaining the "race" and keeping it strong. Eugenics prompted a "cultural traffic in the cultivation of a shared distaste toward 'deviance' and unacceptable human variations" (Snyder and Mitchell 120). A woman's body was seen as not only a creator of, but a miniature instantiation of, the body politic, and this understanding prompted intense policing of women's bodies and sexualities.

Writing about the development of eugenic interest in certain kinds of women, Wendy Kline explains that "by 1915, white womanhood was no longer a marginal player in the evolution of the race but a central figure. As the 'mother of tomorrow' she controlled the makeup of future generations. . . . Specifically, by the early twentieth century, white female fertility had become a potential panacea for the problems of racial degeneracy" (8). While it was mental disability that was specifically targeted for eradication through forced sterilizations, physical disabilities were also seen as hindrances to a "fit" race. Indeed, physical and sensory disabilities often *led* to diagnoses of mental disabilities; Snyder and Mitchell explain that "an inverse analysis was applied, by which physically disabled people presented the visible markers that presumed inferior intelligence, and those who tested positively for inferior intelligence were scrutinized—unclothed—for evidence of accompanying physical stigmata" (80).[11]

Douglas Baynton similarly demonstrates that eugenicists and criminologists saw mental and physical defects as leading one to the other. He quotes a "professor of medicine and criminal anthropology" who "maintained in 1904 that 'defective physique has not received the attention it deserves in the causation of crime'" and a study that concluded that, "by permitting the feebleminded to reproduce, we are not only increasing their number, but we are also increasing the number of [physical] abnormals" ("'These Pushful Days'" 56). In this atmosphere of eugenic surveillance, women's sexuality generally, and disabled women's sexuality in particular, were matters of broad social significance.

While none of the authors considered in this chapter was an advocate of eugenics, none could remain immune to the entrenched eugenic thinking of his or her culture, and each text references ranking people by type.[12] For example, in its insistence on Gerty's "finebred nature" (13.661), "Nausicaa" demonstrates an interest in ranking women according to a biologized understanding of beauty and breeding. Through this motif Joyce mocks—and yet relies on to shape the episode—what Ellen Samuels calls "fantasies of identification," which assume that "embodied social identities such as race, gender, and disability are fixed, legible, and categorizable" (11).

The sexualization of women, the emphasis on walking upright as definitive of humanness, and eugenic ideologies coalesced in literary representations of women with mobility impairments that ostensibly deny their sexuality but that manage to associate, each it its own way, disability with sexuality. In what follows I demonstrate these dynamics of substitution and conjunction in the representations of Laura Wingfield, Hulga Hopewell, and Gerty MacDowell.

Laura Wingfield's Excised Sexuality

Tennessee Williams wrote myriad versions of the tale told in *The Glass Menagerie.*[13] Here I consider the representation of Laura's disability within *The Glass Menagerie* and then widen my focus by turning to two other versions of the story: a short story, "Portrait of a Girl in Glass," and a one-act play, *The Pretty Trap*. Along the way, I reference some draft material for the screenplay of *The Gentleman Caller*. Taken together, these multiple versions of Laura's story reveal the metaphoric meanings of disability in Williams's work.

As critics have noted, *The Glass Menagerie* sets Laura Wingfield against the mechanized world critiqued in the play. Williams's first stage description asserts that the Wingfield apartment is in "one of those vast hive-like conglomerations of cellular living-units." He calls the lower-middle-class people who live there "fundamentally enslaved," forming "one interfused mass of automatism" (3). Laura represents an antidote to this mechanization: rather than being machinelike and fungible, she is delicate and singular. This opposition between the machine and Laura is emphasized by the screen image (in the reading version of the play) of "a swarm of typewriters" (13) when we learn that Laura has secretly dropped out of business college, removing herself from this "swarm." And the opposition is further emphasized in one of the versions of the story Williams drafted for the screenplay of *The Gentleman Caller*: in the "Business College Sequence" we see the swarm of typewriters through Laura's eyes, "which distort it into a virtual phantasmagoria of sinister black machines stretching almost interminably in every direction." Indeed, the typing teacher explicitly enforces the opposition between the individual and the mass: "There are times and places when individuality has to be submerged. Individualism may be the necessity of artists and it is certainly the privilege of lunatics. But in the business-office, what one expects from the good and useful employee is conformity to regulations" ("The Business College Sequence").

In his instructions for the lighting in *Glass Menagerie*, Williams writes that "Laura should be distinct from the others, having a peculiar pristine clarity such as light used in early religious portraits of female saints or madonnas" (xxi–xxii). This lighting confirms her separateness and establishes her innocence or purity. And in his description of the characters, Williams writes that "stemming from [her 'defect'], Laura's separation increases till she is like a piece of her own glass collection, too exquisitely fragile to move from the shelf" (xviii). Furthermore, Laura is clearly associated with her glass unicorn, whose "freakish" difference is also beauty. Laura's disability, then, contributes to her delicacy and accounts for her distinctness from others.

Tom describes Laura as living "in a world of her own" (47). C. W. E. Bigsby writes that "the glass animals of her menagerie transport her into a mythical world, timeless, immune from the onward rush of the twentieth century" (38). Even Laura's history of illness—the pleurosis she had in high school—is linked with her separateness when Jim contrasts the fantastic image of blue roses with weeds: "They're common as—weeds, but—you—well, you're—*Blue Roses!*" (87). In "Good Country People" the gentleman caller (the "bible salesman") similarly flatters Hulga by pointing out how different she is from other people (O'Connor, "Good Country People" 288). This separateness is a version of the isolation commonly associated with disability. As Mitchell and Snyder observe, many fictional plots "emphasize individual isolation as the overriding component of a disabled life" (*Narrative Prosthesis* 19). Bigsby notes that Laura buys her "immunity . . . at too high a price for, in stepping into the fictive world of her glass animals, she steps out of any meaningful relationship with others in the present" (38). We see similar isolation in representations of deaf characters, as I demonstrate in chapter three. But unlike the deaf characters I discuss, Laura's "separation," although understood negatively on the level of plot, prompting pity in the play's viewers, is portrayed positively on the symbolic level of resistant artistry.

On this symbolic level, where conformity is the great evil, Laura's difference is her saving grace. Since she "is unable to conform" to the standardization of modern life, she withdraws into her world of glass animals and old records (Babcock 24). As Granger Babcock points out, this withdrawal has positive connotations because Laura's "inability to standardize herself" (25) constitutes a refusal to become a cog in the great machine of organized society. Such resistance, for Williams, is the job of the artist. Babcock quotes Williams's introduction to *27 Wagons Full of Cotton*: "Art is only anarchy in juxtaposition with organized society. It runs counter to the sort of orderliness on which organized society apparently must be based" (17). Laura, like her brother Tom, represents this type of anarchy in that she resists both a business career and the marriage plot her mother attempts to substitute for it.

I would like to take this observation a step further and assert that Laura symbolizes art, and the newness of Williams's dramatic form, in particular through her disability. Her disability represents artistry not only because it isolates or separates her, but also because it takes the form of a mobility impairment. As Bigsby points out, Williams, like Chekov, conceals the action of his plays "in the very inactivity of his characters" (31). Williams explained this in his notebooks: "A new form, non-realistic, must be chosen. This necessity suggests what I have labeled as 'the sculptural drama.' . . . I visualize it as a reduced mobility on the stage, the forming of statuesque attitudes or tableaux, something resembling a restrained type of dance, with motions honed down to only the essential or significant" (qtd. in Bak 92–93). In his production notes, Williams further describes his play as having a "more or less static nature" (xxii). Seeking a "reduced mobility on the stage," Williams specifically creates a character with a mobility impairment who can represent that "restrained type of dance." Laura's restrained mobility—one leg "held in a brace" (xviii)—is echoed in the assertion that she is "too exquisitely fragile to move from the shelf": she must symbolically *stay put* to help represent a new, sculptural dramatic form.

In the world of the play, Laura's symbolic immobility (within the diegesis she does walk, all day for weeks while pretending to be at business school) is rendered through her status as an unmarried young woman with no career prospects who sits at home polishing and repolishing her glass animals and listening to the same records. Her association with "a restrained type of dance" is reinforced when Jim asks her to dance. She first refuses, saying she doesn't know how to dance. When Jim encourages her, she says, "How—how—how do we start?" highlighting her reluctance to move. As they begin to dance she tells Jim, "I'm afraid you can't budge me." He soon tells her, "Not so stiff—" (85). All of this suggests an immobility that, like the limp itself, needs to be "no more than suggested" (xviii).

Laura's limited mobility in the world is part of what traps Tom. Amanda tells him, "until [you've found a replacement] you've got to look out for your sister. I don't say me because I'm old and don't matter! I say for your sister because she's young and dependent" (35). Williams calls attention to this trap in his character description: "his nature is not remorseless, but to escape from a trap, he has to act without pity" (xviii). Robert Bray describes Tom's choice as one between "sacrifice and personal freedom" (xii). Similarly to H. G. Wells's "The Country of the Blind," discussed in chapter 2, here the text sets up a dynamic where attaining personal freedom requires abandoning a disabled loved one.

In spite of the positive association of disability with resistance and artistry, then, Williams uses Laura's disability to intensify the trap from which Tom must escape. He does this by casting disability as pure need, making Tom's escape even more fraught and difficult. One scene in which Williams stresses disability-as-trap takes place at the end of scene 3, where Tom, storming out of the house after calling his mother an "ugly—babbling old—*witch*," becomes caught in his coat. "His arm catches in the sleeve of the coat as he struggles to pull it on. For a moment he is pinioned by the bulky garment. With an outraged groan he tears the coat off again, splitting the shoulder of it, and hurls it across the room. It strikes against the shelf of Laura's glass collection, and there is a tinkle of shattering glass. Laura cries out as if wounded" (24). This is a scene of metaphoric disability. Tom's arm is pinned; he is unable to use it. As in the more general dynamic of the play, here too disability traps him, and he must wrench free from it. In the process, he damages Laura's glass collection and by implication ("as if wounded") Laura herself.

This scene foreshadows Tom's abandonment of his family. His coat's torn shoulder represents the harm he does to himself as well by tearing himself away. I disagree with Thomas Scheye's claim that this scene indicates that Tom "cannot escape until he finds the way to leave without shattering Laura's fragile self" (209). Instead, the scene symbolizes the damage he *will* do when he leaves and/or *has done* by the time he plays the role of narrator. As Tony Kushner notes, "the monologues in *Menagerie* are spoken by a guilty man who's confessing. The crime Tom confesses is betrayal, which is the central preoccupation of *The Glass Menagerie*. Writing it was an act of betrayal as well" (Introduction 12). The coat scene highlights through Tom's symbolic disability what the play everywhere implies—that disability will immobilize him unless he betrays Laura "without pity." At the end of the scene, as he goes to "collect the fallen glass," he glances "at Laura as if he would speak but couldn't" (25). Now stymied by another type of impairment, Tom remains immobile while music comes up and the lights go down. The symbolic disabilities of this scene convey Williams's sense that writing *Menagerie*, which was "the hardest thing I've ever tried to say," was "like a man performing his own vivisection" (*Gentleman Caller*).

The other scene that most powerfully associates disability with an overwhelming dependence that threatens to hold Tom in its clutches is the final scene, in which Amanda shouts at Tom and he smashes a glass. Until this last scene, Amanda, as I mention above, was invested in rejecting the word *cripple* for her daughter. When Laura defines herself as "crippled," Amanda responds, "Laura, I've told you never, never to use that word! Why, you're not crippled, you just have a little defect—hardly noticeable even!" (17).[14] She also scolds Tom for using the word: "Don't say crippled! You know that I never allow that word to be used" (47). But now that Jim has revealed his engagement and left, and Tom is about to leave for "the movies" yet again, Amanda feels her grasp on Tom slipping. She told him in scene 4 that she knew he would run off, but he had first to find someone to take his place in looking after Laura (35). Now, as Tom seems on the verge of leaving without having found a replacement, Amanda is getting frantic. So she brings out the forbidden word: "Don't think about us, a mother deserted, an unmarried sister who's crippled and has no job! Don't let anything interfere with your selfish pleasure!" (96). The fact that this word emerges when Amanda is desperately trying to hold onto Tom shows its power to elicit pity. Much as "crippled" Tiny Tim succeeds in squeezing pity from Scrooge's stony heart in Dickens's *A Christmas Carol*, Amanda banks on the pathetic power of *cripple* to bind Tom to the home.[15] This return of the repressed word confirms the play's use of disability to intensify the dependence that threatens to suffocate Tom.

If we step back from Laura's representation within the play, we can see that on a broader level, her disability serves Williams as a screen for illicit sexuality. This is suggested first by the fact that in the two alternate versions of the story, Laura is more sexual than she is in *The Glass Menagerie*, and not disabled.[16] And the claim is bolstered by the biographical underpinnings of Laura's character and the role of homosexuality in Williams's work.

In both "Portrait of a Girl in Glass" and Williams's comic version of the story, *The Pretty Trap*, Laura is not quite as innocent as she is in *The Glass Menagerie*, where her interest in Jim is portrayed as a schoolgirl crush. R. B. Parker writes of the multiple early versions of the story that "many of the discarded drafts were much more like what we have come to think of as typical Williams writing: that is, they were more sexually charged, more violent, and more blackly humorous . . . than the final play" (519). In *The Pretty Trap* our first hint that women's sexuality is at issue comes when Jim reads in the paper that it's Sadie Hawkins Day (*Glass Menagerie*, Centennial Ed. 185). Although Laura is shy here too, and dislikes being pushed on a stranger, she quickly loosens up under Jim's banter. When he asks her to dance, she agrees more quickly: "Why, I—yes, I'd love to!" (202). She tells Jim his hair is pretty and insists on this word even after he tells her that *pretty* is for girls. When he kisses her, instead of the brief kiss of *Menagerie*, he "kisses her full and hungrily on the lips" and their "embrace endures" for a couple of moments "with a curious, hesitant intensity" (203). When Amanda enters, Jim tells her that he and Laura would like to go out for a walk. Amanda responds, "What could be nicer?" and Laura echoes her mother: "Oh!—Why—what could be nicer?" (204). This Laura, while starting out shy, is much more comfortable with her desirability and her own desire. She does not have a mobility impairment; the character description reads, "a shy and sensitive girl of eighteen who 'needs to be pushed a little'" (178). This need to be pushed hints at the immobility that is more developed in *The Glass Menagerie.*

The Laura of "Portrait of a Girl in Glass," too, is more of a sexual being. Tony Kushner points out her sexuality in his introduction to the Centennial Edition of *The Glass Menagerie*. He writes that as "she is transposed from unpublished short story to produced play, Laura loses—along with much of her sexuality—autonomy, agency, and a very good line of dialogue" (31).[17] In "Portrait" Laura is very similar to her counterpart in *Menagerie*: sick to her stomach with fear at the business college, prone to stay her in room and wash and polish her glass animals. But here Laura reads and rereads a book called *Freckles*, by Gene Stratton-Porter.[18] "The character Freckles, a one-armed orphan youth who worked in a lumber camp, was someone that she invited into her bedroom now and then for a friendly visit just as she did me" (Centennial Ed., 168). When Freckles becomes romantically involved with "a girl called The Angel," Laura "usually stopped reading. . . . She closed the book or turned back to the lonelier periods in the orphan's story" (169). In one of the early drafts of the screenplay, Jim asks Laura why she is fascinated with Freckles.

> LAURA: I suppose—because—
> JIM: The hero is crippled?
> LAURA: I am too, a little. (*Gentleman Caller*)

Clinging to her identification with Freckles, Laura of "Portrait" refuses to acknowledge her ablebodied fictional rival, instead focusing on the parts of the novel that allow her to project herself into the story to comfort Freckles in his "lonelier periods."

As in the play, in "Portrait" Tom invites Jim for dinner, which proceeds awkwardly. After dinner Laura comments to Jim,

> "Oh—you have freckles!"
> Jim grinned. "Sure that's what my folks call me—Freckles!"
> "Freckles?" Laura repeated. She looked toward me as if for conformation of some too wonderful hope. (Centennial Ed. 173)

Laura sees Jim as the incarnation of her fictional love object. When he asks her to dance, she

> slipped quite naturally into those huge arms of Jim's, and they danced round and around the small steam-heated parlor, bumping against the sofa and chairs and laughing loudly and happily together. Something opened up in my sister's face. To say it was love is not too hasty a judgment, for after all he had freckles and that was what his folks called him. Yes, he had undoubtedly assumed the identity—for all practical purposes—of the one-armed orphan youth (174).

After Jim reveals that he is engaged and leaves, Laura is not as wounded as she is in the play. Instead, "Laura was the first to speak. 'Wasn't he nice?' she asked. 'And all those freckles!'" (175). More confident, more sexual, perhaps less grounded in reality, this version of Laura maintains her desire for Jim in spite of the revelation, just as she turns back to the earlier sections of her novel when the Angel comes on the scene.

Another form of sexuality lingers in this story while being mostly expunged from the finished play. Here the narrator, Tom, is also represented as attracted to Jim. Tom describes Jim: "His big square hands seemed to have a direct and very innocent hunger for touching his friends. He was always clapping them on your arms or shoulders and they burned through the cloth of your shirt like plates taken out of an oven" (Centennial Ed. 170). The burning here indicates the narrator's desire for and concomitant fear of being touched by Jim. When Jim goes through their records, his voice delights the narrator: he reads the titles aloud "in a voice so hearty that it shot like beams of sunlight through the vapors of self-consciousness engulfing my sister and me" (173). The "very good line of dialogue" Kushner mentions, which Laura loses in the play, is Laura's response when their mother asks how Tom could have failed to know that Jim was engaged to be married. When their mother says it's "peculiar," Laura disagrees. "No,' said Laura gently, getting up from the sofa. 'There's nothing peculiar about it.' . . . 'People in love,' she said, 'take everything for granted'" (175). Kushner reads this line as threatening to out Tom's homosexuality, implying that "Tom is in love with Jim, and, because he desires it to be so, he's taken it for granted that Jim isn't the kind to get engaged" (Introduction 27).[19] In *The Glass Menagerie* these lines are removed, resulting in a characterization of Tom's restlessness as intellectual and spiritual, but not overtly sexual.[20]

In these two versions of the story, where Laura is granted sexuality, she is not disabled. Kushner notes about "Portrait of a Girl in Glass" that Laura

> is not physically disabled and doesn't wear a leg brace, nor is she sickly. If she had pleurosis as a girl, it isn't mentioned. The narrator of "Portrait" says his sister is unclassifiable, but he describes her in the grip of an acute, paralyzing agoraphobia: "She made no positive motion towards the world but stood at the edge of the water, so to speak, with feet that anticipated too much cold to move." (Introduction 25)

With its emphasis on feet that do not move, this description gestures toward the "reduced mobility" of *The Glass Menagerie*. The absence of a disability can be explained partly by considering that as Williams moved from the short story to the play, which would be seen on the stage, he needed a visual sign of Laura's misfitness, which could be explained in more detail in the story. Much as Eudora Welty notes that giving a character a disability is "the easiest way" to suggest his or her loneliness (Prenshaw 84), Williams seems to be using a physical disability to call attention and give a visual correlative to Laura's maladaption to the modern world. Most important, the revisions suppress women's sexuality and male homosexuality and replace them with disability.

This suppression seems to have been prompted in part by the role of sexuality in Williams's personal life. As is well known, Laura is based on Williams's sister Rose, who was committed to a mental institution for schizophrenia and lobotomized (Bak 61, 71–72, 99). Rose's mental illness manifested in part through sexual outbursts. Donald Spoto quotes Williams saying that his mother was "frightened most of all by Rose's sexual fantasies" (60). Similarly, in his play *Suddenly Last Summer*, Williams has the doctor tell Mrs. Venable that he was proud after lobotomizing a patient when she commented on how blue the sky was, "because up till then her speech, everything that she'd babbled, was a torrent of obscenities" (19). An analogous suppression of sexuality appears in *The Glass Menagerie* in Amanda returning a book by D. H. Lawrence to the library because she will not tolerate "filth" in her house (21).

But it was not only Williams's mother who was disturbed by Rose's sexual expression. Bak describes Williams "detecting in himself the attitude toward Rose that he had previously only attributed to his parents: 'Visited Rose at sanitarium—horrible, horrible! Her talk was so obscene'" (71). Kushner writes that "the most intolerable aspect of Rose's madness for the Williamses, including Tennessee, seems to have been her sexual acting-out" (Introduction 22). He notes that

> the young Thomas Lanier Williams was very close to his older sister, and when she began to lose her mind he became terrified that he would lose his as well. This terror never left him. That Rose's insanity took the form of an unembarrassed, hyperactive carnality must have intensified her closeted gay brother's identification, as well as his dread. (Introduction 23)

Kushner's insight reveals the link between Rose's sexual "acting-out" and Williams's anxiety about his own sexuality. He hones in on the word *disgust*, "which Tennessee repeatedly used to describe Rose's sexual conduct. In a vicious letter he wrote to Rose when both were in their mid-twenties, regarding the news . . . that she'd come on to a boy, 'I want you to know that you disgusted me'" (Introduction 23). As Kushner points out, this word also applies to homosexuality in Williams's work. In *A Streetcar Named Desire* (1947), "a woman hisses [the word] into the ear of her young husband, whom she's just discovered having sex with another man: 'I know. I saw. You disgust me'" (Introduction 23). And in *Cat on a Hot Tin Roof* (1955), *disgust* is used repeatedly to refer to the "mendacity" that torments Brick, whose sexuality is at issue throughout the play.

In these plays, sexuality is something to be feared, to prompt revulsion. Brick knows that his family believes his relationship with his friend Skipper was homoerotic and insists that they are the ones who dirtied a "clean" friendship. Blanche's mental illness in *Streetcar* manifests, like Rose's, as a threatening hypersexuality. Stella's betrayal of her sister by having her committed echoes Tom's betrayal of Laura in *Menagerie* and Williams's feeling that he betrayed Rose by leaving the family, and by not preventing—though he didn't know about it until afterward—her lobotomy.

In all of these texts, illicit sexuality is associated in some way with disability. Brick, who continually denies his homosexuality, uses a crutch throughout the play. Both his wife and his father take the crutch from him to attempt to control his behavior, highlighting its importance. Blanche is understood as mentally disabled, and her famous final lines confirm her tenuous grasp of what is happening to her. And crucially, Rose's sexual behavior metamorphoses into Laura's mobility impairment, itself associated with disease through the character description: "a childhood illness has left her crippled" (xviii).

In Williams's story, "One Arm" (1948), the association between sexuality and disability becomes more overt. The one-armed protagonist, Oliver Winemiller, is described as "broken," "mutilated," "maimed," and "crippled"—and he is a gay hustler. Like Brick, he is physically beautiful and has the charm of the detached and defeated. Before being arrested, "he had thought of his maimed body as something that, being broken, was only fit for abuse. You God-damned cripple, he used to groan to himself. The excitement he stirred in others had been incomprehensible and disgusting to him" (*One Arm* 19). Disability, disgust, and gay sexuality come together in this story, shedding light on the more subtle links in the major plays.

Disability replaces sexuality in Williams, then, first in that Laura is understood to be unfit for a happily-ever-after ending because she is "crippled." Although her misfitness for the modern world is celebrated on a symbolic level, her mobility impairment nevertheless helps remove her from the ranks of eligible young women so that Jim's departure seems inevitable. Allean Hale notes that Williams "audited playwriting under Dr. Robert Ramsay, who used the *ouroboros* symbol—the snake with tail in mouth—to describe the perfect plot. The end must be implicit in the beginning" (14). Laura's disability serves here as the logical link between the beginning of the play and its devastating end.

Second, insofar as Laura in *The Glass Menagerie* is sexually innocent, her disability stands in for the sexuality that animated her real-life counterpart and the other fictional versions of her character. Illicit sexuality—displays of sexuality from women and male homosexuality—is transmuted into the visually available counterpart of disability. The opposition set up between disability and sexuality on the level of plot is, then, overturned by the metaphoric sexual baggage attached to disability in Williams's work, creating a relationship of identity—where disability *means* illicit sexuality—behind the ostensible opposition.

Hulga Hopewell and the End of Disability Masquerade

O'Connor's "Good Country People" similarly sets up an opposition between disability and sexuality. As I mention above, Hulga Hopewell—a woman with a prosthetic leg whose name was Joy until she changed it without her mother's consent—is portrayed as outside of the realm of "*normal* good times." Although she is thirty-two, she lives with her mother because of a heart condition. She does not date, she wears an old, childish sweatshirt "with a faded cowboy on a horse embossed on it," and she reacts to "nice young men as if she could smell their stupidity" (276). While her mother advocates passing, much as Laura's mother does in *The Glass Menagerie*, Hulga herself engages in what Tobin Siebers calls disability masquerade. She associates her disability with ugliness and cultivates this ugliness in an attempt to define herself as different from the "good country people" who surround her and fend off interest from "nice young men."[21]

Like Amanda Wingfield, Hulga's mother accepts the opposition between disability and sexuality but thinks that the gap could be closed to some degree by charm and a pleasant demeanor.[22] Although she spouts platitudes such as "everybody is different" (273), she finds Hulga's difference disconcerting. As Laura Behling notes, "For Mrs. Hopewell . . . Hulga's difference is too much to bear" (91). The narrator describes her feelings about her daughter's unusual identity: "It seemed to Mrs. Hopewell that every year [Hulga] grew less like other people and more like herself—bloated, rude, and squint-eyed" (276). She is frustrated that she can't label her daughter in a way that conforms to others' expectations: "You could say, 'My daughter is a nurse' or 'My daughter is a schoolteacher,' or even 'My daughter is a chemical engineer.' You could not say, 'My daughter is a philosopher'" (276). Every morning as she watches her daughter cook her breakfast, Mrs. Hopewell thinks "that if she would only keep herself up a little, she wouldn't be so bad looking. There was nothing wrong with her face that a pleasant expression wouldn't help. Mrs. Hopewell said that people who looked on the bright side of things would be beautiful even if they were not" (275). She wishes her daughter would make an effort to pass as a cheerful, normative young woman. And most important, Mrs. Hopewell wishes Hulga would walk more delicately, rather than "stumping" with her wooden leg.[23]

Siebers notes that passing can help powerless people partake of the power of the dominant group: "Erving Goffman defines passing as a strategy for managing the stigma of 'spoiled identities'—those identities discredited by law, opinion, or social convention. . . . People with disabilities find ingenious ways to conceal their impairments and to pass as able-bodied" (*Disability Theory* 97). But, drawing upon Sedgwick's *Epistemology of the Closet*, he acknowledges that "secrets concerning identity are a more complicated affair than Goffman's definition allows" (97). If Hulga were to try to pass in her rural community where everyone knows everyone's business—and where Mrs. Freeman continually prompts Mrs. Hopewell to relate how Hulga lost her leg—she would be fruitlessly concealing an open secret. Moreover, Hulga is too well educated to have any desire to play the role of the southern lady, so she seeks to define her identity otherwise. As Siebers points out, passing "stamps the dominant social position as simultaneously normative and desirable" (101). Since Hulga has nothing but disdain for the norms around her, she refuses to try to pass.

Hulga clearly does not take pains to please or to look "on the bright side of things." She is an atheist and will not let her mother keep a Bible in the parlor (278). She leaves Heidegger lying around seemingly on purpose to work on her mother "like some evil incantation in gibberish" (277). When her mother objects to her "ugly" remarks and her "glum" face as Hulga accompanies her over the fields, Hulga replies, "If you want me, here I am—LIKE I AM" (274). Mrs. Hopewell is sure that when she was deciding on a new name, her daughter "had thought and thought until she had hit upon the ugliest name in any language. Then she had gone and had the beautiful name, Joy, changed without telling her mother until after she had done it" (274). This suspicion is confirmed by the narrator when we learn that Hulga had arrived at the name "first purely on the basis of its ugly sound" (275).[24]

To complete her aggressive self-presentation, Hulga refuses to adopt the "pleasant expression" her mother wishes she would: "Joy, whose constant outrage had obliterated every expression from her face, would stare just a little to the side of her, her eyes icy blue, with the look of someone who has achieved blindness by an act of will and means to keep it" (273). Here Hulga's nearsightedness is linked to her disability identity: not only is she "bloated, rude, and squint-eyed" but she has "achieved blindness"—she has exaggerated her nearsightedness into an aspect of her disability identity.

This identity is emphasized most dramatically through Hulga's refusal to walk delicately with her wooden leg. She "lumber[s] into the bathroom" and slams the door (273); she "stump[s] into the kitchen in the morning (she could walk without making the awful noise but she made it—Mrs. Hopewell was certain—because it was ugly-sounding)" (275). When Mrs. Hopewell says, "It's very good we aren't all alike," Hulga shows the hypocrisy of her mother's statement by getting up and "stump[ing], with about twice the noise that was necessary, into her room and lock[ing] the door" (282).

Hulga's exaggerated "stump" represents the opposite of passing. Siebers writes that people with disabilities often "display their disability by exaggerating it" and labels this phenomenon "masquerade" (*Disability Theory* 100). By exploring the concept of masquerade in feminist theory, especially in Joan Riviere's essay "Womanliness as Masquerade," Siebers examines the reasons for and results of embracing a stigmatized identity. Masquerade, he argues, can serve as a response to the "demand that disabled people overcompensate in public, both to meet the expectation of nondisabled people and to save them from inconvenience. . . . It meets the demand for overcompensation with undercompensation" (108). This describes many of Hulga's behaviors, and especially the stomping, the constant emphasis on her wooden leg.

Indeed, Hulga seems to take her masquerade to the point where she fetishizes her difference. Richard Giannone reads Hulga as motivated largely by an effort to repress shame. He notes that she "mocks herself by exaggerating her physical unattractiveness. In this way she need not admit her fear of being held in contempt" (*Flannery O'Connor* 66). While this self-protective posture does seem to play a role in her disability masquerade, Giannone's discussion doesn't take into account the fact that such an identity, however defensive, can serve Hulga in lieu of a disability community. Her fixation on her difference can be seen as a defiant acceptance of herself as a disabled woman. The text seems of two minds about this masquerade; it is satirized as overdone and childish, but it is also portrayed as a brave refusal to be shamed or cowed by compulsory ablebodiedness. As Tara Powell writes, "important to the success of the story is that O'Connor manages to critique the young woman's intellectual hubris while at the same time loving her strangeness and her courage" (33).

Siebers explores the role prostheses play in the process of masquerade. Citing Cal Montgomery's discussion of prosthetic devices, he writes that "people with disabilities risk becoming their prosthesis" (*Disability Theory* 109). He suggests that "uninvited stares are diverted to prostheses, absorbed there, and satisfied, while disabled limbs spark endless curiosity and anxiety" (110). In "Good Country People" Hulga's wooden leg definitely absorbs uninvited stares, but it also seems to play the role Siebers ascribes to disabled limbs themselves, sparking endless curiosity. Mrs. Freeman, for example, is captivated by the leg: "Something about her seemed to fascinate Mrs. Freeman and then one day Hulga realized that it was the artificial leg. Mrs. Freeman had a special fondness for the details of secret infections, hidden deformities" (275). In this case, the wooden leg is not satisfying in itself because it points to a "hidden deformity"—the stump—which the story emphasizes by using the word *stump* instead of *stomp* to describe the sound of Hulga's wooden leg hitting the floor (275, 282).

When Hulga meets Manley Pointer for the second time, he stands and "gaz[es] at her with open curiosity, with fascination, like a child watching a new fantastic animal at the zoo. . . . His gaze seemed somehow familiar but she could not think where she had been regarded with it before" (283). Pointer's gaze clearly replicates Mrs. Freeman's, and their combined gaze (as Fiona Campbell writes about nondisabled people who desire disabled people *for* their disabilities) "refracts the disabled person as Other (albeit as 'positive'

Other)" (*Contours* 172). Both Pointer and Freeman stare at Hulga with a desire to get under the surface of her self-presentation and come in contact with the disability that is both hidden and revealed by the wooden leg.

The characters' fascination contributes to the way the wooden leg gathers meaning, as O'Connor explains in "Writing Short Stories": "As the story goes on, the wooden leg continues to accumulate meaning. The reader learns how the girl feels about her leg, how her mother feels about it, and how the country woman on the place feels about it; and finally, by the time the Bible salesman comes along, the leg has accumulated so much meaning that it is, as the saying goes, loaded" (*Mystery* 99). O'Connor has portrayed the wooden leg so that Hulga's identity does "risk becoming [her] prosthesis" (Siebers, *Disability Theory* 109). Indeed, she claims that Hulga "believes in nothing but her own belief in nothing, and we perceive that there is a wooden part of her soul that corresponds to her wooden leg" (*Mystery* 99). Within the story, Hulga fetishizes her wooden leg (much as Woolf's dwarf fetishizes her feet), and her own projections onto the leg are echoed in Manley Pointer's; but whereas he fetishizes the leg sexually, with religious reverence serving merely as a cover, she fetishizes it spiritually—or antispiritually, since she uses the leg as a prosthesis or substitute for her own soul.[25]

It is in depicting this fetishization that the story contests the opposition between disability and sexuality and puts forward a dynamic of substitution, in which disability stands in for sexuality. Pointer's main interest is not in Hulga's body (much less her mind or spirit), but in her wooden leg.[26] After looking at her like an animal in the zoo, he invites her on a picnic. As they come to the barn, he says it's a pity they can't go up to the hayloft, because of the "'leg,' he said reverently" (286). After they climb up into the hayloft and begin kissing, he asks her to prove she loves him. She asks how, assuming he means by sexual intercourse but feeling "he should be delayed a little"; in response, he "leaned over and put his lips to her ear. 'Show me where the wooden leg joins on,' he whispered" (288). His seductive whispering indicates that his interest in her disability is a substitute for sexual desire.

Her response echoes his own fascination:

> The girl uttered a sharp little cry and her face instantly drained of color. The obscenity of the suggestion was not what shocked her. As a child she had sometimes been subject to feelings of shame but education had removed the last traces of that as a good surgeon scrapes for cancer; she would no more have felt it over what he was asking than she would have believed in his Bible. But she was as sensitive about

> the artificial leg as a peacock about his tail. No one ever touched it but her. She took care of it as someone else would his soul, in private and almost with her own eyes turned away. (288)

With the words *obscenity* and *shame* this passage links disability with sex. In the comparison of the leg to Hulga's soul, O'Connor suggests what she asserts baldly in the essay, that "the Ph.D. is spiritually as well as physically crippled" and that the leg corresponds to a wooden part of her soul (*Mystery* 99). The passage links shame over the prosthetic leg with religion, with Hulga rejecting both. And it shows that Hulga treats her leg with a devotion that is far more real than Pointer's pretended reverence.

When Pointer has convinced Hulga to let him remove the leg, he returns to kissing her, while repeatedly looking at the prosthesis. "Every now and then the boy, with eyes like two steel spikes, would glance behind him where the leg stood" (289). He has also taken off Hulga's eyeglasses and put them in his pocket, depriving her of her other prosthetic device. The climax of their interaction comes when he grabs the leg, puts it into his valise with the unused condoms, and leaves her, her eyeglasses still in his pocket, in the hayloft of the barn. This ending, like the ending of *The Glass Menagerie*, returns readers to the opposition between disability and sexuality, with the betrayal appearing inevitable given Hulga's mobility impairment. Sara Hosey notes that Hulga's abandonment "in part serves to confirm that Hulga is not desirable (at least not in a 'normal,' non-fetishistic way) and that she has been mistaken in thinking herself so" (34).

The phallic description of Pointer's eyes as "steel spikes" recalls the earlier description of Mrs. Freeman's eyes as "steel-pointed," so that the word *penetrated* from that description (275) resonates here as well. Critics have pointed out that Pointer's theft of the leg is a symbolic and emotional rape. John Gatta calls the scene a "rape of the soul" (274). Carol Schloss writes, "the rape plays against expectations. What is lost is not virginity; yet the weird violation—a wooden leg unjoined and stolen—carries a sense of shame and importance that is probably more pronounced because of its uniqueness" (44). This violation is hinted at slightly earlier when "she gave a little cry of alarm [when he refused to put her leg back on] but he pushed her down and began to kiss her again" (289). It is in this way that the story most strongly uses disability in place of sexuality: Hulga's wooden leg is the emotional counterpart to her virginity, and the real object of Pointer's desire.

The loss of this prosthetic leg/soul, O'Connor writes, "has revealed her deeper affliction to her for the first time" (*Mystery* 99). As Pointer leaves with the leg, he calls up to her: "'And I'll tell you another thing, Hulga,' he said, using the name as if he didn't think much of it, 'you ain't so smart. I been believing in nothing since I was born!'" (291). O'Connor herself repeats this phrase in a letter to Elizabeth Hester (referred to as A. in *The Habit of Being*), writing, "Where do you get the idea that Hulga's need to worship 'comes to flower' in GCP? . . . Nothing 'comes to flower' here except her realization in the end that she ain't so smart" (*Habit* 170). The wooden leg, then, serves as a prosthetic device not only to allow Hulga to walk but to prop up her self-conceit. When it is taken away, her conceit collapses. As Henry Edmondson claims, "The leg, in a perverse sort of way, is the source of Hulga's hubristic self-confidence as well as a commentary on the wounded state of her soul" (79).

When it is stolen, Hulga is left, Edmondson writes, "without a leg to stand on" (90). This critical witticism would be offensive if it weren't for its accuracy to the story. It does seem that O'Connor has portrayed Hulga as using her difference—her wooden leg—to craft an identity of superiority and arrogance, which collapses when the sign of her difference is stolen from her. David Havird outlines the misogyny involved in this violent deflation, as Hulga's "masculine" pride is forced to yield to a more "normal" feminine submission (24).

Violence of various kinds is part and parcel of O'Connor's work. As Giannone explains in the introduction to O'Connor's *Spiritual Writings*, "Severity is the hallmark of O'Connor's understanding of grace and the inner changes it causes. As only a diamond can cut a diamond, so only a devastating blow can get through human hard-heartedness" (18). O'Connor herself wrote similarly that "violence is strangely capable of returning my characters to reality and preparing them to accept their moment of grace. Their heads are so hard that almost nothing else will do the work" (*Mystery* 112).[27]

But as O'Connor notes in her letter, the story ends before any sort of grace can "come to flower." All we get is the devastating blow. Hulga is left suspended not only literally above the barn floor, but also figuratively, as the story ends before she has the opportunity to make use of what she has experienced. This incompleteness, this suspension, is the very uncertainty she had been staving off with her absolute confidence in her atheism and her superiority. The story's incompletion is echoed in her body, which is now unfinished, without a prosthetic leg to fill the space between her "stump" and the ground.

Now the options of passing and masquerade are equally unavailable to her. Having lost the fetish object, she has to face her own incompleteness.

But for O'Connor, this leaves her paradoxically more complete than she was before. The story questions, with Victor Hugo's preface to *Cromwell*, "if, in short, to be incomplete is the best way to be harmonious" (Hugo par. 31). Powell rightly notes that "the loss of the leg is a loss of self with spiritual overtones" (34). Destroying Hulga's misguided self-reliance, O'Connor demonstrates the necessity of the "abandonment of the self" (Giannone, Introduction 48). Giannone links such fictional losses to O'Connor's own "sudden blow":

> The sudden blow of chronic disease that altered the course of O'Connor's life reverberates in her sensibility as a shaping influence on her writing. A comparable calamity recurs in every one of her novels and short stories. Always the physical blow causes a setback that, like lupus, sends the recipient on a new course, one toward self-knowledge that takes into account a conscious relationship with God. (Introduction 23)

Far from cultivating a relationship with God, Hulga had put herself in God's place. As Ruth Holsen points out, the name Hulga is a variant of Helga, which means "holy one" in Norwegian (59). The futility of her presumption is exposed in the story in that someone even more nihilistic than Hulga seizes the tool she used to rely on herself instead of God.

The implications of all this for a disability studies reading are Janus-faced: on the one hand, O'Connor's decision to have Hulga fetishize the leg satirizes what could otherwise have been a politically potent disability masquerade. Her use of Hulga's wooden leg to correspond to the wooden part of her soul is an instance of what Ato Quayson labels "disability as moral deficit" (42). The leg functions, as John Gatta puts it, to "symbolize a crippling moral and spiritual defeat" (275). Behling similarly argues that in this story and "The Lame Shall Enter First," "the disabled body is the modern mirror in which humanity is recognized as hurtling toward ruin and impersonality" (89). The misogyny of the symbolic rape is compounded by its ruthless ableism; insofar as "the average reader is pleased to observe anybody's wooden leg being stolen" (O'Connor, *Mystery* 98), the story seems to enjoy, in the sadistic way described by Patricia Yaeger, the redisabling of a woman who dared to presume she was whole.

On the other hand, O'Connor's strong belief in existential human inadequacy means that Hulga is spiritually better off without her fetishized leg. O'Connor writes that "the basic experience of everyone is the experience of human limitation" (*Mystery* 131) and that "to know oneself is, above all, to know what one lacks" (*Mystery* 35). Hulga is in this sense more complete insofar as she recognizes her incompleteness. David Evans writes, "that bodily impairment should be, in her stories, a privileged sign of [human] incompleteness is not incidental, since it is our condition of embodiment that constitutes our incompleteness" (326).[28]

To use disability in this way, to represent universal human limitation, has quite a different valence than to use it to show an individual spiritual or moral failing that contrasts with the wholeness of other characters.[29] Indeed, if we parse out the metaphoric use of the wooden leg and of the incomplete fleshly leg, we find that it is the *prosthesis* that stands in for Hulga's spiritual defect, not her disabled body itself.[30] The story implies, alongside its disturbing use of the prosthesis, a deep acceptance of disability as a feature of flawed humanity, linking Hulga's disabled body to humanness rather than viewing it as an aberration within or departure from humanness. Resisting the fantasy of and nostalgia for bodily wholeness represented by the prosthetic leg, the story's denouement insists on the fact of the disabled body in nature. It neither endorses Mrs. Hopewell's desire that Hulga should pass, nor approves of Hulga's disability masquerade, but values a disability acceptance that understands the human body, like the human mind and spirit, as by nature imperfect. Like *The Glass Menagerie*, then, "Good Country People" sets up an opposition between disability and sexuality on the level of plot, and then reverses the opposition on a symbolic level where disability is substituted for, or means, sexuality. Diverging from Williams's play, however, the story ultimately wraps sexuality into a broader recognition of the flawed embodiment that gives us our human nature.

Gerty MacDowell and the Melodrama of Revelation

Although *Ulysses* differs dramatically in form and scope from "Good Country People," its "Nausicaa" episode similarly links disability, religion, and sexuality in its portrayal of Gerty MacDowell, a woman with a limp who is ogled on the beach by Leopold Bloom as the sounds of a Benediction of the Blessed Sacrament float down from the Star of the Sea Church. The first part of the episode is written as a mock romance novel, laden with clichés and heavy with idealization of Gerty and of heteronormative romance. Much as Woolf's dwarf values her feet as a signifier of her normalcy, and indeed her worth, Joyce's Gerty MacDowell is represented as seeing her feet as a source of her feminine sexuality.

> Her shoes were the newest thing in footwear (Edy Boardman prided herself that she was very *petite* but she never had a foot like Gerty MacDowell, a five, and never would ash, oak or elm) with patent toecaps and just one smart buckle over her higharched instep. Her well-turned ankle displayed its perfect proportions beneath her skirt and just the proper amount and no more of her shapely limbs encased in finespun hose with highspliced heels and wide garter tops. (13.164–71)

Such narrative focus on the feet of disabled women replicates Mrs. Freeman's fascination with Hulga's wooden leg as that which both veils and gestures toward disability. In "Nausicaa" this fetishization is encouraged by a misogynist consumerism that dictates which aspects of a woman's body should be accentuated and by what commodities (in this case shoes and hose). As Garry Leonard explains, in this episode "Joyce modernizes the romance heroine by showing her as a self-conscious image manipulator who views herself as a commodity that must be carefully packaged and advertised, in accordance with a media representation of what is feminine, in order to attract a male consumer" (99).

The overt emphasis in "Nausicaa" on Gerty's beautiful shoes, feet, hose, and legs draws our attention to Woolf's dwarf's shoe-buying, the materiality of Hulga's wooden leg, and the presence of feet and shoes in *The Glass Menagerie*. There Tom works in a shoe factory, a claw-foot table is mentioned twice (11, 16), a screen image mentions "the accent of a coming foot" when Jim approaches the apartment (51), and when Jim takes out his gum, he wraps it in paper, saying, "I know how it is to get it stuck on a shoe" (81). These references to feet and shoes create a suffocating textual atmosphere in which Laura's braced foot and her limp are continually brought to the fore.

The fixation across the four texts with objects associated with the women's impairments indicates the complexity of the relation between disability and women's sexuality. On the one hand, the objects related to disability are valued as compensation: they deflect attention from the functional limitation (or in the case of the dwarf, her nonnormative size and shape) and serve to replace disability with a normative feminine beauty. On the other hand, these fetishized objects also work to continually remind readers or viewers of the limitations. For the characters themselves, too, objects such as beautiful shoes or a wooden leg both compensate for and point to the absence of a desired state of normalcy.

In the case of "Nausicaa," Gerty's shapely legs in "finespun hose" attract Leopold Bloom, who watches her lasciviously and, when she leans back to watch fireworks, brings himself to orgasm while ogling her thighs and her "knickers." The very objects of his lust, Gerty's legs, are the site of her disability, and as Angela Lea Nemecek points out, they are the source of Gerty's own sexual pleasure (180). When Gerty gets up to join her friends after the fireworks, Bloom sees with apparent shock that she is lame. The narrative switches at this point, halfway through the episode, from focalizing Gerty, back to the Bloomian stream of consciousness familiar to readers from preceding episodes.

In the first half of the episode, narrated from Gerty's point of view, sexual desire builds in both Bloom and Gerty as he watches her, masturbating, and she sees his hand in his pocket and his lustful eyes and responds with her own fantasies and orgasm, facilitated by her swinging legs. As Philip Sicker has demonstrated, there are striking similarities between this episode and the story, told in Havelock Ellis's *Auto-Eroticism* (1897), of a young woman bringing herself to orgasm in public by swinging her legs. In the second half of the episode, narrated by Bloom, he meditates on Gerty's disability in the context of sexuality, gender, and performance as he "recompose[s] his wet shirt" (13.851), thinks about his wife and daughter, and eventually falls asleep on the beach. The style of the chapter is a satire of the shallow idealism of the romance novel, in particular Maria Cummins's *The Lamplighter* (1854), whose protagonist is also named Gerty (Gifford 384). The technique Joyce ascribed to the episode in the schema he gave to Stuart Gilbert in 1921 is "tumescence, detumescence" (Gifford 384), with tumescence clearly corresponding to Gerty's half of the episode and detumescence corresponding to Bloom's. The organs Joyce assigned to this chapter, the eye and the nose, also clearly apply each to one half of the episode, as Bloom uses the gaze to stimulate his desire and considers various smells in his meditative, postclimax musings.

This split structure emphasizes the disjuncture between sexuality and disability. In the first section, where Gerty is sexual object and arguably sexual agent, her disability is hidden. It is alluded to only once: "the years were slipping by for her, one by one, and but for that one shortcoming she knew she need fear no competition and that was an accident coming down Dalkey hill and she always tried to conceal it" (13.650–51). Readers do not know at this point what the "shortcoming" might be. This sets the stage for the drama of the revelation (about which more below). In the second section, where Bloom is thinking about disability and its role in women's marketability, sexuality is in the background: Bloom is satisfied with the encounter but is no longer sexually aroused. Indeed, he remarks on the incompatibility of sexuality and disability: "Poor girl! That's why she's left on the shelf and the others did a sprint. Thought something was wrong by the cut of her jib. Jilted beauty. A defect is ten times worse in a woman. But makes them polite. Glad I didn't know it when she was on show" (13.772–76). The structure of the episode, then, like the more plot-based oppositions in the texts previously discussed, serves to divide disability from sexuality.

The revelation of Gerty's lameness comes at the dividing point between the two halves of the chapter, helping to deflate the excitement of the first half and thereby encourage the text's detumescence. John Bishop argues that Joyce's decision to give Gerty a limp is "more strategic than malicious" because it links her to Bloom, whose penis is described as the "limp father of thousands" in "Lotus Eaters" and as "limp as a boy of six's" by Bella in "Circe" ("Metaphysics" 191–92). He further notes that when Bloom refers to "that little limping devil," it's unclear whether he means Gerty or his penis. "Bloom and Gerty are made to reflect on each other by way of the 'limp' in 'limping' here, which bears the weight of both their real-world deficiencies" ("Metaphysics" 192).[31] If Bishop is right, then Gerty's lameness, like Pat's deafness and possibly the stripling's blindness (both discussed in chapter 4), emerges from wordplay. More importantly, if her lameness serves as a counterpart to Bloom's limp penis, then disability is powerfully linked to the absence of sexual potency.

As is often the case in Joyce, the symbolic meaning of the limp overlays its biographical source. Richard Ellmann describes Joyce's initial observation of a young Swiss woman, Marthe Fleischmann: in 1918 he caught sight of a "young woman walking ahead of him. She moved with a slight limp, her head held high. As she turned to enter a house he saw her face, and his own was lit up. . . . For it seemed to Joyce that he was seeing again the girl he had seen in 1898 by the strand, wading in the Irish Sea with her skirts tucked up" (*James Joyce* 462). Marthe's "haughty, naughty beguilements . . . helped him in composing the episode *Nausicaa*" (R. Ellmann, *James Joyce* 465). In accordance with the mock-heroic mode of the rest of the novel, Marthe's aristocratic origins on her mother's side (R. Ellmann, *James Joyce* 463) are reduced in "Nausicaa" to Gerty's "innate refinement" and "languid queenly hauteur" (13.97), which must suffice because fate has not "willed her to be born a gentlewoman of high degree" (13.99).

The politics of the representation of Gerty's disability have been read in diametrically opposed ways by Vike Martina Plock on the one hand, and Angela Lea Nemecek and Dominika Bednarska on the other. Plock's 2007 article is not informed by disability studies. It reads the use of Gerty's disability in "Nausicaa" as an ironic comment on the Irish nationalist movement, especially the nationalist icon Cathleen Ni Houlihan, who has, in the words of Yeats's and Lady Gregory's play *Cathleen Ni Houlihan*, "the walk of a queen" (Yeats 11). Plock reads Gerty's limp as an ironic "reversal of the proud walk that so conspicuously distinguished Yeats's female nationalist symbol" ("Why" 119). Gerty, she argues, represents Joyce's mockery of the Irish nationalist movement's emphasis on transformation. Instead of an old woman who transforms into a beautiful young queen, Gerty will undergo the opposite metamorphosis, from a young beauty to "a vindictive and cynical old spinster" ("Why" 129). In addition to assuming that being a spinster will make one "vindictive and cynical," Plock's assurance that Gerty's "defect singles her out for a different future from the one desperately desired" (129) echoes the assumption that disability and sexuality cannot coexist. Plock does not comment on the misogyny and ableism of this reading.[32] But the distastefulness of her reading does not mean that it cannot also be an accurate representation of the chapter's body politics. Did Joyce see Gerty's limp as an ironic comment on Cathleen Ni Houlihan's proud walk? Did he use her limp to deflate not just the tumescence of the text but the swollen rhetoric of the nationalist movement? He does describe Gerty as a model "specimen of winsome Irish girlhood" (13.81), and this type of mockery would dovetail with his other representations of Irish nationalism.[33]

Bednarska and Nemecek, however, argue for a disability-friendly reading of Gerty's limp. These two critics independently arrive at readings that understand "Nausicaa" as a "stigmaphilic" space.[34] Bednarska argues that "Gerty MacDowell rehabilitates disability and reveals 'ability' as a central component of the way gender functions and subjectivity is formed" (73). Nemecek similarly writes, "While I am not suggesting that Joyce himself intended a radical critique of ableism, I believe that an examination of Gerty's character reveals her crucial role in shoring up the novel's implicit questioning of compulsory normativity." She reads Gerty as embodying "a powerful resistance to eugenic ideologies of standardization" (173). In her discussion of the revelation of Gerty's limp (which she reads as "planned and intentional" on Gerty's part [180]), Nemecek writes that "Gerty's performance of able-bodiedness reveals the social construction of normativity" (182). While I find these readings a bit too optimistic, there is a sense of acceptance in *Ulysses* for the variations of human being that bolsters their claims that Gerty's disability might be a force of subversion rather than deflation.

But none of these readings of Gerty's limp takes into account the question of the status of Gerty's narration. Indeed, most criticism of the episode reads Gerty's narrative as arising from Gerty's consciousness.[35] While critics notes that, as Bishop puts it, Gerty's narrative is "densely mediated by her immersion in the language of advertising and of sentimental and domestic fiction" ("Metaphysics" 185–86), they do not typically question the notion that Gerty or a detached narrator focalizing Gerty is narrating the first half of the chapter. Margot Norris, for example, writes that Gerty narrates herself "as she would like to be, as she would like people to think about her, and indeed, to write about her, given the conspicuous and emphatic literariness of her narration" (169).

One dissenter from this consensus is John Gordon, who argues that Gerty is a projection of Bloom's fantasy.[36] He notes that Joyce told Arthur Power, "Nothing happened between them. . . . It all took place in Bloom's imagination" (*Joyce and Reality* 73). Providing nine pieces of evidence for his reading, including the "Sense (meaning)" given in the Linati schema, "The Projected Mirage," Gordon persuasively argues that Gerty is a mirage, imagined by Bloom at a time of psychological need (73). He acknowledges that Gerty does exist as a character in the novel but argues that Bloom is likely to have seen her elsewhere and can thus create his fantasy about her in her absence (273n40).

While convinced by Gordon's evidence that Gerty is not narrating her own section, I understand the first half of the episode slightly differently: not merely as Bloom's projection, but as Bloom's narrative, the story he thought about writing in the morning before wiping himself with "Matcham's Masterstroke" (4.502). It seems to me that Gerty is present on the beach but that *Bloom* is the narrator attempting to focalize her as a character based on the romance novels he has read (before and after bringing them to Molly) and that *he* is responsible for the "conspicuous and emphatic literariness of [Gerty's] narration." Having "envied kindly Mr Beaufoy who had written ["Matcham's Masterstroke"] and received payment of three pounds, thirteen and six" (4.516–17), Bloom thinks he "might manage a sketch" (4.518). In "Nausicaa" he is trying his hand at a prize story that also serves his sexual desires.

Seeing Bloom as "author" of this section of the chapter would explain the most obvious feature of the narrative: its relentless banality and sentimentality, so different from the rest of *Ulysses*, even from the "Eumaeus" episode where the language is said to be tired and plodding. In *Aesthetic Nervousness*, Quayson writes that disability often causes the "dominant protocols of representation" to collapse or be short-circuited (26).[37] Certainly in this chapter the stylistic pyrotechnics that are required to represent Bloom's and Stephen's consciousnesses and describe the city of Dublin, the Citizen, the Ormond barmaids, and all the other characters in *Ulysses*—the dominant protocols of the text—have broken down. Bloom's position as the implied writer of the narrative makes it impossible to determine, however, whether the protocols have collapsed in the face of disability or whether they have collapsed because Bloom, rather than Joyce, is "writing" the section.

Bloom does fancy himself a potential writer. In "Calypso," after reading "Matcham's Masterstroke," Bloom considers what he might write for such a feature in the newspaper. He remembers having jotted down, with an eye toward writing, things Molly would say while dressing. Two details here are echoed in Gerty's portion of "Nausicaa": he mentions "a speck of dust on the patent leather of her boot" (4.524)—Gerty's shoes have "patent toecaps"—and he remembers Molly "rubbing smartly in turn each welt against her stocking calf" (4.525), while Gerty's stockinged calves are of obsessive interest to the narrator of Gerty's section. Two of Gordon's points also support the claim that Bloom is the narrator of this section:

> That style itself recalls the namby-pamby parody of Bloom's own "love" speech in "Cyclops" with an admixture of the "costliest frillies" fetishism of *Sweets of Sin* (*U* 13.1492.1501; 10.608–17). Which is to say it has already been established as, under the right conditions, a Bloomian idiom. ([Evidence #] 5) To confirm which, the style twice returns as an outgrowth of Bloom's own voice, in Gerty's absence, as he sinks toward slumber (*U* 13.1166–81, 1292–1302). (*Joyce and Reality* 73)

The lack of firm boundaries between the idiom of the first half and the idiom of the second suggests, in my reading, that Gerty's presence on the beach offers Bloom the opportunity to craft his prize story.

Dermot Kelly observes some features of the narration that similarly provide evidence for the claim that Bloom is narrating Gerty's section, although he does not draw that conclusion. He writes that "even to refer to the first half of the episode as Gerty's discourse is to sail under a flag of convenience, since the descriptions of the temperance retreat and the other girls with the children cannot always be traced directly to Gerty's consciousness" (37). He also notes that "as the fireworks go off and Bloom ejaculates, the Gerty MacDowell style is amended to include the elliptical poetry of 'rain gold hair threads' and 'greeny dewy stars' which, although it cannot be specifically identified with Bloom's language, is more characteristically Joycean in its exuberance than much of the first part of 'Nausicaa'" (38). I would argue that it *can* be specifically identified with Bloom's language, and I would also propose Bloom-as-narrator as the explanation for the paragraph beginning "A last lonely candle" (13.1166ff), in which, as Kelly says, "the language of Gerty's section of 'Nausicaa' is superimposed upon the initial style" (43).

Indeed, the similarity of Gerty's legs in the "transparent stockings" (13.929) to those of the woman Bloom tried to watch in the morning suggests that Bloom crafts his story to pick up the thread (pun intended) of the woman whose legs he didn't get to stare at.[38] In "Lotus Eaters," Bloom was watching a woman with a "wellturned foot" and "silk stockings": "Watch! Watch! Silk flash rich stockings white. Watch! // A heavy tramcar honking its gong slewed between. // Lost it. Curse your noisy pugnose. . . . Always happening like that. The very moment" (5.130–32). After the revelation of Gerty's limp, Bloom considers this similarity: "Made up for that tramdriver this morning" (13.787–88).

The narration of the first part of the episode also represents Bloom very positively; as Gordon puts it, "Gerty's account of Bloom is by far the most flattering of the book" (*Joyce and Reality* 73). In the episode's mock counterpart to Odysseus catching Princess Nausicaa's ball, for example, the Caffrey twins kick the ball down the rocks, "but luckily the gentleman in black who was sitting there by himself came gallantly to the rescue and intercepted the ball" (13.349–50). The narrator then describes Bloom's face as "wan and strangely drawn," seeming to Gerty "the saddest she had ever seen" (13.369–70). This is just how the romantic Bloom, prompted in part by his black funeral suit, would hope to appear to a young woman. Her interpretation of his gaze is as gratifying as Bloom could wish: his "superbly expressive" eyes "burned into her as though they would search her through and through, read her very soul" (13.412–13). Gerty feels "instinctively that he was like no one else" (13.429–30), and the young women compete for his attention (13.493–504). And most of all, Gerty's immediate and sustained sexual response to Bloom's ogling bears all the marks of wish fulfillment (13.513–20, 560–61, 689–740).

Significantly, if Bloom is the author of this narrative, it would also explain why the narrative switches to his head just after the sexual climax. Now that he has finished his story, the narrative shifts back to his stream of consciousness. If the narrative were really Gerty's, how would we explain the switch or its timing? Gordon points out that only in fantasy does the sexual "partner" disappear right after the climax (*Joyce and Reality* 73); but the other realm in which this can happen is the realm of fiction (within fiction). Bloom finishes his story and his sexual escapade and begins thinking about other things.

Additional hints that the narrative is a story "conjured up" by Bloom can be found both in "Nausicaa" and in "Circe." In "Nausicaa" Gerty thinks of a picture of "halcyon days" depicting a gentleman offering flowers to his "ladylove," and the text tells us, "You could see there was a story behind it" (13.333–36). Toward the end of the episode Bloom considers writing a story about a gentleman passing by on the beach: "Ask yourself who is he now. *The Mystery Man on the Beach*, prize titbit story by Mr. Leopold Bloom. Payment at the rate of one guinea per column" (13.1059–61). Bloom has cast *himself* as a mystery man on the beach in his rendering of Gerty's narrative. In "Circe" a Mrs. Bellingham says that Bloom "lauded almost extravagantly my nether extremities, my swelling calves in silk hose drawn up to the limit, and eulogized glowingly my other hidden treasures in priceless lace which, he said, he could conjure up" (15.1051–54). Certainly Bloom can conjure up this kind of romance, as he imagined in the outhouse. After his sexual climax, indeed, he uses the same word, *swell*, to refer to calves, while the "Circe" phrase "drawn up to the limit" echoes the "Nausicaa" phrase "stretched to the breaking point": "Devil you are. Swell of her calf. Transparent stockings, stretched to breaking point" (13.929–30).

In fact, the author of the prize story, Beaufoy, is mentioned a few pages earlier in "Circe." There Bloom announces that "we are just bringing out a collection of prize stories of which I am the inventor" (15.803). Myles Crawford asks, "Who writes? Is it Bloom?" (15.813). But then, according to the stage directions, "(Mr Philip Beaufoy, palefaced, stands in the witnessbox, in accurate morning dress, outbreast pocket with peak of handkerchief showing, creased lavender trousers and patent boots. He carries a large portfolio labeled *Matcham's Masterstrokes*" (15.814–17). Anticipating Shaun's attacks on Shem as an obscene plagiarizer in *Finnegans Wake*, Beaufoy accuses Bloom: "No born gentleman, no-one with the most rudimentary promptings of a gentleman would stoop to such particularly loathsome conduct. One of these, my lord. A plagiarist" (15.820–22). The loathsome conduct is both Bloom's behavior, masturbating on a public beach, and his usurpation of Beaufoy's narrative "baseness" in his story about Gerty MacDowell.

While the phrase *jilted beauty* can be read as Bloom's assumption that a woman with a limp would naturally be rejected by potential suitors, it could also indicate Bloom's knowledge of Reggie Wylie, because he *invented* the story of the boy who no longer rides his bicycle past Gerty's window.[39] This reading would also explain the question "But who was Gerty?" (13.78), which would be oddly self-reflexive if the narrative really originated in Gerty's consciousness. Instead, it could indicate Bloom setting the stage for his romantic inquiry into his "Greekly perfect" heroine.

The most interesting implications of assuming Bloom is the narrator emerge when we analyze the revelation of Gerty's limp. Gerty's ostensible narrative breaks off at "because Gerty MacDowell was . . ." and Bloom's narrative begins, "Tight boots? No. She's lame! O!" Some narrator is clearly quite distant from Gerty's own consciousness when he sets up the drama of that disclosure with the ellipses. Gerty herself, having already mentioned her "one shortcoming," would have no reason to dramatize the information in this way. Rather, a narrator such as Bloom has structured the story so that the disclosure of the limp comes at the end: in the middle of Joyce's episode, but at the end of Bloom's romance/fantasy narrative. The fact that the conclusion to the broken-off sentence is located firmly in Bloom's consciousness further suggests that the story was his all the time. As Mitchell and Snyder remark, "disability is a narrative device upon which the literary writer [here Bloom, with his literary pretensions and prosaic, oversexed mind] depends for his or her disruptive punch" (*Narrative Prosthesis* 49).[40] The revelation of Gerty's limp is a preplanned bit of melodrama that Bloom has inserted into his narrative: his masterstroke.

This leaves open the question of how we are to experience this revelation. Our revision of our former understanding of Gerty may lead to the understanding that a disabled woman can be sexually appealing, as Nemecek has it, or to the sense of deflation that Plock sees in the text. In my view, the text is ambiguous on this point. Bloom's own reactions might serve as a guide to readers, but they are ambivalent. He is relieved that the stage setting of Gerty-on-the-beach sufficed to provide him with his orgasm. He pities her but reminds himself to "be on your guard not to feel too much pity. They take advantage" (13.1095–96). From the manuscript forward, he thinks, "Hot little devil all the same" (*James Joyce Archive* [*JJA*] 13:222).[41] But the line "I wouldn't mind. Curiosity like a nun or a negress or a girl with glasses" was not added until the third typescript (*JJA* 13:284) and is absent from the *Little Review* version of the episode. However, it's not the case that Bloom's reactions became more accepting as Joyce revised the episode: the line "A defect is ten times worse in a woman" was also added in the third typescript (*JJA* 13:284). The ambivalence of Bloom's responses only intensifies as the drafts progress.

It's not clear that the Gerty MacDowell who is a character in *Ulysses* even has a limp. The limp is not mentioned in "Wandering Rocks" or "Cyclops," two episodes where she appears. It is mentioned in "Circe," but since this is a mutual dreamscape of Bloom's and Stephen's, the appearance of Gerty there cannot be taken to indicate anything "real" about her character. If she does have a limp, then Bloom has manipulated the revelation in his melodrama; if she does not, why would he have invented it? Perhaps in his mind a woman with a limp would be more likely to find him attractive, would be easier to please ("But makes them polite" [13.775]). Perhaps *he* intended the parallel between the limping woman and his limp penis. We could take "The Projected Mirage" here to indicate the degree to which Bloom sees himself as defective. In this reading, Gerty's limp does indicate her deflated value and is not, as Nemecek and Bednarska maintain, celebrated by a stigmaphilic text.

Bloom's remark "Glad I didn't know it when she was on show" (13.775) seems to run counter to the suggestion that he *did* know. But the line could easily be disingenuous, a necessity of his fictional drama. Indeed, he also says, "Thought something was wrong with her by the cut of her jib" (13.773–74). And after all, Joyce saw Marthe Fleischmann limping before he caught sight of her face. According to Gordon Bowker, "even [Fleischmann's] slight limp enchanted him" (259). Bloom's later comment, "See her as she is spoil all. Must have the stage setting, the rouge, costume, position, music" (13.855–56), concedes that desire takes place in a performative context (for Joyce, the context of replication of a past narrative; for Bloom, a popular romance story). As Norris points out, Gerty gives a "static performance" that "creates the illusion that beauty is ideal, singular, and timeless" (177). During his fantasy narrative, Bloom allows the ideal and timeless to reign, keeping imperfections in the wings; but when the narrative ends, the imperfections return to center stage. Bloom's musing that his sexual communication with Gerty was "a kind of language between us" (13.944) ties sexuality to textuality in a way that supports a reading of his sexual fantasy as prize story.

Nemecek astutely points out that the "O!" that comes in the revelation ("Tight boots? No. She's lame! O!") echoes and extends the multiple *O!*s of pleasure from the scene of sexual climax just before (184), suggesting a kind of pleasure in the revelation. This pleasure, I would argue, arises from the linkage of sexuality, textuality, and disability: the story reaching its climax. The dramatic climax of Bloom's story is tied to the sexual climax within the episode. This conjunction causes the opposition between disability and sexuality established by the episode's two-part structure to collapse. Both in Bloom's mind and in the text, disability was present within sexuality all along.[42]

The line "Glad I didn't know it when she was on show" reinforces the opposition between disability and sexuality we see in the episode's structure and in the other texts discussed here. But that disjuncture is a false one, in that sexuality requires "stage setting"—fiction—and fiction requires drama, and "Nausicaa" provides that drama through the revelation of disability. Gerty's lameness exposes both the falsity of the dichotomy between disability and sexuality and the degree to which desire is part and parcel of fiction.

In the texts discussed in this chapter, then, the ostensible opposition between sexuality and disability is broken down by the various ways disability inheres within sexuality. We see the power of disability to bring about narrative climax: Tom's abandonment of his family after and in spite of the word *cripple* finally spoken; Pointer's stealing of the wooden leg; the revelation of Gerty's limp. The disavowed association between disability and sexuality emerges or reemerges in the "O!" of pleasure that accompanies the revelation in "Nausicaa"; in the theft of the leg that takes the place of sexual climax in "Good Country People"; and in *The Glass Menagerie*'s use of Laura's disability as proxy for a concealed, illicit sexuality. In the next chapter I explore a related aspect of disability representation in texts where sexuality is subsumed into romantic love, texts that treat blindness as fostering intimacy.

Two

Blindness and Intimacy

> *What the eyes bring is nothing. I have a hundred worlds to create, I am losing only one of them.*
>
> —James Joyce[1]

With the notable exception of Wilkie Collins's *Poor Miss Finch* (1872), Victorian novels tended to depict blindness as something that either ruins one's life or ends one's text.[2] Charlotte Brontë's *Jane Eyre* (1847), for example, by ending with Rochester regaining his sight, "endorses the ocularcentric belief that a person cannot live happily ever after without sight" (Bolt, "Blindman," 285). Discussing *Jane Eyre* and Rudyard Kipling's *The Light That Failed* (1891), Georgina Kleege comments, "These are the old stories of blindness. . . . They show no life after blindness, offer no hope to the blind, except that the condition might prove impermanent or that death might come quick" (*Sight Unseen* 73). In Elizabeth Barrett Browning's *Aurora Leigh* (1856) and Charles Kingsley's *Westward Ho!* (1855), blindness is introduced at the ends of the texts.[3] Although the blind characters' marriages can be assumed to be happy, the texts' failure to represent their ongoing lives gives the impression that blindness is not part of a fully lived life but something beyond "our" understanding—beyond narrative.

By contrast, a variety of early twentieth-century texts such as H. G. Wells's "The Country of the Blind" (1904), J. M. Synge's *The Well of the Saints* (1905), Florence Barclay's *The Rosary* (1909), D. H. Lawrence's "The Blind Man" (1920), and Henry Green's *Blindness* (1926) demonstrate an interest in exploring life *with* blindness. Valuing the interior life, this strand of modernist literature classifies blindness as the inward state par excellence. Although these texts do romanticize blindness, they break from traditional depictions by treating blindness as part of, rather than a frightening departure from, the human condition. Moreover, to varying degrees, these texts suggest that blindness is conducive to romantic love. Unlike earlier representations of blindness as something that "inverts, perverts, or thwarts all human relationships" (Kleege, *Sight Unseen* 71), these texts represent blindness as that which fosters intimacy.[4]

The phrase "blindness and intimacy" is meant to resonate against the phrase "blindness and insight," famously used by Paul de Man and present in many discussions of blindness. De Man used the phrase to describe what he saw as an entanglement of "blind spots" with a scholar's best insights. For example, when he discusses Derrida's account of Rousseau, he traces the moments of what he calls blindness within or alongside moments of insight, writing that "this new interpretation will, in its turn, be caught in its own form of blindness, but not without having produced its bright moment of literary insight" (139). Throughout "The Rhetoric of Blindness" de Man uses blindness to mean obtuseness, delusion, and mistake. As Lennard Davis notes, "while endorsing the cultural continuity that sees blindness as leading to inner vision, de Man nevertheless also endorses the notion that blindness is a metaphor for unwillingness or inability to investigate a point or idea. Thus blindness is only partially enabling" (*Enforcing Normalcy* 102).

The apparent sense of the phrase "blindness and insight" stems from the long history of Western understandings of blindness that position it along an axis of knowledge.[5] That is, blindness is associated (often) with lack of knowledge and (sometimes) with uncanny knowledge, or insight. Michael Davidson points out that "the idea that we are all prisoners in Plato's Cave, seeing only shadows, suggests how powerful the connection between sight and knowledge has been from the outset" (*Concerto* 18). Several denotative meanings of the word *blind* relate to this idea of lacking awareness, understanding, or knowledge (Bolt, "From Blindness" 542). "Our language," Julia Rodas asserts, "bespeaks our unconscious belief that blindness is automatically agnostic, unknowing" (122). This deep association of blindness with lack of knowledge relies on the ableist assumption that knowledge comes through sight.

An example of this assumption can be found in Georg Simmel's "Sociology of the Senses" (1908). Simmel suggests that one of the problems with the modern city is that it gives sighted people so many opportunities to see others without hearing them. This makes them anxious by parading before them the perplexities of human life. Blind people, he asserts, are serene because they are not aware of these perplexities: "The expression of the anxiety and unrest . . . exposed to view in the faces of men, escape the blind, and that may be the reason for [their] peaceful and calm disposition" ("Sociology" 360). In Simmel's version of what Naomi Schor calls the "myth of fortunate blindness" (85), blind people benefit by being excluded from seeing, that is, from *knowing about*, the "anxiety and unrest" of human life.

This attitude persists into the twenty-first century, as can be seen in Kleege's account of an interviewer asking Ray Charles about the attacks on the World Trade Center in 2001. The interviewer asked, "Was this maybe the one time in your life where not having the ability to see was a relief?" Kleege comments that "the interviewer assumed that true horror can only be evinced through the eyes" ("Blindness and Visual Culture" 393). Kleege's "horror" might be broadened to "knowledge," because the interviewer implies that not seeing the collapse of the towers would protect Charles from truly understanding it, and *therefore* from feeling its devastation.[6]

Not as common as the assumption that blind people are excluded from knowledge, but nevertheless powerful and long-standing, is the idea that they are rewarded by a compensatory gift of insight. The blind "seer" Tiresias is the classic example, and Homer's blindness has often been depicted as "transcendent vision" (Barasch 133). Ved Mehta remarks that "the sighted go from one extreme to the other—from assuming that the blind are virtually cut off from all perception to endowing them with extrasensory perception" (3). The attribution of extrasensory perception can also be explained by the ableist assumption that knowledge comes primarily from sight: when blind people demonstrate that they possess knowledge, sighted people conclude that they have come by it through uncanny means.

Deafness is often positioned, in a parallel way, along an axis of communication: for the most part, deaf people are thought to be excluded from communication, and anyone can be stonily "deaf to" someone's pleas. Davis argues that while "blindness has been adopted by Western culture as a metaphor for insight . . . deafness has been a signifier for the absence of language" (*Enforcing Normalcy* 106). Helen Keller provides a case in point, asserting that deafness means "the loss of the most vital stimulus—the sound of the voice that brings language, sets thoughts astir and keeps us in the intellectual company of man" (68). Simmel, for his part, describes deaf people, unlike "serene" blind people, as living in a constant state of perplexity because they cannot fathom the emotions of others: "Indeed, the majority of the stimuli which the face presents are often puzzling; in general, what we see of a man will be interpreted by what we hear from him. . . . Therefore the one who sees, without hearing, is much more perplexed, puzzled, and worried, than the one who hears without seeing" ("Sociology" 360). Both Simmel's and Keller's assertions imply that communication comes only through hearing. They discount both visual (signed) languages and the visual component in oral/aural communication.[7] On the other hand, deaf characters are sometimes seen as having unearthly powers of perception.[8] This indicates that when deaf people do understand the emotions or concerns of others, hearing people assume they have come by that understanding through uncanny means.

One factor in the link between blindness and intimacy, then, is the tight relationship between the "elitc senses" (Kleege, *Blind Rage* 34) of sight and hearing. Blind people are understood as exceptionally auditory and, conversely, deaf people often call themselves "the people of the eye."[9] Since hearing is the privileged mode of communication, blind people are often ascribed—in the modernist period, at least—a special capacity to commune with others. But the axis of knowledge lingers in important ways, underlying this capacity in that being allegedly cut off from knowledge of the world makes possible greater intimacy with a beloved. In this sense, modern British literature is adapting an earlier understanding of blindness as a means to commune with God. In *The Victorians and the Visual Imagination*, Kate Flint details this link between blindness and spirituality, between what one Victorian writer describes as "bodily darkness" and God's "marvelous spiritual light" (80). In the literary texts I consider, this idea is adjusted to a secular world: being "cut off from the world" through blindness brings one closer not to God, but to the beloved.

An important reason blindness was brought to the attention of the postwar writers considered here, Green and Lawrence (as well as Joyce, discussed in chapter 4), was the high incidence of blindness among soldiers returning from the Great War. Gas attacks and explosions damaged the eyesight of thousands of soldiers. St. Dunstan's, "the Blinded Soldiers' and Sailors' Hostel," was established in 1915 to help veterans "learn to be blind." Its location in Regent's Park and its size—"the house, gardens, grounds, and outbuildings whose 15-acre spread was said to make it the largest single piece of property in London next to Buckingham Palace"—brought war-blinded veterans to public notice (Koestler 274). In the midst of press coverage of St. Dunstan's and of wounded and blinded soldiers, John Singer Sargent's painting *Gassed* was exhibited at the Royal Academy of Arts in 1919 and then moved to the Imperial War Museum (Fairbrother 39). The painting depicts a line of soldiers, eyes bandaged, holding each other by the shoulders. "No painting received more press attention that year, and none so starkly divided viewers and reviewers" (Harvey 148). This provocative painting received praise from Winston Churchill and criticism from writers such Virginia Woolf and E.M.

Forster (Harvey 148; McLaurin 27–28). This attention to blinded soldiers and to the politics of representing blindness heightened postwar writers' consideration of the meanings of blindness.

Valuing the Invisible

The association of blindness with *intimacy* in the strand of turn-of-the-century literature considered here is a reversal of the isolation associated with blindness in traditional stories and still, of course, lingering in other modernist texts. Discussing Homer's Cyclops, Tolkein's Gollum, and the witch from the Grimms' Hansel and Gretel, Rodas notes that "the blind are not social creatures, but are turned ever inward on themselves" (125).[10] The reversal evident in the texts discussed here may be contextualized with reference to two related aspects of the period: first, a questioning whether sight gives accurate and factual information, and thus a skepticism about sight's superiority over the other senses, and second, modernism's desire to represent characters' inner lives.

As Martin Jay argues in his magisterial book *Downcast Eyes*, the ocularcentrism characteristic of Western culture—the idea that sight is the "noblest of the senses"—was being undermined in philosophy during this same period, particularly in France. Jay traces the "profound suspicion of vision and its hegemonic role" (14) in several key thinkers of the late nineteenth and early twentieth centuries, including Henri Bergson, Jean-Paul Sartre, and Maurice Merleau-Ponty. He identifies a disenchantment with the eye and its supposed objectivity, stemming in part from new technologies (149–51). Stephen Kern discusses a similar consequence of Nietzsche's "perspectivism," which denied that it was possible for an eye, or seer, to see objectively (150). And Gertrude Stein makes related observations in her book about Picasso and the development of Cubism, writing that in the twentieth century, "the truth that the things seen with the eyes are the only real things, had lost its significance" (10) and that "the faith in what the eyes were seeing . . . commenced to diminish" (12). All this is not to say that sight's supremacy was definitively overturned, but that emerging alongside it, making incursions into its dominance, was a newly important interest in the nonvisual.[11]

Jay's discussion of Bergson relates most closely to literary modernism. Bergson's critique of ocularcentrism, as well as his exploration of private time, or *durée*, influenced modernist authors' focus on consciousness as opposed to material reality (Lehan 47–49). As Mark Antliff explains, Bergson compared *durée* to a melody because "auditory perception is naturally attuned to the soul's inner music" while sight serves more "utilitarian needs" (299). In *Time and Free Will,* Bergson argues that the senses are "intensive," not "extensive"—that is, qualitative, and not quantitative, matters.[12] He explores, for example, how we see color when a source of light is moved closer to and farther away from a colored object. He argues that though we think we're seeing a difference in quantity of color in dimmer light, we're really seeing different colors, differences in quality. He writes: "having made up our minds, once and for all, to interpret changes of quality as changes of quantity, we begin by asserting that every object has its own peculiar colour, definite and invariable. . . . We thus substitute once more, for the qualitative impression received by our consciousness, the quantitative interpretation given by our understanding" (51). What's important for my purposes here is Bergson's assertion that we are not really seeing what we think we're seeing. By arguing that how we understand vision can be distorted by preconceived notions about the steadfastness of color, Bergson undermines the belief that sight is the most accurate and objective sense. As Garin Dowd explains in another context, Bergson's use of the term *image* is "designed to cast into doubt the hegemony of vision in philosophy. . . . He distances himself from several philosophical traditions all constrained by a privileging of the eye" (315).

Such a disenchantment with vision had also been emerging in late nineteenth-century England; Gillian Beer argues that in late Victorian culture "vision was, in quite a new way, subordinate to the invisible" (85). She explains:

> Increasingly the invisible came to declare itself as a condition within which we move, and *of* which we are. . . . Paradoxically, this realization dawned alongside the great advances in microscopes, telescopes, and optics in the mid-nineteenth century.
>
> Even as the domain of sight advanced by means of such instruments, the evidence was mounting that the eye was an uncertain instrument. (88)

As sight's status as the most reliable sense was being called into question, "the invisible" gained in value. The elements of realist fiction that Woolf complains about in famous essays such as "Modern Fiction" and "Mr. Bennett and Mrs. Brown," for example—the details of houses, a "button sewn on as the Bond Street tailors would have it" ("Modern Fiction" 189)—require visual observation. As Jay explains, "nineteenth-century realist fiction . . . called on the author's visual acuity to create its effect of represented reality, the novel's 'holding a mirror to nature'" (173). But modernist writers often dispensed with such aspiration to visual accuracy in order to capture an *invisible* force: "life or spirit, truth or reality, this, the essential thing" (Woolf, "Modern Fiction" 188).[13]

Modernism's emphasis on the invisible was also influenced by developments in technology and physics, whose sweeping effects on understandings of time, space, and perception have been well documented.[14] New, powerful telescopes,[15] the popularity of cinema,[16] and the development of x-rays,[17] among other technologies, contributed to a sense of uncertainty about vision, demonstrating that what we see with the naked eye is far from the whole or true picture. Einstein's special theory of relativity radically changed understandings of time, space, and perspective. The idea that time and space could be relative rather than absolute was, and still is, deeply counterintuitive. If, as Kern puts it, "length is not anything; it is a consequence of the act of measuring. Thus absolute space has no meaning" (136), then how can we trust what we see with our eyes? Impressionism and Cubism in painting were motivated by such changes in our understanding of how visual perception works, as both Jay and Kern discuss.[18] Instead of aiming for visual detail understood as factual, then, many modernist writers sought to depict a more subjective "shower of innumerable atoms" that fall upon the mind (Woolf, "Modern Fiction" 189).

Another clear impetus toward this subjective emphasis of modernism was Freudian psychoanalysis. In the Freudian era, the inner life suddenly appeared both more complex than it had been assumed to be, and more worthy of scientific study and literary representation. As I mention in the introduction, Micale demonstrates that "both psychiatric medicine and creative arts during the late nineteenth and early twentieth centuries were marked by a massive 'turn inward' and a thoroughgoing psychologization of their methods, subjects, and intentions" (2). Artists' desire to delve beneath surface reality to discover unconscious drives and motivations fused with the concurrent attention to what cannot be seen.

In his discussion of paradigms through which modernism has been understood, Astradur Eysteinsson explores the opposition seen to exist between the extreme subjectivity of some modernist works and the efforts toward impersonality touted by T. S. Eliot in "Tradition and the Individual Talent" and evident in many modernist texts.[19] In my view the two ideas are not actually opposed. Impersonality is a way to understand the writer's relationship to his or her material; the type of inwardness called for by Woolf and remarked on by myriad critics, on the other hand, is a way to understand which aspects of their characters writers foreground. While a writer might aim to transcend (her) personality in her work, she could simultaneously represent "the dark places of psychology" in her characters. Eysteinsson also concludes that the differences are overstated, though for a different reason: "what the modernist poetics of impersonality and that of extreme subjectivity have in common (and this outweighs whatever may separate them) is a revolt against the traditional relation of the subject to the outside world" (28).

The representations of blindness discussed here form part of the authors' exploration of this relation of the subject to the outside world—part of their inquiry into the role of the body and its senses in our apprehension of the world around us. In a recent memoir about his blindness, John M. Hull writes that "sighted people live in the world. The blind person lives in consciousness" (202). Such an assertion recalls D. H. Lawrence's claim that "the real activity of life is . . . *developing consciousness*" (*Selected Letters* 428). The romanticized idea that blindness turns a person inward to commune with his own consciousness seems to animate the representations of blindness in the texts discussed here.[20] The concern evinced in early twentieth-century literature, then, about how our inner lives relate to our bodies and to the world outside the self helps account for its fascination with blindness as a means to explore consciousness and communion.

In fact, in a 1914 letter, Lawrence calls for art to be revivified through a "blind knowledge" that can grow out of (hetero)sexual communion: "That is the only way for art and civilization to get a new life . . . men and women—revealing themselves each to the other, gaining great blind knowledge and suffering and joy" (*Letters* 2:181). Later he explicitly links sight to what he calls the "mental consciousness," which he believes is inferior to "blood-consciousness." He writes that there is a "mental consciousness . . . , which depends on the eye as its source or connector. There is the blood-consciousness, with the sexual connection, holding the same relation as the eye, in seeing, holds to the mental consciousness" (*Letters* 2:470).[21]

Lawrence elaborates on these ideas in *Fantasia of the Unconscious*, asserting that "the blood-consciousness is the first and last knowledge of the living soul: the depths. . . . And blood-consciousness cannot operate purely until the soul has put off all its manifold degrees and forms of upper consciousness" (171). These convictions clearly animate his 1920 short story "The Blind Man" as well as his several of his major novels. Lawrence articulates here a strand of thought running through early twentieth-century literature: one that devalues that which can be seen as "the trivial and the transitory" and elevates that which cannot be seen as the "true and the enduring" (Woolf, "Modern Fiction," 187).

One of the ways writers explored this shift in values was through representations of blind characters. In what follows, I first explore representations of blindness in Wells's "The Country of the Blind" and Green's *Blindness*. These fictions establish the connection between blindness and intimacy but veer away from it or revise it to follow their authors' larger agendas. Next I turn to Synge's *The Well of the Saints*, Barclay's *The Rosary*, and Lawrence's "The Blind Man," where the connection is more fully developed. From Wells's disavowal of intimacy to Lawrence's celebration, this set of texts has put aside the association of blindness with ignorance and even its association with uncanny knowledge and proposed instead a way to understand blindness as *contact* with oneself and with a beloved.

Allegories of Independence

In "The Country of the Blind," H. G. Wells portrays a society of blind people in a secluded Ecuadoran valley and mocks his protagonist's pretensions to dominate the village through the power of sight. The story is an anti-imperialist allegory: the intruder, our protagonist Nunez, assumes that he is superior and that the villagers will be thankful for his guidance, only to find that they feel no sense of privation.[22] Repeatedly reciting the adage "in the country of the blind, the one-eyed man is king," Nunez attempts to rule over the village. But not only is he unable to dominate the people as he fantasized; he himself is disabled by the way they have structured their society, as he stumbles in dark houses and is unable to work competently in the cool dark nights.

The anti-imperialist thrust of the story leads it into a progressive representation of blindness as something that can not only be lived with, but lived with well. The society it depicts is efficient. Over many generations, the people have adapted their lives and their village to their blindness. The story exemplifies the social model of disability in its portrayal of a society so well adapted to the needs of blind people that sight, and not blindness, becomes a disability. The anti-imperialist strand of the story invites readers to criticize Nunez for his arrogance and his over-valuation of sight.

But there is another strand of the story, of a piece politically with its anti-imperialism but inviting readers to identify with Nunez instead of criticizing him. In that strand the story celebrates resistance to assimilation. The politics of the story seem to suggest that no one should try to dominate a culture he does not understand (anti-imperialism), but neither should that culture forcibly assimilate the other (antiassimilationism). It is this antiassimilationist strand that most critics focus on; for example, when J. R. Hammond writes that the story is a "parable on conformity" he is referring to the "narrow-minded social order" of the blind society that treats Nunez as an outcast (73). So Nunez is at the same time a colonizer who should be resisted and a foreigner whose difference should be respected. The latter, antiassimilationist strand leads the story into strongly ableist or ocularcentric messages, which sit uncomfortably alongside its more progressive implications.

The antiassimilationist strand asks us to identify with Nunez as he talks to a young woman, Medina-saroté, about sight. While most of the villagers think he is mad, prattling about a sense that does not exist, Medina-saroté takes his stories as a sign of his vivid imagination. Nunez falls in love with her and asks to marry her, but the village elders object because they consider him "a being apart, an idiot, incompetent thing below the permissible level of a man" (562). The villagers' prejudices against him for his incompetence and their dismissal of his explanations of sight also support the social model of disability, demonstrating that what counts as a disability is simply what differs from majority norms. As Abbie Garrington notes (though using *blind* to indicate obtuseness), the story asks that we "contemplate the blind spot within our own 'vision' of the world—the possibly erroneous belief in the central importance of vision" (106).

The village council goes so far along what we can paradoxically call ableist lines that they decide Medina-saroté may marry Nunez only if he will submit to an operation to be normalized: to have his eyes removed. The medicine man tells the council, "Those queer things that are called the eyes . . . are diseased, in the case of [Nunez] in such a way as to affect his brain. They are greatly distended, he has eyelashes, and his eyelids move, and consequently his brain is in a constant state of irritation and distraction" (563). In line with Simmel's assertion that blind people are serene, the village elders assume that it is sight that drives Nunez to distraction. "I think I may say with reasonable certainty," the medicine man continues, "that, in order to cure him completely, all that we need do is a simple and easy surgical operation—namely, to remove these irritant bodies" (563).

Medina-saroté begs him to acquiesce. But Nunez holds to his ocularcentrism. He objects that his "world is sight" and that there are so many beautiful things to see: rocks, lichens, the sky. "And there is *you*. For you alone it is good to have sight. . . . It is these eyes of mine you won, these eyes that hold me to you, that these idiots seek" (564). Finally he agrees to submit to the surgery. But on the night before the surgery, without quite planning to, he leaves the village, wandering into the snowy mountains to meet almost certain death.

While progressive in its representation of a functional blind society, the story is sightist or ocularcentric in crucial ways. First, as Bolt points out about Victorian texts ("Blindman," 272ff), this story understands beauty as a purely visual phenomenon. "Nunez had an eye for beautiful things, and it seemed to him that the glow upon the snowfields and glaciers that rose about the valley . . . was the most beautiful thing he had ever seen. His eyes went from that inaccessible glory to the village and irrigated fields, fast sinking into the twilight, and suddenly a wave of emotion took him, and he thanked God from the bottom of his heart that the power of sight had been granted him" (551). Because of the narrative's many visual descriptions of the landscape, it does not seem that this is a part of Nunez's fantasies of dominance that readers are supposed to reject; instead the story seems to suggest that the appreciation of visual beauty is a supreme gift.

When Nunez escapes and is lying in the snow, moreover, we get this description:

> The mountain summits around him were things of light and fire, and the little details of the rocks near at hand were drenched with subtle beauty—a vein of green mineral piercing the grey, the flash of crystal faces here and there, a minute, minutely-beautiful orange lichen close beside his face. There were deep mysterious shadows in the gorge, blue, deepening into purple, and purple into a luminous darkness, and overhead was the illimitable darkness of the sky. (568)

In addition to this effusion about visual beauty, Wells also emphasizes that light, fire, and beauty are up above, where Nunez is, while the country of the blind is in a symbolic darkness.

Second and more important, Nunez's decision to escape and almost certainly die rather than be blinded cannot but have its effect. The antiassimilationist strand of the story, in which Nunez is forced to choose between escape/death and submission not only to the culture of the blind but to the surgical removal of his eyes, invites sighted readers to shudder at the thought of the surgery and to be relieved that he escapes. J. R. Hammond describes Nunez as a "rebel who refuses to conform with a rigid and narrow-minded social order" (73). Hammond goes so far (and arguably the story does too) as to link sight with freedom and imagination when he writes that Nunez is "faced with a choice between losing his eyesight (and, by implication, his ability to imagine a larger and freer world) and the prospect of escape, even at the risk of physical death" (73). Hammond's reading is representative: according to Patrick Parrinder, even though Nunez's escape from the valley leads to "physical extinction," it is nearly always read as triumphant (71).

Because Wells is writing against the imposition of one set of cultural norms upon another person or persons, he seems to intend readers to celebrate Nunez's refusal of the radical assimilation required by the blind villagers. And if we bracket the villagers' blindness and read them simply as a group of normates insisting on the normalization and cure of an "other," disability studies scholars too can celebrate this refusal. But when we take the villagers' blindness into account and read the ending in line with the strand of the story that casts Nunez as imperialist, we notice that it associates blindness with intimacy and sight with an independence that leads to death. Because of Nunez's foolish chant, "in the country of the blind, the one-eyed man is king" and his futile attempts to dominate the villagers, we are invited *at some points* to be skeptical about his claims for the necessity of vision, and remember that if Nunez had submitted to the surgery, he would have been able to marry the woman he loved. Instead, his eyes intact, he lies dying in the vast snowy mountains. Inverting the trajectory of novels such as *The Light That Failed*, in which blindness leads to suicide, Nunez's stubborn insistence on sight leads to his self-inflicted death. Even though Wells clearly wants readers to endorse Nunez's insistence on sight as a symbol of mental independence and celebrate autonomy over conformity, his double-casting of Nunez as both arrogant imperialist and innocent "other" leaves room for us to read the story against its grain. We can imagine an alternative ending in which Nunez submits to the operation, adapts to his blindness—a feat far easier in "the country of the blind" than anywhere else—and lives happily ever after with Medina-saroté. Associating sight with independence, Wells also links blindness to intimacy as a road not taken.

"I Will Take the Risk": Artistic Self-Communion

Henry Green's first novel, *Blindness*, similarly links blindness to intimacy but rejects romantic intimacy in favor of self-determination; Green's solution is to redefine intimacy as communion with oneself. *Blindness* depicts an English pubic school boy, John Haye, who is blinded in an accident on his way home from Noat, a fictionalized Eton. The novel is structured as an inversion of Joyce's *A Portrait of the Artist as a Young Man*, with the first section, which takes place before John is blinded, written as John's diary, and the rest of the novel told by a third-person narrator. Like Wells, Green remains wary of intimacy as something that threatens to stifle independence. In Green's case, it is artistic independence that is at stake. Influenced by *Portrait*'s celebration of the solitary artist and by the views of his mentor Maurice Bowra, Green removes his artist figure from the proximity of potential romantic partners and leaves him in artistic isolation in London.

The novel is divided into three sections, "Caterpillar," "Chrysalis," and "Butterfly," implying the progressive genre of the *Künstlerroman* (another way in which *Portrait* serves as an intertext). Critics have debated how these section headings should be understood. As Barbara Brothers points out, "The frame of *Blindness*, its progressively labeled parts and its final epiphany, suggests . . . a linear pattern of metamorphic growth for John. But that larger frame is at odds with the episodic development of the novel" (411). This contradiction between the progressively labeled parts and the diegesis raises the question whether the section headings should be taken at face value or read as ironic comments on John's life trajectory.

Readings that understand the section headings as indications that John Haye is poised at the end to write the great novel he imagines are grounded in important aspects of the novel and its context. Brothers notes that "both Kingsley Weatherhead and John Russell, two of Green's earliest admirers and critics, have presented detailed readings of *Blindness* as a *Künstlerroman*" (404). More recently, Benjamin Kohlmann has argued that the trope of visionary blindness and artistic isolation is a result of Green's attempt—due to the influence of Maurice Bowra—to write a Symbolist novel, indeed *the* English Symbolist novel. "Bowra's theoretical writings are concerned with Symbolism as an identifiable set of tropes, including the idea of an 'Absolute of aesthetic joy . . . outside and beyond significant words,' of artistic isolation, of visionary blindness." Kohlmann suggests that critics who view the section headings against their grain may be reading Green's first novel through the lens of his later, much more self-conscious work. Instead, he argues that "the context of Bowra's theories about Symbolism should alert us to the seriousness of this apparently clichéd posture of artistic isolation" (1195).

An alternative reading takes the section headings as ironic signposts that question the very idea of progress and meaning. This reading is supported by some of the ways Haye seems to regress and fall into isolation in the last quarter of the novel. Brothers argues that the novel highlights the "subjective nature of perceptions" (408) and "dramatizes that there is no way to stand outside of time and space, self and event, to render a statement of meaning that is 'true'" (404). Similarly, Rod Mengham, noting that the novel includes "a developmental option" and was formerly titled *Progression*, claims that "the writing itself tends . . . towards retardation; so that the scheme canvassed by the description of contents is a kind of ruse" (1).

Pascale Aebischer argues that both modes exist in the novel—one mode, woven into the *Künstlerroman*, aligns introspection with aliveness and creativity with disability, while the other undermines and exposes this alignment as a myth. In the second mode, "the narrative voice gives the reader access to a series of John's thoughts that cumulatively undermine the notion that his blindness provides the necessary bridge to creativity or that his alienation is ultimately enabling" (519). Indeed, as Aebischer argues, we have no evidence that John Haye is capable of writing much beyond the opening diary. "Structurally the reverse of Stephen Dedalus's diary at the end of *A Portrait of the Artist as a Young Man*, which signals the diarist's maturity and achievement of an independent voice, John Haye's diary in 'Caterpillar' shows the immature schoolboy in search of literary models while failing in his efforts to find a voice of his own" (518).[23] Aebischer points out that the second mode, however, does not erase the first, with the result that Green "uses the trope of blindness to root indeterminacy at the heart of his novel" (512). Aebischer's argument that both modes of the text coexist even though they are contradictory makes sense, especially given Kohlmann's description of Green's interest in Symbolism. In the current context, we can read John Haye's regression as a sort of progression. This paradox results from an understanding of blindness, common to the texts I explore in this chapter, as that which recenters one's values and makes intimacy possible.

Before becoming blind, John Haye begins, in "Caterpillar," by fetishizing his independence. He is an aesthete and a dandy who, when he talks about falling in love or evinces passion or loyalty, is referring not to other human beings but to objects and items of clothing. He writes, "Fell in love with a transparent tortoiseshell cigarette case for three guineas" (4); "Have bought the most gorgeous sun hat for a horse in straw for sixpence, and have painted it in concentric rings" (7); "I have fallen hopelessly in love with the ties in Bartlett's window. I shall have to buy them all, even though they are quite outrageous: the most cunning, subtle and violent checks imaginable" (14). He "glories in his eccentricity," which he says is "true of all of us, in that we glory in ourselves" (5).

He makes a virtue of his status as outsider and disdains public opinion, writing in his diary that "social ostracism which I am experiencing now for the first time for many terms is really incredibly funny" (9). He notices that most of the boys care what others think: "This is what the fear of popular opinion drives the ordinary Public Schoolboy to; that sort of thing is constantly recurring like the plague" (15). He does, however, miss his two friends when he comes back to school after they have left: "They do make a gap, for we three understood each other, and we ladled out sympathy to each other when life became too black. And now I am alone, in a hornets' nest of rabid footballers" (22). John values some company, but ultimately he is alone—for John as for Stephen Dedalus, there is room for a few like minds, but not for any wider fellowship.

John finds beauty in introspection: "And people love money so, and I shall too I expect when I have got out of what our elders tell me is youthful introspection. But why shouldn't one go through something which is so alive and beautiful as that?" (25). He is so aloof that his stepmother (who has raised him because his biological mother died in childbirth) comments: "At dinner to-night Mamma informed me in one of her rare pronouncements on myself, that I always kept people at arm's length. It sounds an awful thing to write, but I seldom meet anyone who interests me more than myself: my own fault, I suppose" (27–28).

Having established John's self-absorption in "Caterpillar," Green invites readers to expect a growth outward, toward other people, in "Chrysalis." And indeed, though John still has his moments of arrogance and separateness, he does begin turning toward other people once he is blind. The link between blindness and intimacy here is cast mostly in terms of dependence on women, which John resents,[24] but also in terms of his obligations to the women in his life. He now thinks about what his stepmother must feel and accepts his role in helping her through the initial crisis of his blindness: "He was blind, finished, on the shelf, that was all. Still, he must carry her through. She must be dreadfully upset about it all." Comparing his stepmother to his birth mother, he realizes that "it was [Mamma, the stepmother] who had brought him up. He belonged to her" (41). In this passage he recognizes an emotional obligation to his stepmother in which she depends on him rather than he on her. In his misogynistic frustration with the women who are trying to take care of him, he even starts to think critically of his earlier insolence: "And this atmosphere of women. There was no male friend who would come to stay, he had always been too unpleasant, or had always tried to be clever" (81).

This newfound sense of obligation, belonging, and interest in the good opinion of others paves the way for his first sustained romantic interest in Joan, the daughter of the local defrocked priest. Green gives us Joan's point of view in the long final chapter of "Chrysalis." Although as critics point out, John makes Joan over in his own image, calling her June and projecting onto her various emotions, he is at least initially interested in her as a subject: "Mamma was horrified at her life, she must have had a queer time, so that she would be interesting" (125). He compares her favorably to everyone he's met since he's been blind. "She had been the first to be almost immediately at her ease, when she spoke it was with an eager note, and there were so few eager people" (127). And he looks forward to discovering in her the qualities he thinks he hears in her voice (129).

This new interest in a woman as subject is concomitant with his gradual acceptance of his blindness. "A whole new set of values had arisen. And being blind did not hurt so long as one did not try to see in terms of sight what one touched or heard" (128). This acceptance and his interest in Joan are linked explicitly when he realizes that he is happy: "The silence had been so full. The rain had stopped falling now, and he was straining to catch the slightest secrets that were in the winds, and before he had never known that. In a way one gained by being blind, of course one did; besides, he was happy to-day, for was she not coming to-morrow?" (129).

John begins planning all of the things he will write about. He sees his life as "beginning again" (135) and looks forward to developing new ways of being in the world. He imagines that his blindness will give him, in time, "a new feeling of companionship with the world. The darkness would be more intimate" (135–36). Here Green explicitly links blindness to artistic expression and to a generalized intimacy with the world that echoes the "pure contact" of Lawrence's "The Blind Man," discussed below. But the context in which John thinks about this "companionship" invites readers to question how seriously to take John's expectations.

> But he had a few interesting things to say, how you would find when you were blind a little longer that you could tell by a feeling in your face when a wall or a chair or even something so low as a footstool was coming. So that you could walk about alone and unaided as he did. It would be wonderful, this new sense, he looked forward to it so, and was often imagining objects in the way when there were none. It would give a new feeling of companionship with the world. The darkness would be more intimate. (135–36)

The idea that John would write out of his own experience of blindness is subtly mocked here in that John is thinking about a sense he does not yet have; clearly he has read or heard about such a sense, which some blind writers call "facial vision."[25] As with the section headings, here too we get a narrative mode that suggests John's blindness will be artistically productive and at the same time a satiric treatment of what Aebischer calls "creative disability."

But the suggestion that blindness leads to intimacy with others and one's surroundings is maintained. John thinks, "This, perhaps, was a beginning with June and the birds and the trees. They were much nearer, and Mummy [his biological mother] was too" (136). About "Mummy" he thinks that she "was nearer than she had ever been before, now that he was blind" (137). When he walks with Joan arm in arm he thinks, "The touch and the warmth were so much finer when one was blind" (141). Joan tells John that he has seen her in the past, in church when they were young, but he never noticed her because he was "too grand" (151). This ties back to the progressively labeled sections, indicating that where once John was self-absorbed and snobbish, now he is able to establish contact with others.

But John does not plan to marry; he views marriage as "the end," as we can see when he worries about his stepmother: "But it was an anxious time for Mamma, waiting to see him settled. And it was the end, to settle down. He could not; one did not dare to. It was not fair to Mamma, but what could one do? . . . But he must go out with June; there was so much to talk about, so much sympathy to be sought after" (131). Here Green makes clear that John wants sympathy from Joan but does not plan equally to give. There are signs all along that he views her as a temporary diversion until he is embarked on his writing career. For instance, he does not plan to share his thoughts about his writing with her because they are "too important" (156).

John thinks self-consciously about his own views of blindness when he tells Joan he will be moving to London and tries to assure her that her suffering at home with her alcoholic father is "fine": "I think perhaps suffering is rather fine, don't you?" / Was it? He did not know. At any rate, it was a way out of blindness" (171). In this assertion, John seems to be questioning whether believing that suffering is productive is a helpful way to deal with his blindness, a "way out." This too compels us to question the novel's suggestion of a natural progression from blindness to creativity. The connection between blindness and intimacy, however, is maintained and revised through the rest of the novel.

In the last chapter of the novel, entitled "Beginning Again," having moved with his stepmother to London, John is again isolated. Without giving up hope, he questions the positive thoughts from previous chapters about what blindness has brought him.

> Oh, why had he gone blind? All these months now he had seen nothing, and he had pretended to others and even to himself that in feeling things he was as well off as one who saw them, but it was not true. For in London so much went on that there was no time to separate or analyze your sensations, everything crowded in upon you and left you dazed. But in a sense life was beginning again, for they would be so happy up here. In time he would learn to understand the streets. (200)

Life in a new city is harder to decode when one has lost sight than life in a familiar country town, and John knows he will need time to adjust. He resolves that writing will be his salvation: "He would write. At Noat he had thought about it, at Barwood he had talked about it, but he must work at it up here, there was nothing else to do, as he was left alone for hours, they were all so busy. In time he could get to understand the streets and so to write about them, for in time one would know more about them than people ever would who had sight. It was so easy to see and so hard to feel what was going on, but it was the feeling that mattered" (202).

Like the writers discussed here, this fictional writer believes that there is a deeper truth invisible to the eye but accessible to one who opens himself to it through feeling. He decides to "start a crusade against people who had eyesight. It was the easiest thing in the world to see, and so very many were content with only the superficial appearance of things; it would teach them so much if they were to go blind, though blindness was a burden at first and he was heavy with memories" (211). At least in this passage, John is not fooling himself that blindness magically brings creativity—he acknowledges that it is "a burden at first"—but he finds greater value in that which can be accessed through the more immediate sense of touch.

At the end of the novel, John has a sort of epiphany of love and joy and then faints away—a fit linked, as critics point out, to the epileptic fits of Dostoyevsky, which John aligns with creativity in his initial diary: "What an amazing man he was, with his epileptic fits which were much the same as visions really" (29). Green describes the fit as a "deeper blindness" (213), returning to the association of blindness with creativity that the novel questions but never abandons. The novel ends with a letter John writes to his old friend B. G., suggesting that John is coming back full circle to himself, but with a difference. For one thing, John shows interest in B. G., writing, "You have led such a different life to mine, I hardly know what you think or feel" (214).

I read John's isolation at the end of the novel as a return to his initial independence but with the difference that he has achieved a deeper and more meaningful isolation than that which characterized him in the first section. When he was sighted, his independence was sterile because he could not truly commune with others or himself; instead he continually fell in love with objects and fetishized his own difference. But by the novel's end he has found a "deeper blindness" that enables him to commune with himself. While blindness is associated with intimacy starting with John's connection with Joan, intimacy is then redefined as a self-communion necessary to artistic practice.

This insistence on intimacy with the self rather than the other stems in part from the influence of Green's mentor Maurice Bowra, for whom marriage was "the ultimate betrayal of artistic independence" (Kohlmann 1207). And it is akin to Stephen Dedalus's willingness to be entirely alone at the end of *Portrait*. When Cranly challenges Stephen, asking him, "And you know what [*alone*] means? Not only to be separate from all others, but to have not even one friend," Stephen assures him, "I will take the risk" (239). For John Haye, blindness enables him to move past superficial appearance to a deeper reality. Green, while self-consciously interrogating the links between blindness and creativity, nevertheless leaves his protagonist poised on the brink of an artistic career that he suggests, but does not promise, will be enriched by the self-communion the text associates with blindness.

Blind Aesthetics

In J. M. Synge's *The Well of the Saints*, blindness is linked with interpersonal intimacy, but here such intimacy is not seen as a threat to artistic achievement; instead, both blindness and intimacy are portrayed as part of an aesthetically fulfilling life. In the play, Mary and Martin Doul, a poor, married blind couple, live contentedly in County Wicklow until a "saint" performs the "miracle" of restoring their sight. In this satirical drama, Synge plays with the notions that "love is blind" and that "ignorance is bliss" (notions astutely analyzed by Naomi Schor). The play employs the traditional axis of knowledge by suggesting a link between blindness and blissful ignorance but then undermines this link in its conclusion. David Bolt reads *The Well of the Saints* as "fundamentally regressive" because it makes "sport" of Martin's obliviousness to his own and his partner's ugliness ("Looking Back" 737). While I find this reading persuasive—Synge does make comedy out of Mary and Martin's blindness—I nevertheless see in the play a defense of blindness as a condition conducive to imagination, aesthetic synesthesia, and intimacy.[26]

While they are blind, the couple believe themselves to be (visually) beautiful. Synge portrays them as overvaluing visual beauty to the point where they use their faith in each other's beauty to smooth over the irritations of living together. For example, the play opens with them bickering, and Martin says, "If I didn't talk I'd be destroyed . . . listening to the clack you do be making, for you've a queer cracked voice . . . if it's fine to look on you are itself" (121). While Mary thinks sighted people are superficial and not to be trusted, she and Martin are at least as obsessed with visual beauty as the sighted people she criticizes.

Knowledge of beauty is depicted as accessible to touch, but not as easily as it is to the eyes. When several characters are waiting for the saint whose holy water will give Mary and Martin sight, Martin mentions that it's a fine thing to be married to "the beautiful dark woman of Ballinatone" (132). A young woman named Molly Byrne responds "scornfully" that "it's little you know of her at all." Martin responds, "It's little surely, and I'm destroyed this day waiting to look upon her face." Martin here assents to the traditional link between sight and knowledge. His friend Timmy tries to soothe him by saying, "It's well you know the way she is; for the like of you do have great knowledge in the feeling of your hands." But Martin points out that such knowledge is comparative, not uncanny. "We do, maybe. Yet it's little I know of faces, or of fine beautiful cloaks, for it's few cloaks I've had my hand to, and few faces" (132). Through this conversation Synge introduces the question of aesthetic knowledge and refuses the idea that blind people have uncanny compensatory insight.

After the saint "cures" Martin, he comes out of the church and passes right by his wife but recognizes several of his friends by sight. As if to invoke the Molyneux question—whether a person blind from birth whose sight is restored could recognize with his eyes shapes he knows with his hands[27]—Synge has Martin translate what he knows about his friends into visual terms: "That's Timmy. I know Timmy by the black of his head. . . . That's Mat Simon, I know Mat by the length of his legs" (136). But he then turns to the most beautiful of the young women, Molly Byrne, and addresses her as if she is Mary. "Love is blind" here in the sense that it cannot be translated into visual terms.

When Mary is in turn "cured" by the saint, she and Martin confront each other and begin to exchange elaborate insults. They each accuse the other of misrepresenting his or her appearance. The saint admonishes them to think about God, not each other's faces, but Mary and Martin angrily split up. At this point in the play, the audience is invited to conclude that blindness is ignorance and ignorance is bliss, since when Mary and Martin did not know they were not beautiful, they could happily assume they were. The play then proceeds to depict sight as giving rise to anger and loneliness. For most of act 2 Mary and Martin are sighted, angry, and separated. Not only has their own relationship broken down, but Martin also antagonizes Timmy and Molly Byrne. There are suggestions that Martin is losing his sight in act 2, and between acts 2 and 3 both Mary and Martin again become blind.

In act 3 they encounter each other and grudgingly begin to reconcile. They have not foresworn the superficiality of visual beauty, but they decide to believe that their visual beauty is still to come. Mary tells Martin that when her hair turns white she will be a beautiful sight, with "soft white hair falling around" her face (160). Martin decides to grow a beard, which, as he ages, will become "beautiful, long, white, silken, [and] streamy" (161). Martin and Mary can recreate their intimacy without "blissful ignorance" by willfully deciding to believe in their own beauty. The audience now realizes that it's not that love is blind—in the sense of ignorant—but that faith requires some will. All of the sighted people who believe in the saint's miracles have chosen to believe; Mary and Martin have chosen to believe in their status as a beautiful couple. Carole-Anne Upton writes that "their irreverent fantasy proves the antidote to that holy poison that opens their eyes" (355). Once blind again, knowing and yet suspending their knowledge of how they really look, the Douls are able to recreate their former intimacy.

Soon the saint comes around again to try to restore their sight with the holy water, promising that the second cure will last "till the hour of death" (165). Hearing his bell, Mary says, "The Lord protect us from the saints of God!" (162), a line whose amusing irony invites the audience to scoff at the notion that the priest is doing the will of "the Lord." Martin asks the saint to go on his way, but the saint and the villagers cannot believe that he does not wish to see again. "Is his mind one that he's no wish to be cured this day, or to be living or working, or looking on the wonders of the world?" (166). Martin replies that "it's wonders enough I seen in a short space for the life of one man only." Mary, at first, also declines. But the people convince Mary that she could be a better wife if she could see. Her capitulation to this persuasion shows an internalized sightism that the play, however, rejects. Martin asks the saint, "What call has the like of you to be coming between married people—that you're not understanding at all—and be making a great mess with the holy water you have, and the length of your prayers?" (170). When Martin hears the splash of the holy water approaching Mary, he "strikes the can from the Saint's hand and sends it rocketing across the stage" (171). Like Brian Friel's *Molly Sweeney* (1994), inspired by Oliver Sacks's "To See and

Not See," Synge's earlier play demonstrates that sight is not always preferable to blindness.

Indeed, Martin's dialogue raises the question, finally, of how beauty is best accessed. When the villagers try to convince him to be cured again by talking about natural beauties such as the "grand glittering sea," Martin responds, "Is it talking now you are of Knock and Ballavore? Ah, it's ourselves had finer sights than the like of them, I'm telling you, when we were sitting a while back hearing the birds and bees humming in every weed of the ditch, or when we'd be smelling the sweet, beautiful smell does be rising in the warm nights, when you do hear the swift flying things racing in the air, till we'd be looking up in our own minds into a grand sky, and seeing lakes, and big rivers, and fine hills for taking the plough" (167–68). In this passage, Martin describes auditory and olfactory beauty *giving rise to* ("till we'd be") a powerfully imagined visual beauty ("looking up in our own minds"). His "vision" is represented not as "impoverished but privileged" (Upton 356). As David Feeney points out, the characters display a "sensory versatility that is integral to the play's achievement" (90).

Beauty, then, is redefined by the play. As much as Martin and Mary need the faith in each other's visual beauty to sustain their relationship, Martin here implies that imagined seeing, combined with the beauty of other sensory input, is better than literal seeing, which he suggests obstructs other sources of aesthetic pleasure. While this implication still participates in ocularcentrism, it refuses the notion that sight is the noblest of the senses, and it is of a piece with a Bergsonian emphasis on inner experience.[28] W. J. McCormack describes the play as "reconciling conjugal love and renunciation of the world in favour of an intellectual vision" (190).[29] Synge adapts the notion that "love is blind" by showing that Mary and Martin's love for each other is willfully "blind" only in the sense that they have placed their faith in it. Their love does not preclude knowledge but puts it aside. Blindness and intimacy are restored at the end of the play, and the senses of smell and hearing and the faculty of the imagination are valued above sight.

In the Ear of the Beholder

The cliché that love is blind operates in a different way in Florence Barclay's *The Rosary*, a sentimental romance novel published in 1909, and the bestselling novel of 1910 (Folks 445). The novel is certainly not modernist by the standards of experimentalism or self-conscious artistry. But according to Martin Hipsky, it does help move the genre of the religious romance closer to modernism by introducing an element of psychologism (127–35). Moreover, as the editors of *Bad Modernisms* point out, there is something to be said for "countering the implication that a few experimental works were somehow the only ones authentically representative of their age" (Mao and Walkowitz 2). What makes the novel particularly worth considering here is its intervention in the tradition of literary representations of blindness: *The Rosary* is in many ways a revision of *Jane Eyre*, and it takes a different view of the hero's blindness.

The novel's heroine, pointedly also named Jane, is, like her predecessor, decidedly plain. Much as in Brontë's novel Jane Eyre believes Edward Rochester will marry the beautiful Blanche Ingram, *The Rosary*'s Jane Champion believes that Garth Dalmain will marry the beautiful Pauline Lister. In both novels the leading men actually love the plain Janes; in both, circumstances and the moral qualms of the heroines delay the marriages; and in both, the male protagonists become blind before the marriages take place. *The Rosary* describes blindness repeatedly as a pitiable "darkness" and helplessness, employing the melodramatic mode of representing disability analyzed by Martha Stoddard Holmes.[30] But it revises *Jane Eyre*'s representation of blindness in two key ways. First, by making music, and in particular Jane's "glorious voice," create the romantic spark between the protagonists, *The Rosary* portrays their intimacy as nonvisual even before Garth is blinded. Second, it rejects the idea that blindness can be conducive to intimacy only by creating dependence. Whereas in *Jane Eyre* Rochester needs to be "brought down" by his blindness (so that his relationship with Jane can rest on terms of equality)[31] and Jane Eyre is moved by his helplessness, in *The Rosary* Garth's blindness only intensifies the communion of two people whose love transcended visuality from the start.[32]

We are first introduced to the protagonists while they are close friends, with no romantic feelings on either side. The Honourable Jane Champion, the thirty-year-old niece of a duchess, has been described by a friend as "a perfectly beautiful woman in an absolutely plain shell" (8). She is forthright, generous, and athletic and has many male friends. She also has a "glorious voice, but her face not matching it, its existence was rarely suspected" (8). Garth Dalmain is an exceptionally handsome and talented painter. He paints all the beautiful young women of his acquaintance and seems to worship their beauty without ever entering a real courtship. It is when Garth finally hears Jane *sing* that he falls in love with her.

Jane has not sung in Garth's presence before because to her music is "a sort of holy of holies in the tabernacle of one's inner being" (20). She soon explains further that singing is like revealing one's soul (24). The chapter in which she finally sings is entitled "The Veil Is Lifted." Her singing is described in terms of personal but also religious revelation. Afterward she sees Garth—his "face was absolutely colorless, and his eyes shone out from it like burning stars" (31). He is "deeply moved," and a "light of adoration" comes into his eyes. He kisses her palms with "an indescribably tender reverence" (33).

Love in *The Rosary* transcends sight even while both characters are sighted. Although Jane has been unmoved by Garth's physical beauty, she now responds to his passion for her musical ability; they talk about music together for days, and she longs for him when they are apart. But when Garth asks her to marry him, she refuses. She does not tell him the real reason: remembering a comment he made about an unattractive preacher, she believes that someone so captivated by visual beauty would soon tire of seeing her plain face at his breakfast table. She runs off to the Continent and tries to soothe her broken heart. Meanwhile, he is involved in a hunting accident while trying to protect a wounded rabbit (sentiment galore!) and is blinded. This event would seem to remove the obstacle of Jane's looks. Indeed, when Jane is first introduced, the narrator describes her as the perfect mate for a blind lover: "She would have made earth heaven for a blind lover who, not having eyes for the plainness of her face or the massiveness of her figure, might have drawn nearer, and apprehended the wonder of her as a woman, experiencing the wealth of tenderness of which she was capable. . . . But as yet, no blind man with far-seeing vision had come her way" (8).

But Barclay includes some plot twists clearly designed to belie the suggestion that Garth's blindness removes the obstacle Jane sees in her plainness. First, Jane decides to go back to England and ask for Garth's hand *before* she learns of his accident and his blindness (73). Second, Garth refuses to receive her because he will not accept pity for his blindness (105, 116). Third, when a mutual friend suggests to Garth why Jane refused him, he claims that he would, if that were the case, never be able to accept her love because without sight he would not be able to prove his fidelity (142). All of this makes Garth's blindness more of a new obstacle to than an enabler of their union.

Meanwhile, the novel explores Garth's new life as a blind man. Although he does need time to adapt to his new condition, he vows to adjust to his new mode of living: "I am receiving no visitors, and do not desire any until I have so mastered my new circumstances that the handicap connected with them shall neither be painful nor very noticeable to other people" (117). Unlike texts such as Rudyard Kipling's *The Light That Failed* and Wells's "The Country of the Blind," where death is preferable to blindness, in this novel Garth determines to adjust, and the text lingers to represent this adjustment.

In the conversation during which the mutual friend, Garth's doctor, suggests the real reason why Jane refused him, Garth first rejects the explanation as unworthy of Jane's great nature. The doctor replies, "Love is blind." "They lie who say so," cries Garth violently. "Love is so far-seeing that it sees beneath the surface and delights in beauties unseen by other eyes" (141). While rejecting the link between blindness and ignorance, Garth articulates the other side of the statement that love is blind. Schor writes, "But there is another way to understand blindness in love, and that is to understand that . . . blindness to the other's physical appearance and gestural language is precisely what enables the lover to see . . . the lover's true soul" (84). The fact that Garth realized he was "blind" to Jane's true, inner beauty (37) while he was still sighted helps to undermine the "myth of fortunate blindness" Schor later critiques.

Since Garth will not let her visit, Jane arranges to be hired as his nurse, using various ruses to conceal her identity. As his nurse, instead of reveling in his dependence on her as Jane Eyre does while Rochester is blind, this Jane encourages Garth's independence.[33] For example, she strings silk cords that he can distinguish by touch along various routes in the house.[34] She invents little tricks for how they will set the table so that he will be able to entertain guests without fumbling with cutlery. And it is only once he has adapted to his blindness and is in good spirits that she reveals herself and begs his forgiveness for not having trusted his love.

Not only does their intimacy flower once he is blind, but Garth's creative power, which before expressed itself in painting, is rerouted into music. Musical talent is a stereotyped attribute of the blind; Kleege points out in her discussion of cinema that when blind people "do have a job, it will probably have something to do with music, confirming the popular misconception that the blind are rewarded with a compensatory musical gift" (*Sight Unseen* 45). In this case, Garth's newfound talent is described slightly differently: "The creative faculty is so strong in you, that when one outlet was denied it, it burst forth through another. When you had your sight, you created by the hand and EYE. Now, you will create by the hand and EAR. The power is the same. It merely works through another channel" (192). The magical quality of his musical talent comes not from blindness but from his creative force itself, which must be expressed through whatever avenues are available to him. While its literary quality is patently inferior to that of *Jane Eyre*, and although it does initially heap pity on Garth for his blindness, *The Rosary* offers a more positive portrayal of blindness, representing it as conducive to intimacy not because it creates dependence and not because "love is blind" in the sense of being capricious or ignorant—but because, it suggests, true love is always already nonvisual.

Blindness as Intimacy

The link between blindness and intimacy in early twentieth-century British literature culminates in Lawrence's "The Blind Man." In this story Lawrence plays out his ideas of "blood-consciousness" versus "mental consciousness" by contrasting the blind, calm farmer Maurice Pervin with the sighted, nervous intellectual Bertie Reid. Maurice, representing blood-consciousness, is at home in his rural setting, at one with the animals and the land, and most importantly, with his wife Isabel, who is pregnant (confirming the consummation of the "sexual connection" Lawrence ascribes to "blood-consciousness"). Lehan explains that Lawrence was influenced by Bergson and Samuel Butler in his belief "that there was an inner self—often identified with sexual consciousness—from which industrial man had become separated, and all of his major work returned . . . to this theme" (52). In line with this belief, Maurice is described as mentally slow but with acute feelings, a well-developed interior life, and the opposite of Bertie, whose mind is quick but whose feelings are "not so very fine" (71).[35]

Maurice's blindness intensifies his intimacy with his surroundings and with Isabel. "Life was very full and strangely serene for the blind man, peaceful with the almost incomprehensible peace of immediate contact in darkness. With his wife he had a whole world, rich and real and invisible" (69).[36] Maurice's blindness is repeatedly described in terms of this immediacy and contact. For example, "Life seemed to move in him like a tide lapping, lapping, and advancing, enveloping all things darkly. It was a pleasure to stretch forth the hand and meet the unseen object, clasp it, and possess it in pure contact" (80).[37] As Tim Armstrong puts it, in this story "the distance implied by sight has collapsed" (*Modernism: A Cultural History* 21). When Bertie, Isabel's closest friend, defines her husband's blindness as "something lacking all the time" (86), Isabel replies that "there is something else, something *there*, which you never knew was there, and which you can't express" (87).

Lawrence seems to use blindness in this story in a way that parallels his use of class in *Lady Chatterley's Lover* (1928). In that novel, too, the idea of "contact" with sexual and spiritual forces is crucial. The upper-class, disabled Clifford Chatterley is repeatedly described as not being "in actual touch with anything or anybody"; he is "just a negation of human contact" (16). His antithesis, the gamekeeper Oliver Mellors, on the other hand, is described in terms of tenderness and contact. During one of the scenes of sexual intimacy between Connie Chatterley and Mellors, the narrator describes the "warm, live beauty of contact, so much deeper than the beauty of vision" (125). Here vision is associated with banal material reality, and "contact" with spiritual depth.

In the short story, the intensity of the intimacy between Maurice and Isabel is sometimes overwhelming. As Lawrence explains in a posthumously published essay entitled "Love," "love is a coming together. But there can be no coming together without an equivalent going asunder. . . . The motion of love, like a tide, is fulfilled in this instance; there must be an ebb" (*Phoenix* 151). Accordingly, sometimes Maurice sinks into a "black misery" and Isabel feels a "dread" and "panic" in response. She worries that when the baby comes, Maurice will feel abandoned. She wants to "luxuriate in a rich, physical satisfaction of maternity" (71) but fears removing her focus from Maurice. She therefore hopes to ignite a friendship between her husband and Bertie.[38] The plot of "The Blind Man" turns on Isabel's efforts in this regard. Toward the end of the story, Maurice and Bertie talk in the dark barn, but "they have come up against the limits of mental consciousness as a means to intimacy" (Delany 30). So Maurice insists that they feel each other's faces. Bertie, who is terrified of intimacy, crumbles under this enforced closeness, and the story ends by describing Bertie as "like a mollusc whose shell is broken" (92).

Kleege notes with satisfaction that with this ending, the blind man has taken the sighted man "in hand" (*Sight Unseen* 90). Indeed, Maurice seems to triumph here even if he is deceived into thinking he and Bertie will be friends from that point forward.[39] Earlier in the story the narrator tells us that "at the centre, [Bertie] felt himself neuter, nothing" (85). The contrast between the two men, made tangible in the moment of touch, casts Maurice as someone who thrives on intimacy instead of "reserve" and lives through direct contact with his surroundings rather than through the mediations of the mind.

Lawrence uses Maurice's blindness, then, as a symbol for immediacy and intimacy, and a way to intensify his alignment of Maurice with the natural world. In his association of Maurice with the farm and Bertie with the town, Lawrence seems to agree with Simmel that rural life is more conducive to harmonious living. In "The Metropolis and Mental Life," Simmel writes that "the metropolitan type of individuality consists in the intensification of nervous stimulation which results from the swift and uninterrupted change of outer and inner stimuli" (410). In this sense, Maurice's blindness cuts him off from the world—the world of visual stimuli—but in another sense, it brings him closer to the world—the natural world, contact with other beings and himself. Just as Maurice is described as slow mentally, Simmel describes the rural life: "here the rhythm of life and sensory mental imagery flows more slowly . . . . [The "emotional relationships" of rural life] . . . grow most readily in the steady rhythm of uninterrupted habituations" ("Metropolis" 410). This idea helps explain Maurice's ability to commune with Isabel.

Bertie, on the other hand, is described as being "ashamed of himself, because he could not marry, could not approach women physically. . . . At the centre of him he was afraid, helplessly and even brutally afraid" (85). This description heightens the contrast with Maurice, whose virility is vouched for by Isabel's pregnancy. Kleege notes that Maurice's "blindness has not impaired his masculinity. He is a big man, massively built, taciturn and sensitive. . . . His blindness seems to have heightened his physicality, instincts, and sensitivity" (*Sight Unseen* 84). Lawrence is clearly overturning the link between blindness and castration suggested by the Oedipus story and instead associating blindness with the heterosexual communion he values as a way to "re-vivify" art. His depiction of blindness arises from his ideas about the nonvisual character of "blood-consciousness" and aligns with a modernist focus on consciousness, on the inner life.[40]

Nonvisual Sensing and Interiority

Representations of blindness are shaped not only by what vision means to the authors, but also by the meaning of the senses that come to the fore in its absence: hearing and touch. Synge's Mary and Martin access the beauties of the natural world through hearing, smell, and touch. In the sentimental last pages of Barclay's novel, Garth puts "up his hand to the dear face, still wet with thankful tears" (286) and then Jane clasps her "hands behind his head—strong, capable hands, though now they trembled a little—and pressed his face against her" (289). The novel ends with Garth singing to a raptly listening Jane, a fitting inversion of Jane's earlier vocal performance. But the fullest exploration of the roles of hearing and touch comes in "The Blind Man." Lawrence's story opens with Isabel Pervin "listening for two sounds" (69)—for her husband to come in from the barn and for Bertie Reid to arrive in a taxi. The initial focus on listening signals the theme of intimacy that permeates the story. The fact that the listener is sighted establishes a link, independent of ideas about blindness, between hearing and communication or communion; and this in turn helps the story resist assumptions of uncanny auditory powers in blind people.

When Isabel goes to the stable to find Maurice before Bertie arrives, she again listens carefully: "She listened with all her ears, but could hear nothing save the night, and the stirring of a horse" (76). She becomes anxious without vision, but relies on her hearing to try to make contact with Maurice. She calls him twice, "musically," and the second time he responds. "She saw nothing, and the sound of his voice seemed to touch her" (77). Here sound leads to an intimacy that sight cannot. In his chapter "The Five Senses" in *Fantasia of the Unconscious*, Lawrence describes hearing as "perhaps the deepest of the senses. . . . Sound acts direct upon the great affective centres" (62). By setting the scene in the dark stable, Lawrence emphasizes the power of hearing to create human contact.

Touch, too, helps Isabel compensate for the darkness. She asks for Maurice's arm, and as he leads her out of the dark barn, "she could feel the clever, careful, strong contact of his feet with the earth, as she balanced against him" (78). This conjunction of blindness, feet, and contact may have been sparked by Lawrence's belief that "the thighs, the knees, the feet are intensely alive with love-desire, darkly and superbly drinking in the love-contact, blindly" (*Fantasia* 56). Indeed, after Maurice leads her back into the house and touches her face "delicately with the tips of his fingers," the "touch had an almost hypnotising effect on her" (79). As Santanu Das notes, Lawrence "championed the sense of touch as the supreme of the senses; to him it could rescue modern man from his cerebral, industrial crust, and put him back in contact with his inner, sensuous being" (233). Indeed, the word *contact*, the dominant metaphor for Maurice's intimacy with his world, is simply another way to describe touch.

Lawrence suggests that vision interferes with the intimacy between a person and his "substantial" surroundings: "So long as he kept this sheer immediacy of blood-contact with the substantial world he was happy, he wanted no intervention of visual consciousness" (80). And he casts hearing and touch as more immediate senses, even occasionally interchangeable, as when Maurice's voice seems to touch Isabel. In focusing his art on consciousness, Lawrence sought states of being that could intensify inwardness. He seems to have agreed that, as Hull puts it, "the blind person lives in consciousness." But "The Blind Man" suggests that he would challenge the first part of Hull's statement: "the sighted person lives in the world." Lawrence would agree that a cerebral sighted person like Bertie Reid lives in one kind of world; but clearly Maurice Pervin lives in "the world" as well—the natural and more meaningful world of physical and emotional connection with the earth and its inhabitants.

Lawrence wrote to his friend Lady Cynthia Asquith, "there is a living unconscious life. If only we would shut our eyes: if only we were all struck blind, and things vanished from our sight: we should marvel that we had fought and lived for shallow, visionary, peripheral nothingness. We should find reality in darkness" (*Letters* 2:455; qtd. in Delany). This understanding of blindness, which clearly informs the depiction of Maurice, romanticizes disability, relying on the assumption that disability is "an 'excessive' sign that invites interpretation" (Quayson 14). But this problematic attitude also results in a complex story in which blindness gives rise to a genuine contact also celebrated in Lawrence's major novels.

The early twentieth-century texts explored in this chapter view blindness as conducive to intimacy, then, in part because the absence of vision makes way for greater attention to hearing and touch, two senses understood to foster human attachment. They participate in the contemporary philosophical devaluation of sight, labeled the "noblest of the senses" but in this period often understood as revealing no more than surface reality. The texts do accept a romantic association of blindness with serenity—that is, they perpetuate a "myth of fortunate blindness." Unlike Simmel, they implicitly ascribe such serenity not to blissful ignorance but to the blind characters' opportunity to ignore surface visual detail and focus on "the essential thing": the inner life. This too is part of the romantic depiction, since blind people are no more likely to focus on "essential" reality than anyone else. They are just as likely as sighted people to be swayed, for example, by physical beauty or by racial prejudice.[41] As Tobin Siebers points out, "it is easy to mythologize disability as an advantage. Disabled bodies . . . bend the rules of representation to such extremes that they must mean something extraordinary" (*Disability Theory* 63). And these portrayals of blind characters certainly ascribe extraordinary opportunity to blindness. But we do find in these representations genuine interest in the experience of blindness and explorations of its possibilities that link it to interiority and communion, both highly valued within the modernist ethos. Conversely, as we will see in the following chapter, characters without the prized sense of hearing were understood to be cut off from communication and positioned in a realm of decidedly unblissful ignorance.

Three

Deafness, Communication, and Knowledge

While the relative devaluation of vision in the early twentieth century resulted in comparatively positive portrayals of blindness in modernist literature, it also led to a heightened valuation of hearing, or what Melba Cuddy-Keane calls a "new aurality" (383). As Tim Armstrong argues, "if modernist aesthetics stress embodiment and contact, sound has a special status" (*Modernism: A Cultural History* 109). In a related claim, Jonathan Sterne asserts that "sound, hearing, and listening are foundational to modern modes of knowledge, culture, and social organization" (2). This increased regard for sound and its associated sense, hearing, stems both from new sound technologies (discussed in detail in Sterne) and from the tradition of understanding sight and hearing as complementary opposites whose values are inversely proportional.[1] In her exploration of vision in late nineteenth-century culture, Gillian Beer writes that "sound began to assume the status as ideal function that sight had earlier held" (91).

Sterne describes an "audiovisual litany" that expresses cultural understandings of the differences between sight and hearing. Like Beer, he notes that the cultural opposition between sight and hearing "idealizes hearing (and, by extension, speech) as manifesting a kind of pure interiority" (15). The authors explored in the previous chapter acclaim hearing, in accordance with Sterne's "litany," as a more immediate and more spiritual sense than sight. And so it is not surprising to find that representations of deafness in modernist literature are more negative than modernist representations of blindness and than the admittedly sparse representations of deafness in Victorian literature.[2] The representations, however, are negative in instructive ways, ways that demonstrate larger attitudes about speech, communication, subjectivity, and means of accessing knowledge.

A key example of Victorian literary deafness can be found in Charles Dickens's 1865 story "Doctor Marigold's Prescriptions." In this popular story, "cheap jack" Doctor Marigold teaches his adopted deaf daughter Sophy to read, starting with the mileposts as they travel through England in their cart. There is no mystical difficulty about this task: it is represented as a practical one. When he takes her to a school for the deaf when she is sixteen, he tells the gentleman there that he would like Sophy "to be cut off from the world as little as can be, considering her deprivations, and therefore to be able to read whatever is wrote with perfect ease and pleasure" (32). While the man objects playfully that he cannot do that himself, Marigold's goal for his daughter demonstrates an ideology that does not require speech—this is a manual school—for adequate, if not perfect, integration into the larger world.[3]

Indeed, in this story communication between deaf and hearing people is depicted as effortless once hearing people learn sign language.[4] When Marigold and Sophy arrive at the deaf school, they can communicate fully with the director using what we would now call the "home signs" they had developed together. Later, when Marigold spies on Sophy conversing with her beau, he "knew every syllable that passed between them as well as they did. [He] listened with [his] eyes, which had come to be as quick and true with deaf and dumb conversation as [his] ears with the talk of people that can speak" (130). After her adoption, Sophy is not isolated or lonely (indeed, it is Marigold who is intermittently very lonely in the story); she is well educated; she marries for love and has a child; her deaf husband has a career that takes them for some years to China. So although the story has been rightly critiqued for ending with the joy of discovering that Sophy's daughter is hearing ("she can speak!") and with Marigold's "happy yet pitying tears" (133),[5] its overall portrayal of deafness as surmountable obstacle highlights by contrast the metaphysical loneliness and epistemological failure surrounding deafness in modernist fiction.

Oralist History

The elevation of hearing during the modernist period interacted with another ideology of the time: oralism. Oralism is not merely the teaching of speech to the deaf, which has been documented in wealthy families since at least the sixteenth century (Lee 35ff). It is, instead, a broader ideology that calls for deaf children to be taught to lipread and speak *exclusively*. It holds that signed language is a lesser, foreign, and for many oralists, subhuman language[6] and that deaf children should be forbidden to use it.[7] Over the course of the nineteenth century, as oral teachers demonstrated some success in teaching deaf children to speak, oral methods of education gained ground. The watershed of oralism was the Milan conference of 1880 (entitled the Second International Conference for Improving the Lot of the Deaf), where several oralist resolutions were "overwhelmingly passed" by the largely handpicked audience (Lee 42). After this conference, most schools for the deaf in England and the United States adopted the "pure oral" method (Lee 42; Baynton, *Forbidden Signs* 4–5).[8]

The first resolution of the conference described "the incontestable superiority of speech over signs, for restoring deaf-mutes to social life and for giving them greater facility in language" (Lee 41).[9] The idea that "articulation" would give deaf people "greater facility in language" demonstrates the erroneous belief that signed language is not really *language* at all but a mere set of coded gestures. It was not until the 1960s that signed languages were shown by linguists to be full, natural languages, although many nineteenth-century educators of the deaf had praised their eloquence.[10]

The other belief encoded in the resolution was that spoken language would restore "deaf-mutes to social life." Susan Burch notes that "enabling Deaf people to talk and, ideally to hear better would supposedly 'restore' them to the broader world. This emphasis on the physical condition as opposed to the cultural identity of Deaf people united oralists and medical specialists" (13). An example of this attitude can be found in a study of the London School Board from 1904, where Hugh Philpott wrote that the "oral system goes further than any other to lessen the tragic isolation of the deaf. It enables them, as no other system could, to take their place in the hearing world, and communicate by the ordinary method of speech with their hearing neighbors" (258). This idea that only speech could lessen the "tragic isolation" of the deaf arose from strong cultural nationalisms on both sides of the Atlantic as England and the United States demanded the assimilation of racial, cultural, and linguistic subgroups.

Douglas Baynton demonstrates oralism's underpinnings in nationalism and xenophobia in this period of mass immigration, focusing particularly on the United States. From the high value people placed on all members of a nation speaking the same language and the low esteem in which foreignness was held grew the emphasis on teaching the deaf to speak English instead of the "foreign" sign language. He explains, "oralists believed sign language was to blame for making deaf people seem foreign, peculiar, and isolated from the nation; oralists also claimed it was an inferior language that impoverished the minds of its users" (32).[11] As Rebecca Sanchez details, Henry Ford's Language School, which opened in 1914, trained Ford's workers in American English while also "regulat[ing] employees' hygiene and social interaction" (11). The nation began requiring fluency in American English for citizenship with passage of the Naturalization Act of 1906, and over the next couple of decades individual states began declaring American English their official language (Sanchez 11–12).

Summarizing the ideologies that supported manualism in the early nineteenth century and oralism in the late nineteenth century, Baynton writes:

> Before the 1860s, deafness was most often described as an affliction that isolated the individual from the Christian community. Its tragedy was that deaf people lived beyond the reach of the gospel. After the 1860s, however, deafness was redefined as a condition that isolated people from the national community. Deaf people were cut off from the English speaking American culture, and *that* was the tragedy. The remedies proffered for each of these kinds of isolation were dramatically different. During the early and middle decades of the nineteenth century, sign language was a widely used and respected language among educators at schools for the deaf. By the end of the century, it was widely condemned and banished from many classrooms. (15)

Alexander Graham Bell was the most influential proponent of oralism, and after starting an oral school for deaf children in Scotland, he hoped his methods would also spread through Great Britain (Rée 222). A major motive for his disapproval of sign language was eugenic: sign language encouraged the deaf to congregate and intermarry and, he feared, bear deaf children, and he believed that "the production of a defective race of human beings would be a great calamity to the world" (Bell 41). Bell's resistance to deaf intermarriage was supported by "staunch British oralists" as well (Lee 42). Banning sign language from deaf schools also helped hearing educators take over deaf education from deaf teachers, who could not teach speech. The resulting absence of deaf teachers gravely damaged deaf culture and pride (Ladd 143). And the educational effects of oralism were disastrous, drastically reducing deaf literacy for more than a century (Ladd 143–44; Lane 165–85).

Language Spoken Here

The strongest message of oralism is that the oral/aural system of communication is essential.[12] Lennard Davis describes this message as "one of the foundational ableist myths of our culture: that the norm for humans is to speak and hear, to engage in communication through speaking and hearing" (*Enforcing Normalcy* 15). During the modernist period, these cultural biases in favor of hearing and speech grew to such a height that in a significant way, signed languages simply did not count. They were not sufficient for communication. They were *too visual*. While purporting to bridge the gap it was actually creating, oralism insisted upon a vast, unbridgeable separation between deaf and hearing people. Instead of the fluid communication we see in Dickens's "Doctor Marigold," where the hearing Marigold listens comfortably with his eyes, modernism, saturated with oralism, offers an array of deaf characters who long to, but cannot, communicate. Even deaf characters who use a signed language are depicted as isolated, lonely, and cut off from communication and access to knowledge.

In Eudora Welty's 1941 story "The Key," Ellie and Albert Morgan's fluent sign language does not prevent the narrator from attributing to them an agonized desire to communicate and a stark lack of access to knowledge. In Carson McCullers's *The Heart Is a Lonely Hunter* (1940), communication is the great problem. The deaf John Singer signs with his friend Antonapoulos, but McCullers shapes the story so that this communication is both doubtful and abruptly truncated. Elizabeth Bowen's representation of deafness is the most complex of the texts considered here. In her last novel, *Eva Trout* (1968),[13] she portrays the deaf boy Jeremy as having a robust subjectivity and an almost supernatural bond with his adoptive mother. But until the end of the novel, Jeremy has no language at all, and the visual world he lives in is ultimately represented as a sort of doom. In all of these texts, the visuality characteristic of deafness is portrayed as insufficient both for communication and for knowledge.

In *What Is Posthumanism?* in the context of a discussion of how autism has been understood, Cary Wolfe critiques

> the too-rapid assimilation of the questions of subjectivity, consciousness, and cognition to the question of language ability—a dogma that is perhaps even more entrenched in the humanities and social sciences than in areas such as medicine. Indeed, as many scholars

> have argued, the shibboleth "where there is reason, there is a subject" morphs, in the twentieth century, into "where there is *language*, there is a subject." (129)

The idea that language is the sine qua non of subjectivity, inadequate in itself, becomes even more reductive in the common slippage—in both everyday and philosophical discourse—from language to speech.

Language *entails* speech for the Western philosophical tradition. Kant famously denied deaf people the ability to reason because they could not speak (Rée 93). As Michael Davidson notes, "in Western theology and philosophy, the Logos or reason is represented as a voice" (*Concerto* 91). Moreover, as Davis points out, even "the act of writing is falsely given the qualities of sonic duration. . . . So many of our assumptions about writing, about language, about communication are based on the premiss that language is in fact sonic, audible, vocalized" (*Enforcing Normalcy* 100).[14] The conflation of language and speech leads people to question or dismiss the subjectivity of those who do not use spoken languages and shapes both fictional representations and real-life understandings of the deaf.

This conflation is also central to oralism, and as a result of it, signed languages are dismissed as inferior modes of communication or not acknowledged as languages at all. As Nicholas Mirzoeff aptly puts it, "hearing remains so normalized as a standard component of humanity that no other means of communication is considered authentic" (75). A recent critic of *The Heart Is a Lonely Hunter* displays this prejudice in his description of McCullers's deaf protagonist—who signs fluently with his deaf friend Antonapoulos, reads the lips of English speakers, and writes grammatical English notes. Charles Bradshaw writes that "Mick Kelly, Doctor Benedict Copeland, and Jake Blount each construct a Self-Other relationship with someone incapable of language—the deaf-mute, John Singer" (119). Indeed, even a critic writing a disability studies analysis of *Heart* conflates language and speech by calling Singer "linguistically impaired" (Berger 42). That these assertions were maintained after peer review and copyediting demonstrates the widespread acceptance of the identification between language and speech.

Another McCullers critic, Michael Merva, ties Singer to a purported lack of understanding, often putting the word *understanding* in quotation marks. In his 2006 article, Merva writes that "Singer's 'eyes' always 'understand.' Of course they do; he is reading lips, 'understanding' with his eyes the words people are saying, although not necessarily their meanings" (13). Merva has slipped from describing "reading lips" to describing a mental incapacity—in his view, Singer can distinguish words but not their meaning, which is to say, Merva assumes that *only through hearing can language have meaning*. He further dehumanizes Singer when he writes that "Mr. Singer is much like a wall—not because he is emotionless or cold, but because one talks *at* him while receiving little more than a smiling visual image" (16).[15] Disregarding Singer's accurate descriptions of his friends' passions (*Heart* 204–5, 215–16), Merva repeatedly dismisses Singer's understanding as an "illusion" (14, 15, 16). He thus follows the nineteenth-century American authors analyzed by Christopher Krentz in placing deafness "outside human language and understanding" ("Hearing Line" 432). These critics' audist dismissals of Singer's ability to use language and to understand his friends bolster Krentz's claim that the belief that "the ability to speak vocally is what makes one human" has contributed to "the oppression and exclusion of deaf people from society for centuries" (*Writing Deafness* 23).[16]

In what follows I trace assumptions about communication, subjectivity, and knowledge through the works by Welty, McCullers, and Bowen mentioned above. In all of the texts, deafness is portrayed as *precluding* genuine communication and knowledge. Like Simmel's imaginary deaf people "perplexed, puzzled, and worried" by the expressions of unrest they see on the faces of others ("Sociology" 360), the deaf characters in these texts are cut off from knowledge of others and the world around them.[17] Oralism's construction of speech and hearing as absolutely necessary makes itself felt in the texts' rejection, in various complicated ways, of signed languages and, more generally, of visuality. Insofar as modernism attempted to forge new modes of expression, new ways of knowing the world and the self, and new connections among real and fictional subjects, deafness is cast as an obstacle to modernism itself.

Shallow Pity

In Welty's story "The Key," published in her first collection, *A Curtain of Green and Other Stories* (1941), deafness is represented first as spectacle. This portrayal ties deafness to the other nonnormative—"freakish"—conditions that make grotesque spectacles of many characters in the collection.[18] Once readers move through several concentric circles of observation to arrive at the deaf couple themselves, we find deafness representing a lack of knowledge and the capacity for communication. The deaf couple respond to this state of affairs differently, with Ellie longing for closer communication and Albert wanting to revel in a sort of "fortunate deafness" (to adapt Naomi

Schor's term for one of the "great myths of blindness") that allows him not to communicate but to live apart in himself. Deafness in this story results in an epistemological crisis: ways of knowing valued by the story—auditory but also existential—are closed to the Morgans, and their minds are portrayed as ultimately inaccessible to the narrator.[19]

Welty makes a spectacle of the Morgans' deafness in several ways. The most innovative is her construction of a series of concentric circles of observers around the Morgans. As Susan V. Donaldson remarks about the stories in this collection, "Welty's volume is full of figures—the poor, the black, the marginal, the deformed, but especially women— . . . who make spectacles of themselves, and they do so in a strikingly panoptic world defined by a merciless collective gaze surveying the odd, the bizarre, and the marvelous" (573). In "The Key" the collective gaze takes a layered form. First, we have a narrator describing a scene to an interlocutor ("you"). Within the scene being envisioned by the interlocutor as he or she listens to the narrator, we have a deaf couple being watched by two other types of observers—the unsympathetic people in the train station and the more sympathetic red-haired young man. That is, in the innermost circle are Albert and Ellie; in the next, the red-haired man; then the rest of the people in the station; then the interlocutor; then the narrator; and in the outermost circle, the readers.

Everyone in all of the circles except for the innermost where Ellie and Albert Morgan reside is hearing and sighted. We know this because the narrator continually remarks, "you could hear" . . . "Or you could listen" . . . "you have seen" . . . "you could observe" (29, 30, 36).[20] The story's opening is *about* sound, in particular the "night sounds of insects." The result is that a community of narrator, interlocutor, characters—except Ellie and Albert—and readers is created around the act of listening to the insects. The interlocutor, in addition, is assumed to want to protect the red-haired observer, an assumption that draws readers' sympathies most to him: "'Take care,' you wanted to say to him, and yet also, 'Come here'" (30–31).

Albert and Ellie, on the other hand, are seen through the panoptic gaze Donaldson describes. They are infantilized, so that readers may initially think they are children. "Their names were ever so neatly and rather largely printed on a big reddish-tan suitcase. . . . They must have been driven into town in a wagon, for they and the suitcase were all touched here and there with a fine yellow dust, like finger marks" (29). The large printed names and the assumption that they were driven to town suggest children, and it is not until the next paragraph that we learn Ellie is a woman of "about forty years old." Albert is called "the little man" (30, 31) and compared to "silent children, who will tell you what they dreamed the night before in sudden, almost hilarious bursts of confidence" (30). After Albert finds the key, his lips tremble (31), and later he thinks that happiness "is something that appears to you suddenly, that is meant for you, a thing which you reach for and pick up and hide at your breast, a shiny thing that reminds you of something alive and leaping" (35). This sense of childishness contributes to the spectacle the text makes of the Morgans.

Two metaphors of disability on the first page of the story add to the vague sense of freakishness about the deaf couple. Some of the bugs inside the station, we are told, "were clinging heavily to the yellow globe, like idiot bees to a senseless smell" (29). And Ellie and Albert's suitcase is "strapped crookedly shut, because of a missing buckle, so that it hung apart finally like a stupid pair of lips" (29). These lines link Ellie and Albert's deafness to mental disability and associate them with the freaks described in "The Petrified Man" and in "Keela, the Outcast Indian Maiden," among other stories in the collection.[21]

To complete the spectacle, Welty has the Morgans' deafness come as a revelation to the others in the station and to readers. After the red-haired stranger drops a key, which makes a "fierce metallic sound," Albert picks it up "as if it had fallen from the sky. Had he failed to hear the clatter? There was something wrong with Albert. . . ." (31). This is readers' first indication that Albert is deaf. The people in the train station must wait a few more paragraphs until Ellie begins to communicate in sign language to Albert. The red-haired man sees this with "sudden electrification." But the "others in the station had seen Ellie too; shallow pity washed over the waiting room like a dirty wave foaming and creeping over a public beach. In quick mumblings from bench to bench people said to each other, 'Deaf and dumb!' How ignorant they were of all that the young man was seeing" (30–31). Here, after the vivid description of the rippling effects of the revelation, the narrator offers a judgment about the ignorance of the people in the station and aligns readers again with the red-haired man, who sees more than the others and feels something more, presumably, than their "shallow pity." As in *Eva Trout*, where Jeremy's deafness comes as a revelation to readers and a character at once (discussed below), here readers are invited to identify with a more positive reaction, while the power of the vividly described alternative reaction ("a dirty wave foaming and creeping") lingers in readers' minds.

Once we move through these layers of spectacle, we find ourselves with a couple whose deafness represents a lack of knowledge and understanding. When the key falls, for example, Albert picks it up and examines it "quite slowly, with wonder written all over his face and hands, as if it had fallen from the sky" (31). As wonder-struck as the blind characters in Wells's "The Country of the Blind" who think Nunez was newly created from the rocks (546–47) and as the deaf Joel Mayes in Welty's own "First Love," who finds that "two men had seemingly fallen from the clouds onto the two stools at his table" (157), Albert cannot simply deduce that someone must have dropped the key. He tells his wife, "The key came here very mysteriously—it is bound to mean something" (32). In the criticism of this story I have not seen anyone mention how ludicrous this is.[22] Indeed, several critics make clear their acceptance of the false link between deafness and the inability to know. For example, Chester E. Eisinger describes "The Key," "A Piece of News," and "First Love" as containing characters who have "limited or impaired capacities for gaining knowledge" (12). Gail L. Mortimer shows that she accepts the link between deafness and the inability to deduce the simplest causes from their effects when she writes, "because he does not hear it fall, it simply appears suddenly in front of him. To Albert the key exists 'as if it had fallen from the sky,' a sort of gift, and he sees in it—instinctively and immediately—a sign of hope" (65). Welty's representation dramatically overvalues hearing as the only means to understanding and, as a result, links deafness tightly to an incapacity to know.

A few other examples make clear the sustained association between deafness and this incapacity. Ellie is portrayed as ignorant to the point of blockheadedness: "she sat there tense and solid as a *cube*, as if to endure some nameless apprehension rising and overflowing within her at the thought of travel" (29, italics added). She believes that if they had not missed the train, they would have arrived at Niagara Falls already; the narrator comments, "she did not even have any idea that it was miles and days away" (36). And Albert too believes they would have arrived so quickly: "It was then, you thought, that he became quite frightened to think that if they hadn't missed the train they would be hearing, at that very moment, Niagara Falls" (36). The Morgans are summed up as existing in reaction to the hearing world, which is unknowable to them: "It was the feeling of conspiracy. They were in counterplot against the plot of those things that pressed down upon them from outside their knowledge and their ways of making themselves understood" (34).

The constant presence of the narrator and the interlocutor ("you thought") casts doubt on the accuracy of the descriptions, but the most powerful effect of their presence is to question the knowability of the deaf characters' minds. The text suggests that they cannot be known for sure any more than they can, themselves, know.[23] This sense that Albert and Ellie are inaccessible, sealed off from the hearing world, is in some ways highlighted by the presence of the red-haired observer. Writing about a later story, "No Place for You, My Love" (included in *The Bride of Innisfallen*, 1955), Welty describes inventing "a single new character, a man whom I brought into the story *to be* a stranger, and I was to keep out of his mind, too. I had double-locked the doors behind me" (*Eye of the Story* 111). By inserting so many layers between herself as writer and Ellie and Albert as characters, and especially by creating the mysterious red-haired observer, she has enacted a similar double locking in "The Key."

Deafness in the story also means a futile longing for communication.[24] This doesn't entirely make sense within the world of the story, since the couple is shown communicating fluently in sign language. But Welty is using their deafness, as she admitted later, to externalize their loneliness and alienation, so she focuses not on the fluid communication among deaf people but on the divide between the deaf characters and the hearing community surrounding them at this moment.[25] Even before we know that the Morgans are deaf, we are told of Ellie's "too explicit evidence of agony in the desire to communicate" (29). The narrator comments repeatedly on this "agony": "How intensified, magnified, really vain all attempt at expression becomes in the afflicted!" (31). "How empty and nervous her red scrubbed hands were, how desperate to speak!" (35). This insistence that communication is an agonizing problem contradicts the descriptions of Albert and Ellie's discussions about the key and Niagara Falls, during which they communicate with ease: "They began again, talking rapidly back and forth, almost as one person" (34). Yet the narrator says that "they were so intent, so very solemn, wanting to have their symbols perfectly understood!" (32).[26]

This self-contradictory description of two people communicating effortlessly and yet longing to be understood demonstrates the prosthetic purpose deafness serves in the story. Insofar as the text offers a purportedly realistic description of a deaf couple, they communicate smoothly. But insofar as their deafness is used as a prop or shorthand for the story's larger theme of loneliness, they can only long futilely for communication. Welty later wrote,

> In those early stories I'm sure I needed the device of what you call the "grotesque." That is, I hoped to differentiate characters by their physical qualities as a way of showing what they were like inside—it seemed to me then the most direct way to do it. This is an afterthought, though. I don't suppose I did it as consciously as all that, and I didn't know it was the easiest way. But it is easier to show somebody as lonely if you make him deaf and dumb than if you go feeling your way into his mind. (Prenshaw 84)

This admission links the "shallow pity" of the people in the train station with the narrative itself. In line with this intention—which she calls an "obvious device" later in the same paragraph—Welty contrasts Ellie's longing to communicate with the red-haired observer's reticence. In his hands, "instead of the craving for communication, [there was] something of reticence, even of secrecy, as the key rose and fell" (30). The narrator, still concerned about the red-haired man, tells the interlocutor, "you felt some apprehension that he would never express what might be the desire of his life in being young and strong, in standing apart in compassion, in making any intuitive present or sacrifice" (33).

At the end of the story, the red-haired man sees that his intuitive gift of the two keys was "useless" and "despises" it; but at least he has the "compassion" that prompted him not only to stand apart but to act to bridge the gap between himself and the deaf couple. The Morgans, on the other hand, are shown to be very inward focused—Albert on himself and Ellie on Albert. The agonizing inability to communicate that the story ascribes to the Morgans, then, rebounds onto the red-haired observer, who has the opposite problem—his reticence will keep him too far apart for his compassion to effect any good in the world around him. It is the observer to whom the narrator grants her compassion and toward whom she directs the attention of the interlocutor. And it is he whom we observe last, as he leaves the station in disillusionment. The deaf couple serve, to some degree, as a catalyst for our understanding of the predicament of the red-haired man.

Within the innermost circle, the descriptions of the Morgans, we find additional aspects of the themes of loneliness and the fragility of human connection. Before they miss the train, Albert is filled with hope that when they get to Niagara Falls they will fall in love, and that maybe they married for love after all, "not for the other reason—both of us being afflicted in the same way, unable to speak, lonely because of that" (32). He tells Ellie that when you lean against the rail at Niagara Falls, you can hear the water's roar. "You hear it with your whole self. You listen with your arms and your legs and your whole body. You'll never forget what hearing is after that" (36). The couple's two goals, then, to understand hearing and to fall in love, are both to be met at the Falls. This confluence implies that the two goals may be related, that hearing may be, for the narrator, a necessary prerequisite for real love.[27]

Indeed, Ellie, whose desperation to communicate the narrator has noted, longs for closer communion with her husband. The "feeling of conspiracy" that holds them together in the counterplot mentioned earlier gives "the wife her greatest pleasure" (34). The narrator imagines that at home she would come to him "to tell him that she did love him and would take care of him always, talking with the spotted sour milk dripping from her fingers." But the narrator comments, "Just try to tell her that talking is useless." The narrator sides with Albert, who thinks, she imagines, that until you talk, "you can be peaceful and content that everything takes care of itself. As long as you let it alone everything goes peacefully. . . . But when you pick up your hands and start to talk, if you don't watch carefully, this security will run away and leave you" (35). In the narrator's speculation, Ellie's need for communication makes security impossible. She does not respect "the secret and proper separation that lies between a man and a woman, the thing that makes them what they are in themselves. . . . This to Ellie was unhappiness" (36).

The couple's deafness, then, represents the tangled problems of communication. While Ellie's longing for it is ascribed to her deafness, Albert's wish not to have to communicate indicates his desire to bask in his "fortunate deafness," remaining apart from others and content in himself. Because of the narrator's sympathy with the red-haired observer, whose reticence is undisturbed, readers are invited to see Ellie's insistence on communication as a misguided threat to the "proper separation" between men and women. Indeed, the story may be primarily about gendered differences in valuing communication, with the conceit of deafness helping Welty to intensify the opposition between communication and separation.

And deafness is linked at least as powerfully in the story to the epistemological crisis sparked by the events in the station. Albert cannot know that someone dropped the key because his deafness, constructed as mental incapacity, shields him from the prosaic truth. Deafness shuts Albert and Ellie off from the auditory knowledge that creates the community of narrator, interlocutor, and other characters at the story's opening. Albert Devlin describes the Morgans' exclusion from the "story" told by the insects as a failure of memory: "hearing has become a simile of remembering, but in 'The Key' the filaments of memory prove too brittle to recover either the hum of the Falls or, more closely at hand, the 'tenuous voices' of insects 'telling a story' in the night" (105).

Deafness prevents the Morgans from knowing not only that the train has come or why a key fell, but how far it is to Niagara Falls and even, by implication, what love is. Deafness also cuts their minds off from the narrator, who indicates throughout the story that the events she is narrating are not fully accessible. The narrator's constant uncertainty, as she "imagines" and "thinks" that this is what is happening, indicates the inaccessibility of the deaf characters, whose minds *we*, interpellated emphatically as hearing readers, cannot expect to understand. The opacity of these deaf characters' minds indicates one way in which deafness is cast as an impediment to modernism's aims—in this case its aim to present with fresh and deep insight the minds of its characters.

Visuality as Psychopathology

In Carson McCullers's *The Heart Is a Lonely Hunter* (1940) there is a similar sense that we readers, and even McCullers herself, cannot be expected to understand the mind of the deaf protagonist, John Singer. In an outline of the novel (then entitled *The Mute*) submitted as part of a successful application for a grant from Houghton Mifflin, McCullers asserts that

> the parts concerning Singer are never treated in a subjective manner. . . . This is partly because the mute, although he is educated, does not think in words but in visual impressions. That, of course, is the natural outcome of his deafness. Except when he is understood through the eyes of other people the style is for the main part simple and declarative. No attempt will be made to enter intimately into his subconscious. (O. Evans 197)

McCullers wrote this outline when she had finished only the first part of the book, and did make changes to her plans as she continued the novel. But her claims about the objective narration of the Singer sections are borne out by the finished product: when the narrative focalizes Singer, the voice and diction are measured, far less idiosyncratic than when it focalizes the other major characters. Her claim that this is "partly because [Singer] thinks in visual impressions" points to a technical problem she decides not to try to solve—how to depict the thoughts of someone who thinks visually—but also suggests that visual thinking, on some level, doesn't give rise to genuine subjectivity.

In the outline, McCullers also writes: "There are five distinct styles of writing—one for each of the main characters who is treated subjectively and an objective, legendary style for the mute. The object in each of these methods of writing is to come as close as possible to the inner psychic rhythms of the character from whose point of view it is written" (O. Evans 215). Taken together these two passages imply that Singer has no "psychic rhythms" or that if he does, they are inaccessible even to his own creator.

Singer's inaccessibility, his mystery, suffuses the text, with the other characters projecting onto him whatever they wish to see. The novel focuses on the struggles of four characters who confide and trust in Singer but whose disparate dreams are portrayed as doomed to failure: a young girl, Mick Kelly, with a talent and passion for music; Jake Blount, an alcoholic Marxist who attempts to organize local labor; Dr. Benedict Copeland, an African-American doctor engaged in fervent attempts to lift up his "race"; and Biff Brannon, the sexually ambiguous owner of a diner who watches all the other characters interact. Each character understands Singer in accordance with his or her own needs; as the narrator asserts, "Each man described the mute as he wished him to be" (223). Biff Brannon wonders about this: "And why did everyone persist in thinking the mute was exactly as they wanted him to be—when most likely it was all a very queer mistake?" (224). This situation continues to puzzle Biff, who repeats, "Owing to the fact that he was a mute they were able to give him all the qualities they wanted him to have. Yes. But how could such a strange thing come about? And why?" (232). I argue that this has come about within the text because the profound influence of oralism, in spite of its efforts to integrate deaf people into "the hearing world," made genuine communication between deaf and hearing people seem impossible, and that McCullers artificially isolates Singer in service to this ideology. When we do not simply take the isolation of deaf characters as a given (as critics of the novel unfortunately do),[28] we are able to see the intricate ways in which authors construct this isolation.

McCullers isolates Singer first by giving him an intimate confidant in his roommate Spiros Antonapoulos in the opening pages and then abruptly removing him (Antonapoulos is sent away to an asylum), leaving Singer without anyone to sign with for the rest of the novel, except during his two visits to Antonapoulos.[29] Second, she has Singer decline to use his voice. We learn that although Singer had learned to speak, he felt uncomfortable doing so: "his tongue was like a whale in his mouth" and he could see from people's faces that his speech was perceived as "disgusting" (11). Therefore, after he met Antonapoulos, with whom he could communicate in sign language (even though he never knows whether Antonapoulos understands him and the text suggests he does not), he never spoke again. Although McCullers's description of his decision not to speak is sympathetic, his continuing not to speak after Antonapoulos has been sent away contributes to the sense of isolation and mystery that surrounds him.

I would not, though, go so far as to say that by not speaking, Singer "seduces the other characters into choosing them as their listener, their god," as Emily Budick does. Budick reads Singer's not speaking as "a refusal to enter the two-way process of communication" (145). This ignores not only the notes Singer writes to his friends and his sympathetic nonverbal responses but also the shame Singer seems to have felt when others found his voice "like the sound of some animal," "disgusting" (McCullers, *Heart* 11). When Budick discusses the passage about Singer's voice, she argues that Singer is afraid to be exposed not as "animalistic or subhuman, but [as] human" (151). While this is an interesting reading, it seems to assume that Singer's speech would be clear, close to "normal." Familiarity with the history of deaf oralism leads to a different interpretation—Singer's deaf speech is not clear to hearing people and prompts their disgust and, in turn, his shame. In *The Deaf-Mute Howls* (1930), deaf artist Albert Ballin describes the embarrassment that results from trying to speak English with imperfect enunciation (30). And as Chris Eagle notes, "Norms of speech . . . can be no less powerful and punitive than those that regulate the body" ("Introduction: Talking Normal" 4).

Third, even though he has friends who are devoted to him and would undoubtedly be willing to learn some sign language (especially Mick, who adores him and longs to know his thoughts), the text never so much as alludes to the possibility that hearing people might be able to sign or even learn the finger alphabet. Critics follow suit, keeping the burden of communication on the deaf character only.[30] In contrast to Dickens's "Doctor Marigold," sign language in this text is for "mutes" only.

Fourth, McCullers represents Singer as uninterested in sharing any of his thoughts and feelings with anyone but Antonapoulos. McCullers's early biographer Oliver Evans claims that "the reason Singer is so highly esteemed by the other characters is that, being mute, he cannot make himself fully known to them" (37). But the novel demonstrates that Singer has no desire to make himself known to his friends. He does not even, for example, leave them a note when he leaves to visit Antonapoulos (or tell them anything about his elaborate plans beforehand). This aspect of his character can explain his failure to speak even a little or to teach any sign language to any of his friends (though the latter probably did not occur to McCullers because of the strength of oralist ideology). His lack of interest in opening up to Biff, Blount, Copeland, or Mick leads directly to the fifth and most interesting aspect of his characterization: McCullers casts Singer as emotionally detached from everything happening around him. His emotional life is fully taken up with Antonapoulos,[31] and even though his friends are emotionally invested in him, the text characterizes his attitude toward them as kindly but unmoved.

When Mick's brother has shot Biff's niece and everything is in chaos, Mick takes Singer's calm to indicate that he "had more sense and he knew things that ordinary people couldn't know" (179). When Doctor Copeland's son Willie is tortured in prison and has to have his feet amputated, Singer stands in the doorway and Dr. Copeland turns to him for solace. "Doctor Copeland gazed up into his face. 'You know of this?' he asked again. The words did not sound—they choked in his throat—but his eyes asked the question all the same. Then the mute was gone" (258). Although the doctor is not dismayed by Singer's disappearance at this terrible moment, readers get the impression that these events simply do not impinge deeply enough on Singer's consciousness to draw him into the other characters' trauma.

McCullers has created a character who is unusually detached from those around him, longing to communicate only with Antonapoulos. In a twist on Welty's nonsensical depiction of the Morgans as both communicating effortlessly *and* longing for communication, McCullers splits Singer's emotional life in two, resulting in his focusing passionately on his fluid communication with Antonapoulos but desiring no disclosure to his hearing friends. McCullers describes him in her outline of *The Mute* as the "simplest" character in the novel. She explains,

> Because of his deaf-mutism he is isolated from the ordinary human emotions of other people to a psychopathic degree. He is very observant and intuitive. On the surface he is a model of kindness and cooperativeness—but nothing which goes on around him disturbs his inner self. All of his deeper emotions are involved in the only friend to whom he can express himself, Antonapoulos. (O. Evans 197)

This comment about Singer's isolation from ordinary human emotions depends on the belief that deaf people cannot communicate in any genuine way with hearing people; the labeling of this isolation as "psychopathic" indicates McCullers's acceptance of the ideology that the aural/oral system of communication is the only one conducive to real human interaction and "normal" emotional development.[32]

Indeed, McCullers grants Singer a chance to make other signing friends only when it is too late: he is so devastated by Antonapoulos's death that he cannot communicate at all. When he meets the three deaf men, having just learned of his friend's death, he can only "clumsily" manage "a word of greeting" (325). He tells the three men where he is from and asks if they knew Antonapoulos. When he finds they did not, the conversation is at an end. "Singer stood with his hands dangling loose" (325). Through this plot device—having Singer meet potential friends only when he is ready to kill himself—McCullers ensures that the only person to whom Singer ever told his thoughts and feelings was Antonapoulos, who never understood him.[33] She thus effectively *empties* sign language of its communicative value.

We get a further sense of an unbridgeable gulf between deaf and hearing people in Mick's musings about Singer's understanding of music. "She wondered what kind of music he heard in his mind that his ears couldn't hear. Nobody knew. And what kind of things he would say if he could talk. Nobody knew that either" (53). Here Singer is a mysterious cipher to whom "nobody" has access (again, there is no suggestion that she could learn sign language to draw out Singer's thoughts, and other signing deaf people simply don't count). Mick articulates here the novel's insistence that sign language isn't really communication and that a nonspeaker's thoughts must forever be inaccessible. One of the ironies in the novel is that those who can and do speak—at great length—such as Jake Blount and Doctor Copeland, cannot achieve communication either, cannot make themselves understood. This is why the "deaf-mute" Singer makes an effective symbol and center for the novel. But his lack of speech is tied by the text to this inhuman separateness, whereas the others keep trying, in spite of everything, to make connections, to make themselves understood. McCullers's symbolic characterization of an inhuman Singer explains her famous refusal to attend a "deaf-and-dumb convention in Macon, Georgia," where reality might impinge on her vision (Carr 19).

Emily Russell reads Singer's disability as a conduit to a "local community as McCullers imagines physical difference as an antidote to the alienating modern world" (62). While a group does form around Singer, calling it a community is dubious because each of the other characters opens up only to Singer. When they all come to his room at the same time, no one has much to say (210ff). But more importantly, what community there is, what "antidote" to the alienation of modernity, benefits the hearing characters exclusively. Not only does Singer not benefit from this community (as can be seen most starkly in his suicide), but it is his constructed isolation that enables him to serve as the "hub" of the wheel composed of the other characters.[34] As Jennifer Murray points out, the relationship of the other characters to Singer is "more akin to that of the patient and the psychiatrist, a site of projection and transfer, where inner conflicts may be aired and worked on" (112). McCullers leaves Singer out of the community for which he paradoxically serves as a center.

Singer's separateness and his position outside of speech give rise to questions about what he knows. Other characters regularly wonder how much he understands—just as Singer wonders how much Antonapoulos understands of what he signs to him—but at other times ascribe to him an uncanny understanding and knowledge. As I argue in the previous chapter, the attribution of uncanny abilities to deaf or blind people implies the ableist assumption that they cannot access knowledge in ordinary ways. Therefore when they demonstrate knowledge, hearing/sighted people assume they came by it through uncanny means. In addition to serving as the symbol of isolation, then, Singer is represented along an axis of understanding or knowledge; he is used to highlight the question of what we can know about each other and our world.

The question of how much Singer understands becomes one of the novel's many motifs. Biff, being the most emotionally detached from Singer, does the most questioning. Biff first takes the question seriously in a scene with some similarities to the moment in "The Key" when pity washes over the waiting room while the red-haired man sees more than the others. The intoxicated Jake Blount is talking to Singer in Biff's cafe, not knowing that Singer is deaf. "The men in the booth were still laughing at the drunk who was trying to hold a conversation with the mute. Only Biff was serious. He wanted to ascertain if the mute really understood what was said to him" (24). Biff, like the red-haired man, remains outside the general reaction, seeking alternative information. Doctor Copeland later similarly wonders whether it is possible to communicate with Singer. He "wanted to talk to the white man and ask him some questions, but he did not know for sure if he could really understand" (85). Much later in the novel Biff is still asking himself what Singer understands: "He sat very still with his hands in his pockets, and because he did not speak it made him seem superior. What did that fellow think and realize? What did he know?" (134).[35]

As I mention in the introduction to this chapter, McCullers answers this question, at least as it pertains to what Singer understands of his friends' obsessions, by having Singer accurately reproduce their concerns both in the objective narration (204–5) and in a letter to Antonapoulos (215–16). While he may not be able to make total sense of Blount's or Doctor Copeland's philosophies, this is because the philosophies are not entirely coherent, marred on the one hand by Jake's alcoholic ramblings and on the other by Copeland's fierce insistence on abstractions. There's little evidence, then, for James Berger's claim that "the novel's central and obvious irony is that the one presumed to understand in fact understands very little. Singer's lipreading skills are imperfect, and he misses a great deal of the language directed at him" (39). It is true that lipreading is a very imperfect art, and it takes some time for

Singer to understand his friends, but the objective narrative voice tells us that "he became so used to their lips that he understood each word they said. And then after a while he knew what each one of them would say before he began, because the meaning was always the same" (205–6). So, though the characters attribute uncanny knowledge to Singer, McCullers explains Singer's knowledge through practical means.

Although Biff Brannon keeps more of a distance from Singer than the other characters and analyzes their deification of him, he too sees something almost mystical about Singer, especially in his eyes: "The fellow was downright uncanny. . . . His eyes made a person think that he heard things nobody else had ever heard, that he knew things no one had ever guessed before. He did not seem quite human" (24). This sense of uncanniness in the deaf character, which we see again with Jeremy in *Eva Trout*, carries through the novel. Jake Blount tells Singer, "'For two days now I been talking to you in my mind because I know you understand the things I want to mean'" (23). Blount thinks Singer will understand not only the things he tells him, but even ideas he has not yet formulated. Blount also thinks, "The eyes seemed to understand all that he had meant to say and to hold some message for him" (69).[36]

Mick, for her part, compares talking to Singer to discovering new things about her passion, music: "Even if he was a deaf-and-dumb mute he understood every word she said to him. Talking with him was like a game. Only there was a whole lot more to it than any game. It was like finding out new things about music" (91). At the end of part 1 an objective narrative voice tells us that Singer's "many-tinted gentle eyes were grave as a sorcerer's. Mick Kelly and Jake Blount and Doctor Copeland would come and talk in the silent room—for they felt that the mute would always understand whatever they wanted to say to him. And maybe even more than that" (94).

The narrator's and characters' emphasis on Singer's eyes indicates the novel's engagement with visuality. Relying on the "tradition of literal sight as a figure for knowledge and insight" (Russell 65), *The Heart Is a Lonely Hunter* both valorizes and denigrates visuality. According to the characters, Singer "sees" more deeply than others—he has uncanny insight—but his visual thinking empties him of subjectivity so that McCullers narrates his sections in an "objective, legendary style," and his visual language is reduced to a secret code that he speaks only with Antonapoulos, who doesn't even understand it. Although the oral/aural system of communication is shown also to have flaws—human beings' most difficult task is to understand each other and make ourselves understood—deafness and visual language serve the novel as the ultimate symbols of isolation, the failure to connect, and the inability to know. As I've demonstrated, this isolation is not the result of deafness itself, not a natural outcome of the inability to hear, but rather a specific, historically bound *construction* of deafness emerging from an oralist culture.

"Without Knowing"

The assumptions about language, knowledge, and subjectivity that we see in Welty and McCullers are complicated but ultimately complemented by representations of deafness in Elizabeth Bowen's *Eva Trout*. In this novel, deafness is associated both with uncanny knowledge and the absence of knowledge, both with authentic understanding and inauthentic mimicry (e.g., "understanding" with quotes around it, as Michael Merva says of John Singer).[37] Deafness in *Eva Trout* begins as a mystical source of knowledge; but such knowledge dissolves into a state of pure visuality defined by its *lack* of, and therefore quest for, knowledge. As I demonstrate below, although Bowen does use deafness to question interiority, she ultimately acknowledges nonlinguistic subjectivity, insisting that the challenges of deafness have less to do with subjectivity than with knowledge. She nevertheless associates deafness with a sense of doom that emerges from the inauthenticity the novel ascribes to the visual world.

The uncanny knowledge associated with deafness takes the form in this novel of an almost magical receptivity to others' thoughts. When Eva brings her illegally adopted deaf son Jeremy from America home to England, they visit her old friends the Danceys. The vicar, Mr. Dancey, and his son Henry invite them in for tea.

> Jeremy's presence . . . was never not to be felt. Eva, habituated, was least aware of it. There he sat, enthroned on a cushion brought from the drawing-room, on a level in every sense with the rest of the company. . . . The effect was not so much of mere intelligence as of a somehow unearthly perspicacity. The boy, handicapped, one was at pains to remember, imposed on others a sense that *they* were, that it was *they* who were lacking in some faculty. . . . A conviction that the vicarage tea table was bugged, if on an astral plane, gained increasing hold on father and son. (172)

With his "unearthly perspicacity" the eight-year-old Jeremy "imposes on others" a sense of lack, of handicap. This passage enlists rich sensory imagery. Jeremy's presence can be palpably "felt" at the table. The word "perspicacity" formerly meant "keen vision" and comes from the Latin word *specere*, to see or to look. The father and son's conviction that the "tea table was bugged" suggests an impossible listener, and the impossibility is conveyed by the phrase "if on an astral plane." At the same time, the very uncanniness of the impression implies a view of Jeremy as lacking an important faculty—it is only that he gives the "effect" that others are "lacking in some faculty." Indeed, in the draft version of this passage more importance is given to the faculty of hearing; the line there reads: "that it was *they* who were lacking in some faculty essential to the conduct of full existence" (Mss of *Eva Trout*). The claim that deafness is "essential to . . . full existence," though deleted for the final version of the novel, is echoed in the dehumanization of Jeremy as a machine that can "bug" the tea table.[38]

The paradoxical nature of Jeremy's character (he is both superhuman and not quite human) is extended through the description of his silences. The narrator tells us that "Jeremy's silentness, usually, had manifold eloquent variations, outgoings, clamourings and insistencies, queries, ripostes. It took much to tie the tongue of his mind" (180). Not only can Jeremy hear on "an astral plane," then, but he can speak with his mind. His silences are expressive not just visually but auditorily: they clamor, they insist, they are eloquent. But occasionally Jeremy is "in a silent mood" (180) or "in one of his silent silences" (210).

The most relevant paradox is the representation of Jeremy's deafness as leading to both uncanny insight and a disabling lack of knowledge. At the Danceys', Jeremy goes out to the ash heap and gathers up a variety of objects—slivers of mirror, fragments of china, a crushed eggshell, buttons—and works absorbedly making them into a pattern. As Henry and Eva talk, "Jeremy put the slivers of mirror into sun-rays surrounding the orange button; *his* patterns made sense" (166). Mr. Dancey is impressed with the pattern, and when he is told that Jeremy is deaf, "the startled man said: 'I should never have known.' He looked the more intently down at the pattern" (169). Mr. Dancey realizes that Jeremy's vision is keen in more than one sense, telling Eva, "'Sight to me is the thing—the thing above all things. And more seeing eyes than his I have seldom seen. And they must be, or he couldn't have made this" (169). Nevertheless, Mr. Dancey asks Eva what has been done to help Jeremy. He believes that modern medicine, accessible through Eva's great wealth, can enable him to speak and to hear. He asks her, "who would not wish to speak?" but she defends Jeremy's resistance to speech training, saying, "*I* have never wished to. What is the object? What is the good?" Mr.

Dancey then turns from speech to hearing, telling Eva, "Crass as sound can be, imagine a soundless world! No, this child has come into your life, however he did, and you must *not* doom him. I do mean 'doom'; you doom if you acquiesce" (169).

I return to the notion of doom below; here I want to note that even though Mr. Dancey believes sight is "the thing above all things" and that Jeremy has exceptionally "seeing eyes," he still believes that Jeremy is "doomed" if Eva cannot find a cure for his deafness. This is not merely the Vicar's personal inconsistency or prejudice; it delineates the structure of the representation. Jeremy has special abilities and yet lacks something fundamental. Because of this lack, Jeremy is depicted as seeking compensatory portents. During their time in America, Eva and Jeremy "lorded it in a visual universe" (208). They rode on horseback "out into forest fires of fall coloring" and felt the "stinging of their same faces by spray from cataracts too loud to be heard even by Eva" (208). During all this, "moments of joyful complicity abounded" (208). But there is an important difference in their experiences of these images: "True, Jeremy looked more deeply into some of the images than she did. Torn skies, curdled waters, hieroglyphic smoke he had had a particular way of scanning: seeking for portents?—if so, rightly" (208). Jeremy seeks knowledge from what he sees in a way Eva need not.

In the drafts there are two earlier versions of the "portents" passage. The earliest one stresses Jeremy's difference from Eva:

> True, he looked more deeply into some of the images than she did <to the extent of following them when they began to disperse>. There began to be moments when his concentration sundered him, though at first by only an infinitesimal degree, from Eva—this had been already beginning when they came to England. Torn skies, battlefields of clouds, for instance, held him. What could he be looking for in them: portents? (Mss of *Eva Trout*)

This passage suggests that the "sundering" of the relationship between Eva and Jeremy that takes place late in the novel may have its origin in their sensory difference. Jeremy must concentrate on the visual world to seek knowledge—"portents." Eva, on the other hand, need not look so "deeply," need not "follow" images "when they begin to disperse," because for this novel, hearing is knowing.

The other passage stresses the function of such seeking:

> True, Jeremy looked more deeply into the dissolving images than she did—some, he was to be felt clutching at, detaining, securing, hauling into the storehouse, which was also the fortress, of his mind. (What *was* he thinking?) Torn skies, wind-curdled waters, hieroglyphic smoke from weedfires, he had a particular way of scanning: seeking for portents?—if so, rightly. (Mss of *Eva Trout*)

While its last sentence is closest to the published version, this passage elaborates more than the other versions the purposes of Jeremy's seeking. He needs to "clutch," "detain," "secure," and "haul" these images "into the storehouse . . . of his mind." This passage, then, emphasizes the relationship of the "portents" Jeremy seeks to information, to knowledge.[39]

Similar imagery characterizes Bowen's description of herself as a child in *Seven Winters*. The young Elizabeth Bowen sought portents not because she could not hear but because she could not read.

> I was not allowed to learn to read: my mother believed that reading would tire my eyes and brain. Actually, frustrations tired me more. I was only allowed picture-books. The pictures in these began to distend themselves, like those on the walls of my nursery and round the dado, till they took on a momentous importance: they were my only clues to a mystery. And, on my walks through familiar quarters of Dublin I looked at everything like a spy. (18)

In a way strikingly similar to Jeremy looking "deeply" at "dissolving images," Bowen as a child looked at images so hard that they "began to distend themselves"; as Jeremy seeks "portents" in visual images, Bowen saw pictures as "clues to a mystery." Because she was always on the alert for clues to what she might be missing due to her inability to read, she "looked at everything like a spy." For Bowen, not being able to read and not being able to hear both lead to a lack of knowledge, and consequent efforts to compensate visually. In the similarities of these passages, then, we uncover an association between two sources of knowledge: hearing and reading.[40]

That hearing should be associated with reading in *Eva Trout* is in line with a claim made about Victorian fiction by Jennifer Esmail. In her article about deafness and sign language in Charles Dickens and Wilkie Collins, Esmail accounts for the dearth of signing deaf characters in Victorian fiction: "the effacement of deafness from Victorian fiction reveals its investment in a particular and normativized relationship between bodies, spoken language, and textuality: one that understands fiction as a record of what was said and heard" (992). In *Eva Trout*, too, we find an association among hearing, speech, and reading: the text of the world is inaccessible to the young, prereading Bowen and to the deaf, nonspeaking Jeremy.

Jeremy is also unable to read: as Eva writes a telegram to Henry, he watches with "impartial interest; he could not of course read, but could write, being a wonderful copyist; line after line of her copper-plate had he reproduced" (225). The narrator's remark that "of course" Jeremy cannot read is odd both in terms of the text's representation of Jeremy's intelligence and in terms of the literary antecedent found in Dickens's "Doctor Marigold," which Bowen very likely read or heard.[41] But this assumption that a deaf boy would be *naturally* unable to read strengthens the text's connection between hearing and reading.

Jeremy's writing is doubly derivative: without understanding it, he copies Eva's "copper-plate," which, as she tells her former teacher Iseult earlier, she learned from her many governesses (60). But in another characteristic paradox, his writing somehow partakes in originality. When Iseult kidnaps Jeremy (after erroneously thinking he was fathered by her former husband, Iseult becomes obsessed with Jeremy, and so she takes him from his sculpture lesson for an outing without Eva's knowledge), they experience what Iseult later describes as a "razor-edged actuality, layers deep" (274). When they go to Westminster Abbey, "he traced the lettering of the inscriptions on monuments he could reach with the point of a finger as though responsible for incising them for the first time" (274). The "as though" simultaneously grants his tracing special status and highlights Jeremy's inability to write anything "for the first time."

With Iseult, Jeremy begins to want to make more of a mark.[42] When she takes him out to eat, he eats "voraciously, as though getting his teeth into the world" (274). The text implies that she implants in him the desire to branch out from his dependence on Eva and interact more directly with others. Later, after Jeremy (who returns to Eva with no explanation that evening) has finally assented to being taught to lipread and speak French by Dr. and Mme. Bonnard, Iseult explains to Father Clavering-Haight that she "roused his genius" and "made him see *why*" (273–74). Clavering-Haight replies, "you may have done what you think you have" (274). The text seems to endorse Iseult's view of the effect she had on Jeremy when Dr. Bonnard too suggests that Jeremy may have "benefited" by the kidnapping, gaining "expanding desires" (249).

Maud Ellmann notes that Iseult destroys "the conspiracy of silence between Eva and her son. . . . Iseult's intervention awakens Jeremy's desire for self-expression" (*Elizabeth Bowen* 218). But the most important thing Iseult has done is recognize the limits—according to the ideology of oralism that infuses the novel—of Jeremy's "seeing eyes." She explains to Clavering-Haight, "I cannot tell you what satiated eyes he had, or how his weariness of seeing, seeing, seeing without knowing, without knowing, without knowing was borne in on me" (273). Challenging the strand of Western thought that links vision to knowledge, the text, through Iseult, articulates the most salient aspect of its representation of Jeremy: his "seeing eyes" are "satiated"; they have taken him as far as they can. As Bowen herself needed to learn to read, Jeremy now needs knowledge beyond what the visual world and his communion with Eva can give him.[43] And this knowledge is figured by the novel as greater access to spoken and written language: reading, lipreading, and speech. It is crucial that there is *no* mention of sign language in the novel, even though several conversations concern Jeremy's education. The absence of sign language as a viable option reflects educational practices at the time Bowen was writing. But the complete erasure of visual language from the text also contributes to the novel's critique of visuality.

"A Depth-Charge": Deafness and Doom

Toward the end of the novel, the relationship between Jeremy and Eva starts to disintegrate. The text chronicles this dissolution without giving an explicit reason for it, but it seems somehow linked to his entrance into language. Once Jeremy starts working with the Bonnards to learn to lipread and speak French, Eva notices that her "accustomed communications" with Jeremy have broken down. "He no longer obeyed her, not out of rebelliousness but from genuine lack of knowledge of what was wanted. His responses were not less willing, but less ready" (239). Their prior methods of communication, labeled "extra-sensory" by Henry (172), have been interrupted by language, but Jeremy and Eva still cannot communicate through language. The text soon baldly states that "his and her universe was over. It had not been shattered; simply, it had ended. It was a thing of the past" (240). The idea that language brings this bond to an end suggests an extreme version of the process of individuation.

Eva wonders what has happened to let through the "roaring" of uncertainty about where they are heading.

> The torrents of the future went roaring by her. No beam lit their irresistible waters. The Deluge: dead arms flailing like swimmers'. Where

> were they on their way to being swept to, she, Henry, Jeremy? Who had opened the sluicegates, let through this roaring? The boy, doing so by the same act by which he heaved the lid from his tomb of silence? Jeremy, whose destiny she had diverted? One does not do such a thing with impunity, the priest had said. The doctor had warned her. (260)

Here the uncertain future is figured through sound, a "roaring" that has replaced the "tomb of silence" Jeremy has lived in until this point. Eva's description of silence as a "tomb" recalls Mr. Dancey's assertion that Eva would "doom" Jeremy if she "acquiesce[d]" to his deafness. Beyond this implied link between Jeremy's entrance into language, figured by the "roaring" sound, and the breakdown of the relationship, the text offers one other possible cause for the "end" of their "universe": the fact of Jeremy's illegal adoption (Eva bought him on the black market in America when he was about three months old). In its references to the warnings of the priest and doctor, the passage suggests some sort of cosmic punishment for that wrongdoing.

This adoption, or appropriation, is the nearest thing to an explicit reason for the sundering offered by the published text. After Jeremy and Eva have been apart for two weeks while he studied with the Bonnards, they reunite in their hotel in London. Their reunion is pleasant but unsettlingly calm:

> And what was disconcerting was, not that there was any question of disillusionment, on either side, but rather that the minute was reigned over by a startling, because unavoidable, calmness—a calmness to which there was no alternative. One could have called it, a disinfected one. They were glad to be seeing each other again: anything beyond that, anything primitive, was gone. . . . Like as they were, they were *not* of each other's flesh-and-blood, and they both knew it. The dear game was over, the game was up. (285)

Here the text suggests that the reason for the loss of the "primitive" bond between them is that they are not biologically mother and son. Since Eva has of course always known that, the implication is that Jeremy now knows it too, and it has destroyed their "dear game." Their relationship, the passage suggests, was built on a false foundation that has now crumbled.

But there is another aspect of falsity in their relationship, according to a draft version of the novel. In both the published novel and the draft version Henry responds viscerally when he discovers that Jeremy is deaf. While Jeremy is making his pattern out of fragments from the trash heap, Henry and Eva stand by chatting, and then Henry compliments Jeremy on his work. When Jeremy does not reply, Henry calls loudly, "*Jeremy!*" "Not a flicker. Over the happy head, Eva confronted Henry. She did so steadily. She said: 'Yes.' // A deaf mute. // Pity mounted in Henry into a wave of hate. He could not contain it. He said: 'You were sold a pup'" (165). Eva says nothing at first, but "with the old hopeless motion, she dragged a fist, bumping, across her eyes" (166). When "the fist dropped, tumbling into her lap" he asks her if she minds so much. "'Mind?' she said. 'Mind that *you* are so cruel?'" (166). With this accusation of cruelty, Eva defends Jeremy from Henry's mixed pity and hatred.

Her feeling of hopelessness, however, suggests some ambivalence in Eva about what Henry has said, and in the draft version we learn more about her emotional response. There, she thinks about the scene later, analyzing her response to Henry's outburst:

> The discovery of what her then very little, then very new little child was had been at the outset dreadful and doomful—what reconciled her to it, as time went on? *Or*, was the dreadful doomfulness buried only? That might be so. All had surged up again, reflected in Henry when *he* made the discovery. There in the vicarage drawing-room Henry's horrified cruelty was a depth-charge, bringing all to the surface—all the original woe, dismay, drastic disappointment, sensation of having been hounded down. She must continue to put a face on things; she had done so. But she could comfort herself no longer. She and the child had lived—as they only could, perhaps—and revelled [*sic*] in, the light of a false dawn. (Mss of *Eva Trout*)

This devastating passage transforms our understanding of how Eva relates to Jeremy's deafness. Her defiance when she tells Mr. Dancey *she* never saw the need to speak (169) is recast as a "face" Eva is putting on her own "woe." The falsity of their relationship is reframed as stemming not from Jeremy's illegal adoption but from Eva's burial of her "drastic disappointment" in his deafness. The assertion that "they were not of each other's flesh and blood" comes to seem a screen for the deeper cause of their separation: Eva's inability to suppress any longer her feelings of "dreadful doomfulness" about Jeremy's deafness.

Bowen deleted this passage. One could surmise that she did so because she decided it was an inaccurate description of Eva's feelings. But Bowen retained in the published text other suggestions that Eva is suppressing strong negative feelings about Jeremy's deafness. The "sculptress," for instance, suggests that Eva may be secretly relieved when Jeremy is kidnapped, that he may be an "encumbrance" on Eva "as he is" (221). Eva herself worries that in her newfound desire to speak she is betraying "the inaudible years" with Jeremy (208). When Clavering-Haight tells her that Jeremy is in her power, she replies, "No, Father Clavering-Haight, I am in his" (206). So it seems more likely that Bowen deleted the scene because it was "over-analytical." In an interview entitled "How I Write," Bowen said, "I revise like one prunes—snipping away dead wood. . . . I make particular war on analysis. My first drafts are always over-analytical. My ideal is, to replace analysis by a pure image—as in poetry" (270). In this case, Bowen may have decided that the buried feelings could more forcefully be gleaned from the "pure image" of Eva, with the "old, hopeless motion," dragging her fist across her eyes.

Another powerful way the text handles the suppressed feelings is by manipulating readers' awareness of Jeremy's deafness. As Davis notes, "deafness is in some sense an invisible disability" (*Enforcing Normalcy* 77). When we first meet Jeremy, he is on the plane with Eva flying from America to England. We are not told that he is deaf. The narrator drops hints, such as that Jeremy watches Eva's lips when she talks, but because the narrator says he shares the quality of "gravity" with Eva, his focus on her lips initially seems merely a symptom of that gravity. Then, when Henry calls "Jeremy!" and gets no answer, Eva says merely "Yes." The text gives the phrase "a deaf mute" its own paragraph; this phrase is not clearly focalized by any particular consciousness. It hangs there—thought by Eva, by Henry, by us—offering readers a way into the text. Through the text's invitation to readers to think "a deaf mute," we are suspended, like the line itself, between Eva's defended, "steady" response and Henry's "pity, mounting into a wave of hate."

As in "The Key," where readers are affected by the description of the "wave" of "shallow pity" and yet invited to transcend it through our identification with the red-haired man, here Henry's "wave of hate" may affect readers who, alongside him, have just discovered Jeremy's deafness, even though we identify more strongly with our protagonist, Eva. This manipulation of readers' reaction to Jeremy's deafness is an example of what Ato Quayson describes as "disability as epiphany" (45). We are suddenly aware of something that changes how we read previous scenes.

Eva's sense of doom comes from her personal "sensation of having been hounded down" when she has adopted (bought) a baby who turns out to be deaf. For the text itself, the doom seems associated with the purely visual world Eva and Jeremy occupy during "the inaudible years" in America. The section of the text from which the "doom" passage was deleted focuses on the ways in which Eva and Jeremy shut themselves off from three-dimensional reality. The published version of the text tells us that Eva and Jeremy "came to distinguish little between what went on inside and what went on outside the diurnal movies, or what was or was not contained in the television flickering them to sleep" (208). The draft version elaborates:

> From screen after screen illusion overspilled on to what should have been three-dimensional but did not seem so. Tracts of country planes they were in dipped over, street-like canyons or canyon-like streets which might happen to overtop them, highways, skyways, parkways and underpasses they hummed along were as though projected. One way or the other—and who cared which?—they had looked, would look or were in the course of looking upon everything conceivable. All was theirs. They were within a story to which they imparted the only sense. The one wonder, to them, of the exterior world was that anything should be exterior to themselves—and did there, indeed, exist anything that quite was? (Mss of *Eva Trout*)

This passage describes a process by which what is three-dimensional comes to seem two-dimensional because of Eva and Jeremy's constant immersion in visual media. The description of a blinkered, even solipsistic, visual existence recalls the self-absorption of Ellie and Albert Morgan. Not understanding that there is a world outside themselves leads Eva and Jeremy to view the world as another movie designed for their entertainment—a process akin to Albert Morgan assuming the key came specially to him. This passage returns us to the links between deafness and not knowing, and between deafness and not reading, that I outline above. "Seeing, seeing, seeing," Eva and Jeremy are locked within visuality; they lack access to the reality that the novel implies sound and language would open up. Jeremy's deafness leads to this immersion in a pure visuality that then comes to seem limiting and inauthentic, "as though projected" for their enjoyment.

"Mimicries": Inauthenticity and Subjectivity

Inauthenticity is thematized in various ways throughout the novel. Neil Corcoran writes that the novel is

> deeply preoccupied with, and plotted around modes of, the inauthentic. The Romantic form of individual identity . . . confronts everywhere

> else in the novel a fundamental insecurity about personal identity. This is sometimes so underminingly severe as to make the novel's modes of characterization congruent with radical postmodern conceptions of the hollowing-out of subjectivity. (128)

Their absorption in visuality prevents Eva and Jeremy from interacting in an authentic way with the world outside themselves. Eva's motherhood is itself labeled "mimicry" by Dr. Bonnard: "What made you prefer mimicry to what could have been the actual continuance of a flesh-and-blood?" (247). Deafness leads to mimicries in that Jeremy's writing, as we saw above, mimics Eva's already derivative "copper-plate." And "mimicries and secret signals" are a component of the "moments of joyful complicity" (208) that Eva and Jeremy enjoy in the United States. The phrase "dear game," used to describe their relationship, plays into this depiction, making mimicry into a multivalenced motif.[44]

These references to mimicry are peppered throughout a narrative that, as Corcoran maintains, is fundamentally concerned with the question of the authenticity of the subject. As Maud Ellmann suggests, Bowen uses Eva to "cast doubt on the very notion of interiority" (*Elizabeth Bowen* 207). Eva is associated from the beginning of the novel with a castle that looks like a mere façade. She has never cried. Although she does speak, she is described as being "unable to speak—talk, be understood, converse" (62). What speech she performs is "unnatural sounding, it's wooden, it's deadly" (64); she talks like "a displaced person" (10). All of this depicts Eva's subjectivity as impaired.[45]

This representation of Eva illuminates the novel's use of Jeremy and its exclusion of sign language. Jeremy serves as a mirror to reflect what the novel casts as Eva's impairments of language and subjectivity. Andrew Bennett and Nicholas Royle point out that Jeremy's "refusal or inability to speak participates in the text's more general questioning of what it is to be a person, to be given a face, a mask, an identity—to become 'real'" (145). Since language is so closely linked to subjectivity in ways I describe above, Jeremy's presence raises the question of how we know when someone "has . . . an inside" (6).

But Bowen's representation of Jeremy differs from many representations of characters with disabilities in that his subjectivity, though it is used as a means for questioning Eva's, turns out to be at least as robust as hers. The text establishes this in its careful delineations of his "clamoring" silences, his "silent silences," his "bereft" feeling when Eva fails to provide him a home (178), his initial resistance to learning to speak, his subsequent hard work on his speech exercises with the Bonnards, and even his murder of Eva in what is arguably a jealous passion at the novel's close.[46] This is a condescending use of a deaf character: even the deaf boy has more subjectivity than Eva, which shows how impaired her subjectivity is. But it is more respectful of Jeremy's humanity than representations, such as those described by Mitchell and Snyder in *Narrative Prosthesis*, that rely on people with disabilities to shore up by contrast the humanity of the other characters.

The humanizing portrayal of Jeremy is overlooked by Bennett and Royle, who go too far along the lines that Bowen reins in. Recognizing the link between Jeremy's deafness and the text's *questioning* of subjectivity, they fail to recognize the text's *answer*: that Jeremy's subjectivity is real. Instead, they dehumanize him when they write that, "deaf and dumb, Jeremy is literally a silent mover, a silent movie, set undecidably flickering" and describe him as "a kind of fictional dummy who does not speak, a mute mutation" (154–55). Their audist description of Jeremy as a "simulacrum" (141) parts ways with Bowen's text.

In fact, *Eva Trout* undercuts the idea that subjectivity depends on language when she has Eva and Jeremy's dual entrance into language (while Jeremy learns to speak and lipread, Eva decides she is "ready to talk") prompt the *disintegration* of their relationship and possibly contribute to Jeremy's murder of Eva. Rather than depict language as enhancing the communication of two subjects, Bowen shows language ruining what was a perfect, "extra-sensory" communion. Maud Ellmann's assertion that "Bowen makes it clear that only language can endow us with an inner life," then, overlooks the way Jeremy's exclusion from language and his abundant interiority cast doubt on that common linkage between language and subjectivity (*Elizabeth Bowen* 206).[47] Indeed, Bowen's representation of deafness as that which prompts a subject to seek *knowledge* refuses such a linkage; it is knowledge rather than subjectivity that Jeremy lacks.

In her final novel Bowen is experimenting, at high stakes, with ideas about language, knowledge, and subjectivity. Resisting the "shibboleth 'where there is language, there is a subject,'" Bowen's nuanced descriptions of Jeremy's emotional states make clear that his inner life is complicated, even tumultuous; Jeremy's subjectivity is depicted as authentic. But *Eva Trout* does assert that for authentic *knowledge*, Jeremy needs spoken language, and that without it, he is condemned to inauthenticity. Omitting all reference to sign language, *Eva Trout* represents deafness as a source of doom, only mitigated by learning to lipread and speak. In this way the novel, for all its insight and compassion, remains a product of its decade: the last before the (partial) reclamation of sign language (Baynton, *Forbidden Signs* 5). If Bowen had Jeremy learn to sign instead of speak—come to knowledge through a visual language—the novel's critique of visuality would lose its force. But its attempt to portray a deaf character with imaginative sympathy would gain transformative power. Overlooking or purposely excluding the possibility of a visual language, Bowen depicts visuality as a sort of epistemological void: "seeing, seeing, seeing without knowing, without knowing, without knowing."

These disparate texts by Welty, McCullers, and Bowen converge in the suggestion that deafness precludes or severely limits the subject's access to the world outside the self, and even in some ways to the self. Influenced by the revaluation of the "elite senses" (Kleege, *Blind Rage* 34) and by the ideology of oralism—itself deeply imbricated in nationalism and eugenics—modernist authors found in deafness and its concomitant visuality obstacles to subjectivity, and insurmountable obstacles to communication and knowledge. In ways unrecognized by most critics, they have constructed their stories *so that* their deaf characters are lonely, cut off, and doomed, and can therefore be used to highlight aspects of other characters (the red-haired man's reticence and loneliness, Singer's friends' inability to make themselves understood, Eva's nonnormative subjectivity), and symbolize central themes (inauthenticity, isolation, and the difficulties of communication). The authors' ideologically driven insistence on the oral/aural system of communication led to their devaluation of visual language and visual ways of knowing. They used deafness, ultimately, as a formidable impediment to modernism's efforts to delve deeply into interpersonal connection and revitalize creative expression. In Joyce's *Ulysses*, however, visuality is returned to a position of prominence as the text explores multiple ways of knowing and their relationships to sight and hearing.

Four

Knowledge Redux

Sensory Disability in Ulysses

In chapter 2 I explore ways in which modernist authors worked to detach blindness from its traditional partner, ignorance, and attach it instead to intimacy—while nevertheless relying on the association between sight and knowledge for their belief that blindness cuts one off from the superficial world. In chapter 3 I demonstrate how additional modernist authors expanded the cultural link between deafness and isolation to include epistemological failure, shutting their deaf characters off from both communication and knowledge. James Joyce's treatments of sensory disability are distinct in important ways from those of his contemporaries. The blind character in *Ulysses* is far from a model of intimacy—he is taciturn with Bloom and bitterly curses the man whose cloak brushes his cane.[1] The deaf character is not isolated—he jokes with the barmaids in the Ormond Hotel, and Bloom speculates that he has a family waiting for him at home: "perhaps he has wife and family waiting, waiting Patty come home" (11.1003). Joyce's treatment is self-conscious and playful, both exposing and relying upon the link between the "elite senses" and knowledge. *Ulysses* recasts the issue of knowledge, associating both its blind and deaf characters not quite with the absence of knowledge but with its suspension. If, as Sara Danius argues, *Ulysses* is "a modernist monument to the eye and the ear" (149), Joyce's representations of blindness and deafness play significant roles in his contribution to modernism.[2]

Joyce's blind and deaf characters are treated, on the surface, quite differently. The blind stripling is portrayed in a semitragic mode and draws sympathy from the barmaids. Although he is unnamed, he is a more prominent character, appearing or being referenced in "Lestrygonians," "Wandering Rocks," and "Sirens" and very briefly in "Circe" and "Ithaca." His curse, laid on Cashel

Boyle O'Connor Fitzmaurice Tisdall Farrell in "Wandering Rocks," echoes three times in "Sirens." And although Joyce does not specify the correspondence, the blind stripling may suggest the character of Tiresias, the blind seer who appears in book 11 of the *Odyssey*. There, Tiresias carries a golden scepter, echoed in the blind stripling's tapping stick. He recognizes Odysseus right away (both the Samuel Butler and the Butcher and Lang translations, on which Joyce relied, give "he knew me"), whereas even the ghost of Odysseus's mother does not immediately know him. In *Ulysses*, when Bloom helps the blind stripling across the street and he says "Thanks, sir," Bloom feels himself recognized: "Knows I'm a man. Voice" (8.1102). While this correspondence may be one of Joyce's red herrings, the blind stripling is nevertheless invested with textual and intertextual resonance.

Deaf bald Pat, the waiter, on the other hand, is treated comically. As David Lodge writes in *Deaf Sentence*, "Culturally, symbolically, [blindness and deafness are] antithetical. Tragic versus comic. Poetic versus prosaic, sublime versus ridiculous" (13). The pun on "bothered" exemplifies the novel's comic use of deafness. Don Gifford points out that *bothered* is an Anglicization of the Irish *bodhar*, deaf (297). As a waiter, Pat is *bothered* by competing demands from patrons, and so his deafness in part emerges from that linguistic joke.[3] Much as in *Portrait*, where Stephen Dedalus's "monstrous reveries" had "sprung up before him . . . out of mere words" (95), Pat's deafness seems to have sprung from Joyce's amusement at this double meaning as he composed *Ulysses*. The text of "Sirens," furthermore, makes sport of Pat: "Pat is a waiter who waits while you wait. Hee hee hee hee. He waits while you wait. Hee hee" (11.916–17).[4] Although Pat appears, like the stripling, very briefly in "Circe," he does not appear in any other chapter, nor is he discussed by other characters. Moreover, the blind stripling is the subject of a handful of critical articles, while Pat has not been discussed at any length.[5] Critics generally settle for pointing out that a deaf character is ironically appropriate to the "Sirens" episode, where the organ is the ear and the art is music. In the *Odyssey* Odysseus stops the ears of his men with wax so they will not be lured by the Sirens' music, and Pat's deafness recalls their immunity. And as Richard Ellmann points out, deafness also adds an appropriate contrapuntal note to the "ear world" of "Sirens" (*Ulysses* 101).

But if we consider the associative logic of *Ulysses*, we find the blind stripling and deaf Pat linked together in meaningful ways. First, in the early draft of "Sirens" held at the National Library of Ireland, Pat is not yet a character in the episode, but Joyce wrote "Enter Pat" in the margin just an inch or so down the page from where the barmaids discuss the blind stripling (NLI MS

36, 639/7/A-B).[6] This contiguity is maintained in the published episode. Pat enters the Ormond bar just when Miss Douce is pitying the blind man:

> —So sad to look at his face, miss Douce condoled.
>
> God's curse on bitch's bastard. [A repeat of the curse the blind stripling bestows on Farrell in "Wandering Rocks."]
>
> Tink to her pity cried a diner's bell. To the door of the bar and diningroom came bald Pat, came bothered Pat, came Pat, waiter of Ormond. (11.284–88)[7]

Miss Douce's pity for the stripling has its musical accompaniment—the bell—which then summons Pat to the room.

Second, both are described through ritualistic, repetitive language: the tapping sound of the stripling's cane and the oddly monosyllabic descriptions of Pat's actions. Brad Bucknell points out that "The monosyllables that accompany Pat . . . are recapitulated in the 'Tap' of the approaching tuner" (260n56). And Alan Shockley writes that "Pat's presence manifests as a choppy, staccato musical performance: 'Bald deaf Pat brought quite flat pad ink. Pat set with ink pen quite flat pad. Pat took plate dish knife fork. Pat went'" (70). The repeated "wait while you wait" further provides Pat a refrain comparable to the tapped refrain of the blind stripling. And the "hee hee" that shapes the text's play with Pat's deafness infects the representation of the stripling at the end of "Sirens" when the narrator rhymes, "Hee hee hee hee. He did not see" (11.1283).

Third, Pat is linked in at least two additional ways to the tapping that represents the blind piano tuner approaching the bar. After Bloom has given Pat a tip, he becomes "tipped Pat": "Listen. Bloom listened. Richie Goulding listened. And by the door deaf Pat, bald Pat, tipped Pat, listened" (11.1028–29). As Angela Leighton points out, "tipped Pat" roughly "condenses to 'Tap'" (208). Furthermore, Pat's name is "tap" backwards, providing a joky link between the two characters.

Fourth, structural parallels link the depictions of the stripling and Pat. Lorraine Wood notes "Joyce's juxtaposition of the *blind* tuner, who can only be *heard* 'tapping' as he returns to the Ormond to retrieve his tuning fork, and the *deaf* waiter Pat, who can only be *seen* by the clientele" (76, original italics). Bloom serves the stripling by helping him across the street in "Lestrygonians," while Pat serves Bloom as his waiter in "Sirens."[8] And then in "Circe," Pat reenacts the stripling's earlier position on the curb (in "Lestrygonians," "a blind stripling stood tapping the curbstone with his slender cane. No tram in sight. Wants to cross" [8.1075–76]), but instead of waiting to cross, he comically waits to wait: "(Bald pat, bothered beetle, stands on the curbstone, folding his napkin, waiting to wait)" (15.506–7). It is as if the image of Pat on the curb is superimposed, in the filmic text of "Circe," on the previous image of the blind stripling.[9]

A fifth connection between the two characters arises from the phrase "deaf beetle," used in "Sirens" (11.911) and repeated in the "Circe" lines just quoted. "Beetle" may refer in part to Pat's bald shiny head. But the phrase "deaf beetle" is similar to "deaf as a post"—a beetle is a wooden implement for driving wedges or pegs. In this sense one can be called "deaf as a beetle" or "dumb as a beetle," and it signifies a heavy or dull stupidity (*OED*). The derogatory phrase is unusual for the generally compassionate Bloom, but it is possible that Joyce wanted the word to suggest yet another associative link between Pat and the blind stripling: there is a beetle called the death-watch beetle, which makes a *tapping* sound that can be heard on summer nights. The *Oxford English Dictionary* (*OED*) tells us that these beetles are associated with "quiet, sleepless nights and are named for the vigil kept beside the dying or dead, and by extension the superstitious have seen the death watch as an omen of impending death." Bloom is not waiting for a literal death, but he does find his own situation echoed in the line Richie Goulding whistles from a Bellini opera: "all is lost now." His vigil is for the potential death of his marriage, and of course in some ways he is still keeping vigil for Rudy.

These links between the deaf waiter and the blind piano tuner provide further evidence for Danius's claim that in *Ulysses* "the act and means of sensory perception . . . have become problems in their own right" (151). The links turn on the cultural association between the "elite senses" and knowledge discussed in the previous two chapters. Instead of giving the *characters* stereotypical qualities of ignorance, however, Joyce uses them metaphorically to signal a sort of willful not knowing. As I demonstrate below, they work textually to signal Bloom's desire not to know what he does know: that his wife has an assignation with Blazes Boylan at 4:00 p.m. that day.

Disabling Metaphors

This metaphoric use of disability is politically multivalent. On one hand, Joyce does not actually suggest that his characters are removed from the realm of knowledge or communication, as do several writers previously discussed. As Andre Cormier points out, Joyce's blind character is "impressively mobile," taking part in the general odyssey of Dubliners on June 16, 1904 (203).[10] Deaf

Pat jokes with the barmaids, taking part in the general social atmosphere of the bar. They are, that is, more integrated into the fabric of the fictional society than most other blind or deaf characters represented in modern literature. On the other hand, the blind piano tuner is pitied by other characters, and the deaf waiter mocked by the text. *Ulysses* does not convey their points of view; almost everything we know about them comes from Bloom's speculation. In "Wandering Rocks," where several minor characters are granted interiority, the stripling is not. The stripling's taciturnity and the text's mockery of Pat exacerbate the sense that we are viewing them from the outside only.

I agree with Clare Barker and Amy Vidali when they advise that disability studies scholars not reject metaphoric representations of disability out of hand; simply "policing" metaphoric representations is not useful (Vidali 34; Barker 20). Moreover, as James Berger reminds us, all language is metaphorical, figurative: "How can there possibly be signification with no residue of meaning—no connotation, ambiguity, no unconscious or ideological upswellings, no imperatives of genre?" (149).[11] But the textual and semantic dynamics of disability metaphors play an important role in literary representations of disabled characters, and so I would like to pause here to consider metaphorization of "othered" characters. At the most basic level, using characters with disabilities *primarily* as metaphors forecloses their identity as rounded fictional characters; they are reduced to carriers of some meaning extrinsic to them. Major characters, though created out of language that is necessarily figurative, are not turned into metaphors to nearly the same degree; they get to aspire to "reality" or "life." Writing about characters in "great novels," Virginia Woolf noted that "if you think of these books, you do at once think of some character who has seemed to you so real (I do not by that mean so lifelike) that it has the power to make you think not merely of itself, but of all sorts of things through its eyes" ("Mr. Bennett and Mrs. Brown" 200). Characters who function too fully as metaphors do not afford us this opportunity to think "through [their] eyes."

However, characters may be used metaphorically at the same time that they are being portrayed as "real." Bloom himself is a good example. There is hardly a more "real" character in modern fiction. He is famously, relentlessly embodied and we spend several hundred pages in his consciousness. I, at least, come away from *Ulysses* each time I read it thinking of "all sorts of things through [his] eyes." At the same time, his Jewishness functions metaphorically to represent a diffuse sort of exile that reflects and highlights Stephen's disconnection from his "home, [his] fatherland, [and his] church" (*Portrait* 268). As Salman Rushdie has remarked, *Ulysses* "has something of the Kafkaesque, the ability to render the real world metaphorical without stripping it of reality" ("Book").[12]

Moreover, in evaluating the political effects of metaphorization, one might consider both the *content* and the *purpose* of a given metaphor. Turning a fictional character into a metaphor is a form of dehumanization (insofar as a fictional character can be dehumanized). As Jay Dolmage notes, metaphors of disability "often function to hide an individual's humanity" ("Between the Valley" 112).[13] Because disability is already a stigmatized state, "the literary traffic in metaphors often misrepresents or flattens the experience real people have of their own or others' disabilities" (Garland-Thomson, *Extraordinary Bodies* 10). However, the dehumanization can carry more or less force depending on the metaphor's content. For example, when a character with a disability represents a sort of death in life, or a Jewish character represents destruction of the social order, the negative political import is much stronger than when the disabled character signals universal human frailty or the Jewish character represents an invigorating outsider status.

Related to the content or meaning is the purpose of the metaphor, or how it is employed in the text. In *Narrative Prosthesis*, Mitchell and Snyder describe the use of disabled minor characters as a "crutch upon which literary narratives lean for their representational power, disruptive potentiality, and analytical insight" (49). Narratives often use this crutch to shore up by contrast the normalcy or, worse, the humanity of the nondisabled major characters. Mitchell and Snyder point out that narrative tends to use disability as a "master trope of human disqualification" (3). In their discussion of David Wills's "fluid notion of prosthesis," they argue that "the deficient body, by virtue of its insufficiency, serves as a baseline of the articulation of the normal body" (7).[14] Similarly, Garland-Thomson analyzes metaphoric representations of disabled characters that "symbolically free the privileged, idealized figure of the American self from the vagaries and vulnerabilities of embodiment" (*Extraordinary Bodies* 7).

But as these critics are aware, it is also possible to use a disabled character metaphorically not for contrast but to suggest commonality with the nondisabled characters. Joyce uses Bloom's Jewishness this way, since one of the main functions of Bloom's Jewishness is to serve as a sort of objective correlative of Stephen's intellectual and spiritual exile. Joyce's metaphoric use of his blind and deaf characters works like this too: Pat and the stripling signal the suspension of knowledge that Bloom is attempting or experiencing, marking a similarity rather than a disparity. This type of metaphoric use is similar to what Ato Quayson sees in Toni Morrison's use of disabled characters; he writes, "the disabled in literature may trade a series of features with the nondisabled, thus transferring some of their significations to the nondisabled and vice versa" (27).[15]

As metaphorization goes, this is a much less stigmatizing form, which may at times "enhance awareness that disability is a complex, resonant human condition" (C. Barker 20). And in fact Joyce demonstrates his awareness of what we would now call ableism through Bloom's second-guessing of his own dismissive thoughts (discussed below). Lawrence Rainey notes that "much of the ethical character . . . of 'content' consists . . . in complex relations binding content and style to audiences and occasions, to interpretive communities in contingent circumstances" (162). One factor that affects the ethical force of this particular "content" is our knowledge that Joyce was dealing with increasing, intermittent blindness. Critics have seen the stripling as a representation of Joyce himself (Morse, Rainsford, Cormier, Garrington); as Garrington puts it, Joyce may have used the stripling as "a prosthetic extension of his author/creator, probing his way through the text" (107). Our assumption that he sympathizes with the blind character further reduces the negative force of the metaphorization.

However, just as biography is not a reliable indicator of views about politics or gender, Joyce's own experiences with blindness do not guarantee a sympathetic portrayal. Garland-Thomson reminds us that "having been acculturated similarly to everyone else, disabled people also often avoid and stereotype one another in attempting to normalize their own social identities" (*Extraordinary Bodies* 15). Ableism is as easily internalized as sexism or racism, and Joyce could as easily express anger and frustration about his blindness in his portrayal of the blind stripling as empathy with him. In fact, as Gordon Bowker points out, the passage early in *Portrait* about Stephen being made to apologize for wanting to marry a Protestant when he grows up establishes an association of blindness with sin. This linkage of disability with sin, an aspect of what Edward Wheatley has called the "religious model" of disability,[16] actually appears in several places in Joyce's work.

About the scene in *Portrait* where Dante says that if Stephen does not apologize, "the eagles will come and pull out his eyes," Bowker writes:

> This savage remark from this emissary of a vengeful God set up in the mind of the embryonic poet a chanted refrain, the lines repeated over and over, round and around in the mind of the haunted young boy:

> "Pull out his eyes / Apologise / Apologise / Pull out his eyes." If his eyes were weak, which they were, the threat, associating blindness with guilt, must have been only too terrifyingly real. (27–28)

The idea that disability can arise from sin also occurs later in *Portrait* when Stephen thinks about the sibling incest that might have produced the "dwarf" with the "blackish monkey-puckered face" (247). And this idea similarly appears in "Grace," where the narrator describes the usurious Harford: "Though he had never embraced more than the jewish [*sic*] ethical code his fellow Catholics . . . spoke of him bitterly as an Irish Jew and an illiterate and saw divine disapproval of usury made manifest through the person of his idiot son" (*Dubliners* 137).

The antisemitism of this *Dubliners* passage links it, too, to the portrayal of usurer Reuben J. Dodd in *Ulysses*. Dodd's son almost drowned in the Liffey (R. Ellmann, *James Joyce* 38n; Bowker 47), but in one of his appearances in "Circe" Dodd bears "on his shoulders the drowned corpse of his son" (15.1918). In these passages both sin and Jewishness are associated with damage to a son—"idiocy" or death. And disability and the sin of usury are linked in another passage about Dodd in "Circe" where "Reuben J Antichrist" "stumps forward" (this time carrying a son *saved* from drowning) and where his presence gives rise to a "hobgoblin" who is "hipshot, crookbacked, hydrocephalic, prognathic with receding forehead" (15.2146–51).[17] Indeed, figures with various disabilities serve to set the scene for "Circe," where both Bloom and Stephen will confront their psychic guilt. In the first page and a half, we get "stunted men and women," a "deafmute idiot with goggle eyes, his shapeless mouth dribbling," a "pigmy woman," a "gnome," and "a bandy child" as well as a "drunken navvy . . . lurching heavily" (15.5–36). These figures, represented as grotesque, associate disability with the sin and guilt that drive the episode.[18]

In "Lestrygonians," furthermore, Bloom thinks about punishment for sin in an ambiguous statement that seems to refer both to the stripling's blindness and to the disaster of the steamer *General Slocum*: "Where is the justice being born that way? All those women and children excursion beanfeast burned and drowned in New York. Holocaust. Karma they call that transmigration for sins you did in a past life" (8.1145–48). This suggestion is echoed when the blind stripling's curse sounds in "Sirens" just after the barmaids mention him: "—So sad to look on his face, miss Douce condoled. / God's curse on bitch's bastard" (11.284–85). Although the curse is shouted *by* the stripling in "Wandering Rocks," in this context it can appear to refer *to* him as a curse, his blindness a result of a mother's sexual sins. All of this is not to say that

Joyce believed disability actually resulted from sin; but these references make clear he was intrigued by the idea of such a linkage. The representation of the blind stripling, then, should not be assumed to be sympathetic merely because Joyce himself was experiencing blindness.

More important, in any case, are the textual dynamics at play, especially the particular ways in which disability is metaphorized in *Ulysses*, and in the remainder of this chapter I explore these dynamics. Rainey's use of the phrase *interpretive communities* reminds us that communities can be formed *through* metaphoric use of othered characters. Philosopher Ted Cohen has argued that any metaphoric utterance initiates some level of intimacy. He claims that "the maker and the appreciator of a metaphor are drawn closer to one another. Three aspects are involved: (1) the speaker issues a kind of concealed invitation; (2) the hearer expends a special effort to accept the invitation; and (3) this transaction constitutes the acknowledgement of a community" (8).[19]

In the case of the blind stripling and deaf bald Pat, Joyce issues a concealed invitation to his readers to understand deafness and blindness as obstacles to knowledge, as a kind of not knowing or ignorance. When readers recognize that Bloom is trying not to know, and when the presence of the deaf and blind characters adds intensity and pathos to that recognition, we have formed a community of normate readers, in some ways at the expense of the disabled characters. One example is Richard Ellmann's comment that Bloom's "being hamstrung finds sympathetic extrapolation in the piano-tuner who cannot see and the 'bothered' (deaf) waiter" (*Ulysses* 104). Without exploring the import of this metaphor (this "extrapolation"), Ellmann assumes a community of readers who will understand sensory disability as a form of being "hamstrung." As Cohen points out, "intimacy sounds like a good thing. . . . [But] some of the most instructive examples will be ones in which intimacy is sought as a means to a lethal and one-sided effect" (11–12).

Bloom and the Blind Stripling

One of Western culture's most powerful one-sided metaphors is "to see is to know," which, in Vidali's words, "represents blindness as misunderstanding and disorder, while seeing is knowledge and coherence" (34). *Ulysses* invites readers to consider this metaphor in its use of the blind stripling, whose presence in the diegesis prompts in Bloom various thoughts about perception, and whose presence in the text prompts in readers closer attention to the use of sight metaphors in the "Lestrygonians" episode where he first appears. As critics such as Whaley (532–33) and Blamires (74) have remarked, in the scene where Bloom helps the blind stripling across the street, he expresses in his everyday language his interest in some of the same issues that occupy Stephen in "Proteus": the role and meaning of sight.

In "Proteus," although Stephen is inquiring into the relationship between sight and knowledge, he privileges sight as that which makes knowledge possible. When he thinks, "Shut your eyes and see" (3.09), as Louise Hornby points out, he "underscores both the coupling of knowledge and sight, even when it is not delivered through the eyes, and . . . the preeminence of vision in his sensory apparatus" (57). In fact, Stephen waits to confirm that the world is "there all the time without you" (3.27) by opening his eyes (Danius 172). Although in many instances "Bloom's prime modalities seem to be taste and smell" (K. Lawrence 120), his musings on the blind stripling, where he considers how sight relates to the other senses and to the objective world, demonstrate that he too privileges vision. When he wonders, "what dreams would he have, not seeing? Life a dream for him" (8.1144–45), he is endorsing the assumption that reality can be accessed only through sight (the cliché "seeing is believing" articulates this assumption).[20] Like Stephen, Bloom does also wonder about nonvisual perception. He speculates whether one can sense volume and weight without sight, whether a blind person can walk in a straight line without a cane, and what impression of Dublin a blind person must have (8.1108–12). He is prompted toward these meditations, characteristically, not by abstract philosophical speculation but by the presence of another human being.

When he meets the stripling, Bloom solicitously asks him twice if he wants to cross the street, telling him where he is and what street he's facing. The language the text uses to describe the stripling—language associated with Bloom's consciousness via the "Uncle Charles principle"—implies blankness and weakness: "His wallface frowned weakly. He moved his head uncertainly. . . . [Bloom takes] the thin elbow gently: then [takes] the limp seeing hand to guide it forward" (8.1078–79, 1090–91). Here blindness is associated with physical and mental weakness, feminizing the stripling in accordance with the Oedipus-castration link. The stripling's lack of certainty about where he would like to go further marks him as deficient in the type of self-determining masculinity that Joseph Valente describes as endorsed by cultural nationalist movements.[21] Bloom's feminization of the stripling prompts his own chivalrous behavior, although he describes his own penis as "the limp father of thousands" at the end of "Lotus Eaters" (5.571) and is himself described as "limp as a wet rag" by the narrator of "Cyclops" (12.1480).

Here Bloom, then, if not the text itself, is using the stripling to shore up his own masculinity in the sort of prosthetic dynamic Mitchell and Snyder describe.

Bloom nervously thinks about what to say to the stripling, admonishing himself not to "do the condescending" but instead to "pass a common remark" (8.1092–93). He "others" the stripling to the degree that he wonders not what the young man's name might be but "if he has a name" (8.1098–99). When he follows him, he describes this as walking "behind the eyeless feet" (8.1106). Given that all feet are eyeless, this phrase serves to insist upon blindness as the only way to understand the young man. Although it does occur to Bloom that blind people can tune pianos, Joyce does not let readers know that the stripling is a piano tuner until we hear his cane tapping in "Sirens" and the barmaids explain that the blind tuner left his tuning fork behind; here in "Lestrygonians," he is only "the blind stripling." This labeling and the stripling's lack of a proper name are examples of the "normate reductionism" and "nominal displacement" Bolt describes in *The Metanarrative of Blindness* (35ff).

In spite of his "othering" of the blind stripling—or maybe because of it, given his own identity as outsider—Bloom seems to feel an affinity with him. The text indicates this affinity when Bloom thinks, "Dark men they call them" (8.1120). This phrase, though commonly used for blind men, also links the stripling to Bloom, who is a "dark horse" (12.1558) and whose Jewishness places him in the category of "dark men of mien and movement" (2.158–59) described by Stephen earlier. In "Circe" Bloom greets the stripling by calling him "My more than brother!" (15.1600). This sense of likeness prompts Bloom to turn his gaze upon himself, so that in addition to musing about the role of sight, he inquires whether he can perceive himself as a blind man might ("See ourselves as others see us" [8.662]). He feels his hair and belly to see if different textures give rise to a sense of colors and to try, generally, to replicate perception without sight. Like participants in most other disability simulation exercises, Bloom emerges from this exercise without insight into being blind and finishes his thoughts about the stripling on a note of pity and disconnection: "Dear, dear, dear. Pity, of course: but somehow you can't cotton on to them someway" (8.1148–50).[22]

Indeed, Bloom's thoughts about the stripling nicely illustrate what Valerie Brew-Parrish maintains about the results of more structured simulation exercises:

Nondisabled people usually come away from disability simulations

- thinking life is a tragedy for persons with disabilities
- thanking the good Lord they are not saddled with a disability
- or falling prey to the "amazing" syndrome: "Ohhhhh just lookie at what disabled people can do! They're better than us at (getting around in the dark, popping wheelies, reading hand signs . . .)." (n.p.)

Bloom assumes that the stains on the stripling's coat are because he "slobbers his food" (8.1096). He compares being blind to the tragic death by fire of a thousand people, mostly women and children, on the *General Slocum* in 1904: "Poor fellow! Quite a boy. Terrible. Really terrible. . . . Where is the justice being born that way? All those women and children excursion beanfeast burned and drowned in New York. Holocaust" (8.1144–47; Gifford 186). He does not explicitly express a feeling of thankfulness that he himself is sighted, but this is implicit in his pity for the stripling.[23] And he "fall[s] prey to the 'amazing' syndrome" when he says, "Look at all the things they can learn to do. Read with their fingers. Tune pianos" (8.1115–16).

But Bloom's reactions are more complex than this. For one thing, he is making a genuine and spontaneous effort to expand his understanding of perception, to speculate about the perception of blind people rather than assuming they cannot perceive much at all. He also criticizes his own "'amazing' syndrome" comments: "Or we are surprised they have any brains. Why we think a deformed person or a hunchback clever if he says something we might say" (8.1116–17). This second-guessing is an afterthought, both for Bloom and for Joyce, who did not add these two sentences until after the chapter was set in placards (*JJA* 18:143). But it does show an awareness of ableist prejudice (*avant la lettre*) and an effort to correct (though not erase) it. In this effort, Joyce is far more progressive than even some recent critics. Dominic Rainsford, for example, ends his article "Pity in Joyce" this way: "And, somewhere in Dublin, Joyce's blighted and rejected alter ego, Dedalus's dead alias, the poor blind stripling, is still tapping dismally, foul-temperedly, along" (54). Here Rainsford far exceeds Joyce's ableism by associating blindness with blight and rejection and using the blind character, though Joyce does not, as a metaphor for death.

Although to some extent Bloom infantilizes the stripling when he compares his hand to Milly's, saying that it's "like a child's hand," Cormier points out that this can be taken as a moment of connection: "Bloom's infantilizing of the stripling is to be understood in the context of his Odyssean quest to reclaim his fatherhood. This context transforms a seemingly patronizing moment into one of paternal care" (207). Bloom also grants sexuality to the stripling, refusing more common discourses that desexualize people with disabilities. He muses, "The voice, temperatures: when he touches her with his fingers must almost see the lines, the curves" (8.1128–29). Here Bloom insists on sight as a metaphor for all perception ("almost see") while at least acknowledging that the stripling is capable of sexual desire and contact. When he thinks, "And with a woman, for instance. More shameless not seeing" (8.1125), the text performs an ambivalence about heterosexuality and the male gaze.[24] *Shameless* is one of those words that can mean opposing things: it can mean brazen, bold (qualities associated with Boylan), unable or unwilling to feel shame. But it can also signal innocence, implying that something does not *warrant* shame. According to the second meaning, the male sexual gaze is indicted as shameful, while the imagined nonvisual sexuality of the stripling is valued more highly.[25]

Sight, Knowledge, and Time

Beyond Bloom's reactions to the stripling, readers' experience of the episode is affected by the text's use of blindness metaphorically to interact with the themes of knowing and time that pepper the chapter. Although "Lestrygonians" focuses on eating and food, while the eye is the organ of the "Nausicaa" chapter, "Lestrygonians" does at times perform an association of sight with knowledge, blindness with ignorance. And it plays with this association by also making the act of looking serve as a way for Bloom to *avoid* seeing and being seen (Bloom decides to accept Richie Goulding's invitation to come into the Ormond because it is a good place to "see, not be seen" [11.357–58]), and to avoid confronting knowledge and Boylan.

As Cormier points out, though without discussing the implications of using blindness in this way, earlier episodes establish a link between not seeing and not wanting to know. He writes,

> Molly tucks away Boylan's letter after Bloom delivers it to her, entering the bedroom with "halfclosed eyes" (*U* 4.247). There is the sense that Bloom refuses to see the evidence of Molly's affair. Ironically, he preoccupies himself by putting the window blinds up, as if informing his own desire to see, but still feeling the need to turn his back on Molly's reaction to the letter. (215)

In "Lestrygonians" seeing becomes one of the motifs through which the text treats Bloom's wish not to know what will happen that day and his desire to reject the maxim "seeing is believing."

When Bloom enters the Burton restaurant and sees all the men feeding like animals, "his eyes said: //—Not here. Don't see him" (8.694–95). As Derek Attridge argues, the unusual syntax in the phrase "his eyes said"—not so unusual for *Ulysses*—removes subjectivity from the "whole" person and ascribes agency to a body part ("Joyce's Lipspeech" 59). In this case the eyes become the speaker, noting an absence. Seeing is knowing here, and "don't see him" means Boylan is not there. Although Boylan is also represented in this chapter through sounds (jingles), as he is more intensely in "Sirens," this eyespeech alerts readers to the chapter's linkage between seeing and knowing.

One of the ways visuality impinges on Bloom's thoughts in this chapter is through the visual coincidences he notes. Bloom thinks of Parnell, then sees Parnell's brother, whom he describes as "unseeing" (8.500–501). He remembers that one of the women who answered his ad claimed that she had the approval of A. E., and then he sees A. E. (8.525). Bloom's "eyes followed" A. E. and he thinks of him as "dreamy, cloudy, symbolistic" (8.543), prefiguring his assertion that life must be a "dream" for the blind stripling. Then, shortly before he meets the stripling, he starts thinking about seeing and not seeing. This third coincidence is left to readers to notice. As Bloom "crossed at Nassau street corner" he prices field glasses at Yeates and Son. He remembers that "there's a little watch up there on the roof of the bank to test those glasses by. // His lids came down on the lower rims of his irises. Can't see it. If you imagine it's there you can almost see it. Can't see it" (8.562–63).

With its use of a watch as the unseen object, this passage connects time with sight and blindness. Bloom's thoughts about vision continue that association by focusing on the passing sun. "The tip of his little finger blotted out the sun's disk. Must be the focus where the rays cross. If I had black glasses" (8.566–67). (Bloom mentions his uncertainty about the meaning of "parallax" earlier and later in the chapter, wondering if he might ask a priest what it means.) All of these references—from the "unseeing" brother of Parnell to the "black glasses"—set the stage for the musings about blindness sparked by his encounter with the stripling. Finally and crucially, just before he meets the stripling, Bloom thinks, "Today. Today. Not think" (8.1063).[26] The proximity of this admonition to the blind stripling's appearance stresses the metaphoric use of blindness even in a chapter where Bloom thinks about the embodied particulars of the stripling's life. In both chapters where Bloom interacts with characters with sensory disabilities, nearby text highlights his efforts not to know.

After the stripling has moved out of Bloom's sight, the text plays with sight and knowledge, seeing and having to know, as Bloom tries to determine whether he is seeing Boylan and whether Boylan has seen him, and then as he tries to avoid seeing and being seen by Boylan by looking in his pockets. Bloom's clue to Boylan's presence here is visual: "Straw hat in sunlight. Tan shoes. Turnedup trousers. It is. It is. // His heart quopped softly. To the right. Museum. Goddesses. He swerved to the right" (8.1168–69). The following passage emphasizes vision: "Is it? Almost certain. *Won't look.* Wine in my face. Why did I? Too heady. Yes, it is. The walk. *Not see.* Get on" (8.1171–72, italics added). This "not see" primarily refers to Boylan (he doesn't see Bloom) but it can also refer to Bloom himself, serving as a repetition of "won't look," a caution to himself not to look at Boylan.

Visual language permeates the remainder of the episode: "He lifted his eyes. . . . Didn't see me perhaps. Light in his eyes. . . . No, didn't see me. . . . His eyes beating looked steadfastly . . . Look for something I. . . . Busy looking. . . . I am looking for that" (8.1173–88). By repeatedly describing Boylan and Bloom not seeing in this scene, the text associates them both with the blind stripling. The phrase *eyes beating* links Bloom's eyes to his heart, which "quopped" when he first saw Boylan and which he thinks of again as he becomes more agitated: "My heart" (8.1190). In order not to look at Boylan, and in order not to be seen, he bends his head to *look for* something in his pockets. He finds first the Zionist pamphlet, then the potato, his change purse, and finally the soap. So while using *not looking at* Boylan as a form of protection from knowledge, a sort of active talisman similar to the potato and the soap, Bloom uses *looking for* the talisman as a form of protection as well. Bloom's use of both seeing and not seeing as ways to protect himself from unwanted knowledge is paralleled in "Sirens," as I describe below, where both hearing and not hearing can offer protection from the fact that 4:00 p.m. has arrived.

As prefigured by the watch on top of the building, these motifs of sight are related to the more prominent theme of time that runs through the chapter and the entire novel. As Mary Ann Gillies observes, "The tension between clock time and inner time provides the framework for the novel: the clock time gives overt structure to Stephen's and Bloom's wanderings; inner time provides the novel's substance, its psychological portraits" (146). We see the workings of this dynamic in lines such as the following: "How time flies, eh?" (8.602–3). "I was happier then. Or was that I? Or am I now I? . . . Can't bring back time" (8.608–10). "Time going on. Hands moving. Two. Not yet" (8.791). "Then about six o'clock I can. Six. Six. Time will be gone then. She" (8.852–53). In his discussion of Bloom's deferral of eating in "Lestrygonians," subheaded "can't bring back time," James McMichael points out "Bloom's resistance to the time it takes for bad things to happen" (179–80).

To an extent, then, not seeing signifies a suspension of time as well as knowledge. Bloom wishes (ambivalently) that four o'clock would never come. He is constantly aware of time passing, of the hour two giving way to three and then to four. He is calculating when he can go home again after Molly's tryst (six o'clock, though he ends up staying out much later), and describes that hour as a time when "time will be gone." This line implies that when the deed has been done, there will be no more waiting and dreading, and so for him, there will in a sense be no more time passing. This feeling is confirmed when he discovers, in "Nausicaa," that his watch stopped at half past four: "What that just when he, she? // O, he did. Into her. She did. Done" (13.848–49).

When Bloom says about the watch on the rooftop, "if you imagine it's there you can almost see it" (8.562–63), he points to the power of will over reality. This is the possibility with which Bloom struggles in both "Lestrygonians" and "Sirens" when he thinks about, hears, or sees Boylan. Can he stop time? Can he change fate? Ought he to try? The use of sight imagery in "Lestrygonians," including the section about the blind stripling, suggests that vision and time are similarly subjective. Gillies and others have shown the influence of Bergson's concept of *durée* on modernists and on Joyce in particular.[27] For Bergson, as for Bloom here, time is not a mechanical progression but a "layered simultaneity synthesizing past and present" (Hornby 55). Bloom's interest in the subjective nature of time interacts with his exploration of the subjective nature of vision, of "seeing as"—seeing yourself as others see you, seeing Boylan as a menacing straw hat, seeing a bar of soap as protection, seeing a blind stripling as "my more than brother!" (15.1600).

This line from "Circe" reinforces the association between Bloom and the stripling that is metaphorically forged in "Lestrygonians." The line alludes to Tennyson's "In Memoriam" (Gifford 477), where the speaker asserts that his friend is more dear to him than his brothers, and more like: "But thou and I are one in kind, / As moulded like in Nature's mint." The likeness between Bloom and the blind stripling, the text suggests, consists in the complex relations among sight and perception, knowledge and time—and in Bloom's attempt to defer sight and its metaphoric accompaniment, knowledge.

Deaf Pat and the Suspension of Knowledge

Deafness appears in *Ulysses* just when Bloom's attempt not to know what he knows is reaching its peak: the time of Molly's assignation with Blazes Boylan has nearly arrived. "Not yet. At four, she said. Time ever passing.

Clockhands turning. On" (11.187–88). As Karen Lawrence comments, in "Sirens" "the prose bides its time, Bloom bides his time; both gestures make us aware of what is not confronted" (41). The power of delay is emphasized when Miss Douce, about to smack her garter, waits, building up suspense and desire: "Delayed. Taunted them still, bending, suspending, with willful eyes" (11.410–11). This pattern of suspension traverses the episode, signaled by a conjunction between motifs of waiting and deafness.

Joyce gives us a model of the dynamic I am outlining toward the opening of the chapter when the barmaids are gossiping together. So as not to hear what Miss Douce is saying, Miss Kennedy "plug[s] both two ears with little fingers. —No, don't, she cried. —I won't listen, she cried. . . . Miss Douce grunted in [the tone of the "old fogey" in Boyd's chemist]. Miss Kennedy unplugged her ears to hear, to speak" (11.129–36). "The plugging and unplugging of the ears, the refusal and yet the willingness to listen" (Valente, *James Joyce* 229), parallel Bloom's fraught relationship with his knowledge of Molly's tryst. Like Miss Kennedy here, Bloom is suspended between refusing and desiring to know, as the text now shifts to representing hearing as the dominant means of gaining knowledge.

While he waits for the fateful hour of four o'clock, Bloom has a meal in the bar of the Ormond Hotel with his acquaintance (and Stephen Dedalus's uncle) Richie Goulding. Their waiter, "deaf bald Pat," is first named in the chapter's overture. The text associates Pat with Bloom first in that he is a waiter who waits while Bloom waits. The narrator or Bloom giggles at this in the overture and then again in the main body of the chapter. "Bald Pat who is bothered mitred the napkins. Pat is a waiter hard of his hearing. Pat is a waiter who waits while you wait. Hee hee hee hee. He waits while you wait. Hee hee. A waiter is he. Hee hee hee hee. He waits while you wait. While you wait if you wait he will wait while you wait" (11.915–19).

It's not clear to what extent this laughter is focalized by Bloom. Richard Ellmann describes the episode as containing an "unknown composer [who] interpolates stray notes at will in Bloom's reflections" (*Ulysses* 109); Dermot Kelly describes a "third voice, in the form of mocking, musical echoes, [serving] to offset the components of the initial style" (26). This repetitive, second-person merriment seems to be one of the interpolations, coming from the mocking musical voice.[28] If we accept Valente's reading, that the real siren song is "a delirious, mellifluent, derisive bout of laughter directed at a prototypical male voyeur, whom the disporting narrative voice insists upon confusing with Bloom" (*James Joyce* 229), then one way to read the laughter at Pat is to assume that the text itself—or the "composer"—is one of the Sirens.[29] As a waiter Pat is associated with Bloom's anxious waiting. And he is also associated with Molly waiting for Boylan. When Bloom sees that Boylan is still in the Ormond bar as 4:00 p.m. approaches, he thinks, "Has he forgotten? Perhaps a trick. Not come: whet appetite. I couldn't do. Wait, wait. Pat, waiter, waited" (11.392–93).[30] Here, replicating the suspense built up by the barmaid waiting to snap her garter, Pat waits on Bloom, who is waiting to be betrayed by Molly, who is waiting for Boylan.

Boylan is represented throughout this episode through sound: his shoes creak identifiably on the floor of the pub, and his car jingles up to the pub and then, in Bloom's or the text's imaginative inner hearing, through the city to Bloom and Molly's house. So a primary way that deafness works in "Sirens" is as metaphorical protection against the knowledge these sounds bring. And conversely, hearing means knowledge Bloom is trying to suppress. When Boylan leaves the bar, the text reads, "Jingle a tinkle jaunted. // Bloom heard a jing, a little sound. He's off. Light sob of breath. . . . Jingling. He's gone. Jingle. Hear" (11.456–58). The final word, *Hear*, stresses that the route to misery here—as in the Shakespearean poison poured in the "porches of their ears" (9.465)—is through the ear. In "Sirens," to hear is to know.

In fact, the association between hearing and misery or danger may suggest an alternative way to interpret the dangerous siren song of the chapter: perhaps the siren song is the music of Boylan's approach to Molly. This suggestion goes against the grain, of course; the Sirens are generally taken to be the barmaids, and the song generally taken to be the music of the Ormond bar or of the chapter itself. Jules Law points out, moreover, that the women of the viceregal cavalcade present additional Sirens and that Boylan "plays the bound Odysseus to the viceregal Sirens" in "Wandering Rocks" (161). But the possibility remains that the jingles could constitute the alluring siren song. After all, Bloom is dangerously lured by Boylan's jingles, as his voyeuristic fantasy in "Circe" demonstrates, while staying metaphorically tied to the mast (in the pub) as Boylan heads off to the Blooms' bedroom. This reading also leads to the intriguing possibility that in spite of Boylan's hypermasculinity, the text is feminizing him by associating him with a Siren. Like the strand of the text that has Bloom, as the outsider horse Throwaway, triumphing over Boylan's "big red brute of a thing" (18.144), or Sceptre, this reading would also suggest that Bloom's woman-manliness will not be conquered by Boylan's manly façade.

In addition to making deafness a metaphor for protection against the knowledge of betrayal, Joyce turns the tables on the metaphor "to hear is to know," suggesting that *hearing* can serve as protection from knowledge as well. In the Bellini opera *La Sonnambula* (which contains the line "all is lost now"), the heroine condemns her lover as faithless because he will not "deign to hear" her (Gifford 292). This phrase brings together deafness and betrayal, suggesting that hearing might bring about reconciliation. And the phrase "tipped Pat" links deafness to betrayal by association with Boylan, who will soon be "tipping her tepping her tapping her topping her" (11.706–7).

Forging another link between hearing and protected ignorance, deafness and knowledge, the text inserts information about Boylan's car within lines about Pat's deafness: "Pat! Doesn't hear. Deaf beetle he is. Car near there now. Talk. Talk. Pat! Doesn't" (11.911–12). Here Bloom is prevented from using his hearing to keep his mind off his predicament because people are not talking, and this state of not hearing leads to unwanted knowledge of the proximity of Boylan's car to Bloom's house and Molly's body. Karen Lawrence suggests that readers too are put into a state of symbolic deafness when the text mishears its own phrases and repeats them with a difference. Lawrence focuses on the process by which "exquisite contrast" becomes "inexquisite contrast" and "with the greatest alacrity" becomes "with grace of alacrity." She calls this "deaf-eared transcribing," suggesting that "instead of the absolute pitch we might expect to find in the chapter about music, we find much less than perfect hearing. At times we seem to be in the same unfortunate predicament as Bald deaf Pat who 'seehears lipspeech'" (38).[31] Although this at first seems persuasive, such linguistic play as the chapter enacts depends on readers' ability to hear, and therefore to be able to play with, the sounds of words. As Lawrence herself notes, the chapter emphasizes "the phonetic rather than the semantic characteristics of words" (38). This emphasis interpellates readers as hearing subjects.[32]

This playful table-turning is one of the ways Joyce demonstrates his awareness of the metaphoric use of deafness. By listening to music, Bloom is able to distract himself from the approaching betrayal: "Wish they'd sing more. Keep my mind off" (11.914). As Stuart Allen observes, "musicality in *Ulysses* allows readers to experience one of music's most striking effects—distraction" (442). Further, the line Allen uses as his title, "thinking strictly prohibited," returns to the blind stripling to draw together hearing, not seeing, and not thinking. Just after the blind stripling "walk[s] tapping by the tap the curbstone tapping, tap by tap" (11.1190), Bloom thinks about "enthusiasts." He describes them as "All ears. . . . Eyes shut. Head nodding in time. Dotty. . . . Thinking strictly prohibited" (11.1192–94). Linking hearing ("all ears") and blindness ("eyes shut") to the prohibition of thought turns the text away from the metaphor that links Pat to the prohibition of knowledge—to hear is to know—and returns it to the metaphor more dominant in "Lestrygonians"—to see is to know.

At the same time, Bloom's attempts not to hear Boylan's progress toward Molly continue to associate him with Pat's deafness, and this conjunction is bolstered by the ways in which Bloom's identity merges with Pat's. Bloom's identity is in question from the beginning of the episode, where the first mention of him is "Bloowho" (11.86). He also merges with the greasy chemist the barmaids are laughing about ("Greasabloom" [11.185]) and with Simon Dedalus and the Lionel character ("Siopold!" [11.752]). Hugh Kenner points out that such mergers are a function of a musical chord: "Music, which can pour many notes into a chord, can fuse souls, fuse identities" (*Ulysses* 92). The music of the text also merges Bloom with Pat. Consider the line "Talk. Talk. Pat! Doesn't." On the surface this is shorthand for "doesn't hear" from earlier in the same passage; but it also raises the question of whether Pat speaks. When Bloom is ready to leave the Ormond and asks Pat how much he owes, the text remains ambiguous about who is speaking aloud: "Much? He seehears lipspeech. One and nine. Penny for yourself. Here. Give him twopence tip. Deaf, bothered" (11.1001–3). This line probably describes Pat "seehear[ing] lipspeech," but by leaving the referent of the pronoun unspecified, the text makes it possible for us to imagine that Pat, like many deaf people, does not speak, but mouths words, leaving Bloom to lipread Pat rather than the other way around. This ambiguity serves as an example of Derek Attridge's claim that "bodily displacements and substitutions are enacted in the displacements and substitutions of language" ("Joyce's Lipspeech" 64).

The possibility that Pat doesn't speak could also be implied by Bloom's comment, "Lot of ground he must cover in the day. Paint face behind on him then he'd be two" (11.914–15): then he would have two faces that do not speak, two "dummy" faces.[33] The image of Pat having two faces further indicates his doubling in Bloom. In a loose page of a "Sirens" draft held in the National Library of Ireland, Bloom thinks instead about painting a face on the back of Richie Goulding's head. The draft passage reads, "Quite bald he is behind. You could paint a second face there for a lark. Thing he'd do himself, then he'd be looking both ways. There is some God" (NLI MS 36,639/7/B). The reference to "some God" suggests Janus, the two-faced Roman god of gates and doors, beginnings and endings.[34] The presence of Janus in the draft passage calls attention to Pat's position in the doorway (11.671–72, 1028–29), a position Leighton makes much of in her essay about listening and thresholds. She concludes that Pat's listening at the door raises the question "What does it mean to listen, without hearing, and therefore with a kind of unfinished expectation? Perhaps that is exactly what is required of us, readers of texts: to listen 'behind a door,' through the difficulties and obstructions of language" (208). Not only does Pat's liminal position as listener parallel readers' work listening to and for "Sirens," but it also underscores the larger issues of unstable identity that run throughout the chapter.

When Bloom walks toward the door, the text gives us another phrase that could be applicable to either Pat or Bloom: "By deaf Pat in the doorway straining ear Bloom passed" (235). Here we assume that the "straining ear" is Pat's, but it could also be that Bloom is straining to hear the music from the other room as he leaves the bar. The line is ambiguous, playfully merging Bloom and Pat into a single entity. And it is the music that, enlisting Bloom's hearing to keep him suspended in a state of not having to know, most fully fuses Bloom with Pat. As Simon Dedalus sings a song from the opera *Martha* in which Lionel laments his lost love, Bloom and Pat merge: "The voice of Lionel returned, weaker but unwearied. It sang again to Richie Poldy Lydia Lidwell also sang to Pat open mouth ear waiting, to wait. How first he saw that form endearing, how sorrow seemed to part, how look, form, word charmed him Gould Lidwell, won Pat Bloom's heart" (11.717–20).[35] Bloom and Pat become "Pat Bloom," hearing and not hearing the music, waiting with trepidation, knowing and not knowing what is about to happen.

Bloom's mutable identity can be compared to the fluctuating representation of Pat's deafness. Although he is called "deaf," "bothered," and "deaf beetle," and Bloom remarks to himself that Pat "doesn't hear," Pat is also represented as listening and hearing. When first introduced, he comes at the sound of a bell (11.286–87). He soon whispers with one of the barmaids (11.318–19). When Bloom asks him for pen and blotting pad, Bloom thinks, "He heard, deaf Pat" (11.823). And Pat listens to music: "And by the door deaf Pat, bald Pat, tipped Pat, listened" (11.1028–29). We can conclude either that Pat is hard of hearing ("hard of hear by the door," as the text puts it [11.671]) or that Joyce is playing with deafness more as a device than a realistic representation. Is Pat "deaf" the way Bloom, who has been baptized three times, is "Jewish"? Perhaps his shifting identity seeps into Bloom's, with his liminal state between hearing and not hearing an echo of Bloom's suspension between knowing and not knowing.

Music, the central theme and structuring device of the episode, offers Bloom the distraction he craves, as he confirms when he "wish[es] they'd sing more" to "keep [his] mind off." The musical overture that opens the chapter parallels the half-knowing Bloom is attempting. Karen Lawrence describes the overture as "an incomplete and abbreviated transcription of reality" (34), and Bloom's desire here is to inhabit such an incomplete reality. When we think about the relationship of the episode's form to Bloom's state of mind, his desire not to know, we might see in a new way the type of music Joyce associated with this chapter: the fugue or *fuga per canonem*. A fugue is "a polyphonic composition constructed on one or more short subjects or themes, which are harmonized according to the laws of counterpoint" (*OED*). Critics have debated whether the chapter really resembles either of these musical forms, with manuscripts discovered in 2001 confirming that Joyce did intend the episode to correspond to the parts of a fugal composition (Groden, "National Library of Ireland" esp. 11–13; Ferrer; and Brown).[36] Joyce wrote to a friend that the chapter is "a fugue with all musical notations: *piano*, *forte*, *rallentando*, and so on" (Martin 281); *rallentando*, like *ritardando*, means to slow down, decrease in tempo. This slowing relates the form of the chapter back to the suspension discussed earlier, the way the chapter emphasizes delay and a reluctance to confront reality.

And there is another meaning for *fugue*: a mental state in which a person flees from his own identity, a state that often involves "travel to some unconsciously desired locality" (*OED*). The word *fugue* in this sense was first used in 1901 as part of a description of hysteria. Perhaps what Bloom wants is not just to hear music and keep his mind off, but to go into a *fugue state*, where he would be fully protected from the knowledge he has but does not want, not only about Molly's acts of adultery but also about his own identity as a cuckold who stays away from home lest he interrupt his wife's tryst. And insofar as music is the device of psychic distraction, the fugue state is fused with the fugue form.

Pat's deafness works in the associative way meanings come together in *Ulysses*. His status as waiter, especially a waiter whose family may be waiting for him at home, highlights Bloom's state of waiting for the dreaded thing to happen at his home. His deafness, through its contradictory relationship to knowledge and its uncertain relationship to music, becomes an analogue to Bloom's state of suspended knowledge and identity. Both of the elite senses work in this chapter to signify an effort to protect against knowledge. Much as Odysseus stopped his men's ears so they would not be susceptible to the Sirens' song, in "Sirens" Joyce plays with ideas about hearing and seeing, deafness and blindness, to protect Bloom, intermittently and with poignant inefficacy, from hearing the siren song of Boylan's jingles as he approaches 7 Eccles St., and from seeing himself as others see him—as a cuckold who submits to his wife's affair as to fate.

In his playful manipulations of these ideas about the senses and knowledge, Joyce demonstrates a self-consciousness about disability representation that many of his contemporaries lacked. I would not, however, go nearly as far as Cormier does when he ascribes to Joyce a "disability consciousness" that enabled him "summarily to defend disability against the parties who abuse its symbolic properties in order to define normalcy" (204). Joyce too "abuses the symbolic properties" of sensory disability—the difference is that *Ulysses* demonstrates an awareness of this abuse. One can read the textual dynamics of *Ulysses* as subverting the metaphoric association of the elite senses with knowledge; but one also has to acknowledge that a portion of the power and pathos of the portrayal of Bloom trying to escape his own knowledge comes from that very association. The text's mirroring of Bloom with deaf and blind characters paradoxically both relegates them to the margins—they serve primarily to give us insight into Bloom's mental processes—and brings them from the margins into the center of the novel, as their metaphoric deafness and blindness help delineate the core of Bloom's emotional experience. Joyce's manipulations of sensory disabilities' relationships with knowledge, then, form part of his modernist project of questioning how bodies shape our interactions with our world.

Five

Deformity and Modernist Form

deformity—
—to be deciphered (a horn, a trumpet!)
an elucidation by multiplicity
—William Carlos Williams, *Paterson*

In H. G. Wells's *The Island of Doctor Moreau* (1896), Edward Prendick is startled when, disoriented from hunger and dehydration after a shipwreck, he meets a "misshapen man" with a "crooked back" and a "singularly deformed" face (6). This man serves as an assistant to a doctor called Montgomery, who has saved Prendick's life. Later Prendick joins Montgomery and Moreau on their deserted island and discovers that Moreau has been attempting to create humans out of animals; the "misshapen man" is one of the most successful. Although all of these creatures are nonhuman, Prendick repeatedly compares them to disabled and deformed human beings. Before he has discovered Moreau's intentions, he wonders how to understand the bits and pieces he has seen and heard: "What could it all mean? A locked enclosure on a lonely island, a notorious vivisector, and these crippled and distorted men?" (24). Even after Moreau explains his purpose ("to make a rational creature of my own"), Prendick uses general antipathy to "cripples" to invite readers to sympathize with his situation: "Imagine yourself surrounded by all the most horrible cripples and maniacs it is possible to conceive, and you may understand a little of my feelings with these grotesque caricatures of humanity about me" (43–44). While labeling the creatures "monstrosities," he notes that "some [are] almost human save in their subtle expression and gestures, some like cripples, some so strangely distorted as to resemble nothing but the denizens of our wildest dreams" (69). The image of the deformed or crippled human being serves Prendick as the transitional figure between the human and the nonhuman, a way to understand the uncanny experience of interacting with the Beast People.

Over time Prendick becomes more used to the Beast People and "a thousand things which had seemed unnatural and repulsive speedily became natural and ordinary to me. I suppose everything in existence takes its colour from the average hue of our surroundings" (63–64). He begins to question the form of his own, formerly normate body: "Most striking . . . was the disproportion between the legs of these creatures and the length of their bodies; and yet—so relative is our idea of grace—my eye became habituated to their forms, and at last I even fell in with the persuasion that my own long thighs were ungainly" (62). By the time he finally returns to London at the end of the novella, his ideas of what is "normal" have shifted. Having seen Moreau's failure to create rational beings, he now doubts that there is a "reasonable soul" (103) within actual human beings. The distinction between humans and animals has broken down, and he even feels himself to be "an animal tormented with some strange disorder in its brain" (103). Wells's exploration of Prendick's feeling that the disfigured Beast Man *c'est moi* may be said to accelerate the exploration of "normal" and "abnormal" bodily configurations found in earlier texts such as Mary Shelley's *Frankenstein* and extended in the literature discussed in this chapter.

The Gothic novel had long inquired into the affinity and even occasionally the interchangeability between the self and the monstrous other. In her introduction to a collection of essays on disability in Gothic literature, Ruth Anolik writes that "the Gothic presents human difference as monstrous, and then, paradoxically, subverts the categories of exclusion to argue for the humanity of the monster" (2). Studies of nineteenth- and early twentieth-century freak shows similarly stress the paradoxical feeling of interchangeability between the audience and the freaks. Rachel Adams, for example, notes that freaks were disturbing because "they reminded the spectator of all the ways she wasn't quite normal" (194).[1] Writing about her own use of "freaks," Flannery O'Connor notes that "it is when the freak can be sensed as a figure for our essential displacement that he attains some depth in literature" (*Mystery* 45).

This interest in the fragility of the boundary between normal and deformed gathered additional meaning for modernists who were engaged in a process of de-forming the novel and who were at the same time being linked to deformity and degeneracy by Nazi art historians and eugenic discourses more generally. Helen Deutsch describes deformity as "a fall from form written by God or nature on the body" (52). In this chapter I discuss three texts whose authors engaged such falls from form as they considered and revised modernist experimentation from the vantage of the 1930s. As John Whittier-Ferguson writes about Woolf and others, modernist writing of this decade was self-consciously reassessing earlier experiments in light of the writers' growing awareness of their bodies as mortal (*Mortality* 1). Their heightened awareness of the body can be seen in their interest in deformed bodies; and as Siebers remarks of modern visual artists, their "experimentation with aesthetic form reflects a desire to experiment with human form" (*Disability Aesthetics* 10).

Tyrus Miller describes late modernist texts: "Precisely in their untimeliness, their lack of symmetry and formal balance, they retain the power to transport their readers and critics 'out of bounds'" (13). A similar lack of symmetry and balance can be seen in the bodies of characters with deformed feet, a curved spine, or "the wrong shoulder higher than the right" that we find in the texts considered here. Indeed, while modernism generally was and is associated with deformity, deforming takes on special resonance in the 1930s when what modernists aimed to unform or deform were not only traditional forms such as the Victorian and Edwardian novel but also (in different ways and for different reasons) the "high modernism" of the 1920s.

In *Spleen* (1930), Olive Moore associates deformity with women's modernism, which she disparages, while nevertheless representing a deformed body in her attempt to supersede the work of other women modernists. Singling out Woolf and Katherine Mansfield for critique, Moore seems especially to target women's modernism of the teens and twenties. Woolf, for her part, after establishing a relation between writing and deformity in earlier texts, revisits deformity in *The Years* (1937). In this novel, where she tentatively and temporarily turns her back on her earlier experimental techniques, Woolf considers the relation between the deformed body and what she saw as the damaged state of the modernist imagination. In the "Shem the Penman" chapter of *Finnegans Wake* (1939), Joyce takes his literary experimentation to a new extreme, revaluing the deformed body as the body of the modernist text. Each of these writers self-consciously links modernist formal experiments to bodily deformity. But only Joyce goes so far as to celebrate deformity in a carnivalesque description of the deformed body of the writer as the body of modernism.

Modernism as Deformity

Modernism's relationship to bodily deformity was shaped by the efforts of modernist authors to de-form the novel. While the dominant rhetoric describing modernist aesthetics calls for newness, breaking with tradition, and getting closer to reality, there is a thin but durable strand of rhetoric about modernist art—from its own time and from ours—that uses deformity as a model for the reshaping modernists set out to perform on traditional art forms. We find Marinetti, for example, writing that art must "detach itself from reality, from photography, from the graceful and solemn. It must become antigraceful, deforming, impressionistic, synthetic, dynamic, freewording" (qtd. in Lewis 81). Franz Kafka commented that Picasso "registers the deformities which have not yet penetrated our consciousness" (Janouch 143), and Stein asserted similarly that "Picasso said once that he who created a thing is forced to make it ugly. In the effort to create the intensity and the struggle to create this intensity, the result always produces a certain ugliness" (9). In a manifesto about "Negro art" Tristan Tzara asserts that "through purity we have first deformed and then decomposed the object, we have approached its surface, we have penetrated it" (Kolocotroni, Goldman, and Taxidou 281). Samuel Beckett wrote about Proust's manipulations of temporality that "there is no escape from yesterday because yesterday has deformed us, or been deformed by us. The mood is of no importance. Deformation has taken place" (Kolocotroni, Goldman, and Taxidou 451). The notion of deforming the contours of what has come before serves as another way to express modernist efforts to "make it new."

Those who were disgusted with modernism used rhetoric of deformity even more persistently. Adolf Hitler, for example, remarked in a 1935 speech that it "is not the mission of art . . . to wallow in filth for filth's sake, to paint the human being only in a state of putrefaction, to draw cretins as symbols of motherhood, or to present deformed idiots as representatives of manly strength" (qtd. in Farago 25). This assertion was displayed on the wall of the Degenerate Art Exhibit of 1937 (Farago 25), where Hitler again attacked modernist painters as having "eyesight deformation" that caused them to see Germans as "rotten cretins; who, on principle, see meadows blue, skies green, clouds sulphur yellow, and so on" (Kolocotroni, Goldman, and Taxidou 562). Hitler pretended to take seriously the possibility of a physical eye "deformity" when he claimed that the "eye deformation" might either be mechanical or inherited and when he said that these artists "quite obviously suffer from an eye disease" (Kolocotroni, Goldman, and Taxidou 562). But his conflation between an eye disease and an insistence on seeing reality in the wrong colors "on principle" demonstrates that he was using the ideas of deformity and disease more for their rhetorical power than for any pretension to accuracy. As Siebers comments, "Hitler's remarks on the modernist palette exemplify the tendency to associate invention in modern art with human impairment" (*Disability Aesthetics* 35).

In a 1937 speech Hitler further "contrasted the new heroic human type represented in the 1936 Olympic Games and Nazi art to the modernist 'degenerate' vision of mankind as monstrous, bestial 'deformed cripples and cretins.' . . . The rhetoric he uses in this speech underlines the conflation fascism endorsed between art and reality, as well as the constant slippage between physical and metaphorical bodies" (J. Barker 34). In these comments, Hitler was drawing on connections between modernist art and bodily deformity made by Nazi art historian Paul Schultze-Naumburg. In his 1928 book *Kunst und Rasse* (*Art and Race*), Schultze-Naumburg displayed ten pages of modernist paintings by artists such as Picasso and Modigliani juxtaposed with photographs of disabled and anomalously formed human beings (106–15). And in a 1932 essay entitled "Bodily Deformations," Schultze-Naumburg wrote that "the one thing this whole art movement seems to have in common is that each work starts to become interesting only if it evokes images of degenerate representatives of humanity or severe bodily deformations" (Wulf 338).[2] As Neil Levi argues,

> If we take Schultze-Naumburg's *Art and Race* as our paradigm, the contours of the Nazi conception of degenerate art (*entartete Kunst*) seem clear: a condemnation of modernism as the wrong kind of representation of the wrong kind of bodies; a racial, eugenic, and biopolitical notion that takes us directly from the expropriation and destruction of paintings and sculptures deemed degenerate to the elimination of life deemed unfit to live. (50)

While modernist artists and critics saw deformity as a rhetorical tool that could describe their transformation of past forms, antimodernist and Nazi critics used the murderous ableism of eugenic thought to express their scorn for avant-garde artworks.[3]

Contemporary critics continue to weave the rhetoric of deformity into their descriptions of modernist aesthetics. Miller writes that late modernist texts come "lame-footed and stuttering into the world" while distinguishing them from the earlier "fractious modernist monster" (6, 11). Danius writes that the ambitions of the modernist text are "monstrous" (26). Richard Murphy writes about the Expressionists that they "shun the conventionally beautiful in favor of the ugly, the deformed, the squalid, the diseased, and the insane" (202). Descriptions of avant-garde painting in particular draw upon this rhetoric. In a discussion of Picasso, Peter Nicholls writes that the archaic and the modern conjoined to create "a network of desires capable of deforming representation from within" (118).[4] And rhetoric of deformity is regularly applied to Joyce, especially in descriptions of *Finnegans Wake*. Finn Fordham writes, for example, that "incestuous desire around [the daughter/sister character] Issy becomes an explanation for the idea that the deformed language of the *Wake* is deformed because it's always trying to shove something out of sight" (Introduction, xx). In *Finnegans Wake*, Seamus Deane notes, we find "deformations of the English language and the traditional form of the novel" (28–29) as "the English language is dismembered and yet reinvigorated" (39).[5]

Although Woolf uses the words "twisted and deformed" negatively in *A Room of One's Own* to describe work that did not "get . . . expressed whole and entire," she does use rhetoric of the non-able body when she describes the newness of modernist writing. In "Mr. Bennett and Mrs. Brown," she warns that for modernists to break new artistic ground, there will be "cost of life [and] limb," sounds of "breaking and falling, crashing and destruction." She admonishes her audience to

> reconcile ourselves to a season of failures and fragments. We must reflect that where so much strength is spent on finding a way of telling the truth the truth itself is bound to reach us in rather an exhausted and chaotic condition. Ulysses, Queen Victoria, Mr. Prufrock—to give Mrs. Brown some of the names she has made famous lately—is a little pale and dishevelled by the time her rescuers reach her. . . . Tolerate the spasmodic, the obscure, the fragmentary, the failure. (211)

Cautioning us to expect loss of limb, for example, or to expect to find truth "exhausted," "pale and disheveled," to accept "the spasmodic," Woolf stops just short of asking us to accept art that will look, to minds accustomed to the shapeliness of Arnold Bennett's novels, "twisted and deformed." This stopping short is important to a reading of Woolf's engagement with deformity because it is replicated, on a larger level, in *The Years*, where the character who most resembles the author, the artist figure, is herself "twisted and deformed."

Deformity, then, is relevant to modernist art in several ways. Modernist artists set out to deform genres and forms; critics used and still use rhetoric of deformity to describe modernist aesthetics; Nazi discourse about art associated modernism with deformed human beings; and modernist fiction represented deformed characters, such as those examined here. Mitchell and Snyder suggest that

> because canonical modernism openly embraced definitions of twentieth-century culture as inherently alienated and fragmented, its narrative method forthrightly sought out working symbols of this degraded malaise. Yeats's "rough beast" in "Slouching towards Bethlehem" announced the arrival of a moment that would find its most powerful expression in the perversion and contortion of physical and literary form themselves. (*Narrative Prosthesis* 145)

Building on this observation, I argue that deformity serves Moore, Woolf, and Joyce as a means to reflect on modernist formal innovations from the vantage of the 1930s. In what follows I explore the relationship between characters with deformities—Richard in *Spleen*, Sara in *The Years*, and Shem in the "Shem the Penman" chapter of *Finnegans Wake*—and broader issues of deformity and form as they relate to each particular fiction.

The Womb in the Forehead: *Spleen*

Olive Moore, whose given name was Constance Vaughan, though until recently almost unknown, was a respected writer in Bloomsbury in the 1930s. A reporter for the *London Daily Sketch*, she was part of "Charles Lahr's Red Lion Street Circle, a literary group that gravitated towards a bookstore specializing in radical literature located at 68 Red Lion Street, Holborn" (*Collected Writings* 422–23).[6] Moore's 1930 novel *Spleen* was reviewed favorably in publications such as the *Times Literary Supplement*, the *New York Times*, and *Twentieth Century*, and she published two other novels, *Celestial Seraglio* (1929) and *Fugue* (1932), and a collection of short essays and aphorisms, *The Apple Is Bitten Again* (1934), the reviews of which were more mixed. Moore mentions in an author's note that she studied art in Italy and literature at the Sorbonne (*Collected Writings* 421). She was well read in English and French literature; of her contemporaries, she was frustrated by Mansfield and Woolf while admiring Lawrence and Joyce. Her dense and intricate style can be off-putting, but she is now the focus of growing critical inquiry, as scholars begin to explore her fascinating aesthetic experiments and political idiosyncrasies.[7]

In *Spleen* (published in the United States as *Repentance at Leisure*), Moore represents an upper-class English woman, Ruth, who, upon giving birth to a son with deformed feet and a "vacant" stare, leaves her husband and goes into exile on an Italian island with the baby, Richard.[8] There she stays for twenty-two years, hiring others to look after her son and only sitting with him in the evenings. She returns to England when her husband, Stephen, has died, just long enough to dispose of his estate. Ruth feels that her son's deformity is her fault. Her exile is meant as penance for her crime: denying her pregnancy as such and trying instead to create something "new and rare" (47). The novel is nonlinear—with memories of her time in England interrupting the Italian present without warning—and elliptical, allowing readers to get their bearings only slowly as the story unfolds. As the reviewer for the *New York Evening Post* describes it, "Rather than construct a plot, Miss Moore has allowed her story . . . to unfold itself, as thoughts unfold themselves in the mind" (Seaver).

As I detail below, Ruth rejects her pregnancy as ordinary reproduction and seeks to create, rather than beget, "something worth having. Something beyond and above it all. . . . Something new" (28). She "ask[s] of life a new form" (58). In so doing, she links her creation—Richard—with modernist art. Richard's body becomes an analogue for an artwork or literary text. Renée Dickinson writes that "Ruth's desire to create something new with her body correlates directly to the modernist impulse to make it new" (22).[9] This raises the following questions: how do Richard's deformity and mental disability relate to art or literature? If Ruth's experiment has failed, why has it failed, and how can we understand its failure in terms of modernist literary experiment?

To begin to answer these questions, it is helpful to explore Ruth's relationships to maternity and creation, and Moore's representations, in *Spleen* and elsewhere, of deformity—especially relating to legs and feet—and of women's role in artistic production. What we find, I argue, is that women's writing is cast as a monstrous distortion of women's reproduction, and Richard's "vacant" body as an artistically empty text. In representing the woman writer's text as monstrous *in* a woman writer's text, Moore demonstrates her anxieties about her role in literary modernism. But she also uses the representation of deformity as proof of her artistry, which she suggests surpasses extant women's modernism.

The novel sharply distinguishes between reproduction and creation when Ruth mentally rejects her pregnancy. She does not want her child and cannot see the point in reproducing herself or her husband: "To what purpose? If I dared ask them that! It will be like Stephen. And what will be the use of that? Or it will be like me. And what will be the use of that?" (22). Reproduction, that is, is represented as mere duplication; to bear a child is to go through the motions "without question," to be a creature "content to have no say in the matter" (25).

Ruth dissociates such reproduction from art when she condemns her pregnancy in aesthetic terms: "What to them is such a wonderful thing is to me fuss and ugliness. Ugliness, she thought, refusing to take back the word. And meaningless too, and dull and hopeless" (22). She wishes, to the point of believing it for a time, that her womb were in her forehead, that she might be able to "create" in both senses of the word simultaneously. "I think, Stephen, said Ruth. I think I carry my womb in my forehead. . . . So that if you came and told me that all the time it is growing in my head I should not be in the least surprised" (24). In this wishful belief, Ruth rejects her female body and aspires to the ability—coded masculine in the story of Zeus's creation of Athena and across Moore's oeuvre—to create in the forehead. She despairs when, one day in the bath, she realizes how large her belly has grown. "She lay back flat again, resting her head against the edge of the bath, contemplating; and had to admit. Had to admit. That it was not happening in her forehead at all, but was happening very much where it was meant to happen" (27). In separating art, which happens in the (male) head, from reproduction, which happens in the (female) belly, Moore rejects the metaphor of gestation for artistic production.

This dissociation of reproduction from art continues when Ruth considers what would result if men reproduced. She wonders

> what women could have done had they brought conscious thought to bear on what had always been dismissed as a preordained and unalterable task. She found herself believing that had it been left to men centuries of creation would have produced something more vital, more exciting. But then men were the active and not the passive instruments of nature. Men questioned. Not from woman that despairing cry: my God what am I in Thy universe? To answer which sails unfurled, wings of birds and angels yielded their secret, the earth rose and parted, was weighed, sifted, spanned from the immensities of its roof to the treacheries of its floor, the moon stuffed in the pocket, the whole held negligently in the hollow of a hand. (25–26)

From the weighty questioning of men would arise, if they were the bearers of children, transcendent beauty (emphasized by the elevated diction of the last sentence) and profound understanding: works of art. Women, however, give birth to children who simply replicate one parent or the other without moving the human species forward in apprehending the earth's "immensities."

After realizing that the baby is indeed growing in her belly, Ruth has a "conversion" experience, deciding that she will be the one to bridge this awful divide between the creating man and the reproducing woman. "An answer had been found to her questioning. Something different, said the message. Something worth having. . . . Something new" (28). Diagnosed with hysteria brought on by pregnancy, Ruth continues to long for, and believe in, her power to bridge the gap. The text indicates her obsession by itself repeating, with variations, her theme: "No, she intended no replica of herself or Stephen. That would indeed be a shocking waste of her new-found and terrible power, laughed Ruth. Something new. Something quite different. Something worth having. Something beyond and above it all. Something free that would defy the dreary inevitable round of years" (30). She anticipates a "new and strange being which she had brought to perfection in her body" (45).

The text reveals Richard's deformity gradually. After he is born, Ruth is ill with a fever for a month. When she is finally well enough to hold the baby, she is at first "astonished and delighted at its winsome and minute perfection" although she also finds that he "stared at her and stared" (48). But after overhearing a nurse say that there's no question the baby will ever walk, she insists on unwrapping him. She finds that he is

> beautifully whole and finished, except for his feet. They hung loose and shapeless from the ankle, soft loose pads of waxen flesh. She stared at them unable to bring herself to take them in her hand or touch them. She knew without knowing how she knew that such a newly created being gathers itself together in its feet, grasps with them, beats at the air with them, eagerly draws them in in small soft folds, and with all the hunger of its new-found energy shoots them out again. . . . Knowing this she raised her eyes from the loose formless pads of waxen flesh that were his feet to his impassive infant face in which two light eyes widely spaced and set stared at her and stared; and this time she understood the vacant fixity of his infant stare and his utter soundlessness and immobility. (49)

In this passage Ruth understands the baby's cognitive disability as arising from his deformed feet. If a newly created being cannot "gather itself together in its feet," she suggests, it cannot develop the mental capacity to interact with the world; this is how she explains his "vacant" staring eyes. The word *finished* connects the baby again with a work of artistic production, but Ruth implies that it cannot come alive. By insisting on creating something "new and strange," she believes, she has willed this to happen; she compares herself to a man who has hit someone in a "drunken stupor," "and they came and said to him: he is dead" (49). Her experiment, she concludes, has failed dramatically.

Upon first reading *Spleen*, I was tempted to see it as a feminist and antiableist intervention that suggests—by displaying and distancing readers from Ruth's prejudices—that maternity can be a valid path to or at least valid metaphor for artistic creation, and furthermore that we can understand a disabled child as representing a new—though to the uninitiated, unsightly—form of artwork. After all, as D. H. Lawrence points out in "The Future of the Novel," audiences aren't always ready for new forms. Lawrence writes that modern art has got to

> break a way through, like a hole in the wall. And the public will scream and say it is sacrilege: because, of course, when you've been jammed for a long time in a tight corner, and you get really used to its stuffiness and its tightness, till you find it absolutely stinkingly cosy; then, of course, you're horrified when you see a new glaring hole in what was your cosy wall. You're horrified. (*Study of Thomas Hardy* 155)

Perhaps, I thought, Richard's immobile body is that shocking but liberating hole in the wall; perhaps it is being celebrated as a new form of modernist art.

Renée Dickinson seems to gesture toward such a reading when she writes that in *Spleen* "Moore both exposes and critiques essentialized notions of the feminine and proposes alternative identities through hybrid embodiments and identities" (77). Jane Garrity makes a similar claim at the end of her essay, when she suggests that Ruth changes her understanding of Richard after encountering the modernist artwork, now famous, that her former lover Hans Uller painted while staying with her: "Like the modern artist who refuses mimetic representation, Ruth too had 'played just such a trick on Nature' (125) by producing a new being who did not conform to corporeal standards of normativity" (310). Garrity sees a productive linkage between disability and creativity in the novel's use of the headless statue, the *Victory of Samothrace*. She writes, "In *Spleen* the image of amputation captures Moore's conflation of disability with female artistic agency, and it simultaneously invokes the larger idea of fracture and violence as a contingent condition of female aesthetic innovation" (312). In a related vein, Matt Franks argues that although *Spleen's* "plot . . . participates in the exploitation of disability" (108–9) the novel's protagonist embraces "disability aesthetics as a radical feminist rejection of able-bodied norms" (112).[10]

But Dickinson acknowledges that all of the "attempts at hybridity ultimately fail to offer satisfactory alternatives" (77), while Garrity's claim is that Ruth's "embrace of abstraction . . . facilitates Ruth's *expiation*" (310, italics added), not that it facilitates Ruth's revaluation of Richard or nonnormativity in human beings. Indeed, as all the critics acknowledge, Ruth's plan for her husband's estate—to turn it into a holiday home for poor children—specifically excludes "mentally defective children," because they are "in no sense, she believed, worth saving" (116). So, despite Ruth's fleeting identification of her own "trick" in giving birth to Richard with Uller's painting, the novel as a whole rejects the comparison, and my hopeful reading of the novel as feminist and antiableist could not be sustained.

Art versus Gestation

An understanding of the novel as feminist would focus on Ruth's refusal to celebrate her pregnancy. It does question, after all, women's destiny as child bearers: "She knew it was not possible to her to love a thing she did not know or had not seen. How can one? Yet I am expected to. All women do. I am a woman. Therefore I do. And if I do not?" (21). Leaving this question unanswered, the text acknowledges the difficult social position of women who do not desire maternity. Ruth links this perceived deficiency to disability, casting it as an invisible impairment: "A woman is expected to have a maternal sense as she is expected to have other womanly attributes. Had I been born blind or deaf they would not expect me to see or hear; that they could understand" (22).

But the novel is deeply misogynist in its insistence on contrasting reproduction with creation and aligning the former with women, the latter with men. In addition to the lines quoted above that assert men would have brought conscious thought to bear on reproduction, giving rise to the secrets of birds and angels and the immensities of the earth, and the passages where Ruth realizes her womb is in her belly after all, the novel endorses Uller's assertion that unless a thing is three times removed from nature, it is not art (78–79). Uller's painting of a local boy, Giovanni, for instance, is blue—blue leaves, blue stones, blue child—whereas "leaves were green and stones were grey and the naked child was brown. And yet for all its absurdity he had caught the browny-blue bloom which Giovanni gave off like a fruit" (77–78). This painting exemplifies Uller's belief that art must not simply reproduce nature and emphasizes the text's distinction between reproduction and creation. In allowing Uller to combine his absurd colors to create art, while Ruth's absurd ideas about the new creature she will birth result in a deformed baby, Moore replicates the long-standing gendering of monstrosity. As Helen Deutsch and Felicity Nussbaum explain in their introduction to *Defects*, "women and men figure differently in cultural equations concerning the reproduction of defects. For example, while monstrosity may be associated with the male imagination's extraordinary creativity, women are accused of imagining themselves into bearing monstrous children" (10).

The text's treatment of the modern woman similarly forecloses the possibility of creativity for women. "There was a novelty and a certain glamour about the new young woman: but was she altogether satisfying? Had she attained anything not previously attained? . . . There was about her a look of impermanence difficult to classify. A look of today. Something momentary. She would grow old and leave the world exactly as she found it" (125). And Ruth, although she did not want her child, cannot understand modern women not wanting children: "How monstrous! she thought, understanding not at all" (126). Ruth also disagrees with someone who suggests that women should have careers: "I hardly agree. A million shorthand-typists remain a million shorthand-typists, but a million mothers can found a nation" (123). These judgments indicate that the politics of the text are not actually about liberating women from compulsory maternity but about sketching the life of an individual odd woman who is impaired in her reproductive desires and abilities but still, as a woman, unable to create. Much as Radclyffe Hall's *The Well of Loneliness* (1928) espouses a deeply conservative view of gender even as it pleads for understanding for inverts, *Spleen* maintains an understanding of women as essentially mothers even as it delineates the situation of a woman who resists maternity and womanliness more broadly. Indeed, Ruth compares herself to an invert, for "surely (she thought) it was a form of mental inversion this loneliness of hers among her fellow-creatures" (125–26).[11]

Moore similarly essentializes women, denying them creativity, in her later novel *Fugue* and her collection of essays and aphorisms, *The Apple Is Bitten Again*. In *Fugue*, a novel clearly influenced by D. H. Lawrence, the protagonist, Lavinia Reade, shares Ruth's prejudice against women. She thinks, for example, that if she were a man she would "love only men. I would not love women with their vacant chatter and soft ornamental bodies. . . . To be only a woman is not worth very much" (*Collected Writings* 273). Men are described as complete in themselves, while women are "scattered in body and scattered in mind" (*Collected Writings* 257).

Fugue divides women into two categories: the "human cow" (*Collected

Writings 282) and the modern woman. Lavinia and her friend Evelyn look at a field of cows and think about the "poor patient beasts on whose broad backs the modern woman had shifted her intimate maternal duty" (*Collected Writings* 282). Indeed, Evelyn thinks that engaging in "the act of love . . . for anything but pleasure . . . was both immoral and unthinkable. Women who desire only to be mothers should be mechanically fertilised. Let them be placed apart and tended and graded like cattle. . . . Let them be content with their yearly child. But let them leave the passionate act to the passionate" (*Collected Writings* 282–3). *Fugue* does not, any more than *Spleen*, grant women an alternate form of creation: "Men might be restless, because men could achieve. But women achieve mostly a half-achievement, and at best nothing that a man cannot better" (*Collected Writings* 309).

In *The Apple Is Bitten Again* Moore goes on several tirades against women's lack of creativity that demonstrate that she shares Ruth's and Lavinia's views of women.[12] For example, she writes that "woman is the vacuum which nature abhors and must see filled. Consequently woman is always slightly ridiculous unless stretched on a bed or with a child in her arms" (*Collected Writings* 343). She sees women who attempt "masculine" activities as, at best, "light-weight" men and asserts that "the only impressively strong-willed women one has met or who exist have been married women with children, who joyfully have done the thinking, earning, acting, and scheming of a half-dozen men" (*Collected Writings* 365). Moore places women in a double bind: they are confined to reproduction, their only route to thinking and acting, with their scope limited to the domestic sphere; if they refuse that role, seeking to transcend the domestic, the most they can aspire to is imitation of men. She believes that women's "creative gift is self-sacrifice. This, their deepest impulse, mitigates against any creative genius they could have. For the creative artist is the supreme selfish being: Art that which you alone can do and to which you will sacrifice all things—but yourself, who must be alone, secure, and impregnable, to create it" (*Collected Writings* 377).

This opposition between the selfishness of the artist and the self-sacrifice of the woman ties womanliness to disability. Women's art, Moore believes, is ruined by their compassion: "For women bring the charitable virtues to the Arts. The lame, the halt, the blind are succoured. They drop pennies only in the bottomless cans of sincerity and good-will" (*Collected Writings* 387). As I demonstrate further below, Moore's writing treats disabled people as, at best, objects of charity, and at worst, subhuman, underserving of consideration. The novel can no more be read as revaluing Richard's disabled body than it can be read as feminist parable.

"Feet above ground": Sentience

In *Spleen*, Ruth dismisses her son as "insentient" (125). This word is odd, because Ruth periodically acknowledges that Richard has feelings, such as when she says that it's clear he likes his new cart (65) or that he is "obviously surprised" when she imitates his cry as an attempt to communicate with him (68). But she insists that her son only *seems* to recognize her: "He stared in exactly the same way at Lisetta, Pasquale, Maria, Concetta, the bowl of noci, the goats. . . . any and every familiar sight of which, though some momentary trick of attention, he seemed suddenly aware for the first time" (68–69). Not recognizing, even if Richard does not, is not the same as not feeling or experiencing, however; so it is unclear whether Moore is using the word *insentient* in the dictionary sense, meaning "destitute of physical feeling, sensation, or consciousness; inanimate" (*OED*). Toward the end of the novel, Ruth compares herself to Richard: "What then was the more culpable: physical or mental insentience? To be unable to understand or to refuse?" (127). Here she concludes that she has been mentally "insentient" in refusing to understand that Richard had never reproached her for, as she believes, accidentally willing his disabilities. In this context the word indicates a lack of understanding, not a lack of feeling or consciousness. Moore's use of *insentient* to describe Richard enacts a blurring between not understanding and not feeling, between a lack of mental acuity and a lack of consciousness.

Continued dismissal of Richard's humanity can be seen in Ruth's description of his vocalizations as "sudden animal sounds" (68), in her description of him as a "corpse" (56), and in her thoughts as she watches him asleep on the sand right before she leaves for England. "Whole he looked lying there in the shadow of the rock: whole and good to look on. How well he looked! Who, seeing him asleep, could believe? At that moment and for the first time it occurred to her how proud a woman she might have been. But he was rootless, null, unproductive; therefore not a living being at all" (108). Denying Richard the status of "a living being" is much the same as denying him sentience. Ruth's technically inaccurate use of the word *insentient*, then, is explained by the fact that she doesn't seem to care about the difference. Since people like Richard don't count as "living beings" and are, as Ruth says to the lawyer about her husband's estate, "not worth saving," they may as well be insentient.[13]

The connection Ruth draws between Richard's deformed feet and his mental incapacity is unusual (even bizarre), but reinforced by the importance given to feet and legs in *Spleen* and Moore's other work. As Garrity insightfully explains, feet are important to Ruth's sense of freedom and personhood, as she remembers running barefoot on the grass while other girls were trapped by norms of propriety and clothing. In her description of her childhood, Ruth remembers how "the soles of her feet would begin to tingle and impelled she knew not how, with Mercury's wings at her heels, she would begin running faster, faster, laughing, elated, breathless, glowing" (37). Ruth's father believes that walking barefoot on grass cures nearly any ill. So feet are associated in the novel with health, inspiration, and flight. Garrity points out that the "focus on Richard's feet as the locus of his deformity and source of his immobility puts him at odds with the chain of associations that link Ruth to images of flight and mobility, namely her ability to 'create . . . something new' while 'seem[ing] to wing across floors and paths leaving no footprints'" (301).

In Moore's first novel, *Celestial Seraglio*, feet and legs are also depicted as signs of humanness. The novel is set in a Catholic boarding school where the girls distrust and dislike one of the nuns. They react by concocting stories about her feet: "when Soeur Marie Thérèse took off her shoes she hadn't any *feet*. Instead she had (whisper-whisper). No! Yes. No! Yes. Truth. Jeanne said so. She was the *Devil*. Or anyway she wasn't human" (*Collected Writings* 98). The implication is that Soeur Marie Thérèse has cloven hooves instead of feet and that one needs normative feet to be understood as human. We see further emphasis on legs and feet when the protagonist, Mavis, and her friend Milly sneak into a freak show at a local fair. They are horrified by all the people they see. But the culmination of their horror comes when they encounter "the half-thing without legs, though one foot dangled somewhere in the middle of it as though it grew from the base of the stomach, and with two half-arms, thin stumps of grey flesh, bound with gold bracelets. And Mavis after one look at the squashed, pushed-in face said: 'Let's get out or I shall be sick or something,' and even Milly looked away" (*Collected Writings* 84). Other performers in the freak show are dehumanized by words such as "doll," and "balloon-like creature," but it is the person without legs and with an anomalous foot who is described most baldly as a "half-thing."

Conversely, in *The Apple Is Bitten Again*, Moore describes her own sense of being alive in terms of her eyes and her feet: "I love life. I would not barter with the most illustrious dead the privilege of being alive; my feet above ground, my eyes in their sockets" (*Collected Writings* 418). She imagines winged feet in her description of great artists: "Why is there none to see the nimbus about our heads, wings at our back and feet, dove above our brows?"

(*Collected Writings* 378). In *Apple* she generalizes her ableist imagery, asserting plainly that a weak body means a weak soul: "The soul must be measured mechanically by the state of the body. // It is absurd to give a great soul to a sickly old man and the proof is given daily in our hospitals. The weak, the old, the drunken, the dissipated, drop their souls at the first shaking. // SOUL AND VITALITY GO HAND IN HAND" (*Collected Writings* 406). Further, Moore ties together ageism and ableism when she dismisses unproductive people entirely: "*The Old*. Never trust the old. The old can only take. That would not matter but that they think it their right. As though unproductive people have any rights!" (*Collected Writings* 372).

Across Moore's oeuvre, then, people with deformities, especially deformed feet, are cast as inhuman, and people who are unproductive—"null," as Ruth says about Richard in *Spleen*—have no rights, no souls, and do not really count as people at all. So we cannot read Richard's deformed body as emblematic of a new form of art, at least not one that we are supposed to approve. But the association remains between art and Ruth's attempt to create something new. And when we consider the femininity of Richard's body and the defects of women's writing according to Moore, we find them linked by a suggestion of monstrosity.

When Ruth sees Richard lying on the sand, she describes him as feminine: "she found him unusually interesting to look at with his fine thin nostrils and well-shaped mouth and the long silky eyelashes of an attractive woman. His shirt was open and the fairish brown hair on his breasts caught lights from the sun and shone like coarse silk. His bare throat was brown as were his hands, long thin-fingered hands like hers: not a man's hands at all" (108–9). In addition to comparing him to an "attractive woman" and noting the femininity of his hands, Ruth uses the word *breasts* rather than the singular *breast* more commonly applied to men. Although she thinks for a moment that he looks "whole" and "good to look upon," she suggests that this is an illusion ("Who, seeing him asleep, could believe?"). And although Ruth too inhabits her gender with great ambivalence, Richard's femininity cannot be a positive thing for a writer who deprecates women's artistic abilities.

In *Apple*, Moore lays out her opinion about women's writing:

> I have read and enjoyed many clever books by many talented women. But I have never yet finished a book written by a woman without, for all its charm and excellence, a sense of limitation. An accurate and deadly knowledge that the writer would rather be taken for a lady than

> mistaken for an artist. A lack of virility; a lack of rebellion; the sad certainty that their literary mock marriages are never consummated. (*Collected Writings* 391)

When she claims that every woman would rather be taken for a lady than mistaken for an artist, Moore may be using Woolf's honesty in texts such as *A Room of One's Own* against her; Woolf admits in *Room* (1929), and essays such as "Professions for Women" (1931) to being brought up short when she thinks of something that it is inappropriate for a woman to express. "Men, her reason told her, would be shocked. . . . She could write no more. The trance was over" ("Professions" 240). Moore shows little sympathy with this broken trance, or with the difficulties of the women Woolf describes in *A Room of One's Own*. She counters, "At no time in the world's history has woman been without a room of her own. But it has always been the kitchen. Then write on the kitchen table! Paint on the kitchen walls! Draw on the kitchen floor! Carve into shape the pastry and the butter! And so she would have had it been essential to her nature" (*Collected Writings* 386).

But creation, Moore claims, is essential only to men's nature, and curiosity is the "most male of male gifts." "Here . . . one comes near to uncovering the source of the failure of women as creative artists. We come near to explaining that mincing elegance, that devoted lifetime of pedantic sterility, that warm monstrous flow of womanly prose, which give to their works all the negative virtues of the male soprano" (*Collected Writings* 388). Describing women's writing as "monstrous" and linking it to gender inversion through the dig at the "male soprano," Moore reminds us that Richard is depicted as both monstrous and feminine, lovely in the way a male soprano's voice might be lovely—displaying that "negative virtue."

Spleen uses Richard's inert body, I suggest, to represent the woman writer's monstrous text. Ruth's reproduction was monstrous because she was trying to create with her mind and will, rather than with her body. In Moore's view, women cannot create anything "new and rare"; they can only reproduce what already is. Furthermore, no human being can *create* another human being—like the Nicene creed, the novel relies on a distinction between begetting and making. A woman can *beget* another, but if she tries to *create*, she will create a monster, much as Frankenstein's created being is monstrous.[14] Women are confined to begetting human beings with the body, while men can create art with the mind. Ruth's attempt to cross this boundary results in "not a living being at all." *Spleen* thus rejects the metaphor of gestation for artistic creation, discarding as monstrous any attempted conjunction of artistic creativity with reproduction.

Writing as a Woman

In representing the woman writer's text as monstrous *in* a woman writer's text, Moore demonstrates her anxieties about her potential role in modernism. Looking back at the extraordinary artistic production of the teens and twenties, Moore may have feared that what she would create, being a woman, would be as "null" as her character Richard. A sense of self-consciousness about her role in modernism is made clear by her attacks on Woolf in *Apple* and can be seen as well in *Spleen*'s allusions to Joyce. Moore aligns Ruth, and by implication herself, with male modernism by associating Ruth with Joyce: we learn that Ruth was six years old in 1888 (33), which tells us that, like Joyce, she was born in 1882. Ruth's husband is named Stephen, the name Joyce gave his alter ego in *Portrait* and *Ulysses*. Ruth's father, the only person she truly loved, "died of paralysis in 1904" after being in a "mental home for more than a year following a stroke" (33). The year 1904 is when Joyce left Ireland with Nora Barnacle, the year he started publishing the stories that would eventually make up *Dubliners* (1916), and the year in which he set *Ulysses* (1922). Moreover, the phrase *died of paralysis* is repeated directly from the first story of *Dubliners*, "The Sisters" (*Dubliners* 5). Joyce's priest's death after the "third stroke" forms another link with Ruth's father.

In fact, the conversion experience Ruth has in the bath, when she rejects the idea of being one in a chain of women begetting children in their own likeness, may be modeled after the conversion experience of Stephen Dedalus, when he rejects the idea of being one in a chain of priests living communally in "order and obedience" (*Portrait* 155). The experiences are linked by their setting in or near water and by the elevated language the authors use to describe them. Joyce repeats exalted words such as "soaring," "impalpable," and "imperishable" (*Portrait* 162, 163). He has Stephen see in the bird-girl an "angel of mortal youth and beauty" whose call to his soul entreats him to "live, to err, to fall, to triumph, to recreate life out of life!" (*Portrait* 165).

Ruth's conversion is described in similarly elevated discourse:

> Conversion, even a mild and imperfect conversion, is an ordeal; but when it is swift and sudden and complete, when, as it were, there is no mistaking the voice that calls from bells and blossoming apple boughs,

> or when, again, in the dark forest the hunted stag turns on the hunter and reveals the crucifix upheld between its antlers, it is such a complete and shocking disintegration of the human soul that few, fortunately, are called upon in a lifetime to endure it more than once. Ruth read her message in the lap-lapping of the water that seemed so far away and in the tightly stretched bubble of a stomach that still seemed to her unreal and not her own; and she understood that the search was ended. An answer had been found to her questioning. (28)

Both texts employ religious discourse (angel, soul, crucifix)[15] and report voices calling to the protagonists to redirect their efforts. Stephen's calling shifts from potential priest of God to potential "priest of the eternal imagination" (*Portrait* 213), while Ruth's shifts from creator of her own or her husband's likeness to creator of something new and rare. And Ruth's "message," that she will create "something worth having. . . . Something new" (28), replicates the prophecy Stephen perceives in his namesake Dedalus, that he must "forg[e] anew in his workshop out of the sluggish matter of the earth a new soaring impalpable imperishable being" (*Portrait* 162).

It is important that Stephen's goals are to forge "anew . . . out of the sluggish matter of the earth" and "recreate life out of life" because these aspirations are couched in vaguely gestational metaphors. Stephen's language is earthy, physical; like Ruth, he suggests that a new form can come from what has always been, until his intervention, merely life. In his talk with Lynch about aesthetics, he asserts that he will seek new ways to understand "the phenomenon of artistic conception, artistic gestation and artistic reproduction" (*Portrait* 202). Usurping women's experience of conception, pregnancy, and birth for his own purposes, Stephen disagrees with Uller that something must be three times removed from nature to be art. But this possibility of re-creating (artistic) life out of (biological) life is foreclosed for Ruth. Male writers, Moore suggests, appropriate female reproduction, but female writers cannot engage in male creation.

Moore's disbelief in women's ability to overcome the limitations she ascribes to their sex brings Ruth's hopes to a crashing halt. Uller's view prevails in *Spleen* insofar as women are connected to biology in a way men are not. Ruth cannot create something in the mind, because she is meant to beget something in the belly. *Spleen* uses Richard's deformed body to represent the monstrosity of women's writing and, indeed, of women's aspirations to transcend biology and step into the shoes of the artist.

I cannot, then, agree with Dickinson's argument that "by fusing the fleshy, female form of textual experimentation to the traditions of male modernist ideas, Moore creates a hybridized text that works to embody female subjectivity as both body and mind, both flesh and intellect" (108). The novel maintains the distinction between body/woman and mind/man even as it depicts a woman trying to overcome that distinction. But Dickinson is right to point out that the form of the novel embodies the "something new and strange" Ruth sought to create. She notes that "the text's internal structure enacts the concerns of the narrative through its inclusion of both fragmentation and fluidity" and describes the novel's form as "broken bits fused together in unfinished sentences and ideas" (103). The question becomes how to read *Spleen*'s experimental form—if it does not represent a feminist intervention in modernist form, how does the novel embody the "something new and rare" its protagonist sought to produce? Clearly the novel is self-consciously putting itself forward as that "something," but its misogyny and ableism mean that the "something" can have little to do with women or with disabled bodies.

Deformed Narrative

If we read the text against its grain, as itself deformed—in spite of Moore's clear antipathy to disabled and unproductive human beings—we can see it as providing a model of modernist fiction as deformation of the novel form. The opening paragraph, for example, is filled with images of distortion and deformity: "goats with long purple udders and sly drooping faces"; a stick brought down "sharply across the undulating hindquarters of her goats, undulating slowly over the long Saracen road"; a woman who would soon be "dwarfed to the size of a child" by distance; a "wild and shrill salute" from church bells (7).[16] Ruth's hair is described as an "elegant misshapen mass of curls" (8). She is described repeatedly as "not a little mad" (11, 14, 81). And her inability to appreciate her pregnancy, as I note above, is described as something "unnatural and not sane" (22) in her.

Moreover, the novel's experimental style can easily be seen as distorted and deformed. The timeline is vague, moving back and forth abruptly and with more confusing transitions than, for example, *Mrs. Dalloway*, where many of Clarissa's memories of the past are prefaced with a phrase such as "at Bourton." The reviewer for the *Times Literary Supplement* rightly remarks that "Miss Moore's method is to give us slices of her heroine's thought and history without regard for strict time-sequence" ("New Books and Reprints"). In the second paragraph of the novel, for example, the narrative suddenly moves back to Ruth's first arrival on the island, and within that narrative there is further confusion because Ruth is sick from the long journey and sees the woman who will become her landlady merely as a "detached blot" that makes soothing noises (10). Sequence is distorted in that readers learn that Ruth has lived on the island for many years but was "never seen to handle her own child" (14) and that the landlady, Donna Lisetta, accepts "the bundle of white clothes that rarely cried and remained motionless for hours on end" (15) before we know about her unwanted pregnancy or Richard's birth. And it is only at the end of the novel, when Ruth has learned that Uller died in 1916 and thinks that that was nearly fourteen years earlier (114), that we understand that Uller was with her on the island of Foria sometime in the years just before World War I and realize that the present of the novel is about 1930, the date of its publication.

The novel genre is further de-formed by its exposition of Uller's views, in long discourses that erupt into the fiction and resemble the aphorisms and expositions of *The Apple Is Bitten Again*. Characters such as Donna Lisetta's children or a housemaid from Ruth's husband's estate are named and incorporated into the narrative without explanation, so that readers only gradually become aware who they are. This confusion is evidenced by the review in the *New York Times*, in which the reviewer describes Stephen as Ruth's father, rather than her husband ("Unhappy Life") and by the review in the *Saturday Review of Literature*, in which the reviewer mistakes the child in Uller's painting—a local boy named Giovanni—for Richard ("New Books"). As Dickinson points out, Moore's sentences are often unfinished. Dickinson writes that "the novel begins with long, chunky, dense, and broken paragraphs and sentences, the paragraphs and sentences interrupted by the use of dashes instead of quotation marks and by frequent insertions of other thoughts and other characters" (103). Repetition adds to the sense of the novel as a "misshapen mass," making it understandable that the reviewer in the *New York Herald Tribune* calls it "devious and occasionally incoherent" ("Idiot's Mother") and the review for the *Saturday Review* questions whether "it can properly be called a novel" ("New Books"). Perhaps Moore intended her text to be three times removed from the "natural" state of the novel.

While Moore associates women's modernism with deformity as a way to dismiss women's artistic production and try to supersede it through her own intellectual gender inversion, she also gives space to deformity in a fiction that can be read as itself formally deformed. Indeed, she seems to be offering her representation of deformity as proof of her modernist artistry, as a triumph in art over the reality of deformity.[17] In her discussion of the relation between national life and artistic outpouring in *Apple*, she argues that

> the lean unstable years are best for the nation's art. . . . No sooner does life become settled than it sags from a Michelangelo (already bad enough) to a Carlo Dolci, a Canova, a Sargent. Then when the despair and gangrene are about to take effect a Goya, a Manet, a Picasso, a Voltaire, a Stendhal, a James Joyce appear, their works bold as the flag of anarchy or the cold gleam of the scalpel. (*Collected Writings* 358)

The juxtaposition of images here suggests that anarchy battles despair, while the cold scalpel roots out gangrene. Though the scalpel cures, it also of course cuts, harms, deforms that which it is curing. Like the work of those artists she admires, Moore's writing cuts into the genre of the novel, exposing a deformed body on which she relies even as she disavows it. While marred by its ableism and misogyny, Moore's effort to make modernism new evinces the productive deformity Michael North sees in the poetry of William Carlos Williams: "the new language really exists in and as the struggle against the old, in the very deformity and strangeness forced on a speaker who has something new to say" (151).

Writing and Deformity in Woolf

Deformity and strangeness similarly occupied Virginia Woolf in the mid-1930s as she decided to "break the mould made by The Waves" (*Diary* 4:233). During this period Woolf worked to leave aside the intense inwardness and poetry of her earlier works in favor of "turn[ing her characters] toward society, not private life" (*Letters* 6:116).[18] This was a difficult shift, prompted by the renewed intrusion of history and politics into private life as fascism gained traction in Europe and war loomed.[19] Herbert Marder describes the effort as a "hard discipline" through which Woolf forced herself to "create new forms of expression to contain new ways of feeling" (138). She worried that the novel she was working on, eventually entitled *The Years*, would be propagandistic, no more than "feeble twaddle" (*Diary* 5:8). She had to constantly "reassure herself that her studied denial of lyricism and inner life [was] not misguided" (Whittier-Ferguson, *Framing* 90). When the book was finished, she noted in her diary that "I myself know why its [*sic*] a failure, & that its failure is deliberate" (*Diary* 5:65). Woolf's ambivalence about this outward turn can be seen in various aspects of *The Years*;[20] one of these is the physical deformity of Sara Pargiter, the artist figure and character closest to Woolf.[21] As I demonstrate in what follows, Woolf maintained an analogy at least since *A Room of One's Own* between deformity and writing.

This analogy was ready at hand when she set out to represent Sara Pargiter in *The Years*, her novel of "fact."

Woolf uses the motif of deformity in *A Room of One's Own* and *The Years*, and briefly in *Three Guineas*, to describe writing and lives that have been thwarted by overpowering obstacles, "crippled" by circumstance. In *The Years*, Sara has a spinal curvature that leaves one shoulder slightly higher than the other.[22] The meanings of her deformity are multilayered and contradictory. The contradictions arise because Woolf has woven two distinct metaphorical deformities into the novel. In one strand, Sara is dissociated from a metaphorical deformity that cripples people who "sign on" to the processions of capitalist London. But in the other strand, Sara is the fulcrum of a metaphoric deformity that the novel implies has hobbled late modernism. She represents, I suggest, the crippling of literary art in the late 1930s, when Woolf felt compelled to surrender the originality and authenticity of vision achieved by high-modernist characters such as Lily Briscoe.

In *A Room of One's Own*, deformity is primarily used to describe writing that has been "twisted and deformed" by the author's battle with the circumstances of her life. Woolf returns to variations of this phrase on four separate occasions, demonstrating that the phrase is no mere figure of speech but indicates Woolf's view of the relationship between outside pressures and the shape of an artwork or artist. In her description of the imaginary Judith Shakespeare, she writes that "had she survived, whatever she had written would have been twisted and deformed, issuing from a strained and morbid imagination" (49). Pointing out that it is not only women writers who must struggle with their material lives, she writes that "if anything comes through in spite of all this it is a miracle, and probably no book is born entire and uncrippled as it was conceived" (51). In her comparison of Lady Winchilsea and Margaret of Newcastle, she notes that "both are disfigured and deformed by the same causes" (60). And about Charlotte Brontë she muses that "if one reads [her books] over and marks that jerk in them, that indignation, one sees that she will never get her genius expressed whole and entire. Her books will be deformed and twisted. . . . How could she help but die young, cramped and thwarted?" (69).

The word *cramped* highlights the connection between this image of deformity and the main focus of the essay: the relation between writing and material reality. Fictions, which she figures as spiders' webs, "are not spun in midair by incorporeal creatures, but are the work of suffering human beings, and are attached to grossly material things, like health and money and the houses we live in" (41–42). Woolf seems to be envisioning, then, a physical pressure that pulls the web "askew," that "deforms" and "twists" the text and "cramps" and "thwarts" the body of the author. Her emphasis on bodily and material circumstances makes possible this conflation of a "cramped and thwarted" soul with physical deformity. The idea that an artwork can be twisted and deformed permeates, too, her description of Charlotte Brontë's imagination "swerve[ing]" and "contract[ing] . . . with a spasm of pain" (72). Throughout *Room*, Woolf describes artworks as having bodies that can be deformed, twisted, and contracted with spasms.

Woolf maintains her use of physical ability as a motif when she talks about how women will write when they do have money and rooms of their own: "No doubt we shall find [the woman writer] knocking that into shape for herself when she has the free use of her limbs; and providing some new vehicle, not necessarily in verse, for the poetry in her" (76). When the woman writer is cured of her symbolic disability, neither her work nor her body will be twisted and deformed; instead, her physically able body will lead to new artistic forms. In Donald Childs's view, Woolf's argument in *Room* depends on a "eugenical logic of inheritance" whose goal is to produce the "right sort of woman: Shakespeare's 'wonderfully gifted sister'" (58, 59). This gifted writer will substitute her symbolically able body for the disabled bodies of the writers Woolf describes as deformed.

In her famous discussion of the fascist poem as an abortion, Woolf develops her disability imagery still further. She writes, "The Fascist poem, one may fear, will be a horrid little abortion such as one sees in a glass jar in the museum of some county town. Such monsters never live long, it is said; one has never seen a prodigy of that sort cropping grass in a field. Two heads on one body do not make for length of life" (102). Fascism, she claims, will produce work far more "twisted and deformed" than women writers "cramped" by their limitations. Here Woolf envisions texts as monstrous bodies and takes it as self-evident that such disability would be "fatal." She uses this imagery to form a community of like-minded and like-bodied readers who accept that bodily ability and integrity are apt metaphors for good literature, literature that will be fit to "live."[23] Childs rightly concludes that *Room* "foregrounds a biological model of women's literary genius—especially in the equation between literary form and woman's body" and that by doing so, Woolf extends "'bio-power' into a site where it had not been seen before" (74).

Woolf uses disability, moreover, as one way to demonstrate the higher value of women when she discusses Oscar Browning, who examined students at Newnham and Girton and declared that they were invariably inferior to male students. Woolf's narrator notes that Browning then went

"Votes for Women." Courtesy of Schlesinger Library, Radcliffe Institute, Harvard University.

back to his rooms and "found a stable-boy lying on the sofa—'a mere skeleton, his cheeks were cavernous and sallow, his teeth were black, and he did not appear to have the full use of his limbs. . . . "That's Arthur" [said Mr. Browning]. "He's a dear boy and really most high-minded."' The two pictures always seem to me to complete each other" (53). The point here is that Browning can see the intelligence and worth in Arthur, in spite of his poverty and his physical disability; but he cannot see them in the ablebodied women he examines. To the narrator, this is an irony that further displays Browning's prejudices against women.

This rhetorical strategy of comparing disabled or otherwise "unfit" men to women in order to point out the ridiculous exclusion of women was a common refrain of suffrage posters. For example, one poster, entitled "Votes for Women," shows a lower-class man leaning against a wall with a pipe in his hand; he has a prominent nose and lower jaw, indicating his degenerate racial status. He is addressing a refined-looking woman with a diploma in her hand. The caption reads, "One of our voters—Wot do you wimmin want the vote for? You ain't fit for it!" As in Woolf's mockery of Browning's praise for the lower-class, disabled Arthur, the poster's power relies on the ironic contrast between the "unfit" man who does have the vote and the more than "fit" woman who does not. Douglas Baynton describes this tactic: "A popular theme in both British and American suffrage posters was to depict a thoughtful-looking woman, perhaps wearing the gown of a college graduate, surrounded by slope-browed, wild-eyed, or 'degenerate' men identified implicitly or explicitly as 'idiots' or 'lunatics.' The caption might read, 'Women and her Political Peers,' or 'It's time I got out of this place. Where shall I find the key?'" ("Disability" 25).

One version of the poster with the latter caption shows a woman locked in a sort of jail cell, a single, outdoor cell with mountains in the background and a set of books outside the bars. The woman, as Baynton mentions, is dressed in a graduation gown with mortarboard and is holding the chains around the doorknob of the cell. Behind her are a large, imposing-looking convict with features that indicate racial difference from the Anglo-Saxon woman and a much smaller man with longish hair and, as Baynton indicates, a sloping brow. The caption reads, "Convicts and Lunatics and Women Have No Vote for Parliament!" and then in smaller letters, "She. It is time I got out of this place. Where shall I find the key?" The man implicitly labeled "lunatic" is portrayed as unmasculine, especially as compared to the hypermasculine "convict." He is reaching toward the woman as if for help, while she seeks to escape his company as much as the convict's. According to Lisa Tickner,

"Convicts and Lunatics." Designed by Emily Harding Andrews and published by the Artists' Suffrage League, 1908. Reprinted in Lisa Tickner, *The Spectacle of Women: Imagery of the Suffrage Campaign, 1907–14*, illustration 4. Courtesy of Schlesinger Library, Radcliffe Institute, Harvard University.

Suffrage Atelier. "What a woman may be, and yet not have the vote. What a man may have been, & yet not lose the vote." 1912. Courtesy of Schlesinger Library, Radcliffe Institute, Harvard University.

> the theme was a popular one, at least since Frances Power Cobbe's "Criminals, Idiots, Women, Minors, is the classification sound?" in *Fraser's Magazine*, vol. 78, 1868. The point is sharpened physiognomically: the woman graduate is given the idealised and regular features of the eugenically superior, while the prisoner and lunatic are clearly portrayed as "degenerate" types. (caption, illustration 4)

Another poster includes physically disabled men when it compares "What a Woman may be, and yet not have the Vote" with "What a Man may have been, and yet not lose the Vote." A woman, the poster asserts, might be a mayor, nurse, mother, doctor, teacher, or factory hand and not be allowed to vote, while the following types of men could vote: "convict, lunatic, proprietor of white slaves, unfit for service, drunkard." The picture of the man "unfit for service" is of a man on crutches, and the small symbol above his head is the crutch (the drunkard's is a bottle, the "lunatic's" a moon). The caption "unfit for service" specifically impugns his masculinity: even those who are too disabled to serve in the military can vote—why can't women? The frequency of this visual rhetoric demonstrates its success at showing that women *are* fit to vote: compared to the varieties of men accepted as unfit, they are clearly deserving of the franchise.

Not only does Woolf draw upon this rhetorical strategy in *Room*, but in *The Years* she has Eleanor Pargiter—who has been attending suffrage meetings and debating whether force is warranted within the suffrage campaign—use similar rhetoric. In the air raid scene of 1917, Eleanor wants to discuss humanity's improvement with Nicholas. "When, she wanted to ask him, when will this New World come? When shall we be free? When shall we live adventurously, wholly, not like cripples in a cave?" (281). Sara had already described the cellar in which the group waited out the air raid as a "cave of mud and dung" (277); Eleanor extends this image by adding the opposition between freedom, wholeness, and adventure on the one hand and cripples on the other. It's as if she's adapting the slogan "It is time I got out of this place [with lunatics and cripples]. Where shall I find the key?" to the broader issue of creating a free society. As in *Room*, the crippling of the body represents for Eleanor a crippling of the soul, a life that is neither free nor whole.[24]

Woolf herself uses deformity with much the same metaphoric meaning in a letter about *The Years*. She writes that "Eleanor's experience though limited partly by sex and the cramp of the Victorian upbringing was meant to be all right; sound and rooted; the others were crippled in one way or another—though I meant Maggie and Sara to be outside that particular prison" (*Letters* 6:122). The word *cramp* returns here, indicating a pressure on Eleanor that stops short of crippling her; she remains "sound." But the other characters, except Maggie and the physically deformed Sara, are "crippled," are inside a "prison"—Woolf's more prosaic version of the cave inhabited by cripples, an image also perhaps influenced by the suffragist's jail cell.

This use of physical disability to indicate spiritual or social corruption is also seen in *Three Guineas*, as Woolf returns to her argument from *Room of One's Own* about the close relationship between physical and spiritual existence. She claims, for example, that "the poverty of the Christian who should give away all his possessions produces, as we have daily and abundant proof, the crippled in body, the feeble in mind. The unemployed, to take the obvious example, are not a source of spiritual or intellectual wealth to their country" (69). But it is not only those without resources who become "crippled" in Woolf's view, but also those who devote themselves to acquiring resources. She suggests that

> if people are highly successful in their professions they lose their senses. Sight goes. They have no time to look at pictures. Sound goes. They have no time to listen to music. Speech goes. They have no time for conversation. They lose their sense of proportion—the relations between one thing and another. Humanity goes. Money making becomes so important that they must work by night as well as by day. Health goes. And so competitive do they become that they will not share their work with others though they have more than they can do themselves. What then remains of a human being who has lost sight, sound, and sense of proportion? Only a cripple in a cave. (72)

This passage provides the most extended explanation of Woolf's deformity imagery. Her ableism is palpable as she links each absent sense or ability to loss of music, conversation, humanity, and health. It is ironic that she uses Dr. Bradshaw's phrase, lacking a "sense of proportion"—which was lambasted in *Mrs. Dalloway*—seriously, even claiming that when one lacks that sense, "humanity goes." The close correspondence of this passage to Eleanor's musings in *The Years* serves as another confirmation of Woolf's claim that *The Years* and *Three Guineas* are "one book" (*Diary* 5:148).[25]

The passage outlines the purpose of Woolf's deformity metaphors by solidifying an imagined link between a person's mental/spiritual and bodily selves. Although Woolf set out to explore the internal life—the atoms that fall upon the mind—she insisted on the connections between the mind and the body, as I discuss in the introduction. This insistence prompted (though it certainly did not necessitate) her use, over the course of several major texts, of these metaphors of bodily unfitness as indicators of spiritual deficiency. While it may be true that the material conditions of a writer's life often contribute to the quality of her output—that a woman writer "must have money and a room of her own if she is to write fiction"—Woolf has conflated material circumstances ("health and money and the houses we live in") with bodily conditions ("twisted and deformed," "cripples in a cave," etc.) in a series of metaphoric repudiations of physical and mental disability. These repudiations, I want to stress, are integral to her feminist arguments in *A Room of One's Own* and *Three Guineas*.

Freedom from Unreal Loyalties: Sara Pargiter

In *The Years* the repudiation reappears in Eleanor's thoughts about living like cripples in a cave,[26] but this novel is complicated by its inclusion of Sara (formerly Elvira)—the artist figure, the character with whom Woolf most identified. Sara is defined primarily by her outsiderness, which comes from an inextricable combination of her will and the social effects of her deformity.[27] Sara embodies, before Woolf has articulated it in *Three Guineas*, the philosophy of the Outsiders Society, whose members make the most of their exclusion from organized society.[28] As Julia Briggs points out, it is in Elvira's/Sara's voice that Woolf imagines herself speaking when she turns down the offer of an honorary degree from Manchester University in 1933: "It is an utterly corrupt society I have just remarked, speaking in the person of Elvira Pargiter, & I will take nothing that it can offer me. . . . I hardly know which I am, or where: Virginia or Elvira, in the Pargiters or outside" (*Diary* 4:148). Briggs notes, "from the moment of her invention, Woolf identified strongly with Elvira" (284).[29]

We learn about Sara's "slight deformity" when we first meet her. Her uncle Abel Pargiter has come to her house to give her sister Maggie a birthday present. The girls' mother, Eugénie, holds out a hand, "partly to coax the little girl, partly, Abel guessed, in order to conceal the very slight deformity that always made him uncomfortable. She had been dropped when she was a baby; one shoulder was slightly higher than the other; it made him feel squeamish; he could not bear the least deformity in a child" (115). Abel's squeamishness is ironic, considering he has lost two fingers in the Indian Mutiny and his hand now resembles the "claw of some aged bird" (13).[30] But as Madelyn Detloff demonstrates, Abel's hand is usually depicted dispensing money or engaging in other masculine activities such as caressing his mistress; his disability, "obtained during military duty, is a signifier of his masculine value" (105–6).[31] This dynamic partakes in the double standard mocked by the suffrage posters described above, in that Abel maintains his masculine privilege while being himself "mutilated" but withholds his approval from Sara because of a "very slight deformity." Such a use of deformity is of a piece with the association of disability with spiritual corruption that we find in Eleanor's musings and in *A Room of One's Own* and *Three Guineas*. It is this metaphoric deformity from which Sara is *dissociated* through her outsider status and her refusal to sign on to the capitalist "procession."

Sara is left out of what Christine Froula calls the "human mating dance" she sees from her window in the 1907 scene (*Virginia Woolf* 244). From the beginning of the novel Sara is outside of the spotlight: it is Maggie's birthday, not hers; her father, Digby (Abel's brother), kisses Maggie but only pats Sara on the head (120); in 1907 she stays home while Maggie and their parents attend a party; then Maggie marries and has babies while Sara lives in a run-down flat in the East End. As Woolf advocates in *Three Guineas*, Sara profits from this exclusion by adopting an alternate vision, identifying with Antigone and refusing to "serve a master" within capitalist patriarchy. In the 1907 section where she lies in bed reading *Antigone*, her identification with Antigone is prompted by her disability. The doctor has told Sara to "lie straight, lie still" (132), presumably (and explicitly in the drafts) because of her spinal curvature.[32] So, reading about Antigone lying "straight out" in the tomb, Sara "laid herself out under the cold smooth sheets" (128) like "a living corpse" (Froula, *Virginia Woolf* 249).

Sara is described as "angular" (132, 164), a word that emphasizes her imitation of Antigone lying straight in her tomb and that highlights descriptions of her as "hunched" (176, 179) and "crooked." We can see this emphasis in one of the draft versions of the same 1907 scene: "Hunch, said Maggie, observing ~~with interest~~ how crooked her sister was, crooked not only in her back, but everywhere, slightly, as if she had been blown upon, made one sided" (*Pargiters* 3:127).[33] Slightly farther on, as Anna Snaith notes, Woolf writes, "'Hunch, as she called her—for it +she+ was a joke, hopping about like a bird, one shoulder higher than another & getting out of everything in consequence'" (*Years*, Cambridge Ed. 774).

In the published version of the 1907 section, the description of Sara as she falls back to sleep after her mother has left retains imagery of a "hump," a "cleft," "sharp folds," and "jutting" angles:

> She curled herself up with her back to the window. She had raised a hump of pillow against her head as if to shut out the dance music that was still going on. She pressed her face into a cleft of the pillows. She looked like a chrysalis wrapped round in the sharp white folds of the sheet. Only the tip of her nose was visible. Her hip and her feet jutted out at the end of the bed covered by a single sheet. (136)[34]

In the drafts, Woolf connects Sara's "stark and angular" body with her deformity: "There was something stark and angular in her position which even ~~which~~ when she was lying down hinted at some slight deformity. Her body seemed to find a ridge in the bed to crouch there" (*Pargiters* 3:117). In the published text the properties of Sara's angular and yet hunched body have been transferred to the humped pillow and the sharp folds of the sheet; her elaborate wrapping of herself in a "chrysalis" of the bedding emphasizes Sara's negotiations with an environment in which her body does not always fit.[35]

Sara's identity as outsider is demonstrated in her lyrical, nonlogocentric speech (often nonsensical or at least non sequitur), in her mockery of North when he tells her he is leaving for the Front (270), in her intimate relationship with Nicholas, who "ought to be in prison" because of his homosexuality (281), and in her decision to remain poor rather than write for money, as the "Jew in the bath" scene makes clear.[36] When Sara tells North in the "Present Day" section that she would not "stain the hand," "sign on, and serve a master" or join the conspiracy of the "pasty; the ferret-eyed; the bowler-hatted, servile innumerable army of workers" (323), even though such a capitulation would allow her to escape from the Jewish neighbor she finds unsavory, she endorses Woolf's call in *Three Guineas* to refuse to prostitute the mind by writing for money (117–18). Sara includes herself when she claims that people who look back on them in their "cave" will say, "Pah! They stink!" And she herself appears to Maggie in this scene "like some great ape, crouching there in a little cave of mud and dung" (179). But it is as if by embodying the image of an ape or a cripple in a cave physically, Sara becomes exempt from it metaphorically. Through her adherence to her own vision of integrity, she is removed from the status of "cripples in a cave" represented by most of the other characters.

In the many draft versions of Sara's scenes, Woolf ascribes her outsider status and intellectual pursuits more directly to her deformity. For example, in 1910, the published novel does not explain why Sara is left at home while Maggie and her parents go to a party. We might conclude, as Snaith suggests, that Sara has not yet been presented to society, so she stays behind much as Virginia Stephen did as a young woman when Vanessa had already "come out" (Cambridge Ed. 453). But in a holograph version, when Maggie comes home, she envies her sister because "being a hump back, she never went to parties" (*Pargiters* 3:126). Elvira also thinks about the fact that Edward had given her his translation of *Antigone*: "Because she was a hump back, she reflected, ~~people always gave her books~~ he gave her books" (*Pargiters* 3:121). These passages confirm that her family does not expect her to occupy herself as other young women do.

Woolf seems to have been ambivalent about how much Elvira's deformity should affect her character, and even her face.[37] In *Between the Acts*, William Dodge's face is described as "twisted" (26) and "twitching" (27), and these descriptions indicate his misfitness as a homosexual who feels himself a "snake in the grass" (51). In the drafts of the 1907 section, Woolf first denies and then confirms that there is a "twist" and a "ripple" to Elvira's face. She writes, "And yet owing to the slight hump that showed itself under her night gown she would never look very young. Her face never had that curious twist which makes the faces of cripples seem to ripple slightly. She would never be the long hands, hanging too far from the sleeves" (*Pargiters* 3:109). This passage appears at the beginning of the scene where Elvira lies in bed listening to music floating in from across the street. Woolf then crossed out this version and restarted the scene, asserting just the opposite: "The face was rippled with the little twist which deformity seems to bring with it. She would never look pretty; she would never look very young. Her wrists stretched out too far beyond the night gown" (*Pargiters* 3:117). Both passages associate disability with a twistedness that recalls the "twisted and deformed" writing discussed in *A Room of One's Own* and anticipates William Dodge's "twisted" face. They draw upon the rhyme of *cripple* and *ripple* to include a sense of motion where there should be stasis. They deny, predictably enough, that disabled women can be pretty or look young. And they link disability with poverty in the image of someone whose sleeves are too short and whose arms therefore appear longer than they "should" be, an image that may be related to that of Sara as "some great ape."

Maggie's envy of Sara's exclusion or exemption from parties confirms Woolf's view that women should embrace "poverty, [mental] chastity, derision and freedom from unreal loyalties" (*Three Guineas* 96). Maggie notes that at parties, "One has to pretend—that's why you're so lucky . . . ~~you say you're~~ a hump back" (*Pargiters* 3:127). Not having to pretend, Sara is free to exercise her integrity and freedom, though of course her scope is quite limited by being "~~in bed perfectly comfortable~~" while Maggie is out at the party (*Pargiters* 3:126). In one passage Maggie attributes Sara's creative imagination to this exclusion: "being a hump back, she never went to parties: then she made up something ~~impossible~~: something that had no relation to ~~her own feelings~~ what had happened" (*Pargiters* 3:126). Sara's imaginative powers, the drafts suggest, come from the exclusion that results from social attitudes toward her disability.

While the two young women embrace a disabled identity for Sara, their mother, much as we saw of the mothers in *The Glass Menagerie* and "Good Country People" discussed in chapter 1, denies that her daughter is a "hump back." In response to a holograph discussion about how women used to bring up their daughters, Elvira replies,

> "But I'm a hump back," said Elvira. She was not ashamed. She did not ask for pity. But her mother flinched.
>
> ~~"I wish I were too," said Maggie~~. Nonsense, Lady Pargiter exclaimed. "You may not be absolutely straight;—but in a year or two, if ~~["]I wish I were" Maggie interrupted~~.

> you would lie flat, instead of jumping about. . . .
> She patted her down.
> "But it's a great advantage ~~being a hump back~~," said Elvira. ["] Maggie has to do the things I don't." (*Pargiters* 3:145)

Eugénie touts a medical model of disability here, placing the emphasis on Sara's compliance with the doctor's orders and looking toward a cure. Her daughters resist that model. The advantage Elvira refers to here is being exempt from social obligations where one must perform femininity and talk about the weather, as described in the published novel. As Clare Hanson argues, Sara is the character who most clearly exposes gender as a performance (62). And the novel also suggests a more comprehensive "disability gain" that arises from Sara's combination of exclusion and self-removal from organized society. Being physically "crippled" contributes to her position "outside that particular prison" of "crippled" souls marching along in the highly gendered capitalist procession.

Deformed Modernism: Sara as Artist

Nevertheless, there is something truncated and unfinished about Sara's lyricism. Like Isa Oliver after her, her artistic expression could be described as "abortive" (*Between the Acts* 11). Sara's intermittent "flashes of insight" (Radin 44) result in no triumphant moment when the artist, even assuming her painting will be hung in an attic, can at least declare "I have had my vision" (*To the Lighthouse* 211). Sue Roe describes Sara's art as a "chaotic and spasmodic capacity to pick the whole fabric to pieces" (140). It is, I suggest, a lyricism or art Woolf views as deformed by the overwhelming pressures of history, which compel repetition and interrupt and preclude imaginative thought. Sara is the locus of this additional metaphoric deformity, through which *The Years* looks back on the heady period of high modernism and acknowledges—with the sort of clear-sighted regret felt by Jinny as she confronts her aging face in *The Waves* (163)—that the belief in originality, in a unique artistic vision, has dissolved as the 1930s brings England closer to a second ruinous war.[38]

John Whittier-Ferguson demonstrates that repetition characterizes Woolf's last two novels:

> Repetition manifests itself in Woolf's writing of the 1930s in a variety of forms, all stemming from her careful attention to social and political forces and to language, not so much as it exists in the sanctity of

> the individual mind, new-minted in the privacy of the imagination, but as it carries out its debased life in the marketplace or its borrowed life in memory, and as it is circulated in the most ordinary of conversations. ("Repetition" 234)

As Whittier-Ferguson points out, this preoccupation with repetition stemmed from Woolf's sense of the coming war as a repetition of the Great War. She wrote in her diary, "1914 but without even the illusion of 1914. All slipping consciously into a pit" (*Diary* 5:170). Whittier-Ferguson uses as an epigraph the passage from *Three Guineas* where Woolf comments, "Things repeat themselves it seems. Pictures and voices are the same today as they were 2,000 years ago."[39] Like the writers Miller discusses, Woolf was "deeply troubled by [her] inability to keep [social context] at a manageable distance" (Miller 32).

Woolf's conviction that history would only repeat itself seems to have led to or at least been intertwined with her loss of confidence in the originality of the imagination. Now instead of an artist figure who clings to her unique vision by insisting "This is what I see" (*To the Lighthouse* 23), she creates an artist figure who does not actually create art and who, rather than redeeming originality in the face of surrounding banality, serves as the "spirit of repetition incarnate" (Whittier-Ferguson, "Repetition" 235). Whittier-Ferguson discusses the scene in the "Present Day" section where Sara and North quote each other's letters from twenty years before: "This textual device—the recipient of a letter quoting that letter back to its author; the author, in turn, verifying the accuracy of the quotation—stands as a fitting emblem for much else that is repetitive in Woolf's late fiction" ("Repetition" 241). Sara's discourse, then, reflects an earlier, authentic expression but is no longer that expression. In a similar way, *The Years*, Woolf's "deliberate" "failure" of a novel (*Diary* 5:65), reflects her earlier authentic art but is no longer that art.[40]

The other major way Woolf conveys the deformity of Sara's artistic expression is by making her the focal point of the interruptions that continually break off imagination and communication in the novel. Much as the work of the writers described in *A Room of One's Own* was "disfigured" by the interruptions that characterized women's lives, Sara's imaginative thought and her communications with others are truncated by intrusions from without. Even when her mother attempts to tell a story *about* Sara, she is interrupted (123). This subtly prepares readers for the various ways in which Sara's own thoughts and communications are curtailed in the rest of the novel.

In the 1907 section Sara is granted the longest time to think as she lies in bed while her family attends the party. She uses the time to read Berkeley and think about thought. But even when she is alone, outside forces interfere. First, dance music from across the road disturbs her solitude. "It was impossible to read; impossible to sleep. First there was the music; then a burst of talk; then people came out into the garden; voices chattered, then the music began again" (124). Then she decides to "*be* thought." But when she imagines herself as a tree putting forth branches and the sun "shin[ing] through the leaves" she is brought up short by the disjunction between her imagined scene and reality. "She opened her eyes in order to verify the sun on the leaves and saw the actual tree standing out there in the garden. Far from being dappled with sunlight, it had no leaves at all. She felt for a moment as if she had been contradicted. For the tree was black, dead black" (125). The fact of the tree outside contradicts the imagined tree and destroys the illusion.

In the 1910 section we are introduced to Sara and Maggie's flat first through the sounds that enter it from without: "The swarm of sound, the rush of traffic, the shouts of the hawkers, the single cries and the general cries, came into the upper room of the house in Hyams Place where Sara Pargiter sat at the piano" (154). In an earlier draft the force of these noises is elaborated upon when the sound of a man crying "Old iron to sell" disturbs Sara so that she gives up playing the piano (Cambridge Ed. 624).[41] When Sara sees Maggie setting three places at the table, she makes a song out of it, dancing about and saying, "Three's the same as two, three's the same as two." But this fancy is broken when Maggie informs her, "'we are three . . . Rose is coming.' Sara stopped. Her face fell" (155). Not only is Sara disappointed that their privacy will be invaded by a cousin she barely knows, but her imaginative play is also halted, again, by reality.

Indeed, many of her conversations with Maggie consist of Sara's flights of fancy checked by Maggie's insistence on facts. When Sara waxes poetic later in the 1910 section, for example, Maggie stops listening, and Sara falls silent (177). What poetic lines she does spout are usually more allusive (in this passage she invokes *The Tempest*) than original. When she invents stories about her outing with Rose, Maggie keeps returning her to the last factual thing she has said:

> "We got onto a bus and went to Holborn," she said. "And we walked along a street," she went on; "and suddenly," she jerked her hand out, "I felt a clap on my shoulder. 'Damned liar!' said Rose, and took me and flung me against a public-house wall!"
>
> Maggie stitched on in silence.

> "You got into a bus and went to Holborn," she repeated mechanically after a time. "And then?" (177)

The conversation continues in this vein, so that any meaning buried within Sara's fanciful assertions is lost.

When Martin runs into Sara in the 1914 section and takes her out to lunch, their conversation is repeatedly interrupted. When he tries to tell her he loathed the army and would have preferred to be an architect, she hushes him, saying, "Somebody's listening" (217). Once they are in the restaurant, the narrative tells us "it was impossible to talk. Too many people were listening" (219). Sara's imaginative outburst is stifled when she sums up the suffrage meeting she'd attended with Rose: "'Roll up the map of Europe,' said the man to the flunkey. 'I don't believe in force!' She brought down her fork. A plumstone jumped. Martin looked round. People were listening. He got up" (220). But when they leave the restaurant seeking the anonymity of the streets, we are told again that "conversation was impossible" (221) and twice more that "it was impossible to talk" (222). When they finally get on a bus and Martin hopes for some kind of "profound" communication, Sara is silent. Her silence indicates that Sara's creativity is not at his command; but in its deflation of Martin's hope for communion, it also suggests that the obstacles they have encountered are more general than Martin understands. It is not simply that they were in the wrong place for genuine communication; it is that the world no longer makes that possible. In its brutal repetition, history has cut into mental privacy and precluded original expression.

The novel links creativity, communion, and mental privacy and figures them all as imperiled in the scene where Sara and North are interrupted by the sounds of "the Jew in the bath." Much as the peddler crying "old iron to sell" in the holograph prevents Sara from playing the piano, here Sara and North are prevented from reciting a Marvell poem because they cannot ignore the sounds of Sara's neighbor Abrahamson bathing. As I argue in "The Jew in the Bath," it matters for understanding Woolf's late fiction and politics that the interrupting force is that of a Jewish male body. Here I want to stress that in these scenes where Sara's ability to communicate is foreclosed, it is because of outside pressures very much like those described in *A Room of One's Own*, pressures that "deform" the output of women writers.

One of the only scenes in the novel where a character can follow a train of thought to its natural conclusion takes place in the first, 1880, section, when Edward is at Cambridge, reading Greek. Edward's brain "gradually warmed; he was conscious of something quickening and tightening in his forehead. . . . His own dexterity at catching the phrase plumb in the middle gave him a thrill of excitement. There it was, clean and entire" (47). Even though he can hear a clock strike, this does not halt Edward's thought process: "his mind went on without the book. It traveled by itself without impediments through a world of pure meaning; but gradually it lost its meaning" (47). This scene clearly recalls Woolf's argument in *A Room of One's Own* that the men's colleges make possible the light, "halfway down the spine" (11), of free and full conversation and thought. Edward's mind lets drop the meaning it was carrying due not to an intrusion from without but to his mind's own natural pattern. The phrase "clean and entire" in this scene echoes the phrase "whole and entire," used multiple times in *Room* to apply to writers who are able to get their genius expressed (51, 56, 69, 72). In 1880, the novel suggests, a man in a protected space that nurtures his body and his intellect can still engage in free and unimpeded thought.

But by the later sections, this sustained concentration is not available to either men or women characters: both Martin and North are frustrated by interruptions and feel their mental privacy endangered (Martin with Sara at the chop house and then with Maggie in the park; North with Sara at her flat). It seems that the demands of history—which prompted Woolf to leave aside her attempts at "vision" and struggle with her novel of "fact"—have erected a barrier between the mind and its expression. Creative output is "deformed" by outside pressures just as it is for earlier women writers in *A Room of One's Own*. And Sara is the focal point of this problem. Her twisted body, while it contributes to her status outside the patriarchy and therefore paints her as *not* spiritually deformed, also symbolizes what Woolf seemed to view as the hobbled state of her own late modernism, which had to abandon private vision in favor of public fact.

One result is that, as an artist, Sara is hostile and mocking: instead of capturing the essence of a loved Mrs. Ramsay in the abstract shape of a purple triangle (corresponding to the wedge shape through which Mrs. Ramsay imagines herself), Sara sums up her loved ones in quick, dismissive phrases (281). Sara seems to represent both Woolf's commitment to external events—to her novel of fact—and her frustration with the social and political circumstances that obliged this commitment. In my discussion of Abrahamson, I argue that he "bear[s] responsibility not just for the threat to Sara's mental freedom, but also for political and artistic pressures on Woolf herself: to abandon her pacifism and to sacrifice her modernism of interiority and 'vision'" ("Jew in the Bath" 349). In a related way, Sara's twisted body bears the weight of Woolf's ambivalent responses to external pressures and interruptions, many of which she coded Jewish by placing Sara in the East End. Sara's deformity as well as her integrity keep her outside the procession of "servile" workers, enabling her, as Woolf recommended in *Three Guineas*, to make a virtue of women's historical exclusion from organized society. But the truncated quality of Sara's creative expressions seems to show that even in that space of Outsiderness there is no real mental privacy or freedom, anymore, to be found.

Compared to modernism of the 1920s, late modernist art would have to negotiate more directly with contemporary political reality. As Wallace Stevens put it, late modernism "has to face the men of the time and to meet / The women of the time. It has to think about war / And it has to find what will suffice" (*Collected Poems* 240). In that more direct engagement with history, evident throughout *The Years*, Woolf's art may indeed have lost something: the triumph of an artist's mind expressing its own vision. Woolf's sense of loss, in spite of her determination to "find what will suffice," is conveyed in this second metaphoric meaning of deformity in *The Years*, the deformity of late modernism.

Here Comes Everycrip

The deformity of late modernism is, in another sense, embodied in the layered, twisted, one might say conjoined words that make up *Finnegans Wake*.[42] With its relentlessly playful manipulations of language, identity, and the body, the *Wake* is no stranger to disability. Its hero (if so he can be called), HCE, is (sometimes) a stutterer and a "humpback" and its writer figure, Shem the Penman, is described by his twin brother Shaun as having a whole litany of disabilities and deformities. In book 1, chapter 7, "Shem the Penman," and to some degree in book 3, chapter 1, "Shaun the Post," Joyce depicts the writer as disabled, degenerate, and dysgenic. But as the writer of *Ulysses* and *Finnegans Wake*, he also functions as a creator, a life-giver. Indeed, "Shem the Penman" ends by asserting that Shem "lifts the lifewand and the dumb speak" (195.5). In *Finnegans Wake*, therefore, the devaluation of disability is overturned; the strong Aryan body of Shaun is seen as brutish and oppressive, and the racialized, disabled, dysgenic body of Shem is celebrated as the source of art and life. Finn Fordham suggests that the pathologies Shaun ascribes to Shem rebound onto Shaun. Shaun's condemnation of Shem "backfires on him: it is so excessive that it seems pathological, an exaggerated parody of the attacks on Joyce after *Ulysses*. The Shem who is described stops seeming real[,] becoming a fantasized other and figment of Shaun's fevered imagination. And so we sympathize with Shem's plea for mercy" (*Lots of Fun* 40).

In some ways this dynamic works because Shem and Shaun are not really fictional people but inchoate beings or sometimes even forces, with Shem representing all that is usually hidden from the conscious mind, all filth and shame, which is nevertheless artistically productive. In his landmark study *Joyce's Book of the Dark*, John Bishop describes the twins as forces battling in the dreamer's dream, one (Shaun) toward wakefulness and the other (Shem) toward sleep, the only state of being where his rejected and repressed qualities can emerge (240). Since, as Bishop maintains, to read *Finnegans Wake* is to enter into the dreamer's dream-consciousness, though, we naturally take Shem and Shaun to be people, though their identities keep strangely shifting.[43]

HCE, in one such shift, is also Tim Finnegan, who in the song from which Joyce adapted his title—"Lots of Fun at Finnegan's Wake"—falls, dies, and then revives when splashed with whiskey at his own wake. Joyce took the song as representative of the great themes of the fall and original sin, death and resurrection.[44] HCE's possession of a humpback can be heard in one of his names, *Hump*hrey Chimpden Earwicker. Fordham describes him in his introduction to the Oxford World Classics edition: "Fat, and in one set of incarnations, having a hunchback (or 'hump') and a stutter, [HCE] has stereotypical qualities of one who is guilty, embarrassed, or ashamed" (xiii). The motif of the fall is also explored through recurring Humpty Dumpty imagery frequently associated with HCE—Humpty Dumpty, who also has *hump* in his name, serves as another model for an archetypal falling being.[45]

This conjunction of disability, guilt, fall, and resurrection contributes to HCE's status as everyman. In his study of stuttering in the *Wake*, Christopher Eagle notes that "as his primary acronym ('Here Comes Everybody') suggests, HCE is a universal, all-encompassing patriarch, a concatenation of all heroes of all eras" ("Stuttistics" 84–85). Or as Patrick Moran puts it, HCE, "by being nothing, is everyone" (300).[46] The presence of disability in the list of what Joyce saw as universal human properties seems to presage what Lennard Davis claims about the "dismodern" subject—that all humans are wounded in one way or another, that the "dismodernist subject is in fact disabled, only completed by technology and by interventions" (*Bending* 30).

In book 2, chapter 3, men sitting around HCE's pub tell a story of a hunchbacked Norwegian sailor, also an HCE figure, who orders a suit from a local tailor and then is angry when it doesn't fit. According to Richard

Ellmann, the story came to Joyce through his father and godfather, Philip McCann. In the story,

> the finished suit did not fit him, and the captain berated the tailor for being unable to sew, whereupon the irate tailor denounced him for being impossible to fit. The subject was not promising, but it became, by the time John Joyce had told it, wonderful farce, and it is one of the parables of native and outlander, humorous but full of acid repartee, which found their way into *Finnegans Wake*. (R. Ellmann, *James Joyce* 22)

In this chapter, when the people in the pub witness the transaction between the sailor and the tailor, we hear "—Hump! Hump! Bassed the broaders-in laugh" (312.13). They seem to be telling the tailor to make the suit to fit the hump, because the tailor replies, "I will do that" (312.15); but their cry sounds like a cheer: "Hip! Hip!" Just after the men cry "Hump! Hump!" the "queriest of the crew" "fear[s] for his own misshapes" (313.31–32). Here and elsewhere *Finnegans Wake* celebrates its transformations and misshapes and, while making sport of the sailor's humpback, also universalizes disability as that which any everyman might have.

Dysgenic Shem

More important for my purposes here are the disabilities ascribed to Shem, the writer figure, a newly carnivalized, and what Margot Norris calls calibanized, portrait of the artist (72). Joseph Campbell and Henry Robinson remark that "Shem, indeed, as the Penman, is the scribe responsible for the actual writing of the mother's letter. He is, in fact, as the reader will immediately perceive, James Joyce himself" (123). The chapter begins, "Shem is as short for Shemus as Jem is Joky for Jacob," pointing out that Shem is a nickname for James (Shemus is Irish for James) (169.1).[47] Rose and O'Hanlon further explain Shem's identity as Joyce:

> The book Shem is said to read in his cell is *Ulysses*, and that which he is writing, *Finnegans Wake*. The titles of the stories in *Dubliners* can be detected spread out over pages 186 and 187. . . . Nobody reading the present chapter could doubt but that Shem's many failings, down to his eye-patch, derive from James Joyce himself. This is in stark contrast to Joyce's self-portrayal in his earlier fiction, an indulgence which Shaun here openly mocks. (104)

As this description makes clear, Joyce's self-portrait as Shem is very different from the self-aggrandizing portrayal of himself as Stephen Dedalus. The primary reason why Shem is depicted in such unsavory terms is that he makes it possible for Joyce to send up the attacks on him as a writer and human being since the publication of *Ulysses* by taking them to ridiculous extremes.

Norris points out that "the many voices that together speak Shaun's malediction of Shem include those of the modernists at their most unmodernistic. Shaun parodies the mean-spirited snobbism of Wyndham Lewis's *Time and Western Man*, Rebecca West's dithery fastidiousness in *The Strange Necessity*, and the hilarious vituperations of Pound's unbridled epistolary play" (73–74). Virginia Woolf's snide remark in "Modern Fiction" about the "poverty of the writer's mind" appears as "horrible awful poverty of mind" (192.10), part of a passage in which Shaun also criticizes Shem for abusing the "Parish funds." Norris glosses the latter phrase: "At the same time that he invokes here the accusations of fraud levied against Parnell for misusing the Paris funds, Joyce gives voice also to the tacit reproaches of Harriet Shaw Weaver and Sylvia Beach for his own abuse of 'Paris funds' . . . wasted on expensive taste in food, wine, and restaurants, while he never ceased to plead hardship and poverty'" (92). This alignment of himself with the maligned Parnell exemplifies Joyce's strategy in this chapter: by attacking himself in others' terms but taking the attacks to an extreme degree, he turns the tables on the attackers, making Shaun appear a nasty, often fascistic bully and Shem an innocent victim. This strategy results, as Norris argues, not only in a calibanized Shem but a calibanized text that is "oblig[ed] to internalize modernist attack" (72).

By rendering the many classist and racialized attacks on himself absurd and fanatical, Joyce sends up attacks on "unfit" human beings generally: he thereby shreds the credibility of eugenic discourses. "Shem the Penman" is saturated with eugenic language, as Shaun attacks Shem for his "lowness"—the word *low* appears in the chapter twenty-one times—and his connections with eugenically despised identities such as blackness, Jewishness, feeblemindedness, degeneracy, and other forms of disability. People hoped, for example, "or at any rate suspected . . . that he would early turn out badly, develop hereditary pulmonary T.B., and do for himself one dandy time" (172.12–14). This statement demonstrates popular linkages between character, hereditary disease, and suicide. And the assertion that people *hoped* he would develop T.B. exposes the wish fulfillment involved in eugenic dismissals of individual people. They hope he will develop this disease so they can justify their sense that he ought to "turn out badly." When a splash heard in the Liffey turns out not to be his suicide, the people around him are frustrated that he is not "true to type" (172.18), but facts do not put a dent in their eugenic condemnations.

Shem's lowness is such that it prevents him from being a man—in the sense both of masculine and of human being. When he poses the first riddle of the universe, asking, "when is a man not a man?" (170.5), the answer, he proclaims, is "when he is a . . . sham" (170.23–24). Shem himself, according to Shaun, who narrates the chapter, is a sham: "Shem was a sham and a low sham and his lowness creeped out first via foodstuffs" (170.25–26).[48] His lowness associates him with dogs, swine, beetles, and apes (171.30–31, 173.5–6, 192.22). We are told that "the pleb was born a Quicklow and sank alowing till he stank out of sight" (175.3–4). In the second draft, this was "but he was born low and sank lower till he sank out of sight" (Hayman 115). As he revised, Joyce transformed the second "sank" to "stank," added the reference to Wicklow, where he lived at Bray with his family when he was young, and adjusted "low" to "alow," which means "below," as in a ship's hold, stressing Shem's position at the bottom rungs of society.

Shem is racialized from the beginning of the chapter when we learn that he is "aboriginally" *not* "of respectable stemming" (169.2–3). This continues throughout the chapter, for example when he's called a "coon" and associated with "darkies" and "piccaninnies" (175.30, 33), when he's called a "hambone dogpoet" (177.21),[49] and when Shaun refers to him as a "nogger among the blankards of this dastard century" (188.13–14). Shem's identity as a Jew is established first in his name, Shem, the ancestor of the Semites, and runs throughout the chapter and indeed throughout *Finnegans Wake*. Shaun describes him as "semisemitic" (191.2–3) and jumbles up his racialization by calling him a "Europasianised Afferyank!" (191.4). As John Gordon notes in his detailed account of Shem's Jewishness, "he is called a sheeny (173.27, 179.6, 626.25), also an ikey (424.3), a jewboy (463.17), a gombeen-man (344.6; cf *Ulysses* 10.890), a yid (318.7), and, countlessly, some variant of 'jew,' 'yude,' 'ju,' 'jewy,' 'yu,' etc." ("Convertshems" 85). Len Platt points out that his Jewish, feebleminded degeneracy is similar to that of a "Jewish degenerate" described in Hitler's *Mein Kampf* (*Joyce, Race* 159).

Shem is a "disinterestingly low human type" (179.12–13) and is referred to as a "blethering ape" and a "simian" (192.4, 192.22) when being addressed by Justius/Shaun. Justius also accuses him of committing a "birthwrong" (190.12); this phrase plays on *birthright*, recalling Shem's identity as Esau.[50] But it also alludes to eugenics: since *eugenic* means well born or good birth, a birthwrong suggests a bad or dysgenic birth. Shem is referred to as a "hybrid"

(169.9) and a "pleb" (175.3) and can be identified as unfit by his walk (172.3–4). He's called a "dirty little blacking beetle" (171.30–31), described as "monstrous" (177.15), and in the most blunt eugenic terms, labeled a "mental and moral defective" (177.16).[51] Indeed, Joyce weaves in several references to the Jukes and Kallikaks, two (invented) families who were the subjects of eugenic treatises. Platt argues that these families are the "most frequently used signifier[s] of eugenics in the *Wake*" (*James Joyce* 139).[52]

According to Platt, R. L. Dugdale's *The Jukes: A Study in Crime, Pauperism, Disease and Heredity, also Further Studies of Criminals* (1877, revised in 1915) "emphasized that 'there was not one "Jukes" family alone in the state— . . . the Jukes family is the type of a great class.' Likewise, Henry Herbert Goddard's *The Kallikak Family—A Study of the Heredity of Feeble-Mindedness* (1912), warned that 'there are Kallikak families all about us'" (*Joyce, Race* 84). As Platt observes, Shem's

> construction as a "mental and moral defective" (177.16), a "hybrid" made up of "an adze of a skull, an eight of a larkseye, the whoel of a nose," and "one numb arm up a sleeve" (169.11–12), is clearly shaped by eugenicist literature of the Juke/Kallikak kind, as is the suggestion that his activities, if allowed to continue unchecked, would have the effect of wiping every "english spooker . . . off the face of the erse" (178.6–7). (*Joyce, Race* 86)

These imaginary families are used to discredit HCE (33.22–25) and his whole family (295n1; 375.3–4) and their names are sprinkled elsewhere in *Finnegans Wake* in a way that, as Platt puts it, transforms the "condition of the Jukes and Kallikaks" from their condition to ours, making it difficult to "tell the 'defectives' from the 'heroes'" (*Joyce, Race* 86).

In book 3, chapter 1, "Shaun the Post," Shem is further condemned in eugenic terms: Shaun describes Shem as "the iniquity that ought to be depraved of his libertins to be silenced, sackclothed and suspended, and placed in irons into some drapyery institution" (421.35–422.1). "Drapyery" is a reference to Jonathan Swift, who had written a series of pamphlets under the pseudonym M. B. Drapier and who left money to found a "lunatic asylum" in Dublin (McHugh 422). Shaun also complains that Shem "has a lowsense for the production of consumption and dalickey cyphalos on his brach premises where he can purge his contempt and dejeunerate into a skillyton be thinking himself to death. Rot him!" (422.6–9).[53]

Platt discusses this passage as a "comic interference with the 'science' of craniometry." Citing the eleventh edition of the *Encyclopedia Britannica*, which Joyce regularly consulted while writing *Finnegans Wake*, Platt explains that in craniometry, "'the skulls of the higher and lower races are compared' and 'various sub-racial types such as the dark and fair Europeans are brought together for the purposes of comparison and contrast.'" He glosses "dalickey cyphalos" as a reference to "Anders Retzius's 'cephalic' (with a play in Joyce's version on 'syphilis') or breadth index which measured the greatest width in a skull expressed as a percentage of the greatest length. Shem appears to his brother to be 'Negroid' or 'dolichocephalic' ('dalickey') as well as 'Samoyed' or 'brachycephalic'" (*James Joyce* 135). Shem is a racialized degenerate, with a skull simultaneously too wide and too narrow, who will "dejeunerate" or make breakfast of himself (French, *dejeuner*) while "thinking" or drinking "himself to death." The final "Rot him!" demonstrates the same wishful thinking involved in the people's hope that Shem would get hereditary T.B. and drown himself. Here Shaun assumes the degenerate will drink himself to death and rot, and believes he should be locked up to protect him from this fate; but his alleged concern fails to hide his murderous desire.

"Smears and Droppings"

Shem's status as defective, degenerate writer links him to the artists lambasted by Nazi art critics from Schultze-Naumburg to Hitler. I have not found direct evidence that Joyce was responding to Nazi art criticism or, later, to the Degenerate Art Exhibition or the Great German Art Exhibition of 1937. Indeed, he was not particularly interested in the visual arts.[54] But he was an avid reader of newspapers and paid close attention to Hitler's political progress and social programs.[55] As John Gordon has documented, he was incorporating Hitler references into *Finnegans Wake* from at least 1927 onward. Indeed, Gordon asserts that "James Joyce and his family aside, the twentieth-century figure most in evidence in *Finnegans Wake* is Adolf Hitler" ("Joyce's Hitler" 179).[56] Joyce was also well acquainted with Wyndham Lewis's changing relations with Nazism (and of course with Lewis's criticisms of Joyce as a member of the time school in *Time and Western Man*); Lewis published his book *Hitler* in 1931 and, as a painter himself, engaged with Nazi theories of art.[57] Moreover, since Nazi art critics were decrying in art all that they and eugenicists more broadly were decrying in human beings, there is necessarily significant overlap between the attacks on Shem as degenerate subject and Nazi attacks on degenerate art and artists.

Shem's racialization, for example, mirrors the Nazis' racialized attacks on

German arts. In 1928 the Militant League for German Culture published a manifesto characterizing the "'German' arts as a life-and-death struggle against the bastardization and niggerization of our existence" (Rabinbach, Gilman, and Friedberg 483). In 1930 William Frick (then Nazi minister of popular education for the state of Thuringia and later Hitler's minister of the interior) "formulated a law forbidding 'nigger culture for the German people'" (Rabinbach, Gilman, and Friedberg 483). In addition to Shem's association with "niggers," "coons," and "darkies" outlined above, Joyce added the line "Niggs, niggs, and niggs again" (183.5–6) in 1937 as he revised the first set of galleys for "Shem the Penman" (*JJA* 49:231). And Shem's work is labeled as foreign filth in "Shaun the Post": "Nothing beyond clerical horrors *et omnibus* to be entered for the foreign as second-class matter. The fuellest filth ever fired" (419.34–35).

In July 1937, at the opening of the Great German Art Exhibition, Hitler described "so-called modern artistic creators, with their abominable paint smears and droppings on canvas that could be bred, propagated, and applauded only by equally unconscionable and unscrupulous literary activity" (Rabinbach, Gilman, and Friedberg 497). These images of "smears and droppings" are echoed in any number of places in *Finnegans Wake* but perhaps especially in Shem's shit-writing, as he produces from his "unheavenly body a no uncertain quantity of obscene matter. . . . through the bowels of his misery, flashly, faithly, nastily, appropriately" (185.29–34). Hitler also described modern artists as "pathetically confused and befuddled paintbrush pushers and scribblers" (Rabinbach, Gilman, and Friedberg 498). Joyce had already written that Shem "scribbled and scratched," but on the galley proofs he intensified this to "scrabbled and scratched and scriobbled and skrevened nameless shamelessness about everybody he ever met" (182.13–14; *JJA* 49:231). And to reinforce his mockery of the idea that literature should serve nationalist aims, he added a clause to the first set of galley proofs: "from the Monster Book of Paltryattic Puetrie" (178.16–17; *JJA* 49:225). Patriotic poetry, it seems, is monstrous, paltry, and puerile and ought to be hidden away in the attic.

Hitler and Adolph Ziegler—the president of the Nazi Visual Arts Chamber, who organized the Degenerate Art Exhibition—also accused modern artists of being swindlers, trying to fool the German people (Rabinbach, Gilman, and Friedberg 499–503). Such accusations in the speeches at the openings of the 1937 exhibitions happened too late to have directly contributed to Shem's identity as a forger, which Joyce had given him from the beginning of *Work in Progress* through his association with the forger Jim the Penman. But Hitler had been attacking modern art since at least 1931, when he "threatened 'to release a tornado' against it" (Chipp 474). In 1933 "official Nazi propaganda organs demanded that 'all artistic productions with cosmopolitan or bolshevist tendencies must be thrown out of German museums and collections.' . . . In 1935, in a speech at Nuremberg, Hitler had threatened: 'One will no longer discuss or deal with corruptors of art. They are fools, liars, or criminals who belong in insane asylums or prisons'" (Chipp 474). These attitudes correspond with the claims that Shem too is a fool, liar, and criminal who should be deprived of his liberty and locked up in an institution, and that his work is a swindle: "what do you think Vulgariano did but study with stolen fruit how cutely to copy all their various styles of signature so as one day to utter an epical forged cheque on the public for his own private profit" (181.14–17). Such similarities between Nazi depictions of modern artists and Shaun's depictions of Shem illuminate Joyce's engagement with these broadly circulating discourses.

In 1937, on the galley proofs of book 1, Joyce added additional references to Hitler, Nazism, and eugenics. He added two variants of *dictator*, for example, to the beginning of "Shem the Penman." He changed "asked" to "dictited" when Shem "dictited to all his little brothron and sweestureens the first riddle of the universe" (170.3–4; *JJA* 49:215). And he added the appositive, "the doctator," merging medical and fascist imagery, when Shem answers the riddle himself (170.22; *JJA* 49:215). He intensified Shem's racialization by adding "*Heali Baboon and the Forky Theagues*" to the list of games (176.13–14; *JJA* 49:223). And most intriguingly, he added a section accusing Shem of violating "the Uncontrollable Birth Preservativation (Game and Poultry) Act" by cooking eggs (184.15–16; *JJA* 49:233). Although ostensibly about food, Shem's crime here is clearly one of miscegenation, with eggs serving as a brilliant symbol. In defiance of the act, Shem cooked and mixed together "whites and yolks and yilks and whotes to the frulling fredonnance of *Mas blanca que la blanca Hermana* and *Amarilla, muy bien*" (184.18–20; *JJA* 49:233). Here Shem is mixing whites with yolks/yellows, with imagery of spring, humming, flutes, egg whisks, whiteness, and yellowness woven into the language, whose mixture of English and Spanish only emphasizes his crime against purity (Glosses of *Finnegans Wake*; McHugh 184). These additions demonstrate Joyce's close attention not only to the Nazis' political progress but to their sociocultural prohibitions.

The following year Joyce continued to strengthen Shem's entrapment by fascistic forces. Just after Shaun attacks Shem for being a "nomad" and a "semisemitic serendipitist," the text reads, "Shall we follow each others a steplonger, drowner of daggers, whiles our liege, tilyet a stranger in the frontyard of his happiness, is taking, (heal helper! one gob, one gap, one gulp and gorger of all!) his refreshment?" (191.5–8). Joyce added the phrases "drowner of daggers," "tilyet a stranger in the frontyard of his happiness," and the parenthetical "Heil Hitler" and mockery of the Nazi slogan in 1938 (*JJA* 50:242–43). As I note in "The Jew's Text," this passage satirizes the slogan "Ein Volk, Ein Reich, Ein Führer" by painting Hitler as a giant mouth ("gob") who will gorge himself on Europe for his refreshment.

Similarly, on the galley proofs of book 3, which he corrected in late 1937 or early 1938, Joyce added further commentary on eugenics and fascism. Where Shaun dismisses Shem as "Mr. Unmentionable," Joyce added a parenthetical appeal: "(O breed not his same!)" (420.4; *JJA* 62:23). This is a reference to the Thomas Moore song "O Breathe Not His Name" (McHugh 420), a song about Robert Emmett, but Joyce has transformed it into a comical eugenic prayer that the unfit Shem not reproduce. On the same set of galleys he added another instance of *dictator*: "Digteter! Grundtsagar! Swop beef!" (423.18; *JJA* 62:27). *Digteter* contains "dig," "eater," and "tater," possibly a reference to Hitler, famously vegetarian, eating vegetables—potatoes—dug from the ground. *Grundtsagar* is a version of the Danish for "green vegetables" (*Finnegans Wiki*) and aptly contains the syllable "grunt," while *sager* is German for "sayer," one who says something—here, perhaps, one who grunts. Given the food imagery woven into this line, the "tsagar" also conjures *Zucker*, sugar.[58] "Swop beef" suggests "stop thief!" (McHugh 423) and returns us to the gobbling imagery of book 1, chapter 7—Hitler is a grunting thief who will dig up Europe's ground ("grundt") as he gobbles up Europe.

Joyce's awareness of Nazi prohibitions also shapes a key addition to Book 3, chapter 1, "Shaun the Post." In the middle thirties, as he edited the version that had appeared in *transition* for the printer of *Finnegans Wake*, Joyce added into Shaun's speech an explicitly eugenic attack on Shem's unfit body: "Never mind his falls feet and his tanbark complexion. That's why he was forbidden tomate and was warmed off the ricecourse of marrimoney, under the Helpless Corpses Enactment" (423.28–31; *JJA* 61:21). This eugenic condemnation is sanctioned, as we can see from its title, by HCE, representing the law of the father or government. In alleging that Shem has false feet (and falls over his feet), Shaun alludes to the accusation that Jews had flat feet, a claim nineteenth-century Germans used to prevent Jews from enlisting in the German military (Gilman 40–41). Hitler was enacting such marriage prohibitions ("forbidden tomate") in the 1935 Nuremberg Laws. Another relevant example of his eugenic policies was asserted in his speech at the Great German Art Exhibition, where he claimed that if the painters really did see the world the way they represented it, doctors would need to determine whether this was due to individual or genetic eye maladies. If the eye diseases were hereditary, such persons would become the concern of the ministry of the interior, "which would be charged with the task of preventing the perpetuation of these horrific diseases of the eye in future generations" (Rabinbach, Gilman, and Friedberg 499).

As I mention above, Hitler described modern artists and their subjects as "deformed cripples." This rhetoric continued throughout the 1930s, culminating in the speeches by Hitler at the Great German Art Exhibition and by Ziegler at the Degenerate Art Exhibition. In his speech Hitler asked, "and what do you continue manufacturing? Deformed cripples and cretins, women whose image can but elicit disgust, men who look more like animals than humans, children who would be considered a curse from God if they were to actually live the way you portray them!" (Rabinbach, Gilman, and Friedberg 498). Hitler also referred to modern artists as "utterly archaic, deplorable retards who have no place whatsoever in our modern times" (Rabinbach, Gilman, and Friedberg 500), while Ziegler described the "degenerate" art works as "miscreants of madness, the mutant by-products of impudence, of ineptitude, and of degeneracy" (Rabinbach, Gilman, and Friedberg 501). Shem's bodily deformations precede these speeches—though Joyce developed and intensified them throughout the 1930s—but the correspondence indicates the degree to which the Nazis were applying to artists and artworks rhetoric of degeneration and deformity that had developed and circulated over the previous half century within the science of eugenics.

Writing on the Body

Shem's body is a wild caricature of a deformed degenerate:

> Shem's bodily getup, it seems, included an adze of a skull, an eight of a larkseye, the whoel of a nose, one numb arm up a sleeve, fortytwo hairs off his uncrown, eighteen to his mock lip, a trio of barbels from his megagegg chin (sowman's son), the wrong shoulder higher than the right, all ears, an artificial tongue with a natural curl, not a foot to stand on, a handful of thumbs, a blind stomach, a deaf heart, a loose liver, two fifths of two buttocks, one gleetsteen avoirdupoider for him, a manroot of all evil, a salmonkelt's thinkskin, eelsblood in his cold toes, a bladder transtended. (169.11–20)

Starting from the top of Shem's skull, this description moves down his body, cataloging his deformities. McHugh explains the origins of many of these words and phrases, which link Shem to untrustworthiness ("something up his sleeve"), sexual perversion ("gleet" is a slimy, morbid discharge from the urethra; "manroot" is slang for penis and conjures "money is the root of all evil"), and subhuman status (McHugh points out that barbels are filaments hanging from the mouths of some fishes and that the goat in *Ulysses* bleats "Megeggaggegg!" Shem is also here compared to a sow, salmon, and eels). The most relevant phrases for my purposes are those in which Joyce plays with the metaphoric meanings that commonly link human foibles to disabilities: "all ears," "a handful of thumbs," "not a foot to stand on," "a blind stomach," and "a deaf heart." By using these phrases in a mock-literal way Joyce calls attention to their inadequacies, even their downright silliness, as metaphors.

As in the case histories of dysgenic families (real or imagined) in eugenic literature, Shem's environment and his body intertwine in a simultaneous explanation for and description of his degeneracy. The Jukes, for example, have a "habitat" that Dugdale describes as consisting of "rude shelters" and "shanties" with "overcrowding so close it suggested that these dwellings were the country equivalents of city tenement houses" (14). Shem's "Haunted Inkbottle" house is similarly designated a "stinksome inkenstink, quite puzzonal to the wrottel" (183.6–7). "Puzzonal" combines "personal" with Italian "puzzone," or stinky, while "wrottel" combines "writer" and Danish "rotte," or rat, and "to the wrottel" suggests "to the letter" or "to the fullest extent" (Glosses of *Finnegans Wake*). The text goes on to describe the house in great and gross detail—it contains, for example, "fresh horrors from Hades, globules of mercury, [and] undeleted glete" (more slimy matter)—until it sounds like the crammed hovel of a hoarder, a space that "has become unliveable because of its failure to discard seemingly valueless objects" (Moran 286). As Norris puts it, Joyce conflates "Shem's mind, house, body, and writing into a single class trope, that of the slum. . . . The writing of the chapter—in its abandonment of modernistic scrupulosity and clarity—becomes itself tenemental, full of junk, filth, brokenness, and squalor" (83).

So, when Shem is trying to or "making believe to read his usylessly unreadable Blue Book of Eccles" (179.26–27)—*Ulysses*—he is prevented by a mixture of bodily and environmental factors.

> But what with the murky light, the botchy print, the tattered cover, the jigjagged page, the fumbling fingers, the foxtrotting fleas, the liabed lice, the scum on his tongue, the drop in his eye, the lump in his

> throat, the drink in his pottle, the itch in his palm, . . . the fog of his mindfag, the buzz in his Braintree, . . . the squince in his suil, the rot in his eater, the ycho in his earer, the totters of his toes, the tetters on his tumptytum, the rats in his garret, the bats in his belfry, . . . and the dust in his ears . . . he was hardset to mumorise more than a word a week. (180.17–30)

Shem's "mind, house, body and writing" are so conjoined that when the text describes the rats in his garret and the bats in his belfry, we cannot be sure whether these are metaphorical conditions of Shem's body or literal conditions of his disgusting house. With "murky light," "botchy print," "the drop in his eye," and "the squince in his suil" (*suil* is Irish for eye), the passage emphasizes Shem's poor eyesight and therefore his identity as Joyce. Joyce has portrayed himself as a racialized, disabled, degenerate figure who has written *Ulysses* and is in the process of writing *Finnegans Wake*.

This writing both emerges from and is written on Shem's deformed body. The occasion for Shem's shit-writing is that a combination of figures from Joyce's publishing history, from Dublin's judicial scene, and from the church, boycotted his use of paper and candles. So "he winged away on a wildgoup's chase across the kathartic ocean and made synthetic ink and sensitive paper for his own end out of his wit's waste" (185.5–8). The description of his process of ink making is "cloaked up" in Latin so as not to scandalize an Anglican "ordinal" (185.10). But within the Latin passage there are English parentheticals that convey pretty much the whole story: "(highly prosy, crap in his hand, sorry!)," "(did a piss, says he was dejected, asks to be exonerated)," and "(faked O'Ryan's, the indelible ink)" (185.17–18, 185.23, 185.25–26). With this ink made from his own waste, but still lacking paper, this

> first till last alshemist wrote over every square inch of the only foolscap available, his own body, till by its corrosive sublimation one continuous present tense integument slowly unfolded all marryvoising moodmoulded cyclewheeling history (thereby, he said, reflecting from his own individual person life unlivable, transaccidentated through the slow fires of consciousness into a dividual chaos, perilous, potent, common to allflesh, human only, mortal). (185.34–186.6)

Writing on his own body, Shem captures, as the first draft had it, "universal history" (Hayman 108). This history is now illustrated as merry, many-voiced, able to mold moods—suggesting the epiklesis Joyce wanted to effect on the people of Dublin through *Dubliners*—and to capture the Viconian cycles of history. As Fordham points out, "manyvoiced" describes *Finnegans Wake* itself, a "polylogue blending different voices and accents and dialects as much as different languages" (*Lots of Fun* 56).[59]

The high-flown rhetoric of "perilous, potent, common to allflesh, human only, mortal" raises the pitch of the passage to a climax similar to that of Stephen's prophecy in *Portrait*. This moment in "Shem the Penman" illustrates Shelly Brivic's assertion that "every particle of the *Wake*'s world is both sacramental and obscene" (472). By writing on his own body, and by serving as the writer of his own "polylogue," Shem becomes the text of *Finnegans Wake*—which is to say the utterly disabled, dysgenic body becomes the body of the text: deformity becomes modernism. When Shaun finishes his long, detailed attack on Shem, "he points the deathbone and the quick are still" (193.29). Shaun's vicious eugenic disqualification of Shem, then, turns life to dust. Shem's disabled creativity, however, "lifts the lifewand and the dumb speak" (195.5). This "alshemist" converts the dull metals of his own body into gold by virtue of his identity as Shem, the Penman, the deformed body of *Finnegans Wake*.

Shem's deformed body-text seems to instantiate Miller's claim that "in the empty spaces left by high modernism's dissolution, late modernists reassembled fragments into disfigured likenesses of modernist masterpieces" (14). Joyce's celebration of deformity as modernism differs from the more negative representations of deformed types of modernism in Moore and Woolf. But it also highlights the connections they too have drawn between modernist literature and deformity. All three authors rely on representations of deformity—Richard's, Sara's, and Shem's—as they reimagine modernism from the vantage of the 1930s. And all three entertain the notion that texts have or are bodies, creating, in their late works, intricately disfigured bodies of modernism.

Epilogue

As modernism enlisted disabled bodies in its myriad attempts to make literature new, it acknowledged the active role of bodies in our subjective lives, imagining links—both positive and negative—between disabled bodies and aspects of modernity. In Jean Rhys's *Good Morning, Midnight* (1939) there is a sense that disability, though constantly disavowed, is the condition of the modern subject. Having decided to drink herself to death in London, the protagonist, Sasha Jansen, looks at a "shop-window full of artificial limbs" and immediately afterward visits a friend "who said: 'I can't bear to see you looking like this'" (11). The conjuncture of prostheses with the comment about Sasha's own condition suggests an identification with disability and sets up her subsequent trip to Paris, paid for by this friend, as a sort of prosthetic limb meant to help her mask her disabled condition and blend into modern society. As Sasha describes it, in Paris she must "get on with the transformation act" (63) in an effort to "look like everybody else" (106).

When, in a flashback, Sasha is confronted by a boss she dubs Mr. Blank, she responds with explicit disability imagery. "Let's say that you have this mystical right to cut my legs off. But the right to ridicule me afterwards because I am a cripple—no, that I think you haven't got. And that's the right you hold most dearly, isn't it?" (29). Sasha's resigned acceptance of capitalism ("you have this mystical right to cut my legs off") ends in a sharp indictment of ableism: her metaphoric way of describing the disgust prompted in the rich and powerful by the poor. Her positioning of herself as a "cripple" because she is "slightly damaged in the fray" (29) ties *Good Morning, Midnight* to the other texts I've discussed in this study that use disability as a way to explore modern identity.

This identification with disability also prompts Sasha's delight in the paintings she encounters in the studio of the exiled Russian Jewish painter

Serge (modeled on Simon Segal, an Expressionist/Cubist painter whom Rhys befriended in Paris).[1] Serge's paintings depict "misshapen dwarfs [who] juggle with huge coloured balloons . . . [a] four-breasted woman" (101), and "an old Jew with a red nose playing the banjo." Sasha describes the banjo player as "resigned, mocking, a little mad"; "double-headed, double-faced"; and "with four arms" (101, 109). These paintings exemplify Siebers's claim that "modern art continues to move us because of its refusal of harmony, bodily integrity, and perfect health. If modern art has been so successful . . . it is because of its embrace of disability as a distinct version of the beautiful" (*Disability Aesthetics* 5–9).

Like Picasso's literally multifaceted representations of his subjects, Serge's modernist paintings use distortion and deformity to depict what the artist understands as our perceptions, in time, of the planes and angles of other human beings. As Ronald Penrose writes, Picasso "was always amazed at the discrepancy between seeing an object and knowing it" (88). Gertrude Stein characterizes this discrepancy as one between seeing and reconstructing:

> Really most of the time one sees only a feature of a person with whom one is, the other features are covered by a hat, by the light, by clothes for sport and everybody is accustomed to complete the whole entirely from their knowledge, but Picasso when he saw an eye, the other one did not exist for him . . . and as a painter, and particularly as a Spanish painter, he was right, one sees what one sees, the rest is a reconstruction from memory and painters have nothing to do with reconstructions, nothing to do with memory. (15)

The deformity of the subjects, then, is cast in such paintings not only as the beautiful but as the true: the way we see when we look without preconceptions of what we are seeing. In the presence of Serge's paintings, Sasha experiences a rare moment of peace: "the room expands and the iron band round my heart loosens. The miracle has happened. I am happy" (99).

This iron band signals the constricting pressure of the normal, the cultural insistence that Sasha do whatever it takes to "look like everybody else." Its loosening in the presence of these paintings indicates the expansive release and relief Sasha experiences when surrounded by the nonnormative figures. She feels freed by the mad, misshapen, double-faced subjects to let fall her metaphoric prosthetic limb and give up—for the moment—her "transformation act." This moment in *Good Morning, Midnight* suggests a way to understand nonnormative bodies in modernist literature (and painting) as agents of freedom in the face of the stifling enforcement of normalcy.

A similar attraction to disability appears in Woolf's *The Waves* (1931), where the emotionally fragile Rhoda prizes deformity. In this "play-poem," as Woolf described it, the six characters who speak are all enamored with a nonspeaking character named Percival. When Percival dies, Rhoda thinks, "The human face is hideous. This is to my liking. . . . I like the passing of face and face and face, deformed, indifferent. I am sick of prettiness; I am sick of privacy" (115). She considers an offering to Percival: violets she will throw at the end of her monologue. "These then are the flowers that grow among the rough grasses of the field which the cows trample, wind-bitten, almost deformed, without fruit or blossom. These are what I bring" (118). In her grief Rhoda identifies with the ugliness of the human and natural worlds, and Woolf uses physical deformity as both a correlative to and a consolation for her distress.

Deformity is associated more subtly with Rhoda through her adoration of one of the teachers in the school episode, Miss Lambert. Miss Lambert has a "hunch," a curved spine:

> "When Miss Lambert passes," said Rhoda, "talking to the clergyman, the others laugh and imitate her hunch behind her back; yet everything changes and becomes luminous. Jinny leaps higher too when Miss Lambert passes. Suppose she saw that daisy, it would change. . . . When Miss Lambert passes, she makes the daisy change; and everything runs like streaks of fire when she carves the beef. Month by month things are losing their hardness; even my body now lets the light through; my spine is soft like wax near the flame of the candle. I dream; I dream." (31)

The other girls' mockery of Miss Lambert's "hunch" means for Rhoda a sense of kinship with the teacher. In a creative alliance with disability, Rhoda transforms her awareness of Miss Lambert's curved spine into the image of her own spine becoming soft like wax, an image that links sexual desire with deformity. Rhoda's image of the waxen spine is carried forward by the writer figure, Bernard, in the final episode. Bernard describes how "the virginal wax that coats the spine melted in different patches for each of us" (178) and how his "waxen waistcoat melted, here one drop, there another" (182). By generalizing Rhoda's image, Bernard validates what began as an association between deformity and Rhoda's susceptibility to her teacher's "luminous" presence.

As this project has made clear, modernism also—often within the same texts in which it interrogates it—acts to *enforce* normalcy. In what we might call its eugenic mode, it associates disability with aspects of human being that it disdains, for example by portraying deaf characters as lacking the usual rhythms of human consciousness. Casting nonnormative embodiment as a degraded state, many early twentieth-century artworks nevertheless suggest that this degradation can be transcended through the superiority of modernist art. Henri Matisse's comment about the woman in his painting *Blue Nude* demonstrates the distinction many artists made between real and aestheticized bodies. As Christopher Butler describes it, "*Nu Bleu* (*Blue Nude*) (1907) [was] a rude challenge to mildly salacious academic painting on the Venus theme. . . . Her 'ugliness'—in the deformation of the bulbous breasts, the spherical head, and elongated torso—echoes common features of African sculpture. Matisse admitted later (in 1939) that should he meet 'such a woman in the street, I should run away in terror'" (107). This blunt statement expresses a revulsion common to many representations of deformity and disability (here strongly gendered and racialized): they are acceptable only to the degree that they have been transformed into and transcended by art.

In "The Rage of Caliban" Davidson quotes Gottfried Lessing, who asserts that a monstrous body provides a welcome challenge to the artist:

> "Who will wish to paint you, when no one wishes to see you?" says an old epigrammatist concerning an extremely misshapen man. Many a more modern artist would say, "Be you as misshapen as is possible, I will paint you nevertheless. Though, indeed, no one may wish to see you, people will still wish to see my picture; not insofar as it represents you, but in so far as it is a demonstration of my art, which knows how to make so good a likeness of such a monster. (611)

The modern artist, Lessing claims, makes beauty out of what in real life would prompt aversion (or even "terror"), much as Moore uses Richard's deformed body not to shatter normative ideas about the body but to showcase her own writerly talent.

Woolf's character Neville demonstrates a similar attitude about the triumph of art over deformity when he describes his quest to "oppose the waste and deformity of the world, its crowds eddying round and round disgorged and trampling. . . . Everything must be done to rebuke the horror of deformity" (131). He reprises this imagery when he determines that he and his friends must "oppose ourselves to this illimitable chaos . . . this formless imbecility" (166). Against the formlessness associated with deformity and imbecility, Neville proposes reading "writers of Roman severity and virtue; [seeking] perfection through the sand" (131). Although *The Waves* offers a highly formal depiction of six consciousnesses that could be said to "rebuke the horror of deformity," it does not wholly endorse Neville's view. Its inclusion of Rhoda and its use of her image of the waxen spine offer counterpoints to Neville's compulsion to iron out the wrinkles in human embodiment with virtuous severity.

A related sense that disability is being transcended through artistic form emanates from Picasso's paintings of blind figures, mostly painted during his Blue Period. Because the figures are not only blind but poor and painted in the muted tones characteristic of this period of Picasso's oeuvre, they portray blindness—with what has been described as "insistent pathos" (Barr 29)—as a condition of sadness and isolation. Penrose notes that "in Barcelona, Picasso found models at almost every street corner for his paintings of the blind." As Patrick O'Brian details,

> Unemployment increased; the fate of the poorer working people and of the outcasts, the old, the blind, the crippled, grew more desperate still. This was reflected in Picasso's painting: 1903 was the year of the "Old Jew" (an ancient blind beggar with a little bright-eyed boy guarding him), the "Blind Man's Meal" (a thin figure, quite young, seated at a table, holding a piece of bread and feeling for the pitcher), and of the "Old Guitar-Player". . . . Picasso was deeply concerned with poverty, with blindness (poverty's ultimate degree), and with solitude. (116–17)

When O'Brian describes blindness as the "ultimate degree" of poverty, he is both expressing cultural assumptions about blindness as a pathetic state and pointing out, as he explains, that blindness in this period often resulted from "the greater and lesser pox," which Spain was "the first to receive" from the New World (117). The spare quality of the paintings does seem to associate blindness with a bleak solitude, even when, as in *Old Jew*, there is an additional figure in the painting.

However, the beauty and formal elegance of the paintings also suggest that blindness may be a route to artistic transformation. About *Blind Man's Meal*, Penrose observes that the blind man's "visual sense finds a substitute in the touch of his hand, and . . . he again sees clearly with his own inner vision" (88). Through these paintings of blind figures, Picasso suggests that "there is a metaphorical inner eye that sees and feels emotionally . . . and this inner seeing may be all the more intense when the windows on the outer world are closed" (Penrose 88–89). *Blind Man's Meal* can be seen as a visual counterpart of Lawrence's story "The Blind Man" in that both portrayals stress the emotional and spiritual benefits of blindness, its allegedly attendant increase in intensity of experience. Likewise, viewers of *The Old Guitarist*, which appears on the cover of this volume, get the sense that the musician's blindness enhances his absorption in the music of the guitar.

In *The Old Guitarist*, one of the most famous of the Blue Period, the guitarist bows over his instrument as though paying it homage. As O'Brian describes it, the painting is structured by a counterbalance between the guitarist's left hand, holding the strings on the neck of the guitar, and the "sharply-bowed blind head" (117). This counterbalance stresses the relation between the man's blindness and his emotional or spiritual investment in music. The Art Institute of Chicago's *Essential Guide* calls the figure "a timeless expression of human suffering. The bent and sightless man holds his large, round guitar close to him; its brown body is the painting's only shift in color" (245). This shift in color centered in the guitar indicates the transformation of "human suffering" into art, a transformation enacted by the guitarist as he plays his instrument and by Picasso as he paints the spare, formally sophisticated, and haunting portrait. This painting was influenced by the Symbolist movement (*Essential Guide* 245), the same movement whose associations between blindness and creativity moved Henry Green in his depiction of John Haye. And it in turn caught the attention of Wallace Stevens, whose poem series "The Man with the Blue Guitar" also emphasizes the theme of transformation.[2]

As Aviram and Harnett describe Stevens's poem series, it "build[s] itself up out of its own musings on how the self and its contingent, ever-changing perceptions of reality may be represented" (208). The first poem of the series reads:

> The man bent over his guitar,
> A shearsman of sorts. The day was green
>
> They said, "You have a blue guitar,
> You do not play things as they are."
>
> The man replied, "Things as they are
> Are changed upon the blue guitar."
>
> And they said then, "But play you must,
> A tune beyond us, yet ourselves,

A tune upon the blue guitar
Of things exactly as they are." (Stevens, *Collected Poems* 165)

In this initial poem Stevens imagines a dialogue with an audience of those who seek realism and object to the artist's shaping of reality. But when the artist responds that reality is transformed "upon the blue guitar," that, in effect, modernist art depicts reality in ways that shed new light on "things as they are," the audience members assent. By conceding that the guitarist must play "a tune beyond us, yet ourselves," they open themselves not only as listeners but as subjects to such transformation. Indeed, in titling the poem series "The Man with the Blue Guitar," Stevens takes part in this transformation by ascribing the color blue to the guitar—the only object in the painting that is *not* blue. Eleanor Cook points out that in Stevens's poetry, the color blue is associated with imagination (113).

The musician's blindness is implicated in the power of these transformations. He may not see things as they are, but like the painter Uller in Moore's *Spleen*, whose painting "for all its absurdity . . . had caught the browny-blue bloom which [its subject] gave off like a fruit," the guitarist catches the bloom of the audience—depicting them as they are and changing them into aesthetic subjects at once. As the audience members later acknowledge, "Ourselves in poetry must take [the] place" of "empty heaven and its hymns" (167). The phrase "ourselves in poetry" reiterates the idea that in art, we are represented "beyond us yet ourselves." Stevens described the poem series as dealing with "the relation or balance between imagined things and real things, which . . . is a constant trouble to me. . . . Perhaps it would be better to say that what they really deal with is the painter's problem of realization: I have been trying to see the world about me both as I see it and as it is" (*Letters* 316). By invoking the blind guitarist Stevens signals the inner vision—imagination—that must be balanced with the world "as it is" in order fully to represent "ourselves in poetry."

When Stevens writes in poem XXXII, "Nothing must stand // Between you and the shapes you take / When the crust of shape has been destroyed" (*Collected Poems* 183), he emphasizes a direct contact—as opposed to the indirect contact created by vision—between an artist and the shape of his subject, a contact that recalls the long, El Greco–like hands of the blind guitarist in Picasso's painting. Much as Lawrence's Maurice Pervin enjoys direct contact with objects, the guitarist's hands in Stevens's representation give him a sense of immediacy, a sense of being outside of the temporality that skews our perceptions and requires us to weigh things as we see them against things as they are.[3] The composite blind guitarist created by Picasso and Stevens, then, offers a "fortunate blindness" (Schor 85) made up of inner vision, immediate contact, and the possibility of transformation, written palimpsestically atop the conception of blindness as symbol of "human suffering."

In "Seeing the Disabled," Garland-Thomson describes distinct modes, or "visual rhetorics," of representing disability in photography: the wondrous, the sentimental, the exotic, and the realistic. She summarizes the four rhetorics: "the wondrous mode directs the viewer to look up in awe of difference; the sentimental mode instructs the viewer to look down with benevolence; the exotic mode coaches the observer to look across a wide expanse toward an alien object; and the realistic mode suggests that the onlooker align with the object of scrutiny" (346). Her taxonomy is helpful in thinking about the use of disability in modernist literature as well. Modernism seems to offer a combination of the latter two modes. It views disability as something radically other: a deaf character whose visual thinking cannot be represented by his creator; a blind character whose sense of contact with his world is "unspeakable"; a deformed person with vacant, indecipherable eyes. And yet through its efforts to remake literature, through its reconception of the body as a crucial aspect of our subjectivity, and through its insistence that the material reality of any body can be transformed into art, modernism at the same time brings this otherness close: a woman with a wooden leg who "just by the grace of god escapes" being identical to her author;[4] a deaf waiter who merges with the protagonist in a literary musical chord; a blind stripling who is the protagonist's "more than brother"; a woman with a twisted spine who comes "straight out of [her author's] psyche" (Radin 42); a deformed outcast who represents his author; a blind guitarist who plays a tune "beyond us, yet ourselves." We might call this paradoxical combination of othering and selving—of casting and reeling in—the modernist mode of representing disability. This mode does understand disability as alien and unfathomable. But it also entertains the possibility that radical otherness is in fact within us: that because of the astonishing variety of human embodiment and experience, our selves are always already inhabited by otherness.

Notes

Introduction

1. The impairment/disability distinction, like the sex/gender distinction, is useful politically but does not hold up under scrutiny. Garland-Thomson gives an example of the social construction of impairment when she remarks that "[p]eople who cannot lift three hundred pounds are 'able-boded,' whereas those who cannot lift fifty pounds are 'disabled'" (*Extraordinary* 7). Georgina Kleege similarly points out that our current definitions of blindness have to do with whether someone can read print and drive a car, and that in other cultures and times, lower levels of vision would be considered adequate (*Sight Unseen* 14–15). In his criticism of what we might call the "strong" version of the social model, Tom Shakespeare counts the "crude distinction between impairment (medical) and disability (social)" as a problem with the model (218).

2. For discussions of the ways contemporary body theory has neglected and even reified disability, see Siebers's chapter "Body Theory" (*Disability Theory*) and Erevelles's chapter "Disability as 'Becoming.'"

3. The Modernist Studies Association centered its 2015 MLA roundtable on "Modernism, Feminism, and Disability," and disability studies panels have begun to appear more frequently at modernist conferences. Books such as Sanchez's *Deafening Modernism* and recent articles such as Davidson's on modernist aesthetics and disabled bodies ("Rage"), Lyon's on Virginia Woolf's responses to intellectual disability ("On the Asylum Road"), and Valente's on autism in Joseph Conrad's *The Secret Agent* ("Accidental Autist") bode well for modernist disability studies.

4. While not using specific disability rhetoric, Levenson's description of the avant-garde's venom can be seen in the same light: "The polemical violence of the avant-garde is only understandable when linked to a vision of the larger social whole, a vision of that whole as moribund, decadent and stifling to creative endeavor" (138). That is, modernist artists felt they must jettison the "moribund" or disabled contemporary scene in order to make art new.

5. Michael Davidson suggests that we call the "close connection between vanguard aesthetic formations and ideas of bodily health and ability" "biopoetics" ("Rage" 612).

6. I don't, therefore, quite agree with Janet Lyon's provocative claim, made in a conference paper at MLA 2015, that while "modernists may be disability-phobes, by and large, modernism isn't, and can't be. Its aesthetics are tied to the generative powers of unhealthy, crookedness, myopia, cracked thinking, perseveration, non-Aristotelian sensoria, disproportion."

7. In a 2015 conference paper, Tobin Siebers stressed the embodied knowledge produced by disability, suggesting that people with disabilities can and should be identified "by their possession and use of the knowledge gathered and created by them as long-time inhabitants of nondisabled society" and arguing that "disability is a body of knowledge" ("Returning the Social"). There are, that is, meaningful interactions between disability and knowledge in disabled people; but as I point out in the chapters that follow, modernist imaginings of disabled people generally misread those interactions.

8. In a chapter of their 2015 study *The Biopolitics of Disability*, Mitchell and Snyder move away from analyzing narrative prosthesis to look at "antinormative novels of embodiment," novels that explore "disability as revelatory of variation's potential for innovation" (181). This is another productive way to use characters as a launching pad to explore broader issues, in this case the creative possibilities of nonnormative embodiment.

9. Grosz describes a group of feminists, including Butler, Irigaray, Cixous, Spivak, Schor, Wittig, and others, for whom "the body is neither brute nor passive, but is interwoven with and constitutive of systems of meaning, signification, and representation" (18). In *The Body and Social Theory* Chris Shilling focuses on the contributions of Mary Douglas and Erving Goffman, in addition to Foucault (and others), to the idea that the body is socially constructed (75–102).

10. Although things have improved on this count since Davis published *Enforcing Normalcy* in 1995, there is still some accuracy in his assertion that while literary and cultural theory celebrates the body's transgressions and rebellions, it envisions an able body. Davis writes that "the nightmare of [critical theory's vision of 'the body'] is one that is deformed, maimed, mutilated, broken, diseased" (6).

11. See E. Donaldson for the beginnings of this re-exploration.

12. Some key examples are given in note 3. In addition, James Berger's *The Disarticulate*, Patrick McDonagh's "Autism and Modernism," Claire Barber-Stetson's "Slow Processing," and my own article about madness in Rebecca West's *The Return of the Soldier* ("Involuntary Cure") consider mental disability.

13. The Australian journalist and disability activist Stella Young remarked in a 2012 blog post that "most journalists seem utterly incapable of writing or talking about a person with a disability without using phrases like 'overcoming disability,' 'brave' . . . or, my personal favourite, 'inspirational.'" Although this attitude circulates powerfully via social media, it did not arise in the digital era. In 1894, to take one example, Britons founded the Guild of the Poor Brave Things to help disabled children. The organization changed its name in 1917 when it turned to serving disabled soldiers, "given that its new beneficiaries were not so little, and the appeal to a literally infantilizing pathos did not accord with the image of the military man" (Burstein 69).

14. The commonly used phrase *inward turn* was introduced by Eric Kahler in *The Inward Turn of Narrative* (1970), though he wasn't discussing modernist works.

15. For explorations of the impact of the new physics on modernism, see, for example, Kern; Schleifer; and Whitworth.

16. McRuer writes that "able-bodiedness, even more than heterosexuality, still largely masquerades as a nonidentity, as the natural order of things" (1). Grosz discusses this phenomenon with regard to gender, asserting that "corporeality must no longer be associated with one sex (or race) which then takes on the burden of the other's corporeality for it. Women can no longer take on the function of being *the* body for men while men are left free to soar to the heights of theoretical reflection and cultural production" (22).

17. For a powerful overview of eugenics, see "The Eugenic Atlantic" in Snyder and Mitchell (100–129). Other excellent sources are Kline; Lombardo; and Stern.

18. Overy details the foundational role eugenics played in the birth control movement in "A Sickness in the Racial Body," a chapter in *Twilight Years*. For a discussion of the close relationship between eugenics and early twentieth-century American feminism, see Lamp and Cleigh.

19. Crip time, on the contrary, "requires reimagining our notions of what can and should happen in time, or recognizing how expectations of 'how long things take' are based on very particular minds and bodies" (Kafer 27).

20. About attitudes toward public "displays" of "unsightliness" in Britain, Schweik writes, "Though no English statute provided the exact template for the ugly law, English precursors existed, in scores" (4).

21. Similarly, Sara Danius argues that "modernist aesthetics from Marcel Proust to James Joyce is an index of a technologically mediated crisis of the senses, a perceptual crisis that ultimately cuts across the question of art as such" (1).

22. E. M. Forster's resonant phrase "only connect" is emblematic here, and the breakdown of language represented by the sounds in the Marabar Caves in *A Passage to India* could be related to modernist treatments of deafness as that which thwarts human communication.

23. Kathryn Geurts's *Culture and the Senses* is a fascinating account of a culture—the Anlo-Ewe people of Ghana—where the senses are understood quite differently. Geurts writes, "From Aristotle to Aquinas and Descartes . . . cultural traditions have sustained a five-senses model that privileges mental representations and external modes of knowing. This construct, I argue, is essentially a folk ideology" (7).

Chapter 1

For research assistance related to this chapter I am grateful to Lisa Belzeski and Elizabeth Wulbrecht, my Purdue University Wilke Interns for academic year 2013–14.

1. I have not found any critic who questions the narrator's assertion that "she needed their kindness," an absence that testifies to the continued strength of this association between disability and dependence. When the "giantesses" ask for shoes

to be brought, the essay continues its association of nonnormative size and shape with incapacity; and when the three women leave, the taller women are called "her guardians," a term that contributes to the infantilization of the woman.

2. Garland-Thomson coined the now-standard term *normate*; it indicates not only an ablebodied person but the "constructed identity" and "cultural capital" of one who is taken to inhabit a position of ablebodiedness (*Extraordinary* 8).

3. As Christina Cogdell points out, clothes (and in this case shoes) were a tool of eugenic normalization, stemming from "machine-based methods of mass production and standardization" (59). The dwarf in "Street Haunting" is depicted as proud not only of her beautiful feet but of their ability to fit in "normal" shoes.

4. This opposition between disability and sexuality does not, of course, apply only to women. D. H. Lawrence's Clifford Chatterley is an example of a fictional man whose physical disability stands for his lack of "warm sympathy" and sexuality. In "A Propos of *Lady Chatterley's Lover*," Lawrence brings up the question of Clifford's disability; he says that when he read over his first draft, he "recognized that the lameness of Clifford was symbolic of the paralysis, the deeper emotional or passional paralysis, of most men of his sort and class today" (*Phoenix II* 514).

5. "Good Country People" was written after what Mao and Walkowitz define as the "core period" of modernism ("New Modernist Studies" 738). Indeed, while O'Connor is often treated as a modernist, she is also sometimes seen as a transitional figure between modernism and postmodernism. I include her here because her exploration of Hulga Hopewell's disability identity and its relation to sexuality shares important features with the treatments of disability and sexuality by the other authors considered here, Williams and Joyce.

6. In one of the versions of the screenplay Williams wrote for this story, this exchange is even more intense:

> Laura (in quiet despair): But, Mother, who would marry a—
> Amanda (furiously interrupting her): You're not crippled! You're not crippled! (*The Glass Menagerie*: Motion Picture Typescript Fragments,box 16, folder 1:29)

7. Siebers goes on to ask, "If sex is walking together on the beach, if it is running across a field of flowers to meet in an embrace, what is the nature of sex apart from the ability to walk or to run?" (*Disability Theory* 139).

8. Even in the early nineteenth century, upright posture was understood to define humanness. As Cynthia Hall writes, "developing evolutionary theories [singled out] the upright human spine as the corporeal site which differentiates the human form from the nonhuman or animal" (38). Popular coverage of early twentieth-century archeological finds brought this defining aspect to wider attention.

9. For discussion of the Piltdown Man's role in popular determinations of the animal-human boundary, see Goulden.

10. Goulden lists forty-one articles about Piltdown Man in major British newspapers during the period from November 1912 to September 1913 (278). The

New York Times also carried many articles about the Piltdown discovery, with headlines such as "Paleolithic Skull Is a Missing Link" (December 19, 1912) and "Primitives' Brains Bigger Than Ours?" (August 12, 1913).

11. Hansen and King similarly note this blurring of categories, writing, "Severe—or not so severe—physical handicaps, blurred speech patterns, and epileptic fits were all bases of decisions to commit people to mental health institutions" (216) where they might then be subjected to forced sterilization.

12. Amanda in *The Glass Menagerie* emphasizes the status of her former gentleman callers; both Hulga and her mother distinguish themselves from "good country people"; and "Nausicaa" uses ideas of breeding throughout to confirm Gerty's value.

13. Brian Parker describes several related published and unpublished texts in his article, "The Composition of *The Glass Menagerie.*"

14. Jim uses the same phrase when he tells Laura to be more confident ("A little physical defect is what you have. Hardly noticeable even!"), and in the typescript fragments from the screenplay, the man in the glass shop says the same thing about some of the glass animals that have imperfections, which he ends up selling to Laura at a discount: "they have little defects in them—some that are hardly even noticeable—but we have to return them to the factory or—sell them at a discount." Here he shows Laura the glass unicorn, which in this version has a tiny bubble in the glass, one that Laura does not see (Williams, "Glass Shop").

15. It may be, too, that Amanda, who accepts the opposition between disability and sexuality, now drops the pretension that her daughter might be able to pass for nondisabled well enough to gain a husband. However, when Bigsby writes that Amanda's use of this word is "her first step toward accepting the truth of her daughter's situation and hence of the need which she must acknowledge and address" (42), he seems to validate the ableist opposition between disability and sexuality.

16. Brian Parker mentions that in one of the draft versions of "Portrait of a Girl in Glass" held in the Ransom Center, University of Texas at Austin, Laura's lameness is included. Williams edited the lameness out of the short story but brought it back for the play. Parker therefore suggests that such details are "reversions, not new insights or additions" (410). The timeline, however, doesn't reduce the force of my argument, which explores a dynamic of substitution and replacement that need not be linear.

17. In one of the typescript fragments of the screenplay, Williams similarly granted Laura more agency. In this fragment she actually tells Tom to leave, because "poets don't belong in a warehouse!"

> TOM: Where do they belong?
> LAURA: I don't know but you have got to find out and go there!
> TOM: —How about you—if I went? What would you do, Laura?
> (She avoids the question, her eyes full of tears)
> TOM: (insistently) Laura! What would you do?
> He follows her. The alarm clock goes off. ("Glass Shop")

This scene would detract from the sense of entrapment Williams developed for *The Glass Menagerie.*

18. For an interesting account of the other book Laura has (but doesn't read), *The Rose-Garden Husband,* see Mann, who explores the similarities between that novel and several of Williams's works.

19. Kushner also considers the possibility that Laura could mean that Tom is in love with her, noting that Williams wrote a play about brother-sister incest, *Purification* (Introduction 27–28). R. B. Parker also suggests that in "Portrait of a Girl in Glass" "there is a distinct, if guarded, hint of incestuous attraction" (520). This attraction gives a slightly erotic tinge to the assertion that Laura invites Freckles into her bedroom for a friendly chat "just as she did me."

20. Mark Lilly reads *The Glass Menagerie* as a gay text, in part through understanding Laura's lameness as "a metaphor for Williams's view of homosexuality" (154). While I agree with this on a general level, my understanding of how the metaphor works differs significantly from Lilly's. He reinforces the ableist assumption that disability precludes sexuality, and this serves his argument in that he associates Laura's "restricted" sexuality with closeted gay sexuality.

21. As Kathleen Patterson points out, this is a in part defensive reaction to her mother's emphasis on normalcy (100).

22. Jolly Kay Sharp mentions that Flannery O'Connor's mother would ask her why she didn't write nicer stories that people would like, a question that is analogous to Mrs. Hopewell's encouragement of her daughter to look more pleasant (28).

23. Sheldon Currie colludes with Mrs. Hopewell in wishing Hulga would try to pass. Writing in an astonishingly ableist, indeed nasty, vein, he writes, "The makers of wooden legs do their best to keep their products from appearing [mechanical] and usually their clients cooperate and dress them up and direct them to appear to be vital and animate adjuncts of a spirited person, and we who watch hope the partnership succeeds, so we won't be tempted to entertain uncharitable thoughts, and perhaps even snigger behind our hands. Hulga, however, does not cooperate" (135).

24. Ralph Wood says that when O'Connor visited East Texas State College in 1962, she said the name came to her "as a hybrid between 'huge' and 'ugly'" (200n26).

25. We see a similar spiritual elevation of a prosthesis, but also in this case of a disabled limb, in "The Lame Shall Enter First" where Rufus Johnson "was as touchy about the foot as if it were a sacred object" (459) and clings to his old "battered" shoe instead of wearing the new one. Donald Hardy points out the similarity between Hulga and Rufus (14–15). And the overidentification with a prosthesis carries through to *The Violent Bear It Away,* where Rayber grabs "the metal part of the hearing aid as if he were clawing his heart" (202).

26. For a nuanced discussion of disability devotees, see F. Campbell, *Contours of Ableism* 179–86. Pointer differs from disability devotees in that he wants not the disabled body but its prostheses (he has stolen a glass eye from another woman in a similar seduction scene).

27. In thus bracketing the misogyny of the text's (not just Pointer's) attack on Hulga, I am admittedly falling prey to the dynamic Patricia Yaeger brilliantly explores in her article "Flannery O'Connor and the Aesthetics of Torture." Yaeger

writes, "She attacks her own characters and deliberately violates or eviscerates their political referents, the narrative coordinates that might help us make sense of her cruelty. Contemplating her fiction, we are left, then, with a primitive sadism that most critics convert into an old and comfortable theology" (191).

28. In his theological reading of O'Connor and disability, Timothy Basselin similarly argues that "a direct correlation exists between the meaning of O'Connor's work and how our culture perceives disability. . . . The heart of O'Connor's critique of modern culture is that she understands we cannot save ourselves, and she declares to us that we must realize our inability (our limitation) before we can be open to a saving force outside ourselves" (14).

29. I discuss the dynamics of disability metaphors further in chapter 4.

30. I disagree, therefore, with Nicole Markotic's claim that readers are intended to laugh at Joy/Hulga because "she is the damaged soul, as signified by her wooden leg and her 'deficiency' without it" (184).

31. John Gordon approaches the "limping devil" phrase from a similar vantage point: "I do not think it a coincidence that she shows up when she does—that Bloom goes from being reduced to 'twisting around all the opposite, as limp as a wet rag' (*U* 12.1497–98), to the telekinetic embrace of a woman with a limp" (*Joyce and Reality* 79).

32. In "Bodies," a later piece in the *Cambridge Companion to "Ulysses,"* Plock discusses disability studies and claims that in his representation of Gerty, Joyce intends "to confront the regulative interventions of modern sciences of the body" (193), a claim that is incompatible with her previous assertion that he's using Gerty as an ironic reversal of Cathleen Ni Houlihan. She still asserts that, "[r]ealistically, Gerty's chances of an advantageous marriage are slim," but in this chapter she notes that Joyce has acknowledged "erotic needs in a character that would conventionally be overlooked by the romantic discourse of courtship" (193).

33. Plock persuasively links "Hoppy Holohan" from "A Mother," for example, to Gerty ("Why" 120).

34. Nemecek uses this term, which originates with Goffman and is also employed by Michael Warner in *The Trouble with Normal.*

35. A fascinating exception is Christine Froula's reading, which understands the narrative as generated by *Stephen*, who creates the style of "Nausicaa" "as an adventure in the artist-son's quest to write himself into 'feminine' positions" (*Modernism's Body* 121). This reading is in part motivated by the idea, put forward by Richard Ellmann, that in "Nausicaa" Joyce parodied his own earlier representation of Stephen's encounter with the bird-girl in *Portrait* (*James Joyce* 385).

36. In her notes to the Oxford World Classics edition, Jeri Johnson implies agreement with Gordon, writing that Gerty is the "object of this discourse, not its subject; . . . she is the fantasy, not the fantasist" (900).

37. Quayson is indebted here to Mitchell and Snyder, who write in *Narrative Prosthesis* that "*disability also operates as the textual obstacle that causes the literary operation of open-endedness to close down or stumble*" (50, original italics).

38. I thank Stephanie Larson for this point. Joyce added the "tramdriver" line in the margins of the manuscript (*JJA* 13:222).

39. Some critics display their ableist prejudice by assuming, as Bloom does, that Gerty is generally rejected by men because of her limp. For example, Cynthia Hornbeck writes that "the blemish of her lameness has repulsed other men long before it draws Bloom's notice" (99). There is no textual evidence for such a claim.

40. Tennessee Williams planned to rely on just such a dramatic revelation in one of the versions of the screenplay of *The Glass Menagerie* (at that time entitled *The Gentleman Caller*). In his treatment of this scene, Laura Wingfield falls for the clerk in the glass shop where she buys her glass animals. This clerk has a disability similar to Laura's. But Williams planned to keep Laura ignorant of this until the end: "Also there is drama in the fact that Laura sees him only from the waist up—his legs hidden by the counter—until the end. Her final recognition of him as one who has gone through the same torments of handicapped singularity that she has will touch and move her more profoundly than anything else could" (Williams, "Glass Shop").

41. In the manuscript included in the *James Joyce Archive* (*JJA*), Joyce wrote "Little hot devil" but drew arrows to indicate that the first two words should be reversed (13:223). In the first version of the line that reveals the lameness, Joyce had written, "Tight boots? NO! She's lame O! Pah!" (*JJA* 13:222).

42. Nemecek makes a related point when she says that "Bloom has desired a cripple all along" (183); but my claim is broader, in that my concern is not with the fact that Bloom has desired a disabled woman but that disability, textuality, and sexuality come together in a way that the episode's two-part structure purports to deny.

Chapter 2

I would like to thank Abigail Godollei, my Purdue Wilke Intern for Fall 2013, for research assistance in the early stages of this chapter.

1. Quoted in R. Ellmann, *James Joyce* 676.

2. Martha Stoddard Holmes calls *Poor Miss Finch* "the century's most radical novel about blindness and sexuality" (*Fictions* 7). In this novel, Lucilla asserts that "my life lives in my love. And my love lives in my blindness" (424). This assertion aligns *Poor Miss Finch* more with the texts I consider here than with contemporaneous representations of blindness.

3. For an analysis of blindness in these texts, see Carpenter.

4. Naomi Schor writes that "what is at stake ultimately in these modern fictions of blindness is intersubjectivity itself" (91). This claim leads into her discussion of the "love is blind" theme in variations on the tale of "Beauty and the Beast" in literature and film from the nineteenth and twentieth centuries.

5. In a review of *Blindness and Insight*, Beth Bjorklund notes that "[s]ighted blindness and blinded sight have been topics at least since Sophocles, and the dialectic is by now familiar" (100).

6. In an interesting parallel, Edward Wheatley describes a medieval blind person praying for sight to see the elevated Host, a prayer that implies that "the elevation of the Host is experienced most intensely" through sight (17).

7. As Davis points out, "linguistic studies routinely tell us that a great part . . . of communication is accomplished through body language" (*Enforcing Normalcy* 20).

8. In Elizabeth Bowen's 1968 novel *Eva Trout*, for example, characters feel that their tea table is "bugged" by a deaf boy's "unearthly perspicacity" (172). In Carson McCullers's *The Heart Is a Lonely Hunter*, the word *uncanny* is repeatedly used to describe the deaf man, John Singer. I explore this phenomenon further in the following chapter.

9. The phrase originates with George Veditz, who used it in a presidential address to the National Association of the Deaf in 1910 (Bahan 97).

10. A reading of blindness as interfering with human closeness is clear in comments by the director of a recent opera entitled *The Blind* and based on Maeterlinck's 1890 play. The composer, Lera Auerbach, is quoted in the *New York Times* as saying, "The message is that we are the blind. With all our means of communication, we see each other less and connect to each other less. We have less understanding and compassion for other people. We have this screen between us" (Schweitzer).

11. It may be helpful to think of the assault on vision's supremacy in these terms—the dominant, emerging, and residual—from Raymond Williams's *Marxism and Literature*: sight's dominance was being questioned by an emerging emphasis on other forms of perception, and we see this questioning in the modernist texts discussed here (121–27).

12. I'm grateful to Daniel Smith for discussing Bergson with me.

13. Conrad may be an exception, in that he describes his highest aspiration as "to make you *see*." We might view Conrad as a transitional figure whose ocularcentric goal later modernist authors moved away from. But it's also worth noting that in many of Conrad's stories and in *Heart of Darkness*, by constructing the tale as told orally to listeners, Conrad wants as much as anything to make us hear. He states his goal, indeed, like this: "by the power of the written word to make you hear, to make you feel—it is, before all, to make you *see*. That—and no more, and it is everything. If I succeed, you shall find there according to your deserts: encouragement, consolation, fear, charm—all you demand—and, perhaps, also that glimpse of truth for which you have forgotten to ask" (14). Though stating this goal in clear ocularcentric terms, Conrad also seems to be using *see* metaphorically, particularly in the "glimpse of truth" that one can apprehend but not actually picture. Further, Michael Levenson points out a tension between Conrad's stated desire to "make you see" and his remark in the same preface that the author "descends within himself, and in that lonely region of stress and strife, . . . he finds the terms of his appeal" (Conrad 12). As Levenson comments, "This tension appears throughout. On the one hand, Conrad makes a rousing rhetorical call for the sensory apprehension of life's surfaces; on the other, he demands inwardness and depth" (1).

14. For example, Jay discusses these forces in *Downcast Eyes*; Kern explores them extensively in *The Culture of Time and Space*; and Michael Whitworth studies the effects of Einstein's theories in *Einstein's Wake*.

15. In *Virginia Woolf and the Discourse of Science* Holly Henry traces the effects of looking through telescopes on Woolf's aesthetics and "global vision." She argues

that "Woolf's aesthetic perspectives, as well as her pacifist politics, were shaped by advances in astronomy and by emerging visualization technologies, ranging from large astronomical telescopes to the inexpensive hand-held camera" (2).

16. Cinema offered, as Armstrong puts it, a "prosthetic extension and investigation of looking" (*Modernism: A Cultural History* 108) that could call "normal" vision into question. During the Boer War, British audiences were presented with staged battle scenes that brought the "indexical quality of the photo-image . . . under suspicion" (Daly 65). Citing Martin Jay and Michael North, Rebecca Sanchez notes that "[if] visual images were privileged through a belief that associated them with truth, the very fact of their exponential proliferation [in cinema for example] seemed to undermine the link" (124).

17. Michael Whitworth details x-ray and radium imagery in Wells, Lawrence, and Woolf, demonstrating that Lawrence uses the mystery of science to replace the mystery of the religious vocabulary he was using in earlier drafts of *The Rainbow* and *Women in Love.*

18. In his discussion of perspective in painting, Kern notes that "under the impact of the Impressionists, Cézanne, and the Cubists that perspectival world broke up as if an earthquake had struck the precisely reticulated sidewalks of a Renaissance street scene" (140).

19. In describing this opposition, Eysteinsson notes that literary "modernism is felt to signal a radical 'inward turn' in literature, and often a more thorough exploration of the human psyche than is deemed to have been probable or even possible in pre-Freudian times" (26).

20. In his essay "Beneficial Blindness," which curiously does not cite Schor's discussion of "fortunate blindness," David Bolt discusses a similar assumption that blind people would be better able to concentrate than sighted people. He calls this assumption sophistry, saying that it relies on an "ocularcentric paradox" because when sighted people shut their eyes to concentrate, it's to redirect "inward the energy that usually would be consumed visually" (84), and this does not apply to people with impaired vision.

21. Lawrence did also think that sight could be linked to sensuality, as he describes in *Fantasia* (60). But he believed that vision in "us" (westerners as opposed to "savages") "becomes faulty because we proceed too much in one mode. We see too much, we attend too much. The dark, glancing sightlessness of the intent savage, the narrowed vision of the cat . . .—these we do not know any more" (61).

22. Terry Thompson reads him as a Lucifer figure who "is compelled by pride" to ruin this blind Eden.

23. Actually, we don't have much evidence in *Portrait* that Stephen will be the great writer he imagines either.

24. At the end of the first chapter of "Chrysalis," John thinks that he will have "[n]othing but women all his life. Better to have died" (52). Later he continues this line of thought when he is frustrated with the nurse: "God blast the woman, why was he always treated as a baby? Oh, how they loved it, now that he was helpless" (79).

25. Ved Mehta writes about riding his bike using facial vision and even once driving a car.

26. Indeed, the saint, who insists upon and serves as the agent of sight, is represented negatively (see McCormack 277, 280).

27. For an astute and witty discussion of the Molyneux question, see Kleege, "Blindness and Visual Culture."

28. Although Synge's biographer does not mention Bergson, he notes that Synge valued the "instant" as that within which morality resides (McCormack 203).

29. Similarly, Robin Skelton says that Martin is "claiming the right to live according to his individual conscience, and to retain his own personal vision" (56).

30. Holmes explores the link between melodrama and disability throughout *Fictions of Affliction* but theorizes it most fully in chapter 1, "Melodramatic Bodies."

31. For a thorough reading of the politics of blindness in *Jane Eyre*, see Bolt, "Blindman."

32. I disagree here with Hipsky's claim that their union is possible only when Garth is "symbolically emasculated by blindness" (136). As Hipsky himself notes, Jane is not afraid of Garth's masculinity, even when she imagines him as a tiger who has tasted blood. There is not the sense, as in *Jane Eyre*, that Garth needs to change to make their union possible. It is Jane who needs to be simultaneously humbled—by a stronger faith in his love—and made proud—by "the realization of her own inner beauty" (Hipsky 136)—to make way for their marriage.

33. In Rosamond Lehmann's *Invitation to the Waltz*, Olivia Curtis meets and dances with a blind, married man named Timmy Douglas. Like Jane Eyre, she is drawn to him by pity: "Imagination stretched shudderingly towards his experience. . . . I'd stay with you. I'd look after you. I'd be your eyes and show you everything. Oh—is she nice enough to you?" (193)

34. Of course, blind people do not need cords to get around their own houses (although cords in public places, delineating a path to a restroom in a restaurant, for example, would be nice), but Barclay is demonstrating Jane's efforts to facilitate his independence.

35. In the sense that they are opposites, Maurice and Bertie represent a variation of the pairings of weak, voluble men and strong, silent men in Victorian fiction described by Karen Bourrier. But in this case, the disabled man is the strong, quiet, and mentally slow one, whereas the nondisabled man is the more talkative and emotionally delicate.

36. As Bolt details in *The Metanarrative of Blindness*, Maurice's name is repeatedly displaced by the label "the blind man," which "evokes a sense of distance" between readers and sighted characters on the one hand and Maurice on the other (42). This distance, I would suggest, works in productive contrast to the contact that Maurice's blindness brings about.

37. In her article about blindness envy in Victorian culture, Mary Ann O'Farrell claims that Victorians sought a more immediate relationship to *things* and understood blindness to give rise to this relationship. "Blindness envy, I argue, bespeaks a craving for a more tactile and bodily—that is, more material—relation to material-

ity" (514). For Lawrence, the "unseen object" is important, but not so much in itself as in its role as a signifier for an unseen spiritual reality.

38. In having Isabel attempt to foster a bond between her husband and another man, the story replicates an aspect of *Women in Love* (1920), where the man needs both a male and a female soul mate. In *Women in Love* Birkin tells Ursula that he wanted a bond with the now-dead Gerald: "You are all women to me. But I wanted a man friend, as eternal as you and I are eternal" (499). Indeed, in the prologue to the novel, not published with it, Lawrence explains their bond in terms that sound like the interchange between Maurice and Bertie in the barn. Much as Maurice says, "We shall know each other now" (91), Lawrence writes that Birkin and Gerald "knew and were known to each other"; but their intimacy makes them nervous and embarrassed, so that they maintain "complete reserve" with each other (*Phoenix II* 92–93).

39. Nils Clausson reads Maurice's mistake as an example of the ways the story deconstructs its own hierarchy of blood-consciousness over mental consciousness (115). Paul Delany also sees the story as showing the "doctrine . . . falling victim to its own premises" (26).

40. In an essay called "On Being a Man," Lawrence asserts that "Bishop Berkeley is absolutely right: things only exist in our own consciousness" (*Phoenix II* 617).

41. An example of a blind person *not* transcending superficial aspects of life is detailed in Ved Mehta's *All for Love*: several beautiful women were drawn to Ved in large part because they felt confident he loved them for who they were. But Ved's psychoanalyst suggests that he was in fact attracted to them precisely because of their beauty, which he thought might bring "lustre" to himself (299). Osagie Obasogie's recent book *Blinded by Sight* demonstrates that blindness does not prevent one from thinking racially, or from thinking race in visual terms. He asserts that "our seemingly objective engagements with the world around us are subordinate to a faith that orients our visual experience and, moreover, produces our ability to see certain things. *Seeing is not believing*. Rather, to believe, in a sense, is to see" (xvi). Physical beauty and race, then, two characteristics that many sighted people assume would be beneath the notice of blind people, have as much influence on the judgments of the average blind person as they do on the judgments of the average sighted person.

Chapter 3

1. Jonathan Rée notes that hearing and sight have tended to be classed together as "distance senses" and points out that Western philosophy accepts the "metaphysical prejudice" that "hearing is specifically concerned with time, and vision with space" (34, 6).

2. For an astute exploration of deafness in Charles Dickens and Wilkie Collins, see Esmail. As Esmail points out, the characterization of deafness as rare in Victorian literature excludes characters who have become hard of hearing with age, who are generally treated comically. For a reading of the ambiguities within Col-

lins's generally positive representation of deafness and sign language, see Anglin-Jaffe.

3. In Collins's *Hide and Seek*, integration into the larger world is not desirable for women. One could argue that disability in this novel, embodied by the deaf Madonna and the mobility-impaired Lavinia Blyth, is represented as an excess of femininity: vulnerability, delicacy, patient endurance, and the need for privacy. For example, Collins's narrator remarks, "In this homely sphere, life, even in its frailest aspects, was still greater than its greatest trials; strong to conquer by virtue of its own innocence and purity, its simple unworldly aspirations, its self-sacrificing devotion to the happiness and the anxieties of others" (92–93).

4. Dickens's representation of sign language demonstrates Douglas Baynton's assertion that many nineteenth-century people understood sign language to be universal. However, the story does acknowledge different *registers* of sign language when Marigold returns to pick up Sophy after two years apart, and hesitates to address her because she has grown so refined. The director tells him, "Address her in your own way. . . . Try if she moves at the old sign" (36).

5. Holmes, *Fictions of Afflictions* 88; Esmail 998–99. Holmes's incisive article "Happy and Yet Pitying Tears" explores the role of tears and pathos in the story's representation of deafness, stressing thematic uses of muteness and speech.

6. Lane quotes the founder of deaf education in German-speaking lands saying that "the breath of life resides in the voice. . . . The voice is a living emanation of that spirit that God breathed into man when he created him a living soul. . . . What stupidity we find in most of these unfortunate deaf. . . . How little they differ from animals" (107).

7. In *Enforcing Normalcy* Lennard Davis discusses the ubiquitous and damaging insistence on the "oral/aural form of communication." He writes, "It is commonly thought that deafness involves the inability to use language properly. If only deaf citizens could speak and understand English, there would be no problem for them in the larger community. Thus, deaf people are schooled arduously in lipreading, speech therapy, and the activities associated with the oral/aural form of communication. However, it is precisely this focusing on the dysfunctionality of the deaf that constitutes a privileging of the aural/oral system of communication" (78).

8. Ladd points out that "oralism's hegemony did not result in an immediate and total implementation. It controlled deaf schools in most of Southern England by 1900, but like the earlier Roman invasion, took time to reach the northernmost parts and the Celtic outposts" (135).

9. Michael Uniacke has written an entertaining fictionalization of the conference, entitled "This Incontestable Superiority."

10. Linguist William Stokoe is widely credited with leading the demonstration that signed languages were natural, complete human languages (Ladd 150). In Britain, Stokoe's work influenced linguist Mary Brennan, who published an important article in 1975 on the pitfalls of oral-only education in which she named the signed language spoken in Britain British Sign Language, or BSL ("Obituary").

11. Burch similarly writes that "Deaf culture had blossomed in the margins of

society during the nineteenth century; America in the late nineteenth and early twentieth centuries was hostile toward such separateness" (3).

12. Discussing the naturalness of signed languages and how some communities use both spoken and signed languages depending on context, Carol Padden points out that "if language is viewed as inherently *multimodal*, then humans' ability to move between different modalities in different communities seems less exotic and more indicative of flexibility" (44).

13. Although *Eva Trout* was published outside what Mao and Walkowitz call the "core period" of modernism, I include it here for three reasons: first, the majority of Bowen's novels were published and her aesthetic was developed in the 1920s and 1930s. Second, as I argue in "Modes of Dislocation," although *Eva Trout* certainly seems to be considering postmodernism, it ends up reaffirming more modernist commitments. Third, and most importantly for my purposes here, sign language was not reintroduced to deaf education until the 1970s; in 1968 oralism was still the dominant paradigm. This historical context suggests that *Eva Trout*'s depiction of deafness would have more in common with depictions of deafness written in the first half of the century than with those written in the 1970s and 1980s. My analysis demonstrates these continuities with McCullers's 1940 novel and Welty's 1941 short story.

14. Nicholas Mirzoeff explains the resistance to sign language as resistance to the materiality of language: "sign pictures language, which modern culture has tried to present as the pure presence of thought, as ineffable and unknowable" (77).

15. A previous critic of this novel, David Madden, describes Singer as a "willing, attentive, supposedly comprehensive listening-post," invoking the dehumanizing phrase "deaf as a post" (139).

16. Michael Davidson defines audism as "the ideological replication of humans as hearing subjects" (*Concerto* 81).

17. In Olive Moore's *Fugue* (1932), a deaf woman is similarly portrayed as cut off from all communication and knowledge. Besides being "deaf and dumb," she lives in an out-of-the-way village in Cornwall and she is illiterate. Within a misogynist economy where women can only hope to create the right atmosphere for male creativity, this woman was a source of peace for her lover, Ollan, who has now committed suicide. "Lying in Ollan's bed he was awake a long time thinking of the woman with her deep upstanding breasts and large unhurried movements and her silence, and of the peace she must have brought him. By god, what a solid and fathomless rock on which to build one's church! And here, in this room, he had written *Self-Portrait*" (265–66). Here the "silence" of deafness brings peace and creativity, more like the blindness of the characters discussed in chapter 2—but not, significantly, to the deaf character herself.

18. For discussions of Welty and the grotesque, see Yaeger, *Dirt and Desire*, chapter 5; S. Donaldson; Gleeson-White, "Peculiarly Southern."

19. Christopher Krentz notes similarly, about the deafness rhetoric associated with the whale in *Moby-Dick*, that the whale is "essentially unknowable and beyond language, characteristics that [Melville] implicitly equates with deafness" ("Hearing Line" 428).

20. Citations to "The Key" are from Welty's *Collected Stories.*

21. These metaphors also link Ellie and Albert to Flannery O'Connor's Lucynell Crater (in "The Life You Save May Be Your Own"), whose deafness is easily (and commonly) conflated with intellectual disability.

22. Almost as unrealistic is the fact that the Morgans sit in the station while the train pulls up and departs again. Is there no window? Were there no vibrations that could be felt to indicate the train's arrival? Did no one else get on the train? In fact, the story indicates that others did get on the train, because after the train draws in and rolls away again, "people were gone, or turned in sleep" (62). Deaf people would either sit where they could see the train or, noticing others getting up, go and see if it was their train. This plot detail exemplifies, again, Welty's desire to portray deafness as that which precludes knowledge.

23. Reine Dugas Bouton takes a different, productive approach to the unreliability of the narrator. Comparing the story to Woolf's "An Unwritten Novel," she explores Welty's manipulations of readers and her insistence that readers "become aware that the narrator indeed is creating a narrative, making up a fiction" (183).

24. Critics for the most part take this at face value, as for example in Kreyling: "the Morgans's physical inability to speak or hear is the metaphor for human separateness" (29).

25. Within Deaf culture, communication, which requires sustained eye contact and often includes bodily contiguity, could be said to be more intimate than communication among hearing people (see Burke 13–16).

26. Aldous Huxley's *Crome Yellow* uses deafness similarly to indicate the difficulty of human connection. When the deaf woman Jenny responds with a non sequitur to Denis's question, he thinks, "Parallel straight lines . . . meet only at infinity. He might talk for ever of care-charmer sleep and she of meteorology till the end of time. Did one ever establish contact with anyone? We are all parallel straight lines. Jenny was only a little more parallel than most" (16).

27. In Welty's "First Love" (published in *The Wide Net*, 1942), there is a similar link between love and hearing when the deaf boy Joel Mayes suddenly hears the music played by the wife of Harman Blennerhassett—"the only thing he had ever heard" (*Collected Stories* 164). This moment integrates his memories of his mother with his newfound love for Aaron Burr and brings about a painful sensation in the tips of his fingers, as if he is able to feel in a new way.

28. Every critical treatment of the novel I've read does take this isolation for granted; critics do not seem to realize that deaf characters placed in deaf, signing communities would not be isolated (McCullers actually gives us a glimpse of deaf characters who do not seem isolated in the three mutes Singer meets when Antonapoulos has died). Even Emily Russell's disability studies reading of the novel seems to take the equation of deafness and isolation at face value.

29. I am indebted to John Lee Clark for pointing this out to me when I was reading the novel for the first time.

30. Ballin points out the unfairness of asking a deaf person to spend years learning to lipread and speak orally, sacrificing "all other branches of learning" when even "after years of study and work he is likely to fail in the end. All these years are

given to save you and those like you [hearing people] some thirty minutes of your whole life [to learn the finger alphabet]" (79).

31. For a compelling reading of their relationship as homosexual, see Gleeson-White, *Strange Bodies*, chapter 2.

32. Noting how commonplace are metaphors of disability in literature, Lennard Davis cites several phrases about disability from Conrad's *Lord Jim*. Two of them indicate this link between deafness and emotional incapacity: "he was made blind and deaf and without pity"; "unmoved like a deaf man" (*Enforcing Normalcy* 44).

33. McCullers writes in her outline of *The Mute* that Antonapoulos's "mental, sexual and spiritual development is that of a child of about seven years old" (O. Evans 206). His cognitive disability is explored from a disability studies perspective by Heidi Krumland.

34. The image of Singer as the hub of a wheel is used in the novel (211), and in McCullers's outline she compares the characters to the "spokes of a wheel" (O. Evans 211).

35. Singer usually keeps his hands in his pockets, an apparent effort to repress his desires to communicate manually, especially with Antonapoulos. The text's recurrent hand imagery may owe something to Sherwood Anderson's story "Hands" (from *Winesburg, Ohio*, 1919), in which the homosexual Wing Biddlebaum constantly uses his expressive hands. Sanchez discusses "Hands" in the context of manual language, focusing on Biddlebaum's embodied style of communication (86–90). And in *Strange Bodies*, Gleeson-White discusses the similarities between Singer and Biddlebaum and the texts' use of hand imagery (53–54).

36. A similar focus on eyes and on secret connection shapes Frankie's relation to the "freaks" in McCullers's *The Member of the Wedding*. Frankie "was afraid of all the Freaks, for it seemed to her that they had looked at her in a secret way and tried to connect their eyes with hers, as though to say: we know you. She was afraid of their long Freak eyes" (20).

37. In "Seeing, seeing, seeing" I explore a similar link between deafness and knowledge in Bowen's 1942 short story "Summer Night." There is a suggestion of solipsism attached to the deaf character's ability to remain "immune" from political history that is similar to the solipsism of Eva and Jeremy.

38. The idea that people with disabilities cannot live "full" lives is a key component of ableism. For discussions of ableism, see F. Campbell, "Ability"; Linton.

39. In Welty's "First Love," the boy similarly seeks knowledge: "Where did people learn things? Where did they go to find them? How far?" (*Collected Stories* 163).

40. Bennett and Royle suggest that Jeremy is a "figure of reading," explaining that "to the extent that no sound comes out of a written text, we are, like Jeremy, lipreaders" (143). Their subsequent claim that "[t]hrough Jeremy, reading in *Eva Trout* becomes a telepathic, extra-sensory reading of faces," however, is compatible with my claim that his deafness is aligned with the inability to read. *Searching* a face for information is not as successful as reading and thereby attaining that information.

41. Dickens is a major figure in *Eva Trout*: he is one of Iseult's models and

she and Eva meet after their estrangement at Dickens's house in Broadstairs. He was one of Bowen's favorite writers, and she noted that his influence on her was great because his stories had been read to her before she could read (M. Ellmann, *Elizabeth Bowen* 225n26). In 1965, after visiting the same Broadstairs house she incorporates into *Eva Trout*, she wrote to Charles Ritchie that rereading *David Copperfield* "has given me an almost terrifying illumination about my own writing. Here really are the roots of so many things I have felt, or perhaps my way of feeling things and seeing them" (Glendinning 440). Bowen also wrote about Dickens in *English Novelists* (28–30).

"Doctor Marigold" was one of Dickens's most popular stories. It was published first in a special Christmas issue of *All the Year Round* in 1865 and then republished in collections of Dickens stories in 1873, 1896, and 1908; it was also published in 1908 as a standalone illustrated piece. Any one of these collections could have been among those read to the young Bowen. The story was also performed regularly during and after Dickens's lifetime. *Eva Trout* may owe much to Dickens's story; both feature an unofficially adopted deaf child who forms an exceptionally close bond with the adoptive single parent and is later removed from that parent to learn to communicate more widely (through sign language in "Doctor Marigold" and through speech in *Eva Trout*).

42. The desire to make a mark on the world motivates several characters in Bowen's earlier novel *The House in Paris* (1935).

43. An Eden motif, beginning with Eva's name, runs through the novel. Jeremy's need to exit the Eden he inhabits with his mother participates in this strand of the narrative. I discuss this motif in "Modes of Dislocation."

44. It may be that male homosexuality is represented as another form of mimicry in the novel. Bowen may have intended the relationship between Constantine and the late Willy Trout to be understood as a mimicry of marriage. If so, this might help to explain why homosexual men, infrequent in Bowen's work, are included alongside deafness in both *Eva Trout* and Bowen's short story "Summer Night."

45. I more thoroughly examine Eva's subjectivity and the novel's thematics of inauthenticity in "Modes of Dislocation." But more recently I have begun to see Eva as autistic; this would explain dozens of textual details, such as her visual patterns of memory, her difficulties with spoken language, her discomfort with sudden noises, her misunderstanding of social cues and idioms, her focus on certain details—what Joseph Straus calls "strong local coherence" (467ff)—her vague but agreed upon "handicap" and other characters' frustrated responses to her. So it may not be that her subjectivity is impaired but merely that it is expressed in nonnormative ways. Bowen may, however, have seen those possibilities as synonymous.

46. Eva is setting off to be married to Henry when Jeremy kills her, perhaps accidentally, perhaps not. I explore the murder in "Matricide and the End of Nostalgia in Elizabeth Bowen."

47. Ellmann does go on to ask, "Yet is this innerness merely an illusion concocted out of words?" (*Elizabeth Bowen* 206). She thereby returns to the text's questioning of interiority or subjectivity itself.

Chapter 4

I would like to thank Michael Groden for his generous responses to my queries about Joyce manuscripts; John-Whittier-Ferguson for reading and commenting helpfully on a draft of the chapter, and especially for alerting me to the existence of the "death-watch" beetle; and Lisa Belzeski for research assistance relating to this chapter. I would also like to thank the Purdue graduate students in my Joyce seminar of fall 2013 for their wonderful insights into *Ulysses*.

1. Siân White argues that the stripling represents an intimate aesthetics, in part because Bloom is prompted by holding the stripling's hand to think about his daughter and his own history. But this is rather a one-sided intimacy, and White has to explain away the fact that we do not get any information about the stripling's perspective.

2. In spite of *Ulysses*'s many disabled characters, there is surprisingly little work on Joyce from a disability studies perspective. I know of two articles about Gerty MacDowell (Plock, "Why"; and Nemecek) and one about the blind stripling (Cormier).

3. If Aida Yared is right that in "Lestrygonians" Bloom's movements imitate the progress of food through the digestive tract, there may also be a pun animating the stripling's blindness. Yared points out that "Dawson Street [where Bloom meets the stripling] becomes the caecum (the first portion of the large intestine, commonly called the 'blind' intestine)" (472). As I mention in chapter 1, furthermore, Gerty's lameness may similarly arise from a pun, in that Bloom's penis has been referred to as "limp."

4. The "hee hee" directed at the stripling at the end of the chapter, in my view, does not alter the general seriousness of the representation of the blind stripling. It does, as I mention below, serve as one of several links between Pat and the stripling.

5. Critics who have written articles about the stripling include Cormier, Rainsford, Morse, Whaley, and White. Critics who briefly discuss Pat include Leighton and Shockley.

6. For more information about the "Sirens" drafts in the National Library, see Ferrer, "What Song." For a chart detailing extant manuscripts of *Ulysses*, see Groden, *Ulysses*, appendix 2.

7. In the first draft of this passage, the line was "tink to her compassion"; this word lacks the condescension implied by *pity* but also lacks the pithy rhythm needed for this musical chapter (NLI MS 36,639/7/A-B).

8. I thank Joe Valente for this insight.

9. Robert Ryf explores Joyce's filmic visual techniques and points out several examples of his texts superimposing images one on another (38–40).

10. Angela Lea Nemecek argues convincingly that Cormier overvalues mobility without noting the gendered implications of his claims (189).

11. Berger inaccurately characterizes disability studies as simply rejecting metaphoric representations and adhering to a naïve understanding of language as able to "symbolize only itself, without remainder" (149). The first part of this is belied by

scholars firmly within disability studies, such as C. Barker, Vidali, and Dolmage, who provide nuanced readings of metaphor. And the claim that critiquing the ways disabled characters are metaphorized implies an understanding of fictional language as potentially nonfigurative is also unfounded; disability scholars such as Tobin Siebers, whom Berger critiques on this ground, are not seeking unmetaphorical representations. Instead, they are pointing to a continuum of metaphoricity on which many disabled characters (certainly not all) serve far more thoroughly as metaphors than their nondisabled counterparts, who are granted a roundedness I discuss briefly here. Berger then acknowledges that Siebers and other scholars whom he criticizes do know that language is figurative, but seems to imply that their political struggle for the ownership of disability has prevented their acknowledging this (149).

12. Rushdie also has his character Saleem Sinai in *Midnight's Children* point out that "reality can have metaphorical content; that does not make it less real" (230); also quoted in C. Barker (1).

13. Dolmage points out, quoting Thomas Kuhn and Lakoff and Johnson, that metaphors generally highlight one feature and suppress others ("Between the Valley" 110).

14. For a recent, nuanced discussion of "narrative prosthesis," see Bérubé 41–53.

15. This comment appears in his introduction without reference to Morrison, but Quayson returns to the idea in his discussion of Morrison, where he claims that "the disability becomes like a fulcrum or nexus point that radiates variant processes of signification . . . across various representational scales and locations" (114).

16. Wheatley posits and explores the religious model in detail (including ways of understanding disability as a manifestation of God's glory).

17. Even in the more realistic "Hades" episode, Reuben J Dodd, here unnamed, is described as "bent on a stick, stumping round the corner" and Simon Dedalus curses him in terms of further disability: "The devil break the hasp of your back!" (6.252, 6.256).

18. In her article "Self and Other in *Finnegans Wake*," Kimberly Devlin discusses the relation of stuttering and deafness to guilt in the Mutt and Jute episode (41).

19. In his explanation of this process, Cohen sounds like the Arranger of "Ithaca": "In both tasks—realizing that the expression is intended metaphorically, and seeing what to make of it—the hearer typically employs a number of assumptions about the speaker: what the speaker believes, what the speaker believes about what the hearer believes (which includes beliefs about what the speaker thinks the hearer can be expected to believe about the speaker)" (8).

20. Bolt discusses the blindness-dream confusion, remarking, "Though far from being profound, this question has been raised *by* (if not *in*) many philosophical works" (*Metanarrative* 71).

21. See Valente, *Myth of Manliness* 220–36, for a fascinating discussion of *Ulysses*'s treatment of "metrocolonial" masculinity and the different reigning versions of masculinity promoted in cultural nationalist circles.

22. Toward the end of "Nausicaa" Bloom has a very similar thought about Gerty MacDowell: "Sad about her lame of course but must be on your guard not to feel too much pity" (13.1094–94).

23. The Arranger of "Ithaca" compounds this sense of tragedy later when he lists "blind stripling" as a possible identity for Bloom if "all positive values" were eliminated from his life and he ended up a mendicant (17.1941).

24. The line "more shameless not seeing" was a very late addition to the text; it was added in the fourth set of page proofs (out of five) for "Lestrygonians" (*JJA* 23:189).

25. Bloom's interaction with the stripling prompts him to finally recall the name—Penrose—of the "priestlylooking chap was always squinting in when he passed" (8.175–76) because the stripling's "[b]loodless pious face [is] like a fellow going in to be a priest" (8.1112–13), as well as because Penrose "squint[ed]" and had "[w]eak eyes" (8.176). As Maud Ellmann points out, Penrose's name "evokes such loaded terms as pens, rising penises, and roses, the last of which is Bloom's term for menstruation, as well as a pun on his own flowery name" ("*Ulysses*" 61).

26. This line was closer to his meeting with the stripling in the typescript, before Joyce expanded the two brief paragraphs (*JJA* 12:320). Before the typescript, the only extant draft is the Rosenbach manuscript, in which the line "Today. Today. Not think" does not yet appear (Levin 172).

27. For discussions of Bergson's influence on modernism and on Joyce (in *Time and Western Man*, Wyndham Lewis placed Joyce in the "time-school" of Bergson), see, in addition to Gillies, Hornby, Kumar, and Lehan, the collection edited by Ardoin, Gontarski, and Mattison.

28. In an earlier draft, Joyce created a sort of prelude to this laughter by rhyming Pat's name: "Pat. How much is that?" (*JJA* 13:39).

29. In "Circe," Pat is substituted for the mocker and laughs at the pun: "Hee hee hee. Wait till I wait" (15.510).

30. In the second draft held at the National Library of Ireland (which is the first half of a manuscript held at the State University of New York at Buffalo and reproduced in the *James Joyce Archive*), Pat is not yet described as deaf, but he is already associated with Bloom's (and Molly's) waiting: "He sat with Richie Goulding. Near. At four. Is he not? Forgotten. Wait. Pat, waiter, came to wait" (NLI MS 36,639/9). By the time Joyce was midway through this draft, he had conceived of Pat as deaf, as evidenced in *JJA* 13:33ff.

31. Lawrence's description of Pat's "unfortunate predicament" and her labeling of the chapter's wordplay "deaf-eared transcribing" are themselves unfortunate, but I do think the question of the role of hearing for readers of "Sirens" is compelling.

32. In an argument that interestingly inverts Lawrence's, Roy Gottfried explores Joyce's wordplay as a function of weak vision: "Joyce's visual weakness includes misreading as probable meaning, error as possible interpretation" (44).

33. In "Clay" there is a "dummy," or deaf, nonspeaking person, who is the object of hostility from one of the women in the laundry: "Ginger Mooney was always saying what she wouldn't do to the dummy who had charge of the irons if it wasn't for Maria" (*Dubliners* 83).

34. I am grateful to Daniel Ferrer for helping me decipher the draft passage and pointing out the allusion to Janus.

35. These lines contain phrases from the song "M'appari" from Flotow's opera *Martha*. The lyrics Simon Dedalus sings were freely translated by Charles Jeffreys (Gifford 292).

36. On the inside cover of a notebook in which he drafted "Sirens" Joyce wrote out the parts of a *fuga per canonem*, a musical form distinct from a fugue; he listed this as the technique of the chapter in the schemata as well. But he also used the term *fugue* to describe the chapter, seemingly interchangeably.

Chapter 5

For assistance with research for this chapter I am indebted to Elizabeth Wulbrecht, Kelsey Johnson, and Ryan Buss, my Purdue Wilke Interns for Spring 2014, Fall 2014, and Spring 2015, respectively. Elizabeth Wulbrecht did excellent work with Woolf's manuscripts. I am also grateful to Douglas Baynton for helping me locate suffrage posters and to John Whittier-Ferguson, Michael Groden, and John Gordon for assistance with matters Joycean.

1. Leslie Fiedler similarly writes that "the distinction between audience and exhibit, we and them, normal and Freak, is revealed as an illusion, desperately, perhaps even necessarily, defended, but untenable in the end" (36).

2. Thanks to Jennifer William for finding and translating sections of this essay for me.

3. In *Disability Aesthetics*, Tobin Siebers points out that Nazi insistence on "a bombastic perfection of the body" is one of the main reasons we view it as kitsch. "The perfection of the bodies is the very mark of their unreality and lack of taste" (5).

4. In their book about Cubism, Thomas Vargish and Delo Mook consider the common claim that "every deformity has its formal justification." They comment, "We are tempted to agree, but then what can we mean any more by 'deformity'? And where does the necessity for deformity come from?" (62).

5. Derek Attridge and Marjorie Howes both use the same term, *deformations*, in their contributions to the *Cambridge Companion to James Joyce* (Attridge 15, 257). To give another representative example, Juliette Taylor-Batty writes that in *Finnegans Wake* "the English language is deformed almost beyond recognition" (117).

6. Lahr published pamphlets by writers such as D. H. Lawrence, T. F. Powys, and Rhys Davies and included in his series an essay by Moore about D. H. Lawrence.

7. Critical works in print on Moore are so far limited to a single book—Renée Dickinson's study of Woolf and Moore—and two articles: Jane Garrity's "Olive Moore's Headless Woman" and Matt Franks's "Mental Inversion, Modernist Aesthetics, and Disability Exceptionalism in Olive Moore's *Spleen*."

8. Moore's choice of the title *Spleen* may owe much to Baudelaire's "Spleen," in which he describes a kind of ennui, associated with limping, that resonates with

Spleen: "Nothing is longer than the limping days / When under heavy snowflakes of the years, / Ennui, the fruit of dulling lassitude, / Takes on the size of immortality" (147).

9. Garrity writes similarly: "In displacing her pregnancy from the body to the mind, Ruth aligns herself with the rhetoric of innovation that is the founding impetus for modernist aesthetics and implicitly answers Pound's injunction to 'Make It New'" (299).

10. Franks argues that Ruth appropriates a disability aesthetics by "taking up her son's supposedly 'arrested' and 'debilitated' modes of perception" (112). I don't see this process in the novel because Richard is not understood by Ruth's narration to have *any* modes of perception (an absence that Franks acknowledges [118] and that I discuss further below). Further, I don't see Ruth adopting any point of view other than, temporarily, Uller's, when she finally appreciates his painting as capturing the essence of Giovanni by *not* replicating him as he appears in nature. Franks suggests that Uller "borrows disabled ways of perceiving such as color-blindness and visual impairment" (122); but even if one can see his modernist painting in those terms, there is little to link visual impairment with Richard.

11. In an astute conference paper that focuses on a scene in *Spleen* where Richard moves his chair, Rebecah Pulsifer suggests that Ruth "occupies a trans position in that she desires to transform the material conditions of her body into new forms of gender expression."

12. The reviewer in the *Forum and Century* asserts that Moore "belies her own wit by professing a contempt for women" (Rev. of *The Apple Is Bitten Again*).

13. Curiously, Garrity uses the word as though it is merely descriptive (301, 302) and questions whether Richard may in fact be "sentient" (303).

14. The reviewer for the *Book World* calls Richard an "infant monstrosity" (Rev. of *Repentance at Leisure*).

15. At least two saints are said to have had visions of stags with crucifixes between their antlers: Saint Eustace, who was converted when, serving as a Roman general, he was hunting a stag until this vision stopped him; and Saint Hubertus, who was similarly converted by a stag with a crucifix held in his antlers, this one advising him verbally to turn to God (Catholic Online).

16. Franks perceptively links the passage with eugenics, describing the woman becoming "dwarfed" and some goats becoming their own droppings as they recede into the distance: "While the figures she watches are walking forward, away from her, she 'incorrectly' perceives them as getting smaller, as if they are retreating into their own devolution" (119).

17. I discuss this dynamic of aiming to transcend deformity further in the epilogue.

18. In its first incarnation, *The Years* was a novel-essay with fictional episodes interspersed with expository prose. Woolf abandoned this experiment early on, however, waiting to write *Three Guineas* and keeping *The Years* focused on what she thought of as "fact" as opposed to characters' imaginative lives.

19. As Woolf put it in a diary entry in March 1938, after *The Years* was pub-

lished, "The public world very notably invaded the private at M[onk's] H[ouse] last week end. Almost war" (*Diary* 5:131).

20. One such aspect is the intrusion of the male Jewish body into Sara Pargiter's mental privacy, as I explore in *Modernism, Feminism, and Jewishness*, especially 180–89.

21. Radin describes Elvira, who became Sara in the published novel, as seeming to "come straight out of Woolf's own psyche" (42).

22. Sara's slight deformity may be indebted to that of Olive in Dinah Maria Mulock Craik's novel *Olive* (1850). Olive has a mildly twisted spine, is for a long time emotionally rejected by her parents (with whom she later becomes close), and becomes an artist. The novel is intensely conservative on gender and marriage, but does make a heroine out of a disabled woman. Woolf may have read this novel; she mentions another Craik novel, *John Halifax, Gentleman*, in a 1907 review of *The Weavers* by Sir Gilbert Parker (*Essays* 6:340). Thanks to David Bradshaw for alerting me to this review.

23. A contemporaneous reviewer of *The Years*, Theodora Bosanquet, applies such eugenic logic when she asks in *Time and Tide*, "What will it profit us if we eliminate all the causes of war, equalize everybody's income, sterilize all the unfit, if the jet of that fountain [of life] is plugged up?" (Majumdar and McLaurin 368).

24. Peggy later makes the same point with some of the same words, though without the metaphor of deformity. She feels she can envision "not a place, but a state of being, in which there was real laughter, real happiness, and this fractured world was whole; whole, vast, and free. But how could she say it?" (*Years* 370). Evelyn Chan describes this as "one of the most important moments in *The Years*, the writing of which excited Woolf so much that she described her own reactions as 'my cheeks burn; my hands tremble'" (609). The importance of this moment highlights the significance of Eleanor's ableist version of the same idea.

25. Woolf partially reprises this image of disability caused by the pursuit of wealth in *Between the Acts*: "So we answer to the infernal, age-long and eternal order issued from on high. And obey. 'Working, serving, pushing, striving, earning wages—to be spent—here? Oh dear no. Now? No, by and by. When ears are deaf and the heart is dry'" (82).

26. *The Years* also contains four deaf characters: Mrs. Potter (93–94), Mrs. Chinnery (Morris's mother-in-law, 198–99), Uncle Patrick (333–34), and Rose, once she's older (340). Mrs. Potter, one of Eleanor's tenants, is also arthritic, her hands "knotted and grooved like the gnarled roots of a tree." The depiction of her as a "large tousled ape" who looks about her "wildly, suspiciously" is the most obviously ableist portrayal in the novel, reminding us how "humanity goes," as *Three Guineas* has it. When Eleanor and the contractor, Mr. Duffus, tell Mrs. Potter they have come to look at her ceiling, "the words conveyed nothing" (93–94). Deafness, then, symbolizes the breakdown of (spoken) language that the novel everywhere explores, and indeed explores most persistently through the character of Sara.

27. As Elvira her outsider status was even more pronounced, in that she and

Maggie had "lived abroad for years. . . . To them the social codes of England [were] like the peculiar rituals and taboos of an unknown tribe" (Radin 51).

28. Alice Wood notes that in drafts of the 1910 section Elvira and Maggie "debate their outsider status and discuss whether they are, or would want to be 'Englishwomen'" (50).

29. Mitchell Leaska suggests that the reason Woolf feared Elvira becoming "too dominant" was that she sensed that "too much of the author was being siphoned into the figure of Elvira" (225).

30. Several characters comment on Abel's missing fingers, the "knobs of his mutilated fingers" (13), the "smooth knobs" (48), the "shiny stumps" (318).

31. Sarah Cole argues that Abel's hand participates in the violence diffused throughout the novel; in the scene where he fumbles at Mira's neck, she writes, his hand's "groping action and the odd decapitating imagery ('where the neck joins the shoulders') holds undertones of an unspecified violence" (258).

32. The textual apparatus in Snaith's Cambridge Edition of *The Years* gives, "What did the doctor say about your back? Lie straight, lie still, he said" (615). Woolf removed "about your back" from the final version.

33. Another passage uses similar language: "Sally laughed. Maggie looked round. When she laughed she was crooked, like something blown on one side" (Cambridge Ed., 613).

34. Cole, too, notes the relationship of this passage to Sara's "hump" (260).

35. I am thinking not only of Garland-Thomson's description in "Misfits" of the misfit between a person and an environment but also of Nicholas's question, with the word *fit* supplied by Eleanor: how, if we do not know ourselves, can we make laws and religions that fit? (266, 299).

36. See my *Modernism, Feminism, and Jewishness* 180–89. Kathy Phillips discusses Sara's positions against war and empire, noting that she "points up the paradox of using force to repel force" and that she's the only character who directly speaks out against empire (33–35).

37. For example, Woolf writes two versions of a passage that attributes Elvira's "irascibility" to her deformity: "Another waltz crashed out from the house at the back. That was entirely wrong[.] With all the irascibility which so often goes with deformity Elvira seized her pillow and beat it on the bed" (*Pargiters* 3:113). The second version of this passage is more hesitant about the linkage: "Elvira started up in bed, with the sudden irascibility ~~which might have some connection with~~ from perhaps her deformity, dashed her pillow down. The milk rolled over the books" (*Pargiters* 3:114).

38. Miller describes the late modernist authors he considers as "bringing modernism to a close" through their "different handling of literary form and in their works' . . . more direct response to the historical currents in which they were written and read" (23). This description is accurate for Woolf as well.

39. *Between the Acts* contains a similar line, stressing Woolf's sustained awareness of historical repetition: "The Guide Book still told the truth. 1830 was true in 1939" (37).

40. I hope it is clear that I'm not myself judging the earlier and later novels

as authentic or inauthentic, but inferring Woolf's embrace of authenticity in, for example, *To the Lighthouse* and her disillusion with authenticity in *The Years*.

41. Since a man in the East End crying out "Old iron to sell" is a likely portrait of a Jewish peddler, this interruption foreshadows the interruption by the Jew in the bath in the "Present Day" section.

42. Indeed, "the *Wake* makes a mess not just of English as it is commonly maintained, but also of what was in many ways *the* science of the nineteenth century—the historical linguistics that tried to construct language in terms of historiography and racial order. . . . 'Pure' language is entirely compromised not just by the fact of cross-language puns and portmanteaus, but inasmuch as the *Wake* revels so much in its own 'contamination'" (Platt, *Joyce, Race* 19–20).

43. Bishop writes that "Shem's writing is symptom-making, the most efflorescent variety of which is the dream, the most common of which is mere living" (*Joyce's Book* 249).

44. Fordham relates a comment by Maria Jolas, who heard Joyce say that the title of the novel indicates "that the little people of the Erse will awaken. The Finnegans. Do wake up, you see. And it was almost a warning, if you want, to the people who regarded the Finnegans as non-essential and not worth taking into account" (*Lots of Fun* 36).

45. "The Ballad of Persse O'Reilly" begins and ends with Humpty Dumpty and casts the lines about being unable to put Humpty together again in terms of resurrection: "And not all the king's men nor his horses / Will resurrect his corpus / For there's no true spell in Connaught or hell / (bis) That's able to raise a Cain" (47.26–29).

46. This sense of universalization emerges from Joyce's deft manipulations and transmutations of stereotypes, as Hugh Kenner points out: "*Finnegans Wake* is a book of stereotypes, and we'd get nowhere with it at all if it wasn't" ("Shem" 153).

47. In April 1924 "Joyce even sent a picture of himself to Sylvia Beach with the note: 'Here is the passport photo of Shem the Penman'" (Landuyt 144).

48. Knuth points out that the Hebrew *asham* means "sin" or "sin offering," indicating Shem's status as sacrificial victim (82).

49. The website Glosses of *Finnegans Wake* glosses *hambone*: "a performer doing an imitation of negro dialect; negro in American comic strip; amateur (*Slang*)."

50. In addition to Esau, Shem is Cain, and his siglum, a squared-off *C*, suggests this identity, as Seamus Deane has pointed out; one of Shaun's identities is, correspondingly, Abel, and his siglum is a stylized *A* (Crispi, Slote, and Van Hulle 18).

51. As Landuyt points out, some of these terms also stem from a review of *Ulysses* by Dr. Joseph Collins. Collins called Bloom a "moral monster, a pervert and an invert, an apostate to his race and his religion" (Landuyt 145).

52. The influence of *The Jukes* was such that in an introduction to the fourth, 1910 edition, Columbia University professor Franklin H. Giddings writes that "'The Jukes' has long been known as one of those important books that exert influence out of all proportion to their bulk." He goes on to praise its method: "It is not too much to say that when the first edition of 'The Jukes' was published, it was the best example of scientific method applied to a sociological investigation" (Dugdale iii).

53. Joyce added the scientific racism/craniometry term "dalickey cyphalos" and made some other changes to the passage in March 1928 (*JJA* 57:327).

54. I am grateful to John Gordon for discussing with me the absence of direct references in Joyce to Nazi theories of art and the meanings of that absence. Gordon points out that *Finnegans Wake* 182.4–29 brings together a "mishmash" of theories of art, especially in the word *stipple*, which brings Shem's writing together with Impressionist art (email communication, February 2015).

55. In *Joyce, Race, and "Finnegans Wake"* Len Platt also makes clear Joyce's extended responses to claims of racial and linguistic purity made by Nazism and race science. Jesse Schotter similarly explores Joyce's rejection of Aryan assertions of linguistic purity.

56. Platt remarks that "the *Wake* registers many references to German race pride and Nazism, almost all of them insulting. . . . Storm troopers, the Gestapo, the Strength Through Joy movement, Hitler's road building programme and so on, are all meted out a similar treatment" (*James Joyce* 144–45).

57. For an astute exploration of Lewis's complex reactions to Nazi aesthetics, see Hewitt 171–98.

58. I am grateful to Jennifer William for discussing this phrase with me.

59. Fordham insightfully explores the development of this passage about Shem writing on the body through the draft and published versions in *Lots of Fun* 39–65.

Epilogue

1. Born in Bialystock in 1898, Segal lived in Paris and other parts of France beginning in 1925 (Roditi 24).

2. Although Stevens said he had no particular Picasso painting in mind, the poem is regularly and reasonably associated with *The Old Guitarist* (Cook 113). In its lack of specificity, Stevens's poem's reference to "this picture of Picasso's" blurs the boundaries between *The Old Guitarist* and the later Cubist paintings that, as Aviram and Hartnett point out, are more accurately described as "hoarde[s] / of destructions" (209).

3. Aviram and Hartnett describe a related aspect of the poem: "This meditation on blindness extends . . . to the possibility that '[t]hings as they are have been destroyed' by passing away into time. . . . [O]nce a thing is observed, it has been fixed by the memory; it is past, gone, in a sense 'destroyed' because it is no longer present" (217).

4. "In a 1 March 1955 letter to Caroline Gordon and Allen Tate, O'Connor confessed, 'as for Hulga I just by the grace of God escape being her'" (Sharp 28).

Works Cited

Adams, Rachel. *Raising Henry: A Memoir of Motherhood, Disability, and Discovery.* New Haven: Yale University Press, 2013.

Aebischer, Pascale. "Creative Disability / Disabled Creativity in Henry Green's *Blindness. Studies in the Novel* 35.4 (Winter 2003): 510–25.

Allen, Stuart. "'Thinking Strictly Prohibited': Music, Language, and Thought in 'Sirens.'" *Twentieth-Century Literature* 53.4 (Winter 2007): 442–59.

Anglin-Jaffe, Hannah. "From 'Freak Show' to 'Charity Case': The 'Containment' of Deafness in Wilkie Collins's *Hide and Seek.*" *Journal of Literary and Cultural Disability Studies* 7.1 (2013): 53–69.

Anolik, Ruth Bienstock, ed. *Demons of the Body and Mind: Essays on Disability in Gothic Literature.* Jefferson, NC: McFarland, 2010.

Antliff, Mark. "Bergson on Art and Creativity." *Understanding Bergson, Understanding Modernism.* Ed. Paul Ardoin, S. E. Gontarski, and Laci Mattison. New York: Bloomsbury Academic, 2013. 299–300.

Ardoin, Paul, S. E. Gontarski, and Laci Mattison, eds. *Understanding Bergson, Understanding Modernism.* New York: Bloomsbury Academic, 2013.

Armstrong, Tim. *Modernism: A Cultural History.* Malden, MA: Polity Press, 2005.

Armstrong, Tim. *Modernism, Technology, and the Body: A Cultural Study.* New York: Cambridge University Press, 1998.

Art Institute of Chicago. *The Essential Guide.* 4th ed. Foreword by Douglas Druick. Chicago: Art Institute of Chicago, 2013.

Attridge, Derek, ed. *The Cambridge Companion to James Joyce.* 1990. New York: Cambridge University Press, 2004.

Attridge, Derek. "Joyce's Lipspeech: Syntax and the Subject in 'Sirens.'" *James Joyce: The Centennial Symposium.* Ed. Morris Beja, Phillip Herring, Maurice Harmon, and David Norris. Urbana: University of Illinois Press, 1986. 59–65.

Aviram, Amittai, and Richard Hartnett. "The Man with the Blue Guitar: Dialogism in Lyric Poetry." *Dialogism and Lyric Self-Fashioning: Bakhtin and the Voices of a Genre.* Ed. Jacob Blevins. Selinsgrove, PA: Susquehanna University Press, 2008. 204–20.

Babcock, Granger. "*The Glass Menagerie* and the Transformation of the Subject." *Journal of Dramatic Theory and Criticism* 14.1 (Fall 1999): 17–36.

Bahan, Benjamin. "Upon the Formation of a Visual Variety of the Human Race." *Open Your Eyes: Deaf Studies Talking*. Ed. H-Dirksen L. Bauman. Minneapolis: University of Minnesota Press, 2008. 83–99.

Bak, John. *Tennessee Williams: A Literary Life*. New York: Palgrave Macmillan, 2013.

Ballin, Albert. *The Deaf-Mute Howls*. 1930. Washington, DC: Gallaudet University Press, 1998.

Barasch, Moshe. *Blindness: The History of a Mental Image in Western Thought*. New York: Routledge, 2001.

Barber-Stetson, Claire. "Slow Processing: A New Minor Literature by Autists and Modernists." *Journal of Modern Literature* 38.1 (Fall 2014): 147–65.

Barclay, Florence L. *The Rosary*. Cirencester, England: Echo Library, 2005.

Barker, Clare. *Postcolonial Fiction and Disability: Exceptional Children, Metaphor, and Materiality*. New York: Palgrave, 2012.

Barker, Jennifer Lynde. *The Aesthetics of Antifascist Film: Radical Projection*. New York: Routledge, 2013.

Barr, Alfred H. Jr. *Picasso: Fifty Years of His Art*. New York: Museum of Modern Art, 1966.

Basselin, Timothy. *Flannery O'Connor: Writing a Theology of Disabled Humanity*. Waco, TX: Baylor University Press, 2013.

Baudelaire, Charles. *Flowers of Evil*. Trans. James N. McGowan. New York: Oxford World Classics, 1998.

Bauman, Zygmunt. "Allosemitism: Premodern, Modern, Postmodern." *Modernity, Culture, and "the Jew."* Ed. Bryan Cheyette and Laura Marcus. Stanford: Stanford University Press, 1998. 143–56.

Baynton, Douglas. "Disability and the Justification of Inequality in American History." *Disability Studies Reader*. 4th ed. Ed. Lennard Davis. New York: Routledge, 2013. 17–33.

Baynton, Douglas. *Forbidden Signs. The Campaign against Sign Language*. Chicago: University of Chicago Press, 1996.

Baynton, Douglas. "'These Pushful Days': Time and Disability in the Age of Eugenics." *Health and History* 13.2 (2011): 43–64.

Bednarska, Dominika. "A Cripped Erotic: Gender and Disability in James Joyce's 'Nausicaa.'" *James Joyce Quarterly* 49.1 (Fall 2011): 73–89.

Beer, Gillian. "'Authentic Tidings of Invisible Things': Vision and the Invisible in the Later Nineteenth Century." *Vision in Context: Historical and Contemporary Perspectives on Sight*. Ed. Teresa Brennan and Martin Jay. New York: Routledge, 1996. 83–98.

Behling, Laura. "The Necessity of Disability in 'Good Country People' and 'The Lame Shall Enter First.'" *Flannery O'Connor Review* 4 (2006): 88–98.

Bell, Alexander Graham. *Memoir upon the Formation of a Deaf Variety of the Human Race*. Washington, DC: National Academy of Sciences, 1882.

Bennett, Andrew, and Nicholas Royle. *Elizabeth Bowen and the Dissolution of the Novel: Still Lives*. New York: St. Martin's Press, 1995.

Berger, James. *The Disarticulate: Language, Disability, and the Narratives of Modernity*. New York: New York University Press, 2014.

Bergson, Henri. *Time and Free Will: An Essay on the Immediate Data of Consciousness*. Trans. Frank Lubecki Pogson. London: G. Allen, 1913.

Bérubé, Michael. *The Secret Life of Stories: From Don Quixote to Harry Potter, How Understanding Intellectual Disability Transforms the Way We Read*. New York: New York University Press, 2016.

Bigsby, C. W. E. "Entering *The Glass Menagerie*." *The Cambridge Companion to Tennessee Williams*. Ed. Matthew C. Roudané. New York: Cambridge University Press, 1997. 29–44.

Bishop, John. *Joyce's Book of the Dark: "Finnegans Wake."* Madison: University of Wisconsin Press, 1986.

Bishop, John. "A Metaphysics of Coitus in 'Nausicaa.'" *Ulysses: En-gendered Perspectives: Eighteen New Essays on the Episodes*. Ed. Kimberly J. Devlin and Marilyn Reizbaum. Columbia: University of South Carolina Press, 1999. 185–209.

Bjorklund, Beth. Rev. of *Blindness and Insight: Essays in the Rhetoric of Contemporary Criticism*, by Paul de Man. *German Quarterly* 58.1 (Winter 1985): 100–103.

Blamires, Harry. *The New Bloomsday Book*.3rd ed. New York: Routledge, 1996.

Bolt, David. "Beneficial Blindness: Literary Representation and the So-Called Positive Stereotyping of People with Impaired Vision." *New Zealand Journal of Disability Studies* 12 (2006): 80–100.

Bolt, David. "The Blindman in the Classic: Feminisms, Ocularcentrism, and Charlotte Brontë's *Jane Eyre*." *Textual Practice* 22.2 (2008): 269–89.

Bolt, David. "From Blindness to Visual Impairment: Terminological Typology and the Social Model of Disability." *Disability and Society* 20.5 (August 2005): 539–52.

Bolt, David. "Looking Back at Literature: A Critical Reading of the Unseen Stare in Depictions of People with Impaired Vision." *Disability and Society* 20.7 (December 2005): 735–47.

Bolt, David. *The Metanarrative of Blindness: A Re-reading of Twentieth Century Anglophone Writing*. Ann Arbor: University of Michigan Press, 2014.

Bourrier, Karen. *The Measure of Manliness: Disability and Masculinity in the Mid-Victorian Novel*. Ann Arbor: University of Michigan Press, 2015.

Bouton, Reine Dugas. "Woolf and Welty, Readers and Writers, Writing and Unwriting." *Literature and the Writer*. Ed. Michael J. Meyer. New York: Rodopi, 2004. 175–90.

Bowen, Elizabeth. *English Novelists*. 1942. London: Collins, 1947.

Bowen, Elizabeth. *Eva Trout; or, Changing Scenes*. 1968. New York: Anchor Books, 2003.

Bowen, Elizabeth. *The House in Paris*. 1935. New York: Anchor Books, 2002.

Bowen, Elizabeth. "How I Write: A Conversation with Glyn Jones." *Listening In: Broadcasts, Speeches, and Interviews by Elizabeth Bowen*. Ed. Allan Hepburn. Edinburgh: Edinburgh University Press, 2010. 267–73.

Bowen, Elizabeth. Manuscripts of *Eva Trout*. Elizabeth Bowen Collection. Harry Ransom Center, University of Texas at Austin.

Bowen, Elizabeth. *Seven Winters: Memoirs of a Dublin Childhood* and *Afterthoughts: Pieces on Writing*. New York: Alfred A. Knopf, 1962.

Bowker, Gordon. *James Joyce: A New Biography*. New York: Farrar, Straus and Giroux, 2011.

Bowlby, Rachel. *Feminist Destinations and Further Essays on Virginia Woolf*. Edinburgh: Edinburgh University Press, 1997.

Bradshaw, Charles. "Language and Responsibility: The Failure of Discourse in Carson McCullers's *The Heart Is a Lonely Hunter*." *Southern Quarterly* 37.2 (Winter 1999): 118–26.

Brain, C. K. "The Day the Missing Link Turned Up in the Post." *Guardian* December 17, 2003.

Brew-Parrish, Valerie. "The Wrong Message—Still." *Ragged Edge Online*. Web. August 9, 2004.

Briggs, Julia. *Virginia Woolf: An Inner Life*. New York: Harcourt, 2005.

Brivic, Shelly. "Bitter Milk: Joyce's Shem Nursed Hysterically." *James Joyce Quarterly* 48.3 (Spring 2011): 457–76.

Brothers, Barbara. "*Blindness*: The Eye of Henry Green." *Henry Green*. Spec. issue of *Twentieth-Century Literature* 29.4 (Winter 1983): 403–21.

Brown, Susan. "The Mystery of the Fuga per Canonem Solved." *European Joyce Studies* 22.1 (2012): 173–93.

Bucknell, Brad. *Literary Modernism and Musical Aesthetics: Pater, Pound, Joyce, and Stein*. New York: Cambridge University Press, 2001.

Budgen, Frank. *James Joyce and the Making of "Ulysses."* Bloomington: Indiana University Press, 1960.

Budick, Emily Miller. *Engendering Romance: Women Writers and the Hawthorne Tradition, 1850–1990*. New Haven: Yale University Press, 1994.

Burch, Susan. *Signs of Resistance: American Deaf Cultural History, 1900–World War II*. New York: New York University Press, 2002.

Burke, Teresa Blankmeyer. "Armchairs and Stares: On the Privation of Deafness." *Deaf-Gain: Raising the Stakes for Human Diversity*. Ed. H-Dirksen L. Baumann and Joseph J. Murray. Minneapolis: University of Minnesota Press, 2014. 3–22.

Burstein, Jessica. *Cold Modernism: Literature, Fashion, Art*. University Park: Pennsylvania State University Press, 2012.

Butler, Christopher. *Early Modernism: Literature, Music, and Painting in Europe, 1900–1916*. New York: Oxford University Press, 1994.

Campbell, Fiona Kumari. "Ability." *Keywords for Disability Studies*. Ed. Rachel Adams, Benjamin Reiss, and David Serlin. New York: New York University Press, 2015. 12–14.

Campbell, Fiona Kumari. *Contours of Ableism: The Production of Disability and Abledness*. New York: Palgrave Macmillan, 2009.

Campbell, Joseph, and Henry Morton Robinson. *A Skeleton Key to "Finnegans Wake."* 1944. New York: Penguin Books, 1980.

Carpenter, Mary Wilson. "Blinding the Hero." *Differences: A Journal of Feminist Cultural Studies* 17.5 (2006): 52–68.

Carr, Virginia Spencer. *The Lonely Hunter: A Biography of Carson McCullers*. Athens: University of Georgia Press, 2003.

Catholic Online. "St Hubert" and "St Eustace." Web. August 2, 2014.

Chan, Evelyn T. "Professions, Freedom and Form: Reassessing Woolf's *The Years* and *Three Guineas*." *Review of English Studies* 61 (February 2010): 591–613.

Childs, Donald. *Modernism and Eugenics: Woolf, Eliot, Yeats, and the Culture of Degeneration*. New York: Cambridge University Press, 2007.

Chipp, Herschel Browning, ed. *Theories of Modern Art: A Source Book by Artists and Critics*. With contributions by Peter Selz and Joshua C. Taylor. Berkeley: University of California Press, 1968.

Clausson, Nils. "Practicing Deconstruction, Again: Blindness, Insight, and the Lovely Treachery of Words in D. H. Lawrence's 'The Blind Man.'" *College Literature* 34.1 (Winter 2007): 106–28.

Cogdell, Christina. "Design." *Keywords for Disability Studies*. Ed. Rachel Adams, Benjamin Reiss, and David Serlin. New York: New York University Press, 2015. 59–60.

Cohen, Ted. "Metaphor and the Cultivation of Intimacy." *Critical Inquiry* 5.1 (Autumn 1978): 3–12.

Cole, Sarah. *At the Violet Hour: Modernism and Violence in England and Ireland*. New York: Oxford University Press, 2012.

Collins, Wilkie. *Hide and Seek*. 1854. New York: Dover, 1981.

Collins, Wilkie. *Poor Miss Finch*. 1872. New York: Oxford University Press, 2000.

Conrad, Joseph. Preface. *The Nigger of the Narcissus*. 1897. Garden City, NY: Doubleday, 1914. 11–16.

Cook, Eleanor. *A Reader's Guide to Wallace Stevens*. Princeton: Princeton University Press, 2007.

Corcoran, Neil. *Elizabeth Bowen: The Enforced Return*. Oxford: Clarendon Press, 2004.

Cormier, Andre. "'Our eyes demand their turn. Let them be seen!' The Transcendental Blind Stripling." *Joyce Studies Annual* (2008): 203–25.

Crispi, Luca, Sam Slote, and Dirk Van Hulle. Introduction. *How Joyce Wrote "Finnegans Wake": A Chapter-by-Chapter Genetic Guide*. Ed. Luca Crispi and Sam Slote. Madison: University of Wisconsin Press, 2007. 3–48.

Cuddy-Keane, Melba. "Modernist Soundscapes and the Intelligent Ear: An Approach to Narrative through Auditory Perception." *A Companion to Narrative Theory*. Ed. James Phelan and Peter Rabinowitz. Malden, MA: Blackwell, 2005. 382–98.

Currie, Sheldon. "Freaks and Folks: Comic Imagery in the Fiction of Flannery O'Connor." *Antigonish Review* 62–63 (July 1985): 133–42.

Daly, Nicholas. *Literature, Technology, and Modernity, 1860–1920*. New York: Cambridge University Press, 2004.

Danius, Sara. *The Senses of Modernism: Technology, Perception, and Aesthetics*. Ithaca: Cornell University Press, 2002.

Das, Santanu. *Touch and Intimacy in First World War Literature*. New York: Cambridge University Press, 2008.

Davidson, Michael. *Concerto for the Left Hand: Disability and the Defamiliar Body*. Ann Arbor: University of Michigan Press, 2008.

Davidson, Michael. "The Rage of Caliban: Disabling Bodies in Modernist Aesthetics." *Modernism/modernity* 22.4 (November 2015): 609–25.

Davis, Lennard. *Bending over Backwards: Disability, Dismodernism, and Other Difficult Positions*. New York: New York University Press, 2002.

Davis, Lennard. *Enforcing Normalcy: Disability, Deafness, and the Body*. London: Verso, 1995.

Deane, Seamus. "Joyce the Irishman." *The Cambridge Companion to James Joyce*. Ed. Derek Attridge. 1990. New York: Cambridge University Press, 2004. 28–48.

Delany, Paul. "'We Shall Know Each Other Now': Message and Code in D.H. Lawrence's 'The Blind Man.'" *Contemporary Literature* 26.1 (1985): 26–39.

De Man, Paul. *Blindness and Insight: Essays in the Rhetoric of Contemporary Criticism*. Minneapolis: University of Minnesota Press, 1983.

Detloff, Madelyn. "'The Law Is on the Side of the Normal': Virginia Woolf as Crip Theorist." *Interdisciplinary / Multidisciplinary Woolf: Selected Papers from the Twenty-Second Annual International Conference on Virginia Woolf*. Ed. Ann Martin and Kathryn Holland. Clemson, SC: Clemson University Digital Press, 2013. 102–8.

Deutsch, Helen. "Deformity." *Keywords for Disability Studies*. Ed. Rachel Adams, Benjamin Reiss, and David Serlin. New York: New York University Press, 2015. 52–54.

Deutsch, Helen, and Felicity Nussbaum. Introduction. *"Defects": Engendering the Modern Body*. Ed. Helen Deutsch and Felicity Nussbaum. Ann Arbor: University of Michigan Press, 2000. 1–28.

Devlin, Albert J. "Eudora Welty's Mississippi." *Eudora Welty: Thirteen Essays (Selections from Eudora Welty, Critical Essays)*. Ed. Peggy W. Prenshaw. Jackson: University Press of Mississippi, 1983.

Devlin, Kimberly. "Self and Other in *Finnegans Wake*: A Framework for Analyzing Versions of Shem and Shaun." *James Joyce Quarterly* 21.1 (Fall 1983): 31–50.

Dickens, Charles. "Doctor Marigold's Prescriptions." 1865. *Boots at the Holly-Tree Inn and Other Stories*. London: Vision Press, 1969. 17–133.

Dickinson, Renée. *Female Embodiment and Subjectivity in the Modernist Novel: The Corporeum of Virginia Woolf and Olive Moore*. New York: Routledge, 2009.

Dolmage, Jay. "Between the Valley and the Field: Metaphor and Disability." *Prose Studies* 27.1–2 (April–August 2005): 108–19.

Dolmage, Jay. "Disabled upon Arrival: The Rhetorical Construction of Disability and Race at Ellis Island." *Cultural Critique* 77 (Winter 2011): 24–69.

Donaldson, Elizabeth. "Revisiting the Corpus of the Madwoman: Further Notes toward a Feminist Disability Studies Theory of Mental Illness." *Feminist Disability Studies*. Ed. Kim Q. Hall. Bloomington: Indiana University Press, 2011. 91–113.

Donaldson, Susan V. "Making a Spectacle: Welty, Faulkner, and Southern Gothic." *Mississippi Quarterly* 50.4 (1997): 567–83.

Dowd, Garin. "Bergson on Image and Representation." *Understanding Bergson, Understanding Modernism*. Ed. Paul Ardoin, S. E. Gontarski, and Laci Mattison. New York: Bloomsbury Academic, 2013.

Dugdale, Robert L. *The Jukes: A Study in Crime, Pauperism, Disease, and Heredity*. 1877. Reprint ed. New York: Arno Press and the *New York Times*, 1970.

Eagle, Chris. "Introduction: Talking Normal." *Literature, Speech Disorders, and Disability: Talking Normal*. Ed. Chris Eagle. New York: Routledge, 2014. 1–8.

Eagle, Chris. "'Stuttistics': On Speech Disorders in *Finnegans Wake*." *Literature, Speech Disorders, and Disability: Talking Normal*. Ed. Chris Eagle. New York: Routledge, 2014. 82–99.

Edmondson, Henry T. *Return to Good and Evil: Flannery O'Connor's Response to Nihilism*. Lanham, MD: Rowman and Littlefield, 2002.

Eisinger, Chester E. "Traditionalism and Modernism in Eudora Welty." *Eudora Welty: Thirteen Essays (Selections from Eudora Welty, Critical Essays)*. Ed. Peggy W. Prenshaw. Jackson: University Press of Mississippi, 1983. 3–25.

Ellmann, Maud. *Elizabeth Bowen: The Shadow across the Page*. Edinburgh: Edinburgh University Press, 2003.

Ellmann, Maud. "More Kicks Than Pricks: Modernist Body-Parts." *A Handbook of Modernism Studies*. Ed. Jean-Michel Rabaté. John Wiley & Sons, 2013. 255–80.

Ellmann, Maud. "*Ulysses*: The Epic of the Human Body." *A Companion to James Joyce*. Ed. Richard Brown. Hoboken, NJ: Blackwell, 2008. 54–70.

Ellmann, Richard. *James Joyce*. 1959. New York: Oxford University Press, 1972.

Ellmann, Richard. *Ulysses on the Liffey*. New York: Oxford University Press, 1972.

Erevelles, Nirmala. *Disability and Difference in Global Contexts : Enabling a Transformative Body Politic*. New York: Palgrave Macmillan, 2011.

Esmail, Jennifer. "'I Listened with My Eyes': Writing Speech and Reading Deafness in the Fiction of Charles Dickens and Wilkie Collins. *ELH* 78.4 (Winter 2011): 991–1020.

Evans, David H. "Cut! . . . Flannery O'Connor's Apotemnophiliac Allegories." *American Literature* 81.2 (June 2009): 305–31.

Evans, Oliver. *The Ballad of Carson McCullers: A Biography*. New York: Coward-McCann, 1966.

Eysteinsson, Astradur. *The Concept of Modernism*. Ithaca: Cornell University Press, 1990.

Fairbrother, Trevor J. *John Singer Sargent: Sensualist*. Seattle: Seattle Art Museum, 2000.

Farago, Jason. "Degenerate Art: The Attack on Modern Art in Nazi Germany, 1937. Review." *Guardian* March 13, 2014: 25.

Feeney, David. "Sighted Renderings of a Non-visual Aesthetics: Exploring the Interface between Drama and Disability Theory." *Journal of Literary and Cultural Disability Studies* 3.1 (2009): 85–100.

Ferrer, Daniel. "What Song the Sirens Sang . . . Is No Longer beyond All Conjecture: A Preliminary Description of the New 'Proteus' and 'Sirens' Manuscripts." *James Joyce Quarterly* 39.1 (Fall 2001): 53–68.

Fiedler, Leslie. *Freaks: Myths and Images of the Secret Self.* New York: Simon and Shuster, 1978.

Finger, Anne. *Call Me Ahab.* Lincoln: University of Nebraska Press, 2009.

Finnegans Wiki. Web. finneganswеb.com

Flint, Kate. *The Victorians and the Visual Imagination.* New York: Cambridge University Press, 2000.

Folks, Jeffrey J. "William Faulkner's 'The Rosary' and Florence L. Barclay." *Studies in Short Fiction* 18.4 (Fall 1981): 445–47.

Fordham, Finn. Introduction. *Finnegans Wake.* By James Joyce. New York: Oxford World Classics, 2012. vii–xxxiv.

Fordham, Finn. *Lots of Fun at Finnegans Wake: Unraveling Universals.* 2007. New York: Oxford University Press, 2013.

Franks, Matt. "Mental Inversion, Modernist Aesthetics, and Disability Exceptionalism in Olive Moore's *Spleen.*" *Journal of Modern Literature* 38.1 (Fall 2014): 107–27.

Froula, Christine. *Modernism's Body: Sex, Culture, and Joyce.* New York: Columbia University Press, 1996.

Froula, Christine. *Virginia Woolf and the Bloomsbury Avant-Garde: War, Civilization, Modernity.* New York: Columbia University Press, 2005.

Garland-Thomson, Rosemarie. *Extraordinary Bodies.* New York: Columbia University Press, 1997.

Garland-Thomson, Rosemarie. "Integrating Disability, Transforming Feminist Theory." *Disability Studies Reader.* 4th ed. Ed. Lennard Davis. New York: Routledge, 2013. 333–53.

Garland-Thomson, Rosemarie. Introduction. *Freakery: Cultural Spectacles of the Extraordinary Body.* Ed. Rosemarie Garland-Thomson. New York: New York University Press, 1996. 1–19.

Garland-Thomson, Rosemarie. "Misfits: A Feminist Materialist Disability Concept." *Hypatia* 26.3 (Summer 2011): 591–609.

Garland-Thomson, Rosemarie. "Seeing the Disabled: Visual Rhetorics of Disability in Popular Photography. *The New Disability History: American Perspectives.* Ed. Paul K. Longmore and Lauri Umansky. New York: New York University Press, 2001. 335–74.

Garland-Thomson, Rosemarie. *Staring: How We Look.* New York: Oxford University Press, 2009.

Garrington, Abbie. *Haptic Modernism: Touch and the Tactile in Modernist Writing.* Edinburgh: Edinburgh University Press, 2013.

Garrity, Jane. "Olive Moore's Headless Woman." *Modern Fiction Studies* 59.2 (Summer 2013): 288–316.

Gatta, John. "*The Scarlet Letter* as Pre-text for Flannery O'Connor's 'Good Country People.'" *Hawthorne and Women: Engendering and Expanding the Hawthorne Tradition.* Ed. John L. Idol Jr. and Melinda M. Ponder. Amherst: University of Massachusetts Press, 1999. 271–77.

Geurts, Kathryn Linn. *Culture and the Senses: Bodily Ways of Knowing in an African Community.* Berkeley: University of California Press, 2002.

Giannone, Richard. *Flannery O'Connor and the Mystery of Love*. Chicago: University of Chicago Press, 1989.

Giannone, Richard. Introduction. *Flannery O'Connor: Spiritual Writings*. Ed. Robert Ellsberg. Maryknoll, NY: Orbis Books, 2003. 15–48.

Gifford, Don. *"Ulysses" Annotated: Notes for James Joyce's "Ulysses."* With Robert J. Seidman. Berkeley: University of California Press, 1988.

Gillies, Mary Ann. *Henri Bergson and British Modernism*. Montreal: McGill-Queen's University Press, 1996.

Gilman, Sander. *The Jew's Body*. New York: Routledge, 1991.

Gleeson-White, Sarah. "A Peculiarly Southern Form of Ugliness: Eudora Welty, Carson McCullers, and Flannery O'Connor." *Southern Literary Journal* 36.1 (Fall 2003): 46–57.

Gleeson-White, Sarah. *Strange Bodies: Gender and Identity in the Novels of Carson McCullers*. Tuscaloosa: University of Alabama Press, 2003.

Glendinning, Victoria, ed. *Love's Civil War: Elizabeth Bowen and Charles Ritchie*. New York: Simon and Schuster, 2009.

Glosses of *Finnegans Wake*. Web. finwake.com

Gordon, John. "The Convertshems of the Tchoose: Judaism and Jewishness in *Finnegans Wake*." *James Joyce's "Finnegans Wake": A Casebook*. Ed. John Harty. New York: Garland, 1991. 85–98.

Gordon, John. *Joyce and Reality: The Empirical Strikes Back*. Syracuse, NY: Syracuse University Press, 2004.

Gordon, John. "Joyce's Hitler." *Joyce through the Ages: A Nonlinear View*. Ed. Michael Patrick Gillespie. Gainesville: University Press of Florida, 1999. 179–98.

Gottfried, Roy. *Joyce's Iritis and the Irritated Text: The Dis-lexic "Ulysses."* Gainesville: University Press of Florida, 1995.

Goulden, Murray. "Boundary-Work and the Human-Animal Binary: Piltdown Man, Science, and the Media." *Public Understanding of Science* 18.3 (2009): 275–91.

Green, Henry. *Blindness*. 1926. Victoria, TX: Dalkey Archive Press, 2001.

Groden, Michael. "The National Library of Ireland's New Joyce Manuscripts: A Narrative and Document Summaries." *Journal of Modern Literature* 26.1 (Fall 2002): 1–16.

Groden, Michael. *"Ulysses" in Focus: Genetic, Textual, and Personal Views*. Gainesville: University Press of Florida, 2010.

Grosz, Elizabeth. *Volatile Bodies: Toward a Corporeal Feminism*. Bloomington: Indiana University Press, 1994.

Hahn, Harlan. "Love, Sex and Disability: Maintaining Interest and Intimacy." *CODI: Cornucopia of Disability Information*. Web. March 6, 2014.

Hale, Allean. "Early Williams: The Making of a Playwright." *The Cambridge Companion to Tennessee Williams*. Ed. Matthew C. Roudané. New York: Cambridge University Press, 1997.

Hall, Cynthia. "'Colossal Vices' and 'Terrible Deformities' in George Lippard's Gothic Nightmare." *Demons of the Body and Mind: Essays on Disability in Gothic Literature*. Ed. Ruth Bienstock Anolik. Jefferson, NC: McFarland, 2010. 35–46.

Hammond, J. R. "The Country of the Blind." *An H. G. Wells Companion: A Guide to the Novels, Romances, and Short Stories*. London: Macmillan, 1979. 71–73.

Hansen, Randall, and Desmond King. *Sterilized by the State: Eugenics, Race, and the Population Scare in Twentieth-Century North America*. New York: Cambridge University Press, 2013.

Hanson, Clare. "Virginia Woolf in the House of Love: Compulsory Heterosexuality in *The Years*." *Journal of Gender Studies* 6.1 (March 1997): 55–62.

Hardy, Donald E. *The Body in Flannery O'Connor's Fiction: Computational Technique and Linguistic Voice*. Columbia: University of South Carolina Press, 2007.

Harvey, Benjamin. "Virginia Woolf, Art Galleries, and Museums." *The Edinburgh Companion to Virginia Woolf and the Arts*. Ed. Maggie Humm. Edinburgh: Edinburgh University Press, 2010. 140–59.

Havird, David. "The Saving Rape: Flannery O'Connor and Patriarchal Religion." *Mississippi Quarterly* 47.1 (Winter 1993): 15–26.

Hayman, David, ed. *A First-Draft Version of "Finnegans Wake."* Austin: University of Texas Press, 1963.

Henry, Holly. *Virginia Woolf and the Discourse of Science: The Aesthetics of Astronomy*. New York: Cambridge University Press, 2003.

Herman, David. "1880–1945: Re-minding Modernism." *Emergence of Mind: Representations of Consciousness in Narrative Discourse in English*. Ed. David Herman. Lincoln: University of Nebraska Press, 2011. 243–72.

Hewitt, Andrew. *Political Inversions: Homosexuality, Fascism, and the Modernist Imaginary*. Stanford, CA: Stanford University Press, 1996.

Hipsky, Martin. *Modernism and the Women's Popular Romance in Britain, 1885–1925*. Athens: Ohio University Press, 2011.

Holmes, Martha Stoddard. *Fictions of Affliction: Physical Disability in Victorian Culture*. Ann Arbor: University of Michigan Press, 2009.

Holmes, Martha Stoddard. "'Happy and Yet Pitying Tears': Deafness and Affective Disjuncture in Dickens's 'Doctor Marigold.'" *Victorian Review* 35.2 (Fall 2009): 53–64.

Holsen, Ruth. "O'Connor's 'Good Country People.'" *Explicator* 42.3 (March 1984): 59.

Hornbeck, Cynthia. "Greekly Imperfect: The Homeric Origins of Joyce's 'Nausicaa.'" *Joyce Studies Annual* (2009): 89–108.

Hornby, Louise E. J. "Visual Clockwork: Photographic Time and the Instant in 'Proteus.'" *James Joyce Quarterly* 42–43.1–4 (Fall 2004–Summer 2006): 49–68.

Hosey, Sara. "Resisting the S(crip)t: Disability Studies Perspectives in the Undergraduate Classroom." *Teaching American Literature: A Journal of Theory and Practice* 6.1 (Spring 2013): 23–44.

Hugo, Victor. "Preface to *Cromwell*." *Prefaces and Prologues to Famous Books*. Ed. Charles William Eliot. New York: P. F. Collier & Son, 1909–14. Harvard Classics, vol. 39. Bartleby.com, 2001. August 19, 2014.

Hull, John M. *Touching the Rock: An Experience of Blindness*. New York: Vintage, 1990.

Huxley, Aldous. *Crome Yellow*. 1921. Minoala, NY: Dover, 2004.

"Idiot's Mother." *New York Herald Tribune*. October 12, 1930: XI, 17.

Janouch, Gustav. *Conversations with Kafka*. 2nd ed. New York: New Directions, 1971.

Jay, Martin. *Downcast Eyes: The Denigration of Vision in Twentieth-Century French Thought*. Berkeley: University of California Press, 1994.

Johnson, Jeri. "Explanatory Notes." *"Ulysses": The 1922 Text*. New York: Oxford World Classics, 2008. 763–980.

Joyce, James. *Dubliners*. Ed. Margot Norris. New York: W. W. Norton, 2006. Norton Critical Edition.

Joyce, James. "Episode XIII (Continued)." *Little Review* (August 1920): 42–58.

Joyce, James. *Finnegans Wake*. 1939. New York: Penguin Books, 1976.

Joyce, James. *"Finnegans Wake": Book 1, A Facsimile of the Galley Proofs*. Vol. 1. Vol. 49 of *The James Joyce Archive*. Michael Groden, General Ed. New York: Garland, 1978.

Joyce, James. *"Finnegans Wake": Book 3, Chapters 1 and 2: Drafts, Typescripts, and Proofs*. Vol. 57 of *The James Joyce Archive*. Michael Groden, General Ed. New York: Garland, 1978.

Joyce, James. *"Finnegans Wake": Book 3, A Facsimile of the Galley Proofs*. Vol. 62 of *The James Joyce Archive*. Michael Groden, General Ed. New York: Garland, 1978.

Joyce, James. Manuscripts of "Sirens." James Joyce Collection. National Library of Ireland. Dublin, Ireland.

Joyce, James. *A Portrait of the Artist as a Young Man*. 1916. Ed. Hans Walter Gabler with Walter Hettche. New York: Random House, 1993.

Joyce, James. *Ulysses*. 1922. Ed. Hans Walter Gabler. New York: Vintage Books, 1986.

Joyce, James. *"Ulysses": "Aeolus," "Lestrygonians," "Scylla and Charybdis," and "Wandering Rocks": A Facsimile of Placards for Episodes 7–10*. Vol. 18 of *The James Joyce Archive*. Michael Groden, General Ed. New York: Garland, 1978.

Joyce, James. *"Ulysses": "Aeolus," "Lestrygonians," and "Scylla and Charybdis": A Facsimile of Page Proofs for Episodes 7–9*. Vol. 23 of *The James Joyce Archive*. Michael Groden, General Ed. New York: Garland, 1978.

Joyce, James. *"Ulysses": Notes and "Telemachus"—"Scylla and Charybdis": A Facsimile of Notes for the Book and Manuscripts and Typescripts for Episodes 1–9*. Vol. 12 of *The James Joyce Archive*. Michael Groden, General Ed. New York: Garland, 1978.

Joyce, James. *"Ulysses": "Wandering Rocks," "Sirens," "Cyclops," and "Nausicaa": Manuscripts and Typescripts for Episodes 10–13*. Vol. 13 of *The James Joyce Archive*. Michael Groden, General Ed. New York: Garland, 1977.

Kafer, Alison. *Feminist, Queer, Crip*. Bloomington: Indiana University Press, 2013.

Keller, Helen. *Helen Keller in Scotland: A Personal Record Written by Herself*. Ed. James Kerr Love. London: Methuen, 1933.

Kelly, Dermot. *Narrative Strategies in Joyce's "Ulysses."* Ann Arbor: UMI Research Press, 1988.

Kenner, Hugh. "Shem the Textman." *The Languages of Joyce: Selected Papers from the 11th International James Joyce Symposium, Venice 1988*. Ed. Rosa Maria Bollettieri

Bosinelli, Carla Marengo, and Christine van Boheemen. Philadelphia: John Benjamins North America, 1992. 145–54.

Kenner, Hugh. *Ulysses*. London: George Allen & Unwin, 1982.

Kern, Stephen. *The Culture of Time and Space, 1880–1918*. Cambridge, MA: Harvard University Press, 1983.

Kleege, Georgina. "Blindness and Visual Culture." *Disability Studies Reader*. 3rd ed. Ed. Lennard Davis. New York: Routledge, 2010. 522–30.

Kleege, Georgina. *Blind Rage: Letters to Helen Keller*. Washington, DC: Gallaudet University Press, 2006.

Kleege, Georgina. *Sight Unseen*. New Haven: Yale University Press, 1999.

Kline, Wendy. *Building a Better Race: Gender, Sexuality, and Eugenics from the Turn of the Century to the Baby Boom*. Berkeley: University of California Press, 2001.

Knuth, Leo. "Shem's Riddle of the Universe." *A Wake Newslitter* 9.5 (October 1972): 79–89.

Koestler, Frances A. *The Unseen Minority: A Social History of Blindness in the United States*. 1976. New York: American Foundation for the Blind, 2004.

Kohlmann, Benjamin. "'The Heritage of Symbolism': Henry Green, Maurice Bowra, and English Modernism in the 1920s." *Modern Language Notes* 124 (2009): 1188–1210.

Kolocotroni, Vassiliki, Jane Goldman, and Olga Taxidou, eds. *Modernism: An Anthology of Sources and Documents*. Chicago: University of Chicago Press, 1998.

Krentz, Christopher. "The Hearing Line: How Literature Gains from Deaf People." *Deaf Gain: Raising the Stakes for Human Diversity*. Ed. H-Dirksen L. Bauman and Joseph J. Murray. Minneapolis: University of Minnesota Press, 2014. 421–35.

Krentz, Christopher. *Writing Deafness: The Hearing Line in Nineteenth-Century American Literature*. Chapel Hill: University of North Carolina Press, 2007.

Kreyling, Michael. *Understanding Eudora Welty*. Columbia: University of South Carolina Press, 1999.

Krumland, Heidi. "'A big deaf-mute moron': Eugenic Traces in Carson McCullers's *The Heart Is a Lonely Hunter*." *Journal of Literary Disability* 2.1 (2008): 32–43.

Kulick, Don, and Jens Rydström. *Loneliness and Its Opposite: Sex, Disability, and the Ethics of Engagement*. Durham, NC: Duke University Press, 2015.

Kumar, Shiv Kumar. *Bergson and the Stream of Consciousness Novel*. New York: New York University Press, 1963.

Kushner, Tony. Introduction. *The Glass Menagerie*. New York: New Directions, 2011. Deluxe Centennial Edition.

Ladd, Paddy. *Understanding Deaf Culture: In Search of Deafhood*. Clevedon, UK: Multilingual Matters, 2003.

Lamp, Sharon, and W. Carol Cleigh. "A Heritage of Ableist Rhetoric in American Feminism from the Eugenics Period." *Feminist Disability Studies*. Ed. Kim Q. Hall. Bloomington: Indiana University Press, 2011. 175–89.

Landuyt, Ingeborg. "Cain–Ham–(Shem)–Esau–Jim the Penman: Chapter I.7." *How Joyce Wrote "Finnegans Wake": A Chapter-by-Chapter Genetic Guide*. Ed. Luca Crispi and Sam Slote. Madison: University of Wisconsin Press, 2007. 142–62.

Lane, Harlan. *The Mask of Benevolence: Disabling the Deaf Community*. 1992. San Diego: DawnSign Press, 1999.

Law, Jules. "Political Sirens." *"Ulysses": En-gendered Perspectives: Eighteen New Essays on the Episodes*. Ed. Kimberly J. Devlin and Marilyn Reizbaum. Columbia: University of South Carolina Press, 1999. 150–66.

Lawrence, D. H. "The Blind Man." *England My England*. London: Heinemann, 1950. 69–92.

Lawrence, D. H. *Fantasia of the Unconscious* and *Psychoanalysis and the Unconscious*. Toronto: William Heinemann, 1961.

Lawrence, D. H. *Lady Chatterley's Lover*. Ed. Michael Squires. New York: Penguin Books, 1994.

Lawrence, D. H. *The Letters of D. H. Lawrence*. Vol. 2. Ed. George J. Zytaruk and James T. Boulton. Cambridge: Cambridge University Press, 2002.

Lawrence, D. H. *Phoenix: The Posthumous Papers of D. H. Lawrence*. Ed. Edward D. McDonald. New York: Viking Press, 1936.

Lawrence, D. H. *Phoenix II: Uncollected, Unpublished, and Other Prose Works by D. H. Lawrence*. Ed. Warren Roberts and Harry T. Moore. London: Heinemann, 1968.

Lawrence, D. H. *The Selected Letters of D. H. Lawrence*. Ed. James T. Boulton. Cambridge: Cambridge University Press, 1997.

Lawrence, D. H. *Study of Thomas Hardy and Other Essays*. Ed. Bruce Steele. New York: Cambridge University Press, 1985. The Cambridge Edition of the Works of D. H. Lawrence.

Lawrence, D. H. *Women in Love*. New York: Modern Library, 2002.

Lawrence, Karen. *Who's Afraid of James Joyce?* Gainesville: University Press of Florida, 2010.

Leaska, Mitchell. *The Novels of Virginia Woolf: From Beginning to End*. New York: John Jay Press, 1977.

Lee, Raymond. *A Beginner's Introduction to Deaf History*. Feltham, UK: British Deaf History Society, 2004.

Lehan, Richard. *Literary Modernism and Beyond: The Extended Vision and the Realms of the Text*. Baton Rouge: Louisiana State University Press, 2009.

Lehmann, Rosamond. *Invitation to the Waltz*. London: Virago, 1981.

Leighton, Angela. "Thresholds of Attention: On Listening in Literature." *Thinking on Thresholds: The Poetics of Transitive Spaces*. Ed. Subha Mukherji. New York: Anthem Press, 2011. 199–212.

Leonard, Garry. *Advertising and Commodity Culture in Joyce*. Gainesville: University Press of Florida, 1998.

Levenson, Michael H. *A Genealogy of Modernism: A Study of English Literary Doctrine, 1908–1922*. New York: Cambridge University Press, 1984.

Levi, Neil. *Modernist Form and the Myth of Jewification*. New York: Fordham University Press, 2014.

Levin, Harry. *"Ulysses": A Facsimile of the Manuscript*. Philip H. & A. S. W. Rosenbach Foundation. New York: Octagon Books, 1975.

Lewis, Pericles. *The Cambridge Introduction to Modernism*. New York: Cambridge University Press, 2007.

Lilly, Mark. "Tennessee Williams: *The Glass Menagerie* and *A Streetcar Named Desire*." *Lesbian and Gay Writing: An Anthology of Critical Essays*. Ed. Mark Lilly. Philadelphia: Temple University Press, 1990. 153–63.

Linett, Maren. "Involuntary Cure: Rebecca West's *The Return of the Soldier*." *Disability Studies Quarterly* 33.1 (2013). Web.

Linett, Maren. "The Jew in the Bath: Imperiled Imagination in Woolf's *The Years*." *Modern Fiction Studies* 48.2 (Summer 2002): 341–61.

Linett, Maren. "The Jew's Text: 'Shem the Penman' and 'Shaun the Post.'" *James Joyce Quarterly* 45.2 (Winter 2008): 263–80.

Linett, Maren. "Matricide and the End of Nostalgia in Elizabeth Bowen." *Modernism and Nostalgia: Bodies, Locations, Aesthetics*. Ed. Tammy Clewell. New York: Palgrave/Macmillan, 2013. 71–90.

Linett, Maren. *Modernism, Feminism, and Jewishness*. New York: Cambridge University Press, 2007.

Linett, Maren. "Modes of Dislocation: Jewishness and Deafness in Elizabeth Bowen." *Studies in the Novel* 45.2 (Summer 2013): 259–78.

Linett, Maren. "'Seeing, seeing, seeing': Deafness, Knowledge, and Subjectivity in Elizabeth Bowen." *Twentieth-Century Literature* 59.3 (Fall 2013): 465–93.

Linton, Simi. *Claiming Disability: Knowledge and Identity*. New York: New York University Press, 1998.

Lodge, David. *Deaf Sentence*. New York: Penguin Books, 2008.

Lodge, David. *The Modes of Modern Writing: Metaphor, Metonymy, and the Typology of Modern Literature*. Ithaca: Cornell University Press, 1977.

Lombardo, Paul A., ed. *A Century of Eugenics in America: From the Indiana Experiment to the Human Genome Era*. Bloomington: Indiana University Press, 2011.

Lyon, Janet. "On the Asylum Road with Woolf and Mew." *Modernism/modernity* 18.3 (September 2011): 551–74.

Lyon, Janet. Paper presented at the Modernist Studies Association Roundtable on Modernism, Feminism, and Disability. Modern Language Association Conference, Vancouver, BC, January 2015.

Madden, David. "The Paradox of the Need for Privacy and the Need for Understanding in Carson McCullers's *The Heart is a Lonely Hunter*." *Literature and Psychology* 17.2–3 (1967): 128–40.

Majumdar, Robin, and Allen McLaurin, eds. *Virginia Woolf: The Critical Heritage*. London: Routledge, 1997.

Mann, Bruce. "Tennessee Williams and *The Rose-Garden Husband*." *American Drama* 1.1 (Fall 1991): 16–26.

Mao, Douglas, and Rebecca L. Walkowitz, eds. *Bad Modernisms*. Durham, NC: Duke University Press, 2006.

Mao, Douglas, and Rebecca L. Walkowitz. "The New Modernist Studies." *PMLA* 123.3 (May 2008): 737–48.

Marder, Herbert. *The Measure of Life: Virginia Woolf's Last Years*. Ithaca: Cornell University Press, 2000.

Markotic, Nicole. "Re/presenting Disability and Illness: Foucault and Two 20th Century Fictions." *Disability Studies Quarterly* 23.2 (Spring 2003): 178–92.

Martin, Timothy. "Music." *James Joyce in Context*. Ed. John McCourt. New York: Cambridge University Press, 2009. 275–84.

McCormack, W. J. *Fool of the Family: A Life of J. M. Synge*. London: Weidenfeld & Nicolson, 2000.

McCullers, Carson. *The Heart Is a Lonely Hunter*. 1940. New York: Houghton Mifflin, 2000.

McCullers, Carson. *The Member of the Wedding*. 1946. New York: Houghton Mifflin, 2004.

McDonagh, Patrick. "Autism and Modernism: A Geneological Explanation." *Autism and Representation*. Ed. Mark Osteen. New York: Routledge, 2008. 99–116.

McHugh, Roland. *Annotations to "Finnegans Wake."* 3rd ed. Baltimore: Johns Hopkins University Press, 2006.

McLaurin, Allen. *Virginia Woolf: The Echoes Enslaved*. New York: Cambridge University Press, 1973.

McMichael, James. *"Ulysses" and Justice*. Princeton: Princeton University Press, 1991.

McRuer, Robert. *Crip Theory: Cultural Signs of Queerness and Disability*. New York: New York University Press, 2006.

Mehr, Jessica. "Time and the Disabled Mind." Unpublished dissertation prospectus. Purdue University, 2015.

Mehta, Ved. *All for Love*. New York: Thunder's Mouth Press/Nation Books, 2001.

Mengham, Rod. *The Idiom of the Time: The Writings of Henry Green*. New York: Cambridge University Press, 1982.

Merleau-Ponty, Maurice. *The Primacy of Perception: And Other Essays on Phenomenological Psychology, the Philosophy of Art, History and Politics*. Ed. James. M. Edie. Evanston: Northwestern University Press, 1964.

Merva, Michael. "An Illusion of Understanding: Listeners and Tellers in Sherwood Anderson's *Winesburg, Ohio* and Carson McCullers's *The Heart Is a Lonely Hunter*." *Midamerica* 33 (2006): 9–20.

Micale, Mark S., ed. *The Mind of Modernism: Medicine, Psychology, and the Cultural Arts in Europe and America, 1880–1940*. Stanford, CA: Stanford University Press, 2004.

Miller, Tyrus. *Late Modernism: Politics, Fiction, and the Arts between the World Wars*. Berkeley: University of California Press, 1999.

Mitchell, David T., and Sharon L. Snyder. *The Biopolitics of Disability: Neoliberalism, Ablenationalism, and Peripheral Embodiment*. Ann Arbor: University of Michigan Press, 2015.

Mitchell, David T., and Sharon L. Snyder. *Narrative Prosthesis: Disability and the Dependencies of Discourse*. Ann Arbor: University of Michigan Press, 2000.

Mirzoeff, Nicholas. "Paper, Picture, Sign: Conversations between the Deaf, the Hard of Hearing, and Others." *"Defects": Engendering the Modern Body*. Ed. Helen Deutsch and Felicity Nussbaum. Ann Arbor: University of Michigan Press, 2000. 75–92.

Moore, Olive. *Collected Writings*. Normal, IL: Dalkey Archive Press, 1992.

Moore, Olive. *Fugue*. 1932. *Collected Writings*. Normal, IL: Dalkey Archive Press, 1992.

Moore, Olive. *Spleen*. 1930. Normal, IL: Dalkey Archive Press, 1996.

Moran, Patrick W. "An Obsession with Plenitude: The Aesthetics of Hoarding in *Finnegans Wake*." *James Joyce Quarterly* 46.2 (Winter 2009): 285–304.

Morse, J. Mitchell. "Joyce and the Blind Stripling." *Modern Language Notes* 71.7 (November 1956): 497–501.

Mortimer, Gail L. "'The Way to Get There': Journeys and Destinations in the Stories of Eudora Welty." *Southern Literary Journal* 19.2 (Spring 1987): 61–69.

Murphy, Richard. "Expressionism." *A Companion to Modernist Literature and Culture*. Ed. David Bradshaw and Kevin J. H. Dettmar. Malden, MA: Wiley-Blackwell, 2008. 198–203.

Murray, Jennifer. "Approaching Community in Carson McCullers's *The Heart Is a Lonely Hunter*." *Southern Quarterly* 42.4 (Summer 2004): 107–14.

Nemecek, Angela Lea. "Reading the Disabled Woman: Gerty MacDowell and the Stigmaphilic Space of 'Nausicaa.'" *Joyce Studies Annual* (2010): 173–202.

"New Books, The." *Saturday Review of Literature*. December 20, 1930: 475.

"New Books and Reprints." *Times Literary Supplement*. October 23, 1930: 867–. Times Literary Supplement Historical Archive.

Nicholls, Peter. *Modernisms: A Literary Guide*. Berkeley: University of California Press, 1995.

Norris, Margot. *Joyce's Web: The Social Unraveling of Modernism*. Austin: University of Texas Press, 1992.

North, Michael. *The Dialect of Modernism: Race, Language, and Twentieth-Century Literature*. New York: Oxford University Press, 1994.

Obasogie, Osagie. *Blinded by Sight: Seeing Race through the Eyes of the Blind*. Stanford, CA: Stanford University Press, 2014.

"Obituary: Mary Brennan." *Journal of Deaf Studies and Deaf Education* 11.1 (Winter 2006): 1–2.

O'Brian, Patrick. *Pablo Ruiz Picasso: A Biography*. 1976. New York: W. W. Norton, 1994.

O'Connor, Flannery. "Good Country People." *The Complete Stories*. New York: Farrar, Straus and Giroux, 1971. 271–91.

O'Connor, Flannery. *The Habit of Being: Letters of Flannery O'Connor*. Ed. Sally Fitzgerald. New York: Farrar, Straus and Giroux, 1979.

O'Connor, Flannery. "The Lame Shall Enter First." *The Complete Stories*. New York: Farrar, Straus and Giroux, 1971. 445–82.

O'Connor, Flannery. *Mystery and Manners: Occasional Prose*. Ed. Sally Fitzgerald and Robert Fitzgerald. New York: Farrar, Straus and Giroux, 1961.

O'Connor, Flannery. *The Violent Bear It Away*. 1960. New York: Farrar, Straus and Giroux, 1988.

O'Farrell, Mary Ann. "Blindness Envy: Victorians in the Parlors of the Blind." *PMLA* 127.3 (May 2012): 512–25.

Overy, Richard. *The Twilight Years: The Paradox of Britain between the Wars*. New York: Viking Press, 2009.

Padden, Carol. "Communication." *Keywords for Disability Studies*. Ed. Rachel Adams, Benjamin Reiss, and David Serlin. New York: New York University Press, 2015. 43–45.

Parker, Brian. "The Composition of *The Glass Menagerie*: An Argument for Complexity." *Modern Drama* 25.3 (Fall 1982): 409–22.

Parker, R. B. "The Circle Closed: A Psychological Reading of *The Glass Menagerie* and *The Two Character Play*." *Modern Drama* 28.4 (Winter 1985): 517–34.

Parrinder, Patrick. "Wells's Cancelled Endings for 'The Country of the Blind.'" *Science Fiction Studies* 17.1 (March 1990): 71–76.

Patterson, Kathleen A. "Negotiating Elevators and Haylofts: Disability and Identity in Flannery O'Connor's Short Fiction." *Literature and Sickness*. Ed. David Bevin. Amsterdam: Rodopi, 1993. 95–103.

Penrose, Roland. *Picasso: His Life and Work*. 3rd ed. Berkeley: University of California Press, 1981.

Phillips, Kathy. *Virginia Woolf against Empire*. Knoxville: University of Tennessee Press, 1994.

Philpott, Hugh B. *London at School: The Story of the School Board, 1870–1904*. London: T. Fisher Unwin, 1904.

Platt, Len. *James Joyce: Texts and Contexts*. New York: Continuum, 2011.

Platt, Len. *Joyce, Race, and "Finnegans Wake."* New York: Cambridge University Press, 2007.

Plock, Vike Martina. "Bodies." *The Cambridge Companion to "Ulysses."* New York: Cambridge University Press, 2014. 184–99.

Plock, Vike Martina. "Why Does Gerty Limp?" *Joyce in Trieste: An Album of Risky Readings*. Ed. Sebastian David Guy Knowles, Geert Lernout, and John McCourt. Gainesville: University Press of Florida, 2007. 119–30.

Powell, Tara. *The Intellectual in Twentieth-Century Southern Literature*. Baton Rouge: Louisiana State University Press, 2012.

Prenshaw, Peggy Whitman, ed. *Conversations with Eudora Welty*. Jackson: University Press of Mississippi, 1984.

Price, Margaret. "The Bodymind Problem and the Possibilities of Pain." *Hypatia* 30.1 (Winter 2015): 268–84.

Pulsifer, Rebecah. "'It was a strange and unreal sight': Disability in Olive Moore's *Spleen*." Paper presented at University of Illinois Disability Studies Colloquium, May 2014.

Quayson, Ato. *Aesthetic Nervousness: Disability and the Crisis of Representation*. New York: Columbia University Press, 2007.

Rabinbach, Anson, Sander L. Gilman, and Lilian M. Friedberg, eds. *Third Reich Sourcebook*. Berkeley: University of California Press, 2013.

Radin, Grace. *Virginia Woolf's "The Years": The Evolution of a Novel*. Knoxville: University of Tennessee Press, 1981.

Rainey, Lawrence. *Institutions of Modernism: Literary Elites and Public Culture*. New Haven: Yale University Press, 1998.

Rainsford, Dominic. "Pity in Joyce: The Significance of the Blind Stripling." *English Language Notes* 34 (September 1996): 47–55.

Reader, John. *Missing Links: In Search of Human Origins*. New York: Oxford University Press, 2011.

Rée, Jonathan. *I See a Voice: Deafness, Language, and the Senses, A Philosophical History*. New York: Metropolitan Books, 1999.

Relethford, John. "The First Hominins." *The Human Species: An Introduction to Biological Anthropology*. New York: McGraw-Hill, 2012. 235–63.

Rev. of *Repentance at Leisure* [*Spleen*], by Olive Moore. *Book World* November 16, 1930: 3e.

Rev. of *The Apple Is Bitten Again*, by Olive Moore. *Forum and Century*. 94.3 (September 1935): iv. Proquest American Periodical Series. August 12, 2014.

Rhys, Jean. *Good Morning, Midnight*. 1939. New York: W. W. Norton, 1999.

Rodas, Julia Miele. "On Blindness." *Journal of Literary and Cultural Disability Studies* 3.2 (2009): 115–30.

Roditi, Edouard. "Simon Segal's 'Songs of Innocence.'" *Jewish Quarterly* 5.3 (1958): 24–26.

Roe, Sue. *Writing and Gender: Virginia Woolf's Writing Practice*. New York: Prentice-Hall, 1990.

Rose, Danis, and John O'Hanlon. *Understanding "Finnegans Wake."* New York: Garland, 1982.

Rushdie, Salman. "Book of the Century." *London Telegraph* January 10, 1988.

Rushdie, Salman. *Midnight's Children*. New York: Random House, 2006.

Russell, Emily. *Reading Embodied Citizenship: Disability, Narrative, and the Body Politic*. New Brunswick, NJ: Rutgers University Press, 2011.

Ryf, Robert S. "Joyce's Visual Imagination." *Texas Studies in Literature and Language* 1.1 (Spring 1959): 30–43.

Sacks, Oliver. "To See and Not See." *An Anthropologist on Mars*. By Sacks. New York: Vintage Books, 1996. 108–52.

Samuels, Ellen. *Fantasies of Identification: Disability, Gender, Race*. New York: New York University Press, 2014.

Sanchez, Rebecca. *Deafening Modernism: Embodied Language and Visual Poetics in American Literature*. New York: New York University Press, 2015.

Scheye, Thomas E. "*The Glass Menagerie*: 'It's No Tragedy, Freckles.'" *Tennessee Williams: A Tribute*. Ed. Jac Tharpe. Hattiesburg: University of Southern Mississippi, 1977.

Schleifer, Ronald. *Modernism and Time: The Logic of Abundance in Literature, Science, and Culture, 1880–1930*. New York: Cambridge University Press, 2000.

Schloss, Carol. *Flannery O'Connor's Dark Comedies: The Limits of Inference*. Baton Rouge: Louisiana State University Press, 1980.

Schor, Naomi. "Blindness as Metaphor." *Differences: A Journal of Feminist Cultural Studies* 11.2 (1999): 76–105.

Schotter, Jesse. "Verbivocovisuals: James Joyce and the Problem of Babel." *James Joyce Quarterly* 48.1 (Fall 2010): 89–109.

Schultze-Naumburg, Paul. *Kunst und Rasse*. München: Lehmann, 1928.

Schweik, Susan. *The Ugly Laws: Disability in Public*. New York: New York University Press, 2010.

Schweitzer, Vivien. "Listening to a Disconnected Society." *New York Times* July 7, 2013: AR8.

Seaver, Edwin. "Passing in Brief Review." *New York Evening Post* October 11, 1930: 4d.
Sharp, Jolly Kay. *Between the House and the Chicken Yard: The Masks of Mary Flannery O'Connor*. Macon, GA: Mercer University Press, 2011.
Shilling, Chris. *The Body and Social Theory*. 3rd ed. Thousand Oaks, CA: SAGE, 2012.
Shockley, Alan. *Music in the Words: Musical Form and Counterpoint in the Twentieth-Century Novel*. Burlington, VT: Ashgate, 2009.
Sicker, Philip. "Unveiling Desire: Pleasure, Power, and Masquerade in Joyce's 'Nausicaa' Episode." *Joyce Studies Annual* 14 (Summer 2003): 92–131.
Siebers, Tobin. *Disability Aesthetics*. Ann Arbor: University of Michigan Press, 2010.
Siebers, Tobin. *Disability Theory*. Ann Arbor: University of Michigan Press, 2008.
Siebers, Tobin. "Returning the Social to the Social Model." Paper presented at a panel entitled "Toward a Methodology of Critical Embodiment." Modern Language Association Conference, January 2015.
Simmel, Georg. "The Metropolis and Mental Life." *The Sociology of Georg Simmel*. Trans. and ed. Kurt H. Wolff. New York: Free Press, 1950. 409–24.
Simmel, Georg. "Sociology of the Senses: Visual Interaction." *Introduction to the Science of Sociology*. Ed. Robert E. Park and Ernest W. Burgess. Chicago: University of Chicago Press, 1924. 356–61.
Shakespeare, Tom. "The Social Model of Disability." *The Disability Studies Reader*. 4th ed. Ed. Lennard Davis. New York: Routledge, 2013. 214–21.
Shumaker, Jeanette. "Bruised Boys and 'Fallen' Women: The Need for Rescue in Short Stories by Elizabeth Bowen." *South Carolina Review* 32.1 (1999): 88–98.
Skelton, Robin. *J. M. Synge*. Lewisburg, PA: Bucknell University Press, 1972.
Snyder, Sharon L., and David T. Mitchell. *Cultural Locations of Disability*. Chicago: University of Chicago Press, 2006.
Spoto, Donald. *The Kindness of Strangers: The Life of Tennessee Williams*. New York: Little, Brown, 1985.
Stein, Gertrude. *Picasso*. 1938. New York: Dover, 1984.
Stern, Alexandra Minna. *Eugenic Nation: Faults and Frontiers of Better Breeding in Modern America*. Berkeley: University of California Press, 2005.
Sterne, Jonathan. *The Audible Past: Cultural Origins of Sound Reproduction*. Durham, NC: Duke University Press, 2003.
Stevens, Wallace. *The Collected Poems of Wallace Stevens*. New York: Vintage Books, 1990.
Stevens, Wallace. *The Letters of Wallace Stevens*. Ed. Holly Stevens. Berkeley: University of California Press, 1996.
Straus, Joseph N. "Autism as Culture." *The Disability Studies Reader*. 4th ed. Ed. Lennard Davis. New York: Routledge, 2013. 460–84.
Synge, John M. *The Complete Plays of John M. Synge*. New York: Vintage Books, 1960.
Taylor-Batty, Juliette. *Multilingualism in Modernist Fiction*. New York: Palgrave, 2013.
Thompson, Terry W. "Wells's 'The Country of the Blind.'" *Explicator* 63.1 (Fall 2004): 34–37.

Tickner, Lisa. *The Spectacle of Women: Imagery of the Suffrage Campaign, 1907–14*. Chicago: University of Chicago Press, 1988.

"An Unhappy Life." Rev. of *Repentance at Leisure*, by Olive Moore. *New York Times*. November 2, 1930. BR4.

Uniacke, Michael. 'This Incontestable Superiority." *Deaf Lit Extravaganza*. Ed. John Lee Clark. Minneapolis: Handtype Press, 2013. 63–82.

Upton, Carole-Anne. "Visions of the Sightless in Friel's *Molly Sweeney* and Synge's *The Well of the Saints*." *Modern Drama* 40 (1997): 347–58.

Valente, Joseph. "The Accidental Autist: Neurosensory Disorder in *The Secret Agent*." *Journal of Modern Literature* 38.1 (Fall 2014): 20–37.

Valente, Joseph. *James Joyce and the Problem of Justice: Negotiating Sexual and Colonial Difference*. New York: Cambridge University Press, 1995.

Valente, Joseph. *The Myth of Manliness in Irish National Culture, 1880–1922*. Champaign: University of Illinois Press, 2011.

Vargish, Thomas, and Delo E. Mook. *Inside Modernism: Relativity Theory, Cubism, Narrative*. New Haven: Yale University Press, 1999.

Vidali, Amy. "Seeing What We Know: Disability and Theories of Metaphor." *Journal of Literary and Cultural Disability Studies* 4.1 (2010): 33–54.

Wells, H. G. "The Country of the Blind." *The Country of the Blind, and Other Stories*. By Wells. London: T. Nelson and Sons [1913?]. Photocopy at Northwestern University Library.

Wells, H. G. *The Island of Doctor Moreau*. 1896. New York: Dover, 1996.

Welty, Eudora. *The Collected Stories of Eudora Welty*. New York: Harcourt, 1980.

Welty, Eudora. *The Eye of the Story: Selected Essays and Reviews*. New York: Vintage, 1990.

Whaley, Helen R. "The Role of the Blind Piano Tuner in Joyce's *Ulysses*." *Modern Fiction Studies* 16:4 (Winter 1970/1971): 531–35.

Wheatley, Edward. *Stumbling Blocks before the Blind: Medieval Constructions of a Disability*. Ann Arbor: University of Michigan Press, 2010.

White, Siân. "'O Despise Not My Youth': Senses, Sympathy, and an Intimate Aesthetics in *Ulysses*." *Texas Studies in Literature and Language* 51.4 (Winter 2009): 503–36.

Whittier-Ferguson, John. *Framing Pieces: Designs of the Gloss in Joyce, Woolf, and Pound*. New York: Oxford University Press, 1996.

Whittier-Ferguson, John. *Mortality and Form in Late Modernist Literature*. New York: Cambridge University Press, 2014.

Whittier-Ferguson, John. "Repetition, Remembering, Repetition: Virginia Woolf's Late Fiction and the Return of War." *Modern Fiction Studies* 57.2 (Summer 2011): 230–53.

Whitworth, Michael. *Einstein's Wake: Relativity, Metaphor, and Modernist Literature*. New York: Oxford University Press, 2001.

Williams, Raymond. *Marxism and Literature*. New York: Oxford University Press, 1977.

Williams, Tennessee. "The Business College Sequence." Tennessee Williams Collection. Harry Ransom Center, University of Texas at Austin.

Williams, Tennessee. *The Gentleman Caller*: Early Drafts. Tennessee Williams Collection. Harry Ransom Center, University of Texas at Austin.

Williams, Tennessee. *The Glass Menagerie*. 1945. Introduction by Robert Bray. New York: New Directions, 1999.

Williams, Tennessee. *The Glass Menagerie*. New York: New Directions, 2011. Deluxe Centennial Edition.

Williams, Tennessee. *The Glass Menagerie*: Motion Picture Typescript Fragments, 1947–1949. Tennessee Williams Collection. Harry Ransom Center. University of Texas at Austin.

Williams, Tennessee. "The Glass Shop." *The Glass Menagerie*: Motion Picture Typescript Fragments, 1947–1949. Tennessee Williams Collection. Harry Ransom Center, University of Texas at Austin.

Williams, Tennessee. *One Arm and Other Stories*. 1948. New York: New Directions, 1954.

Williams, Tennessee. *Suddenly Last Summer*. 1958. *Tennessee Williams: Four Plays*. New York: Signet Classics, 1976.

Winterson, Jeanette. "How Would We Feel If Blind Women Claimed the Right to a Blind Baby?" *Guardian* April 8, 2002.

Witemeyer, Hugh. "Introduction: Modernism Resartus." *The Future of Modernism*. Ed. Hugh Witemeyer. Ann Arbor: University of Michigan Press, 1997. 1–8.

Wolfe, Cary. *What Is Posthumanism?* Minneapolis: University of Minnesota Press, 2010.

Wood, Alice. *Virginia Woolf's Late Cultural Criticism: The Genesis of "The Years," "Three Guineas," and "Between the Acts."* New York: Bloomsbury, 2013.

Wood, Lorraine. "Joyce's Ineluctable Modality: (Re)reading the Structure of 'Sirens.'" *Joyce Studies Annual* (2007): 67–91.

Wood, Ralph C. *Flannery O'Connor and the Christ-Haunted South*. Grand Rapids, MI: Eerdsmans, 2004.

Woolf, Virginia. *Between the Acts*. Annotated and with an introduction by Melba Cuddy-Keane. New York: Harcourt, 2008.

Woolf, Virginia. *The Diary of Virginia Woolf*. 5 Vols. Ed. Anne Olivier Bell with Andrew McNeillie. New York: Harcourt, Brace, Jovanovich, 1984.

Woolf, Virginia. *The Essays of Virginia Woolf*. Vol. 3. Ed. Andrew McNeillie. New York: Harcourt, Brace, Jovanovich, 1988.

Woolf, Virginia. *The Essays of Virginia Woolf*. Vol. 6. Ed. Stuart N. Clarke. London: Hogarth Press, 2011.

Woolf, Virginia. *The Letters of Virginia Woolf*. 6 Vols. Ed. Nigel Nicolson and Joanne Trautmann. New York: Harcourt, Brace, Jovanovich, 1980.

Woolf, Virginia. "Modern Fiction." *The Common Reader: First Series*. London: Hogarth Press, 1951. 184–95.

Woolf, Virginia. "Mr. Bennett and Mrs. Brown." 1923. *The Virginia Woolf Reader*. Ed. Mitchell A. Leaska. New York: Harcourt, 1984. 192–212.

Woolf, Virginia. *On Being Ill*. 1930. Ashfield, MA: Paris Press, 2002.

Woolf, Virginia. *The Pargiters: A Novel-Essay Based upon a Paper Read to the London National Society for Women's Service*. Holograph, unsigned, dated October 11, 1932—November 15, 1934. 8 vols. Virginia Woolf Manuscripts from the Henry

W. and Albert A. Berg Collection of the New York Public Library. Reel 10. Woodbridge, CT: 1993.

Woolf, Virginia. "Professions for Women." *The Death of the Moth and Other Essays.* New York: Harcourt, Brace, 1942. 235–42.

Woolf, Virginia. *A Room of One's Own.* Annotated and with an introduction by Susan Gubar. New York: Harcourt, 2005.

Woolf, Virginia. "Street Haunting." *The Death of the Moth and Other Essays.* New York: Harcourt, Brace, 1942. 20–36.

Woolf, Virginia. *Three Guineas.* Annotated and with an introduction by Jane Marcus. New York: Harcourt, 2006.

Woolf, Virginia. *To the Lighthouse.* Annotated and with an introduction by Mark Hussey. New York: Harcourt, 2005.

Woolf, Virginia. *The Waves.* New York: Harcourt, 1959.

Woolf, Virginia. *Women and Writing.* Edited and with an introduction by Michèle Barrett. New York: Harcourt, 1979.

Woolf, Virginia. *The Years.* Annotated and with an introduction by Eleanor McNees. New York: Harcourt, 2008.

Woolf, Virginia. *The Years.* Ed. Anna Snaith. New York: Cambridge University Press, 2012. The Cambridge Edition of the Works of Virginia Woolf.

Wulf, Josef. *Die bildenden Künste im Dritten Reich* [The visual arts in the Third Reich]. *Eine Dokumentation von Joseph Wulf.* Gütersloh: Sigbert Mohn Verlag, 1963.

Yaeger, Patricia. *Dirt and Desire: Reconstructing Southern Women's Writing, 1930–1990.* Chicago: University of Chicago Press, 2000.

Yaeger, Patricia. "Flannery O'Connor and the Aesthetics of Torture." *Flannery O'Connor: New Perspectives.* Ed. Sura P. Rath and Mary Neff Shaw. Athens: University of Georgia Press, 1996. 183–206.

Yared, Aida. "Eating and Digesting 'Lestrygonians': A Physiological Model of Reading." *James Joyce Quarterly* 46.3–4 (Spring/Summer 2009): 469–79.

Yeats, W. B. *Cathleen Ni Houlihan: Modern Irish Drama.* With Lady Augusta Gregory. Ed. John P. Harrington. New York: W. W. Norton, 1991.

Young, Stella. "We're Not Here for Your Inspiration." *Ramp Up: Disability, Discussion, Debate.* Blog of the Australian Broadcasting Corporation. July 2, 2012.

Index